Salesforce Lightning Web Component Cookbook

More than 70 expert hands-on recipes to help you build dynamic and high-performance Salesforce apps

Evelyn Maguire

<packt>

Salesforce Lightning Web Component Cookbook

Portfolio Director: Pavan Ramchandani
Relationship Lead: Alok Dhuri
Content Engineer: Esha Banerjee
Technical Editor: Vidhisha Patidar
Copy Editor: Safis Editing
Proofreader: Esha Banerjee
Indexer: Rekha Nair
Production Designer: Shankar Kalbhor
Growth Lead: Nivedita Singh

First published: March 2026

Production reference: 1200326

Published by Packt Publishing Ltd.
Grosvenor House
11 St Paul's Square
Birmingham
B3 1RB, UK

ISBN 978-1-83546-986-6
`www.packtpub.com`

To my parents – all of them – without their love and support I would not be here. Especially to my mom, Fran, and my dad, Lindy. Thank you for everything. To my wonderful husband, James, who brewed the coffee (and the beer) that kept me motivated. And to my high school Java teacher, Mr. Tank, whose teachings kept me coming back for more code. I finally found my way back to it.

– Evelyn Maguire

Contributors

About the author

Evelyn Maguire is a 10x certified developer and architect. They started working as a Salesforce developer in 2019 after a decade in various service industries, including hospitality and communications. While attending school for network and systems management, Evelyn pivoted into a career in Java, Apex, and Kotlin development and never looked back.

In their spare time, Evelyn coaches for RAD Women Code, an organization that upskills women from Salesforce administrators to developers, and Clicked, an early career program to empower Salesforce professionals to gain practical experience in the field.

Their favorite subjects to teach are asynchronous Apex and the principles of object-oriented programming as they pertain to Apex. When they aren't bouncing around the wider Salesforce community, Evelyn can be found knitting, roller skating, playing with their dogs, Boudin and Bernie, or snuggling with their cats, Cujo and Gizmo.

I would like to thank all the members of Ladies Be Architects, Scale Up Architects, and RAD Women Code for pushing me to be a better developer and architect, and all of the members of the Salesforce community who have poured into me to make this book a reality. Thank you especially to the team at Packt for their patience with me.

About the reviewers

Adam Olshansky is a Salesforce technical Architect and a member of the Salesforce MVP Hall of Fame based in San Francisco. He has 17 Salesforce certifications, including System Architect, Application Architect, and Platform Developer II. He is passionate about teaching people how to code on the Salesforce Platform. As an 11X RAD Women coach, he works as a gender equality ally to help teach Salesforce development to female Salesforce administrators. Adam loves sharing his Salesforce knowledge with the world and has presented at nine Dreamforce conferences, as well as conferences in Uruguay, India, Poland, and the United Kingdom.

Edith Valencia is a senior Salesforce developer with over a decade of experience in the Salesforce ecosystem and more than 20 years of experience in software engineering. She focuses on building clean, scalable solutions and brings a pragmatic, business-aligned approach to Apex, LWCs, and platform architecture. She's also an active community contributor, serving as a RAD Women coach, conference speaker, and developer group co-organizer.

Table of Contents

Chapter 9: Creating Custom Lightning Web Components 295

Chapter 10: Designing Polymorphic Lightning Web Components 315

Preface

Salesforce developers strive to build fast, scalable, and efficient apps—whether to streamline business processes, enhance user experience, or modernize legacy systems. But mastering **Lightning Web Components (LWCs)** can be complex. *Salesforce Lightning Web Development Cookbook* simplifies this journey with 70-plus recipes that guide you through every stage of LWC development with step-by-step solutions to real-world challenges faced by Salesforce developers. This book covers key concepts such as component composition, data retrieval, event handling, and performance optimization. You'll explore advanced topics such as writing accessible components, migrating from Visualforce and Aura, and testing LWCs using Jest and Apex. Each recipe is carefully crafted to provide clear explanations, concise code snippets, and best practices to ensure that you can immediately apply what you learn to your projects. By the end of the book, you'll be able to successfully build and scale LWCs for enterprise-grade applications. Whether you're developing new features, troubleshooting performance issues, or transitioning legacy code, this book will equip you with the expertise needed to streamline development and create high-performance applications.

Who this book is for

This cookbook is for Salesforce developers looking to expand their frontend programming expertise by advancing their skills in LWCs. Whether you're a seasoned Salesforce developer or just starting your journey, this cookbook offers a wealth of practical knowledge and insights that will take your LWC development skills to new heights. Apex and JavaScript knowledge is preferred.

What this book covers

Chapter 1, Getting Ready for Lightning Web Component Development, explains how to set up Visual Studio Code for Salesforce LWC development and seed your org with the data necessary to complete the projects in this cookbook.

Chapter 2, Writing Apex for Lightning Web Components, teaches about the Persistence, Service, and Presentation layer classes, which help to break out Apex for LWC development with the use of wrapper classes.

Chapter 3, Working with a Selector Class, defines a more effective pattern for building LWCs using Selector and Domain classes, setting yourself up for effective integration and unit testing.

Chapter 4, Synchronous and Asynchronous Processing in Components, translates between legacy and modern frameworks for asynchronous JavaScript and explains when to use each to make asynchronous JavaScript run semi-synchronously.

Chapter 5, Accessing External Data Sources via Lightning Web Component, utilizes Salesforce's REST API and the JavaScript Fetch API to show you multiple ways to call out to external data sources, while weighing the requirements of each.

Chapter 6, Composing Lightning Web Components, covers how JavaScript events can be composed in Salesforce LWCs, and how they travel up the Document Object Model.

Chapter 7, Building Secure Components with Lightning Locker and Lightning Web Security, covers building a backward-compatible modal component that works with Lightning Locker and Lightning Web Security while implementing a modest example of feature flagging.

Chapter 8, Implementing Reactivity in Lightning Web Components, shows you how to create components that collapse based on form factor and screen width, while learning how to identify and utilize legacy media queries.

Chapter 9, Creating Custom Lightning Web Components, extends the functionality of the base `lightning-datatable` component by adding custom columns.

Chapter 10, Designing Polymorphic Lightning Web Components, explains polymorphic serialization in JavaScript and polymorphism in Apex by building a custom drop-down component that searches across multiple sObjects.

Chapter 11, Writing Accessible Lightning Web Components, covers the importance of accessibility in applications by testing a custom component for accessibility and amending the functionality to bring it up to code.

Chapter 12, Migrating Aura to Lightning Web Components, maps legacy Aura Component functionality into the modern Lightning Web Components framework.

Chapter 13, Testing Apex with Mocking and Stubbing, explores a simple implementation of the Apex stub provider, while slowly building up to full unit testing with the `apex-mockery` framework.

Chapter 14, Testing Lightning Web Components with Jest, shows you how to write tests for your JavaScript with the Jest framework and learn what tests are recommended for your org.

Chapter 15, Debugging Lightning Web Components, recreates common errors in Apex in our components so that you can easily identify them when they occur in your org.

To get the most out of this book

Software/hardware covered in the book	**OS requirements**
Salesforce (Developer, Pro Suite, Professional, Enterprise, or Unlimited Edition)	Windows, macOS
Visual Studio Code (version 1.82 or higher) or Salesforce Code Builder	
Java JDK 21 (recommended) or greater than JDK 11	
Salesforce Extension Pack for Visual Studio Code	
Salesforce CLI	
Git and GitHub	

If you are building the projects in this cookbook as written, you will need to seed your Salesforce Developer Edition org with test data. Detailed instructions for seeding your org are located in *Chapter 1, Getting Ready for Lightning Web Component Development*, in the *Setting up the Salesforce Lightning Web Components Cookbook org* section.

If you are using the digital version of this book, we advise you to type the code yourself or access the code via the GitHub repository (link available in the next section). Doing so will help you avoid any potential errors related to the copying and pasting of code.

Download the example code files

You can download the example code files for this book from GitHub at `https://github.com/PacktPublishing/Salesforce-Lightning-Web-Component-Cookbook`. In case there's an update to the code, it will be updated on the existing GitHub repository.

All of the code is organized into folders by chapter under the `force-app` directory. Each chapter folder contains the relevant sub-folders for deployment of a project into a Salesforce org, such as `classes` and `lwc`. To deploy to your Salesforce org, you must have the **Salesforce Extension Pack for Visual Studio Code** installed, as well as the **Salesforce CLI**.

To access the code in the repository, fork the repository and clone your fork into your local **VS Code**. From there, authorize a free Salesforce Developer Org and deploy the `force-app` folders for `force-app/chapter00` to `force-app/chapter12` and `force-app/chapter12_setup`.

Note

The *Chapter 13, Testing Apex with Mocking and Stubbing* code is dependent on the open source `apex-mockery` framework, which must be deployed to deploy the `force-app/chapter13` directory. `apex-mockery` is available at `https://github.com/salesforce/apex-mockery`.

We also have other code bundles from our rich catalog of books and videos available at `https://github.com/PacktPublishing/`. Check them out!

Download the images

We also provide a PDF file that has color images of the screenshots/diagrams used in this book. You can download it here: `https://packt.link/gbp/9781835469866`.

Conventions used

There are a number of text conventions used throughout this book.

`Code in text`: Indicates code words in text, database table names, folder names, filenames, file extensions, pathnames, dummy URLs, user input, and X/Twitter handles. Here is an example: "Once we have our class definition, we will add a constant, denoted by a designation of `public static final String`, for an `assetsByAccount` variable."

A block of code is set as follows:

```
static customTypes = {
    picklistColumn : {
        template : picklistPlaceholder,
        editTemplate: picklistSelector,
        standardCellLayout: true,
        typeAttributes: ['label', 'placeholder', 'options', 'value']
    }
};
```

Any command-line input or output is written as follows:

```
00:00:00:000 USER_DEBUG [4]|DEBUG|001000000000001AAA
```

Bold: Indicates a new term, an important word, or words that you see onscreen. For example, words in menus or dialog boxes appear in the text like this. Here is an example: "Similar to how we have **Assert** statements in Apex, there are **matchers** in Jest. Matchers allow us to test our code against various assumptions.

> **Note**
>
> Warnings or important notes appear like this.

> **Tip**
>
> Tips and tricks appear like this.

Sections

In this book, you will find several headings that appear frequently (*Getting ready*, *How to do it...*, *How it works...*, *There's more*, and *See also*).

To give clear instructions on how to complete a recipe, use these sections as follows.

Getting ready

This section tells you what to expect in the recipe and describes how to set up any software or any preliminary settings required for the recipe.

How to do it

This section contains the steps required to follow the recipe.

How it works

This section usually consists of a detailed explanation of what happened in the previous section.

There's more

This section consists of additional information about the recipe in order to make you more knowledgeable about the recipe.

See also

This section provides helpful links to other useful information for the recipe.

Get in touch

Feedback from our readers is always welcome.

General feedback: If you have questions about any aspect of this book, mention the book title in the subject of your message and email us at `customercare@packtpub.com`.

Errata: Although we have taken every care to ensure the accuracy of our content, mistakes do happen. If you have found a mistake in this book, we would be grateful if you would report this to us. Please visit `www.packtpub.com/support/errata`, selecting your book, clicking on the **Errata Submission Form** link, and entering the details.

Piracy: If you come across any illegal copies of our works in any form on the Internet, we would be grateful if you would provide us with the location address or website name. Please contact us at `copyright@packt.com` with a link to the material.

If you are interested in becoming an author: If there is a topic that you have expertise in and you are interested in either writing or contributing to a book, please visit `authors.packtpub.com`.

Share your thoughts

Once you've read *Salesforce Lightning Web Component Cookbook*, we'd love to hear your thoughts! Scan the QR code below to go straight to the Amazon review page for this book and share your feedback.

`https://packt.link/r/1835469868`

Your review is important to us and the tech community and will help us make sure we're delivering excellent quality content.

Free benefits with your book

This book comes with free benefits to support your learning. Activate them now for instant access (see the "*How to Unlock*" section for instructions).

Here's a quick overview of what you can instantly unlock with your purchase:

Complete Code Bundle

Download the full source code for this book's examples and projects.

DRM-Free PDF Version

Download DRM-free PDF and ePub copies of this book.

7-Day Packt Library Access

Get 7-day unlimited access to 8,000+ books and videos. No credit card required.

Available for first-time Packt+ trial users only.

Next-Gen Reader Access

Read this book on Packt Reader with progress sync, dark mode and note-taking.

How to Unlock

Scan the QR code (or go to `packtpub.com/unlock`). Search for this book by name, confirm the edition, and then follow the steps on the page.

UNLOCK NOW

Note: Keep your invoice handy. Purchases made directly from Packt don't require one

Part 1

The Basics of Lightning Web Component Development

Whether you are new to Lightning Web Components development or an expert refreshing on the basics, there are a number of steps that must be completed to ensure you are ready to develop. You'll prepare yourself to use **Visual Studio Code** (**VSCode**) or Salesforce Code Builder, learn about the makeup of LWCs, and set up a solid foundation for the rest of the cookbook. All learners will benefit from the org seeding instructions contained in *Chapter 1, Getting Ready for Lightning Web Component Development*, which will prepare a set of test data and deploy the necessary metadata for use throughout this cookbook.

This part has the following chapters:

- *Chapter 1, Getting Ready for Lightning Web Component Development*
- *Chapter 2, Writing Apex for Lightning Web Components*
- *Chapter 3, Working with a Selector Class*

1

Getting Ready for Lightning Web Component Development

Hello, and welcome to the *Salesforce Lightning Web Component Cookbook*! If you are reading this book, you are likely a Salesforce professional who is looking to increase your knowledge of frontend development in Salesforce. Whether you are a seasoned architect or developer, an admin developer looking to grow your skills, or an **object-oriented programming** (**OOP**) developer who is dipping your toes into the wild world of Salesforce, this book aims to introduce patterns of development that allow for secure and scalable code while providing a cohesive user experience.

If you are reading this chapter, you are likely setting up your machine for Salesforce development, possibly for the first time! Unlike Apex, Aura, and Visualforce development, which can all be completed within the Salesforce Developer Console, Lightning Web Component requires an integrated development environment (**IDE**). The most common IDE in use for Salesforce development is Microsoft's **Visual Studio Code**, commonly known as **VSCode**, which is what we will be using to build the recipes in this book.

Setting up VSCode for development is a crucial part of the process that can be a little bit tricky because it is hard to rehearse, so this chapter breaks down the basics. Use this chapter as a reference when you need to set up your IDE on a new-to-you machine.

In addition to VSCode, we will be installing and setting up **Git**, a version control tool that will allow us to track our changes as we work through this cookbook. We will be utilizing **GitHub**, a free developer platform that uses Git for version control, so we can copy the cookbook code and host our projects as we work our way through the recipes.

In this chapter, we are going to cover the following main recipes:

- Forking the repository
- Setting up your IDE
- Setting up VSCode on Windows
- Setting up VSCode on macOS
- Setting up Salesforce Code Builder
- Retrieving and deploying metadata from Salesforce
- Linting for Salesforce
- Setting up the *Salesforce Lightning Web Component Cookbook* org
- Building your first Lightning web component

Note

Your purchase includes a free PDF copy + exclusive extras

Your purchase includes a DRM-free PDF copy of this book, 7-day trial to the Packt+ library (no credit card required), and additional exclusive extras. See the *Free benefits with your book* section in the *Preface* to unlock them instantly and maximize your learning.

Technical requirements

To complete the recipes in this book in VSCode, you must have admin access to a computer with a 1.6 GHz or faster processor and 1 GB of RAM, with 500 MB of download space available. VSCode is supported on 64-bit Windows 10 and 11, as well as the latest release of macOS (Sequoia) or the two previous versions (Sonoma or Ventura). These operating system requirements are accurate as of the writing of this book. To download VSCode, visit `https://code.visualstudio.com/download`.

Once you have VSCode installed, your window will look similar to the following:

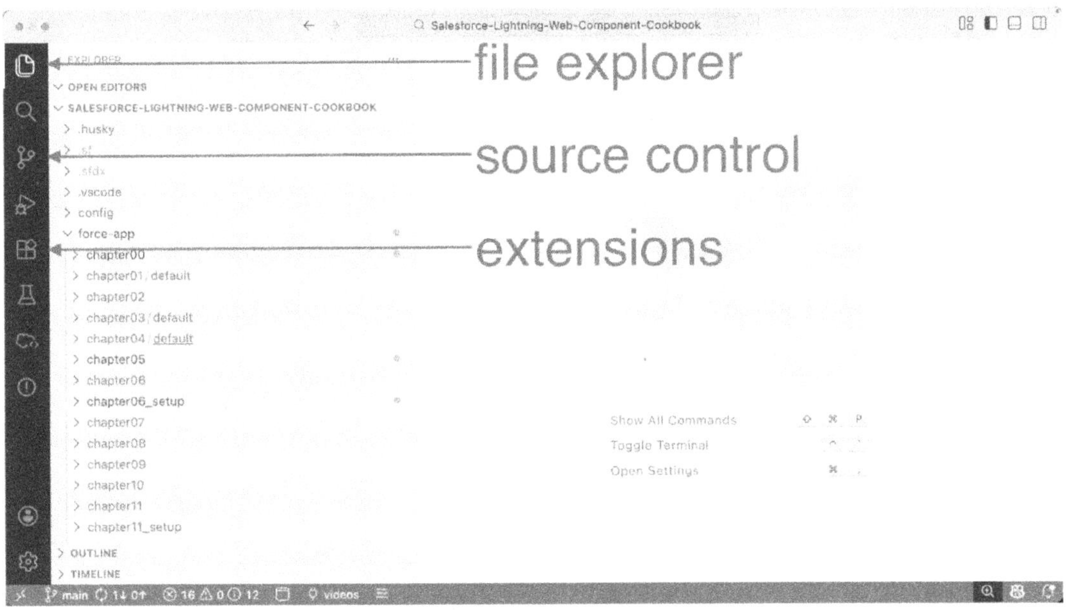

Figure 1.1: A screenshot of the VSCode window on a Mac, showing the locations of the File Explorer, File Viewer, Source Control icon, and Extensions icon.

In addition to VSCode, you will need to download and install the most recent stable **Java Development Kit (JDK)**, which can be downloaded directly from Oracle at `https://www.oracle.com/java/technologies/downloads/`. This JDK is required for use of the **Salesforce Developer Experience (SFDX) Command-Line Interface (CLI)**, which can be downloaded from `https://developer.salesforce.com/tools/salesforcecli`.

To complete the recipes in this book in **Salesforce Code Builder**, you must be a user in an Enterprise, Performance, Professional, or Unlimited edition org. Salesforce Code Builder is not currently available in **Salesforce Developer Edition orgs**. The minimum system requirements to run Salesforce are at least 5 GB of RAM and a download speed of 1 Mbps or greater. For the best results, do not use Microsoft Internet Explorer.

The recipes for this book can be found at `https://github.com/PacktPublishing/Salesforce-Lightning-Web-Component-Cookbook`, where each chapter has its own folder under the `force-app` folder. This GitHub repository is structured in the form of an **SFDX project**, which will allow you to easily fork the repository, essentially copying the repository for personal use, to prepare it for deployment in a free Salesforce Developer Edition org. For example, the code for this chapter is located at `https://github.com/PacktPublishing/Salesforce-Lightning-Web-Component-Cookbook/tree/main/force-app/chapter01`.

If you do not have Git installed on your local machine for version control, it can be downloaded and installed via `https://git-scm.com/downloads` for Windows or Mac. The easiest way to install Git for Mac is via **Homebrew**, which can be installed via the CLI using the instructions at `https://brew.sh/`. Once Homebrew is installed, the following command can be issued, which will install the Git version control system:

```
brew install git
```

These instructions are documented in the Homebrew formulae, located at `https://formulae.brew.sh/formula/git`.

Lastly, the edition of Salesforce required to implement the recipes in this book must be Developer, Performance, Unlimited, Enterprise, or Database.com. If you are planning to build the project in the book as written, you can sign up for a free Salesforce Developer Edition org at `https://developer.salesforce.com/signup`. In order to use a Developer Edition org, which does not come complete with Salesforce Code Builder, we must also install VSCode. To prepare ourselves for development, we will start by copying the cookbook code for our personal use.

Forking the repository

The version control system that this cookbook utilizes is Git, which is an open source tool that allows you to track changes in your code. GitHub is a complementary Software as a Service (SaaS) platform that hosts Git repositories and provides additional features. A fork of a Git repository grants access to a copy of an original upstream repository so that changes can be made without affecting the upstream. For the purposes of building out the projects covered in this cookbook, we are going to fork the cookbook repository so that we can make our own changes in a separate developer org.

How to do it...

We are going to start by making a copy of the cookbook repository that we can play with. In order to do so, we must set up a GitHub account.

1. Navigate to `https://github.com` and sign up for a free account if you don't have one already. Once you have an account, or if you have an account already, sign in and proceed to step 2.
2. Enter the repository for this cookbook, located at `https://github.com/PacktPublishing/Salesforce-Lightning-Web-Component-Cookbook`.

3. Fork the repository by selecting the **Fork** button to the right of the repository title, **Salesforce-Lightning-Web-Component-Cookbook**. This will allow you to have your own copy of the code for this cookbook.
4. Leave the default options for the name for the repository, and select the green **Create Fork** button. This will create a fork of the repository at `https://github.com/YOUR_GITHUB_USERNAME/Salesforce-Lightning-Web-Component-Cookbook`. We will use this fork later in the chapter to build out a free Developer Edition org with the necessary features and test data.
5. If you haven't already, sign up for your free Salesforce Developer Edition org at `https://developer.salesforce.com/signup`. It usually takes around 5–10 minutes for the Developer Edition to be instantiated, which will give us enough time to set up our IDE while we wait.

Note

Setting up your IDE

To enable Salesforce **Lightning web component** (**LWC**) development, first, we must install an IDE on our local machine. This can be a tricky task! This chapter aims to serve as a reference for a process that most developers only complete when they get a new computer. This cookbook provides a step-by-step guide for two major operating systems, Windows and Mac, as well as Salesforce Code Builder, which is generally available in many Salesforce editions as of the Winter '23 release.

Setting up VSCode on Windows

If you are one of the nearly two-thirds of developers who use Windows, you'll need to start by selecting the appropriate Windows download from `https://code.visualstudio.com/download`. From there, it can get a little tricky, so I have done my best to compile the steps.

How to do it...

1. Download the appropriate installer to your preferred directory from `https://code.visualstudio.com/download`, and open the installer. This will open a pop-up window.
2. Accept the licensing agreement and select **Next**.
3. Select a destination folder for your install, with the default being `C:\Users\YOUR_NAME\AppData\Local\Programs\Microsoft VS Code`.

4. If you would like to create a Start menu folder, make no changes on the **Select Start Menu Folder** page. Alternatively, check the **Don't create a Start Menu folder** checkbox at the bottom left of the popup. Select **Next**.
5. Under the **Select Additional Tasks** menu, select the following options. These selections will allow you to right-click files and folders within your Windows directory and select **Open with Code** to open them in a VSCode window. The final **Add to PATH (requires shell restart)** selection will allow us to automatically set our system PATH variable for VSCode, which is required for use with the Salesforce extensions we will be installing in a moment.
   - (Optional) Create a desktop icon
   - Add the **Open with Code** action to the Windows Explorer file context menu.
   - Add the **Open with Code** action to the Windows Explorer directory context menu.
   - Register **Code as an editor** for supported file types.
   - **Add to PATH (requires shell restart)**
6. Complete the remainder of the steps for installation, and restart Visual Studio Code.
7. While inside the VSCode app, navigate to the Extensions icon (four squares building a larger square) on the left-hand side of the window.
8. Search for the Salesforce Extension Pack (Expanded), which has every extension necessary to complete the recipes contained within this cookbook, including the Salesforce Developer Experience (SFDX) suite of tools. Click Install.
9. While the extension pack is installing, navigate in your browser to `https://developer.salesforce.com/tools/salesforcecli` to download and install the Salesforce CLI. Select the appropriate build for your Windows architecture.
10. Run the downloaded executable file and complete the required steps for installation.
11. Restart VSCode to activate the CLI.
12. Verify your CLI install by opening a terminal within VSCode (**Terminal** > **New Terminal**, or *Ctrl* + *Shift* + `` ` ``) and issuing the `sf` command within the terminal. If there is an error with the install, you will receive a message stating that the command does not exist. If this occurs, attempt steps 13-16 again.
13. Issue the `sf update` command. This will update your version of the CLI to the latest stable version. You can check which version you are on with the `sf version` command.
14. If this is a wholesale new install, you will need to create a folder for your Salesforce projects. Navigate to **File Explorer** with the icon that looks like two pieces of paper on

the left-hand side of the screen, and select the **Open Folder** button. Alternatively, use **File** > **Open Folder** to open file navigation for your PC.

15. Create a new folder in your chosen directory, such as `Documents`, and label it `VSCode`. This folder is named generically so that it can house all our future coding projects! Open your new `VSCode` folder in Visual Studio Code using **File** > **Open Folder**, and allow **Read** access as well as **trust the authors of the files** in your new folder if prompted.
16. Once you are in your VSCode directory, you can optionally create a new Salesforce project by typing *Ctrl* + *Shift* + *P* and selecting **SFDX: Create Project With Manifest**, and then **Standard Project Template**. This will create a new project in a subfolder of your `VSCode` folder. This step is not necessary for the installation of the cookbook project, but it will be helpful to know for the future!
17. Because we are utilizing GitHub for version control, we will open a terminal in the newly created `VSCode` folder by right-clicking on the `VSCode` folder in your VSCode **File Explorer**, selecting **Open In Integrated Terminal**, and issuing the following command, which contains the link to your forked repository:

```
git clone https://github.com/YOUR_GITHUB_USERNAME/Salesforce-Lightning-Web-
Component-Cookbook
```

18. Substitute `YOUR_GITHUB_USERNAME` with your GitHub username. This will clone the repository for this book into a subfolder within your `VSCode` folder. Git must be installed locally for this command to work. If you do not have Git installed, visit `https://git-scm.com/downloads` to view the download instructions for Windows.

> **Note**
>
> The exact link to clone your forked repository (or any other repository) can be copied directly from the GitHub **user interface** (**UI**). Navigate to your forked repository in GitHub, and select the green **Code** button, which will display a dropdown. Copy the link under the **HTTPS** tab and issue the `git clone [COPIED_URL]` command.

19. Open your newly cloned repository by going to **File** > **Open Folder** and opening the `Salesforce-Lightning-Web-Component-Cookbook` subfolder under your `VSCode` directory.
20. To utilize the **Salesforce Apex Extension for VSCode**, we must lastly install **Java** as a **Java Development Kit** (**JDK**).

21. Return to your browser and navigate to `https://www.oracle.com/java/technologies/downloads/`. You may be prompted to create a free Oracle account, which is expected.
22. Navigate to the latest stable version of the JDK, and download the appropriate executable installer for your Windows architecture. Follow the prompts to install, and restart VSCode once complete.
23. Once the appropriate JDK files are installed, you may receive an error pop-up like the following:

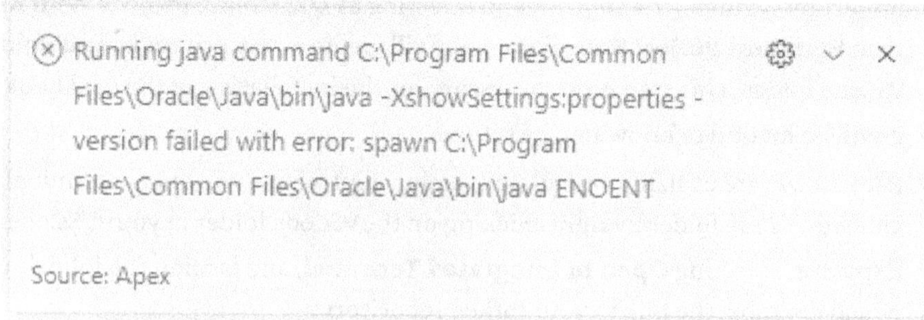

Figure 1.2: Error pop-up indicating that the Java PATH variables need to be set

24. To correct this, we must set our JAVA_HOME variable for Windows. Navigate to `C:\Program Files\Java` in your Windows File Explorer and copy the path to the folder for your JDK install. It should look similar to `C:\Program Files\Java\jdk-21` or `C:\Program Files\Java\jdk-17`, depending on the version you selected.
25. Access the Windows **Start** menu, and search for **Environment Variables**. Select **Edit the system environment variables**, and click the **Environment Variables...** button.
26. Under **System Variables**, select **New**, and create a variable named `JAVA_HOME` with a value of the path to your JDK files. This should look like the following:

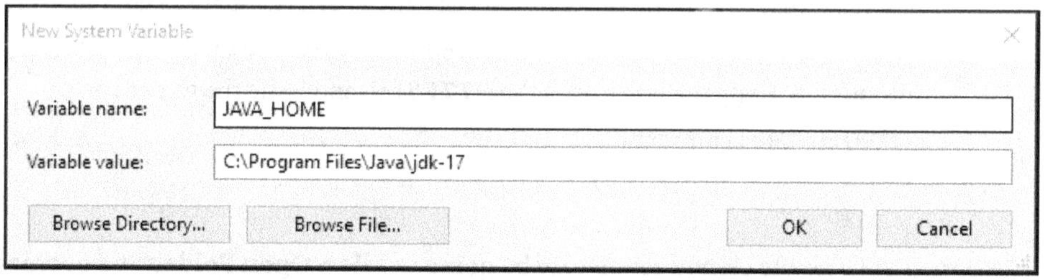

Figure 1.3: New System Variable popup allowing us to set the JAVA_HOME path variable

27. Save your environment variables and restart VSCode.
28. Press *Ctrl* + *Shift* + *P* one more time, this time selecting **SFDX: Authorize an Org**.

29. Select how you would like to authorize, typically using either **login.salesforce.com** for a production or Developer Edition org, or **test.salesforce.com** for a sandbox.
30. In the next prompt, enter a descriptive alias, such as your Developer Edition org username, which will allow us to easily identify our org later. Upon hitting *Enter*, the CLI will open a browser window allowing you to log into your Salesforce org.
31. If there is a window that prompts you to enter an 8-digit code from a device or app, select the **Connect** button. This code will be automatically filled in by the CLI.
32. Log in with your Salesforce org credentials.
33. If you have not yet authorized the org with the Salesforce CLI, you will be prompted to allow access to the Salesforce CLI. Select **Allow**, followed by **Continue**, once your org has been authorized.

You are now ready for Salesforce Lightning Web Components development on your Windows machine.

Setting up VSCode on macOS

If you are using the preferred operating system of FAANG software development, good news! The process of installing VSCode for macOS tends to be a little simpler than installing it for Windows, as the path variables are set within VSCode itself. Let's dive in.

How to do it...

1. Start by selecting the download file for the macOS version that matches your processor chip from `https://code.visualstudio.com/download`. To find out what kind of chip your Mac has, either an Intel chip or a Mac chip, select the Apple icon in the top-left corner, select **About This Mac**, and view the **Processor** settings in the resulting pop-up.
2. Download the `.zip` file and double-click the downloaded file in your **Downloads** folder in **Finder** to automatically unzip it.
3. Double-click the **Visual Studio Code** application to open it. If you receive a popup asking if you would like to open an app downloaded from the internet, select **Open**.
4. Once you have verified that VSCode is operating, drag the application icon from your `Downloads` folder in Finder to your `Applications` folder.
5. While inside the VSCode app, navigate to the **Extensions** icon (four squares building a larger square) on the left-hand side of the window.
6. Search for **Salesforce Extension Pack (Expanded)**, which has every extension necessary to complete the recipes contained within this cookbook. Click **Install**.

7. While the extension pack is installing, navigate in your browser to `https://developer.salesforce.com/tools/salesforcecli` to download and install the Salesforce CLI. Once again, select the installer for the appropriate chip for your Mac.
8. Double-click the `.pkg` file in your `Downloads` folder and follow the prompts for installation.
9. Verify your CLI install by opening a terminal within VSCode (**Terminal** > **New Terminal** or *Ctrl* + `) and issuing the `sf` command within the terminal. If there is an error with the install, you will receive a message stating that the command does not exist. If this occurs, attempt steps 7-9 again.
10. Issue the `sf update` command. This will update your version of the CLI to the latest stable version. You can check which version you are on with the `sf version` command.
11. If this is a wholesale new install, you will need to create a folder for your Salesforce projects. Navigate to **File Explorer** with the icon that looks like two pieces of paper on the left-hand side of the screen and select the **Open Folder** button. Alternatively, use **File** > **Open Folder** to open file navigation on your Mac.
12. Create a new folder in your chosen directory, such as `Documents`, and label it `VSCode`. This folder is named generically so that it can house all our future coding projects! Open your new `VSCode` folder in Visual Studio Code and allow read access, as well as **trust the authors of the files** in your new folder if prompted.
13. Once you are in your `VSCode` directory, you can optionally create a new Salesforce project by typing *CMD* + *Shift* + *P* and selecting **SFDX: Create Project With Manifest**, and then **Standard Project Template**. This will create a new project in a subfolder of your `VSCode` folder. This step is not necessary for the installation of the project, but it will be helpful to know for the future!
14. Because we are utilizing GitHub for version control, we will open a terminal in the newly created `VSCode` folder by right-clicking on the `VSCode` folder in your Visual Studio Code File Explorer, selecting **Open In Integrated Terminal**, and issuing the following command, which contains the link to your forked repository:

```
git clone https://github.com/YOUR_GITHUB_USERNAME/Salesforce-Lightning-Web-Component-Cookbook
```

15. Substitute `YOUR_GITHUB_USERNAME` with your GitHub username. This will clone the repository for this book in a subfolder within your `VSCode` folder. Git must be installed

locally for this command to work. If you do not have Git installed, visit `https://git-scm.com/downloads` to view the download instructions for Mac.

> **Note**
>
> The exact link to clone your forked repository (or any other repository) can be copied directly from the GitHub **user interface** (**UI**). Navigate to your forked repository in GitHub, and select the green **Code** button, which will display a dropdown. Copy the link under the **HTTPS** tab and issue the `git clone [COPIED_URL]` command.

16. Open your newly cloned repository by going to **File** > **Open folder** and opening the `Salesforce-Lightning-Web-Component-Cookbook` subfolder under your `VSCode` directory.
17. If you are completing your VSCode install on a brand new personal or company-issued Mac, you might receive the following error popup at this point, meaning that you will need to install a JDK on your machine:

Figure 1.4: Error popup indicating that a JDK needs to be installed

18. Return to your browser and navigate to `https://www.oracle.com/java/technologies/downloads/` to download the latest stable version of the JDK. You may be prompted to create an Oracle account, which is expected.
19. Download the appropriate Apple **Disk Image file** (**DMG**) for your computer's architecture, x64 or ARM64. The good news is, if you download the wrong one, your

computer will let you know. Follow the prompts to install, and restart VSCode once complete.

20. Set the `salesforcedx-vscode-apex.java.home` variable to the pathname of your Java runtime install by navigating to **Code** > **Settings...** > **Settings** and searching for **java home**. To find the pathname of your Java runtime, open your VSCode terminal and issue the following command:

```
/usr/libexec/java_home
```

21. Copy the output, which should look similar to `/Library/Java/JavaVirtualMachines/jdk-21.jdk/Contents/Home` or `/Library/Java/JavaVirtualMachines/jdk-17.jdk/Contents/Home`, depending on the version you downloaded, and paste it in the text input box for the **Java: Home** variable.

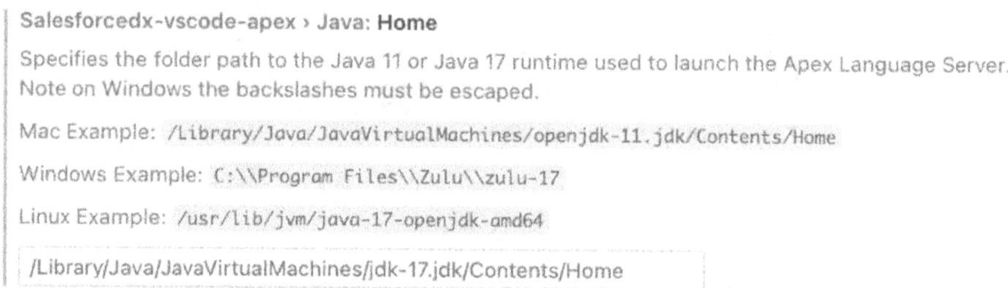

Figure 1.5: Java Home variable location in VSCode settings

22. Having set our **Java: Home** variable, we can close out of the **Settings** tab in VSCode and return to **File Explorer**.
23. Press *CMD* + *Shift* + *P* one more time, this time selecting **SFDX: Authorize an Org**.
24. Select how you would like to authorize, typically using either **login.salesforce.com** for a production or Developer Edition org, or **test.salesforce.com** for a sandbox.
25. In the next prompt, enter a descriptive alias, such as your Developer Edition org username, which will allow us to easily identify our org later. Upon hitting return, the CLI will open a browser window allowing you to log in to your Salesforce org.
26. If there is a window that prompts you to enter an 8-digit code from a device or app, select the **Connect** button. This code will be automatically filled in by the CLI.

27. Log in with your Salesforce org credentials.
28. If you have not yet authorized the org with the Salesforce CLI, you will be prompted to allow access to the Salesforce CLI. Select **Allow**, followed by **Continue**, once your org has been authorized.

You are now ready for Salesforce Lightning Web Components development on your Mac.

Setting up Salesforce Code Builder

If you are a user in an Enterprise, Performance, Professional, or Unlimited edition, you may have access to **Salesforce Code Builder**. Code Builder brings all the functionality of VSCode to your browser as a web-based IDE, preventing the need for a local IDE. This is a good option if you are developing on a **Chromebook**, as you do not need to meet the system requirements of VSCode, but note that you must be a user in an Enterprise, Performance, Professional, or Unlimited edition org. Salesforce Code Builder is not currently available in Developer Edition orgs.

It is important to note that Code Builder is also not available in the EU **Operating Zone** (**OZ**) due to an enhanced level of data residency commitment, but it is supported in EU orgs that are not part of the EU OZ.

How to do it...

1. If you are installing Code Builder in your org, log into your Salesforce production instance as a System Administrator (or user with baseline administrator permissions). Otherwise, skip to step 7.
2. Navigate to **Setup** > **Development** > **Code Builder**.
3. Enable Code Builder and read the Product Terms popup. Note that Code Builder may operate on separate infrastructure than your Salesforce org. If this is agreeable with your org's information security policies, click **Accept**; otherwise, click **Cancel**.
4. Install the Code Builder managed package for the appropriate profiles in your organization—for example, profiles housing developers and administrators.
5. Approve **Third-Party Site Access**, which is necessary for Code Builder to run.
6. Navigate to **Setup** > **Users** > **Permission Set Groups**, and assign the **CodeBuilderGroup** permission set group to applicable users.
7. Now that Salesforce Code Builder is available for use in your org, navigate to **App Launcher** and select the **Code Builder** app. Select the **Launch** button on the right-hand side of the screen. Once loaded, you will see your web-based IDE.
8. In the bottom left-hand corner, you will be able to set your default org for development. Click on the **No Default Org Set** indicator, which will open the org selector for Code

Builder. Alternatively, press *Ctrl* + *Shift* + *P* (Cmd + *Shift* + *P* on Mac) to open the org selector.

9. Select **SFDX: Authorize an Org** and select **Sandbox**. For our use case, we are going to be utilizing a Developer Sandbox named **Cookbox**.
10. In the next prompt, enter the name `Cookbox` as an alias, which will allow us to easily identify our org later. This will open a browser window allowing you to log into your Salesforce Sandbox at `https://test.salesforce.com/`.
11. If there is a window that prompts you to enter an 8-digit code from a device or app, select the **Connect** button. This code will be automatically filled in from Code Builder.
12. Log in with your appropriately suffixed sandbox credentials (in this example, `user@org-name.com.cookbox`).
13. Similarly to other methods of authorizing VSCode, if you have not yet authorized the sandbox with the Salesforce CLI, you will be prompted to allow access to Code Builder. Select **Allow**, followed by **Continue** once your sandbox has been authorized.

As soon as you have set your Code Builder configurations, you are ready for Lightning Web Components development. Unlike setting up VSCode, Code Builder comes pre-installed with the necessary extensions for Salesforce development. This allows you to jump straight into building components without any additional installations, enabling lightweight, web-based LWC development on any machine that can access Salesforce.

> **Note**
>
> If you are utilizing an edition of Salesforce that has Code Builder, it is safe to assume that you are likely developing on an employer-issued machine, and thus, should not deploy the repository into this Salesforce org, but use the recipes in this book as an example.

Retrieving and deploying metadata from Salesforce

Now that we have our IDE set up with the appropriate settings and extensions, whether we are utilizing VSCode or Code Builder, we're going to want to know how to retrieve and deploy metadata. Metadata, or data about data, is the underlying code that tells our Salesforce org what to do. The main metadata types that we will be concerned with in this cookbook are Apex classes, LWCs, Aura components, and Visualforce pages.

> **Note**
>
> The **Salesforce Extension Pack** can occasionally take some time to load upon opening VSCode. This can be a source of frustration at the start of the day, as the extensions are

required to authorize an Org, create new metadata types, or retrieve and deploy metadata. To check if your extension pack is loading successfully, press *Ctrl + Shift + P* (*CMD + Shift + P* on Mac) and search for **Developer: Show Running Extensions**. This tool will let you view which extensions are still loading and the startup activation time for each extension. If necessary, extensions can be disabled or restarted from this menu.

How to do it...

There are two ways to retrieve and deploy metadata: through the UI and through the CLI.

To push and pull data via the UI, right-click on the file, folder, or package.xml file that you would like to retrieve or deploy. To deploy the code for this cookbook from your fork into your Salesforce Developer Edition Org, right-click on the `force-app` folder in your cloned repository in VSCode, and select **SFDX: Deploy Source to Org**. This is the easiest way to deploy the metadata for this cookbook, and we can check our deployment's progress on the Deployment Status page in the Setup menu. As we add and change individual files, we can right-click on those files to deploy them individually.

To utilize the Salesforce CLI for Windows or Mac, make sure that it is installed by issuing the sf command in a terminal. If you have followed the steps in this chapter for Windows or Mac, it should already be installed. If the CLI is not installed, you will receive an error message stating that the sf command does not exist. The CLI can be installed from `https://developer.salesforce.com/tools/salesforcecli`.

Once the CLI is installed, let's practice deploying the setup code from our repository via the CLI. Issue the following command:

```
sf project deploy start --source-dir force-app/chapter00
```

This can also be achieved by right-clicking on the `force-app/chapter00` folder and selecting **SFDX: Deploy This Source to Org**.

To practice retrieving specific components, such as the components we just deployed in the `force-app/chapter00` directory, issue the following command:

```
sf project retrieve start --source-dir force-app/chapter00
```

This can also be achieved by right-clicking on the `force-app/chapter00` folder and selecting **SFDX: Retrieve This Source from Org**.

As we make changes in our Salesforce Developer Edition Org, we can use the `retrieve` command to pull down components that we have built within the **Setup** menu, such as custom objects, custom fields, or custom metadata types. This won't show any changes yet, because we just deployed and retrieved our unaltered `force-app/chapter00` directory, but we'll keep this information in our back pocket!

> **Note**
>
> If you have made changes locally, retrieving from the Org can overwrite those changes, while deploying to the Org can overwrite changes that have been made within the **Setup** menu. Be sure to **commit** your local changes often, effectively saving them so that these changes can be retrieved if necessary. To see if there is a **diff**, or **difference**, between what is stored locally and in your target Org, you can right-click on a file or folder and run the **SFDX: Diff File/Folder Against Org** command.

The full Salesforce CLI Command Reference is available at `https://developer.salesforce.com/docs/atlas.en-us.sfdx_cli_reference.meta/sfdx_cli_reference/cli_reference_top.htm`.

How it works...

We've spent a fair bit of time in this chapter talking about metadata. You may be wondering, what exactly is **metadata**? As the Salesforce documentation likes to put it, metadata is **data about data**. If our records in Salesforce are our data, then the metadata in our org is how we structure and transform that data. There are a number of types of metadata that we will be touching on in this cookbook, the most important being **Apex classes** and **Lightning web components**. Before we can get into these types of metadata, let's set up some common terminology so that we can understand the necessary pieces of each, starting with the languages we will be using.

Apex is the proprietary language used by Salesforce developers to interact with the relational database that is Salesforce. Apex is loosely based on Java, and as such, each Apex file has variables and methods organized into a class structure. Each Apex file, suffixed with `.cls`, represents an Apex class. You'll notice that each Apex class has its own corresponding `.cls-meta.xml` file, which determines how we can use our class. The markup in this file makes it an **XML file**, which we will define in a moment.

Next, we have Lightning web components. Each LWC will, at a minimum, contain an **HTML file**, a **JavaScript file**, and a `.js-meta.xml` file. Similarly to the `.cls-meta.xml` file, the `.js-meta.xml` file is an XML file that determines how our LWC can be used.

Since we've now mentioned two types of XML files, what is an XML file? **XML** stands for **Extensible Markup Language**, which is a markup language that allows us to set rules for defining our data. In later chapters, we will see that we can use our XML files to determine the placement of an LWC, such as what pages it is allowed to be placed on, and even what sObject records and device form factors it can interact with.

A **markup language** is a way to encode text, which allows us to define the presentation of a file. We use XML files, suffixed by either `.xml` or `.type-meta.xml`, as well as **HTML files**, suffixed by `.html`, to do this. **HTML**, or **HyperText Markup Language**, allows us to create and render web pages. In the context of LWCs, we build the UI of our components with HTML. Markup languages utilize **elements** and **tags** to structure their files. In the context of an XML or HTML file, an element is formed by an opening and closing set of tags, denoted by **angled bracket characters** (**<tag>**, **</tag>**, or **<tag />**), and each tag is defined using **attributes**. A tag may also optionally contain **content**. Here is an example of an HTML `<a>` tag that contains an `href` attribute and link content:

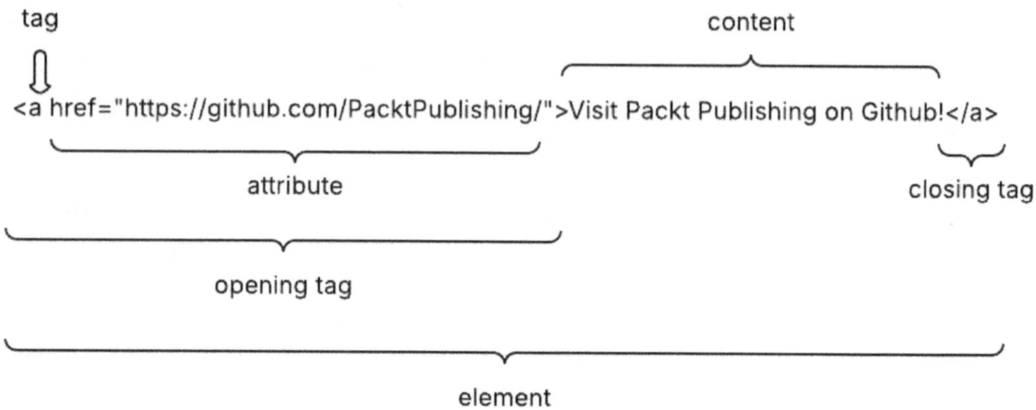

Figure 1.6: A diagram showing the parts of an HTML tag that display a link

In *Chapter 11, Writing Accessible Lightning Web Components*, we will see the importance of using appropriate tags to format our LWCs to make them accessible to people using assistive devices.

Now that we know how our backend and frontend are written, how do we make them talk to each other? This is where **JavaScript** comes in. **JavaScript** is one of the cornerstone languages of the web, allowing us to add frontend logic to our components, as well as to communicate with our database via Apex. JavaScript files are suffixed by `.js`, and most JavaScript files in our LWCs will have a corresponding `.js-meta.xml` file as well. It is important to note that JavaScript is a **case-sensitive** language. Many a night has been wasted by developers looking for a lowercase letter where it shouldn't have been!

Similar to Apex, JavaScript files are built in a class structure that can contain variables and actions that can be taken. Unlike Apex, the action mechanism of JavaScript is called a **function**, not a **method**. And, unlike Apex, JavaScript runs in the browser, which means that it can process records on the frontend very quickly. We will see the difference between frontend and backend processing very clearly in *Chapter 4, Synchronous and Asynchronous Processing in Components*, and we will learn a frontend optimization technique called **lazy-loading** in *Chapter 8, Implementing Reactivity in Lightning Web Components*.

There's more

If you would like to use a VSCode extension that will allow you to automatically generate a `package.xml` file, which is a definition of what metadata to retrieve and deploy by default for your org, the **Salesforce Package.xml Generator Extension for VSCode** by Vignaesh Ram A. is an excellent tool. To install it, search for this extension under the **Extensions** menu in VSCode, and select **Install**. Alternatively, the extension documentation and download can be found at `https://marketplace.visualstudio.com/items?itemName=VignaeshRamA.sfdx-package-xml-generator`. The prerequisites for this extension are the Salesforce Extension Pack and VSCode `v1.26` or later.

To utilize this extension after installing it, hit *Ctrl* + *Shift* + *P* (*CMD* + *Shift* + *P* on Mac) and search for **SFDX Package.xml Generator: Choose Metadata Components**. This will open a UI that shows the metadata types in your org and allows you to pick and choose which components to include in your `package.xml` file.

> Note
>
> To see the components in your org, you must have authorized an org with Salesforce. To authorize an org, hit *Ctrl* + *Shift* + *P* (*CMD* + *Shift* + *P* on Mac), and select **SFDX: Authorize an Org**. If you forgot to authorize an org, complete the steps to authorize, and restart the **SFDX Package.xml Generator** extension.

If you are utilizing the SFDX Package.xml Generator extension to pull all metadata, it is important to note that your package.xml file will need to be refreshed when new metadata, such as a new sObject or permission set, is added to your org. The way to mitigate this is to utilize wildcards in the members tag of your XML file, such as the following package.xml file that is written to pull all `ApexClass` metadata:

```
<?xml version="1.0" encoding="UTF-8" standalone="yes"?>
<Package xmlns="http://soap.sforce.com/2006/04/metadata">
   <types>
     <members>*</members>
     <name>ApexClass</name>
   </types>
   <version>63.0</version>
</Package>
```

This tool is especially beneficial if you are utilizing a Git-based **continuous integration and continuous delivery** (**CI/CD**) process, as all components must be retrieved and deployed to keep environments in sync.

In order to deploy or retrieve all metadata specified in your `package.xml` file, right-click on the `package.xml` file and select **SFDX: Deploy/Retrieve Source** in **Manifest** from **Org**.

See also

- The full Salesforce CLI Command Reference is available at `https://developer.salesforce.com/docs/atlas.en-us.sfdx_cli_reference.meta/sfdx_cli_reference/cli_reference_top.htm`.
- If you would like to do more reading on the types of metadata available in a Salesforce org, the full list of Salesforce metadata types is available at `https://developer.salesforce.com/docs/atlas.en-us.api_meta.meta/api_meta/meta_types_list.htm`.

Linting for Salesforce

Knowing the basics of VSCode, we are ready to start developing. If, while you are developing, you would like to check the code you are writing against a set of standards or for errors, linting may be a good option for you. **Linting** allows programmers to check their written code for style issues and programmatic errors utilizing static code analysis. Salesforce has its own linting tool, **ESLint**.

> Note
>
> If you are working on a company-issued computer, you may have different linting requirements from those listed in this chapter.

How to do it...

To utilize Salesforce's linting tool, ESLint, you must have the latest stable release of **Node.js**, which is a **JavaScript runtime environment** (**JRE**) where a JavaScript program can be executed, installed on your local machine. Node.js can be installed utilizing the package manager and instructions at `https://nodejs.org/en/download/package-manager`.

Once Node.js is installed, issue the following command in a terminal in your project's root directory:

```
npm install --save-dev @salesforce/eslint-config-lwc @lwc/eslint-plugin-lwc
@salesforce/eslint-plugin-lightning eslint-plugin-import eslint-plugin-jest
```

Don't worry if you don't want to type this; it is copyable from Salesforce's GitHub README for the LWC linter at `https://github.com/salesforce/eslint-config-lwc`.

If you receive errors while running this command in the directory for your fork of the cookbook repository, add the `--force` token to the end of it. This will overwrite the included `package.json` and `package-lock.json` files to include the most up-to-date version numbers for **ESLint**. If there are errors after running this command, issue one more command:

```
npm audit fix
```

This will automatically run `npm install`, which will ensure you have a stable version of Node.js installed and attempt to fix any errors in dependencies.

Now that **ESLint** has been installed in your project, we can set up our linting file. Verify that your project has the `.eslintrc.json` file in the root directory. If this file does not exist, it can be created from scratch or downloaded from the cookbook repository here: `https://github.com/PacktPublishing/Salesforce-Lightning-Web-Component-Cookbook/tree/main/.eslintrc.json`.

If you are creating your `.eslintrc.json` file from scratch or copying it from another source, configure your linting level by editing the `extends` key-value pair of the `.eslintrc.json` file.

There are three standard configuration levels: **Base**, **Recommended**, and **Extended**. Base flags common **anti-patterns** in Lightning Web Components, as well as other Salesforce platform restrictions. Recommended flags common issues in JavaScript and enforces all Salesforce best practices. Extended flags the use of older JavaScript syntax that may slow down older browsers, such as Internet Explorer.

For more details on the configuration levels of ESLint, you can visit the Salesforce GitHub repository here: `https://github.com/salesforce/eslint-plugin-lwc`.

For the purposes of this cookbook, we are going to set our configuration level to **Recommended**. The reason for this is that we want to ensure that all of our components are following best practices. As a result, our `.eslintrc.json` file will look like the following:

```
{
  "parser": "@babel/eslint-parser",
  "extends": ["@salesforce/eslint-config-lwc/recommended"],
  "overrides": [
    {
      "files": ["*.test.js"],
      "env": {
```

```
                "node": true
            }
        }
    ]
}
```

The necessary `.eslintrc.json`, `package-lock.json`, and `package.json` files can be downloaded from the cookbook repository at `https://github.com/PacktPublishing/Salesforce-Lightning-Web-Component-Cookbook` and are included when the repository is cloned.

Once the linter is installed and configured, we can run it.

Issue the `npm run lint` command, which will run the linter. If there are any errors flagged by the linter, you will see them in your terminal. Hopefully, you aren't seeing any to start! Run this command as you update your code to check for new errors.

See also

- The full documentation for Salesforce ESLint can be found here: `https://developer.salesforce.com/tools/vscode/en/lwc/linting`
- The GitHub repository for Salesforce ESLint can be found here: `https://github.com/salesforce/eslint-config-lwc`

Setting up the Salesforce Lightning Web Components Cookbook org

Now that we have forked our repository metadata and deployed it to our Developer Edition org, let's create some test data.

Imagine you are a Salesforce developer for an art broker who has been tasked with transporting artworks (**Assets**) between different museums (**Accounts**). Each artwork is required to document the history of its residencies (**Asset Residencies**), which are created by a record-triggered flow upon insertion or update of an Asset record. Each artwork also carries documentation for the artist who primarily completed the work (**Constituents**) and the classification of the artwork (**Tags**). A general **Entity Relationship Diagram** (**ERD**) for our purposes follows:

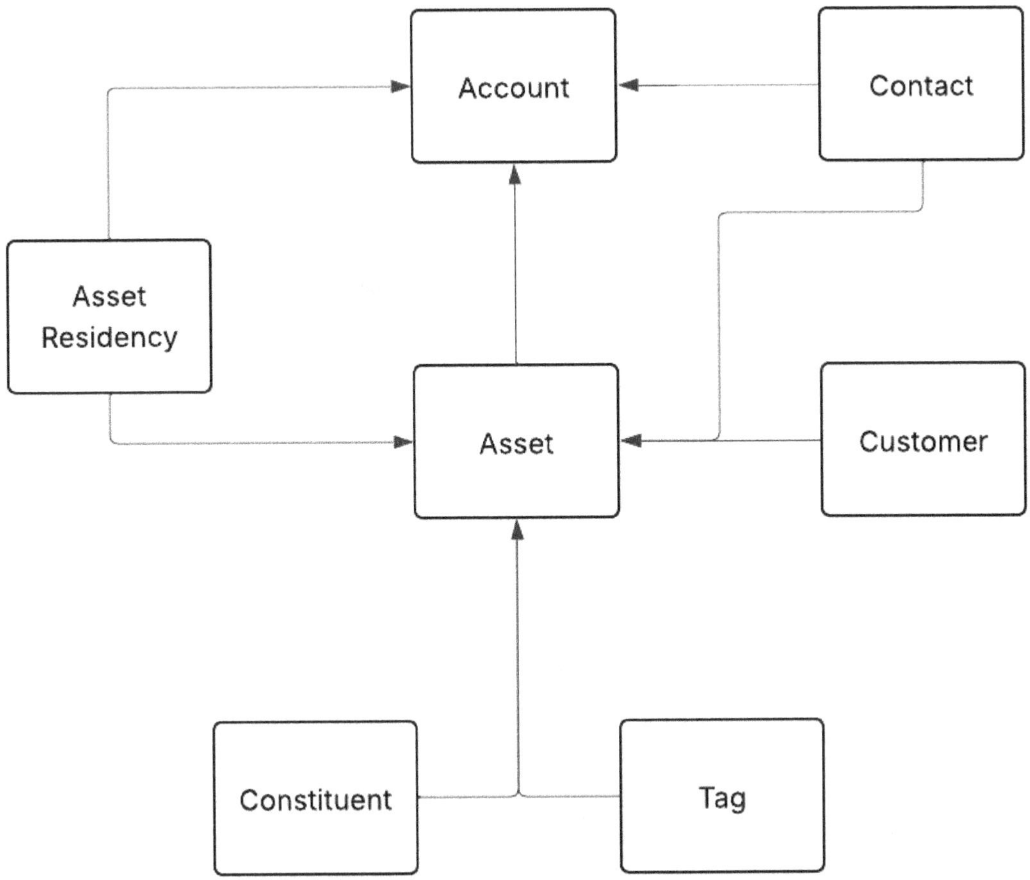

Figure 1.7: An Entity Relationship Diagram (ERD) showing the general relationships that will be utilized for the use case presented in this cookbook.

Your job as the developer is to make sure that your end users are able to complete tasks such as transferring artworks between museums, viewing the museums that an artwork has had residency at on a map, tracking errors that occur in the transfer and acquisition of artworks, and more. We will be building out a Developer Edition Org to satisfy a number of related requirements for this fictional use case throughout this cookbook.

How to do it...

Hopefully, by now, you have forked the repository for the cookbook and have it located in a repository similar to *https://github.com/YOUR_GITHUB_USERNAME/Salesforce-Lightning-Web-Component-Cookbook*, where `YOUR_GITHUB_USERNAME` is your GitHub username. If you haven't, go back to the *Forking the repository* section at the top of the chapter and review the Retrieving *and deploying metadata from Salesforce* section as well. Once you have forked and deployed the repository to your Developer Edition Org, you'll have everything you need to get started with custom objects, flows, and metadata files to insert sample accounts, contacts, customers, and more. We'll just have to do a few manual steps to load some data from our deployed metadata.

> Note
>
> The datasets we are loading were generated using the open source software (**OSS**) solution **GenerateData.com** at `https://generatedata.com`, where more sample data can be generated if desired. The test data is completely random, so the cities and geolocations on the accounts may not be geographically accurate. This is expected behavior.

1. In your Salesforce Developer Edition Org that you signed up for at the start of this chapter, ensure that you have authorized your Org and deployed the setup code for this cookbook by right-clicking the `force-app/chapter00` folder and selecting **SFDX: Deploy This Source to Org**.
2. Open your Developer Console to execute anonymous Apex. If preferred, execute anonymous Apex through VSCode.
3. Issue the following anonymous Apex snippet. This snippet will grant you the permissions necessary to complete the next step:

```
OrgSetupClass.getPerms();
```

4. Next, we will insert 10 of my favorite pieces of public domain art into your Developer Edition Org as assets and associate them with a new top account that will be inserted, **Ultricies PC**. To do this, issue the following snippet:

```
OrgSetupClass.dataSetup();
```

Now that you have completed these steps, you should have at least 25 accounts, 25 contacts, and 25 customers, as well as 10 asset records associated with the **Ultricies PC** account in your org. We will be adding more asset records in later chapters.

Building your first LWC

Once we have our IDE set up and configured for development, and now that we understand how to retrieve and deploy metadata, we are ready to develop our own metadata to deploy!

How to do it...

1. Navigate to your IDE and right-click on the `lwc` folder in the `force-app/chapter01/default` path. If you have forked the repository for this book, there will be an `lwc` folder under each of the chapters—for example, the `lwc` folder for *Chapter 1, Getting Ready for Lightning Web Components Development*, will be under the `force-app/chapter01/default` path.
2. From the drop-down menu that appears after right-clicking `force-app/chapter01/default/lwc`, select **SFDX: Create Lightning Web Component**.
3. When your Salesforce Extensions Pack loads, enter a name for your new LWC, such as `yourFirstLWC`. For example, I will be using `evelynsFirstLWC` for mine. Hit *Enter*, and either choose a custom directory, such as `force-app/chapter01/default/lwc`, or hit *Enter* one more time without selecting a custom directory, meaning that the Salesforce Extensions Pack will create all the necessary files for your LWC under the default path of `force-app/main/default/lwc`. If you have forked the cookbook repository and created your LWC under the custom directory of `force-app/chapter01/default/lwc`, your IDE File Explorer will look similar to the following:

Figure 1.8: The folder structure of the forked Chapter 1, Getting Ready for Lightning Web Components Development, repository

4. Once the files have been created, double-click the `yourFirstLWC.html` file. This will open your file in a new tab in your IDE with the following code:

```
<template>
</template>
```

5. In between the two `template` tags, which are LWC-specific HTML tags, add a **lightning-card** tag. Documentation for this tag can be found at `https://developer.salesforce.com/docs/component-library/bundle/lightning-card/documentation`. To auto-insert the template utilizing the Salesforce extensions we installed earlier, type `lwc-card` and hit *Enter*. We now have the following base template:

```
<template>
    <lightning-card icon-name="standard:account" variant="base">
        <div slot="title">
            Card Title
        </div>
        <div slot="actions">
        </div>
        <div slot="footer">
        </div>
        <div>
            <!-- Card Body  -->
        </div>
    </lightning-card>
</template>
```

6. Navigate to the **Salesforce Lightning Design System** (**SLDS**) Icon Library, located at `https://www.lightningdesignsystem.com/icons/`, and select an icon for the header of your LWC by browsing the **Icon Library** tab. Note the type of icon (**Utility**, **Doctype**, **Standard**, or **Action**), and copy your icon name. Replace the `standard:account` text within the `icon-name` attribute of the `lightning-card` tag with your `type:icon`. For example, if I were to choose the `component_customization` icon, I would enter `utility:component_customization`.
7. Replace the **Card Title** text in the `div` tag, which is a tag that represents a group of content that can be easily styled, where the slot attribute is `title`, with a title for your **lightning-card**. An ideal card title is something descriptive, like `My First Component`.

8. Next, let's add a standard first program greeting inside our body `div`. On the line after the `<!-- Card Body -->` comment, enter the following: `Hello World! My name is {userName}!`. The curly brackets allow us to access a variable in our JavaScript file, which we will look at next.
9. Let's also add some padding so that our greeting prints properly. In the `div` tag surrounding **Hello World!**, add the attribute `class="slds-p-around_medium"` to the opening tag.
10. Under your **Hello World!** greeting, but within the `div` tags surrounding it, enter the following to add a **template if:true directive** followed by a **lightning-formatted-date-time** component, which will format and display a date variable, `currentDate`, as a 2-digit, 2-month, 2-year date and a long-form weekday:

```
<template if:true={currentDate}>
   <br/>
   The date is currently:
   <lightning-formatted-date-time
        value={currentDate}
        day="2-digit"
        month="2-digit"
        year="2-digit"
        weekday="long"
   ></lightning-formatted-date-time>!
</template>
```

11. We will learn more about **template directives** in later chapters, but for now, know that this date will display if we have a **truthy** (read: non-`null` or non-`false`) value for the variable `currentDate`.
12. Let's also replace the `actions div`, right below our `title div` and highlighted in the code snippet in step 8, with the following **lightning-button** tag:

```
<lightning-button label="Get Date" slot="actions" onclick={updateDate}></
lightning-button>
```

13. This will add a button that calls a JavaScript function, `updateDate`, to get the current date from the browser.

14. Lastly, for our HTML file, to go with our button, let's add some descriptive text in the footer `div` of our **lightning-card**. Add the following text between the tags: `Press the button to get the date.`
15. In all, our HTML file should look like the file in the `force-app/chapter01/default/lwc/myFirstLWC/myFirstLWC.html` directory of the cookbook repository, linked in the *See also* section for this recipe.
16. Now, let's look at the `yourFirstLWC.js` file, which is going to start off looking like this:

```
import { LightningElement } from 'lwc';
export default class evelynsFirstLWC extends LightningElement {}
```

17. Within our first set of curly brackets, let's add some more decorators to import. Change `LightningElement` to `LightningElement, api, wire`. The `@api` decorator will allow us to access the `recordId` of the record page that we place our LWC on, and the `@wire` decorator will allow us to wire an Apex function for use in our LWC. We will dive into what each of these mean in depth in later chapters.
18. Under our first `import` statement, let's import the `getRecord` and `getFieldValue` methods from `'lightning/uiRecordApi'`. These methods will allow us to grab the record using our `recordId` and get the field values of that record based on field names. This line will look like the following:

```
import { getRecord, getFieldValue } from 'lightning/uiRecordApi';
```

19. Under our import statements, but before the definition of the `yourFirstLWC` class, we are also going to add the following two lines of code. These will import the `User.Name` field schema from our Salesforce org and store it in a variable called `USER_NAME`, in all caps to indicate a constant variable. We will then instantiate another constant, `fields`, which we will declare as an array storing the `USER_NAME` constant.

```
import USER_NAME from '@salesforce/schema/User.Name';
const fields = [USER_NAME];
```

20. Let's start building out our class. Directly under the class definition, within the curly brackets, add two variables: `@api recordId` and `currentDate`. The `@api` decorator paired with the exact text of `recordId` allows us to grab the `recordId` of the sObject

record page that our LWC is placed on, while the `currentDate` variable will store the current date as pulled from our browser.

```
@api recordId;
currentDate;
```

21. Next, let's wire our `getRecord` method that we imported into a variable called `user`. We will go into this in more depth in *Chapter 2*, but for now, all we need to know is that our `wire` function will look like this:

```
@wire(getRecord, { recordId: "$recordId", fields })
user;
```

22. Once we have wired the result of the `getRecord` method to our `user` variable, let's write a getter function that imperatively calls the `getFieldValue` method from our import statement. We are going to use dot notation to grab the data property of our `user` variable, and we are going to pass in `USER_NAME` as another parameter, like so:

```
get userName() {
  return getFieldValue(this.user.data, USER_NAME);
}
```

23. Finally, we are going to write the function for the button on our LWC, `updateDate`. We are going to utilize the `Date.now()` function in JavaScript, which will grab the current date from our browser. The snippet of code `this.currentDate` is the same `{currentDate}` as we included in our HTML file, and we are setting it to the value of `Date.now()`, which is a built-in function.

```
updateDate() {
  this.currentDate = Date.now();
}
```

24. The `this` keyword lets our JavaScript know the scope in which the variable can be utilized. Put simply, because we declared `currentDate` as a class variable, we need to let our `updateDate` function know that it's okay to use it!
25. In all, our code will look like the JavaScript file in the `force-app/chapter01/default/lwc/myFirstLWC/myFirstLWC.js` directory, linked in the *See also* section of this recipe.

26. Once our JavaScript file has been completed, we can turn our eyes to the `yourFirstLWC.js-meta.xml` file, commonly referred to as the `meta-xml-file`. The only changes that we are going to make here are to set `isExposed` to `true` and to add a target of `lightning__RecordPage` nested within a set of `targets` tags. These additions to our file will allow us to drop our LWC on a Lightning Record Page utilizing the Lightning App Builder. This will yield the following for our `js-meta.xml` file:

```
<?xml version="1.0" encoding="UTF-8"?>
<LightningComponentBundle xmlns="http://soap.sforce.com/2006/04/metadata">
    <apiVersion>63.0</apiVersion>
    <isExposed>true</isExposed>
    <targets>
        <target>lightning__RecordPage</target>
    </targets>
</LightningComponentBundle>
```

> **Note**
>
> The `apiVersion` in your file might be different from what is in the cookbook and cookbook repository. This is expected. As Salesforce releases new versions, the apiVersion changes. As of the editing of this chapter, we are on `apiVersion` 63.0. It is best practice to use the latest API version, although there are some use cases for using an older API version, which we will see in *Chapter 7, Building Secure Components with Lightning Locker and Lightning Web Security*.

27. Once we have saved all three of our LWC files, we can deploy our LWC to our target org that we specified while setting up our IDE. Right-click on the `yourFirstLWC` folder and select **SFDX: Deploy Source to Org**. Any errors preventing deployment will appear as output in your IDE and can be debugged using *Chapter 15* of this book.
28. Now that our component is deployed, we can add it to the **User** record page. Navigate to your **User** record page by clicking the logo (or your profile picture) in the top-right corner of the Salesforce home page, and click on your name to view your profile.
29. From the **User** record page, click the **Setup** cog in the top-right corner, and select **Edit Page**. This will take you to Lightning App Builder for the **User** record page.
30. On the left-hand **Components** pane of Lightning App Builder, scroll down until you get to the **Custom** components dropdown. Drag and drop `yourFirstLWC` onto the record page above the **Related** module.

31. Save and activate the Lightning Record Page for the **User** sObject and return to your **User** page. You should see `yourFirstLWC` on the left-hand side of the page, like so:

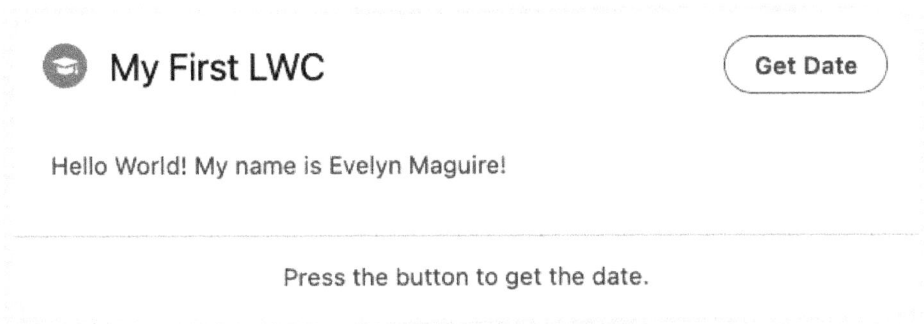

Figure 1.9: The evelynsFirstLWC component on page load

32. If you click the **Get Date** button, your browser will supply the date to your LWC, which will conditionally render our `currentDate` value when it is not `null`:

Figure 1.10: The evelynsFirstLWC component after pressing the Get Date button

33. When we refresh the page, we see that `currentDate` is, once again, set to `null`, and we only see our greeting.
34. Now that we have built our first LWC, we can optionally run our newly configured linter by issuing the `npm run lint` command in our project directory, which will show us if there are any stylistic errors or anti-patterns in the code.
35. In order to compare your code to mine, you can now deploy the `force-app/chapter01` folder. While this component was fairly straightforward, our components will be rapidly gaining in complexity!
36. Finally, now that we are satisfied with our changes, let's commit our project code to our forked repository. In the left-hand sidebar for VSCode, select the **Source Control** icon,

represented by three circles in a loose triangle, with the two upper circles connected to the bottom third. This icon represents a Git branch with two nodes.

37. Once you have clicked into the **Source Control** tab, you'll see all the changes you've made to your files! To make these changes easier to view, you can hover over the **CHANGES** tab right above the **Message** input and select the **View As Tree** icon, which looks like several lines stacked on top of each other. This will organize your changes as they are structured in your directory, which makes it easier to parse exactly which files have been changed.

38. For now, we won't worry about creating a **new branch** because this is a personal project and we won't be submitting **pull requests** to the original repository. However, if we were committing changes in an **open source** project or a work repository, we would want to create a **new branch** and follow the remote repository's **branching strategy**. You can read more about branching and branching strategies in the GitHub documentation at `https://docs.github.com/en/get-started/using-github/github-flow`.

39. To **stage** the changes that you have made, hover over the **CHANGES** list and select the **plus** (+) icon. To **unstage** any changes, such as changes that aren't quite ready to be made public, you can hover over an individual file name and select the **minus** (-) icon. We have only made changes to our first LWC project, so there should be four files to stage to start. Add a descriptive commit message, and select the **Commit** button:

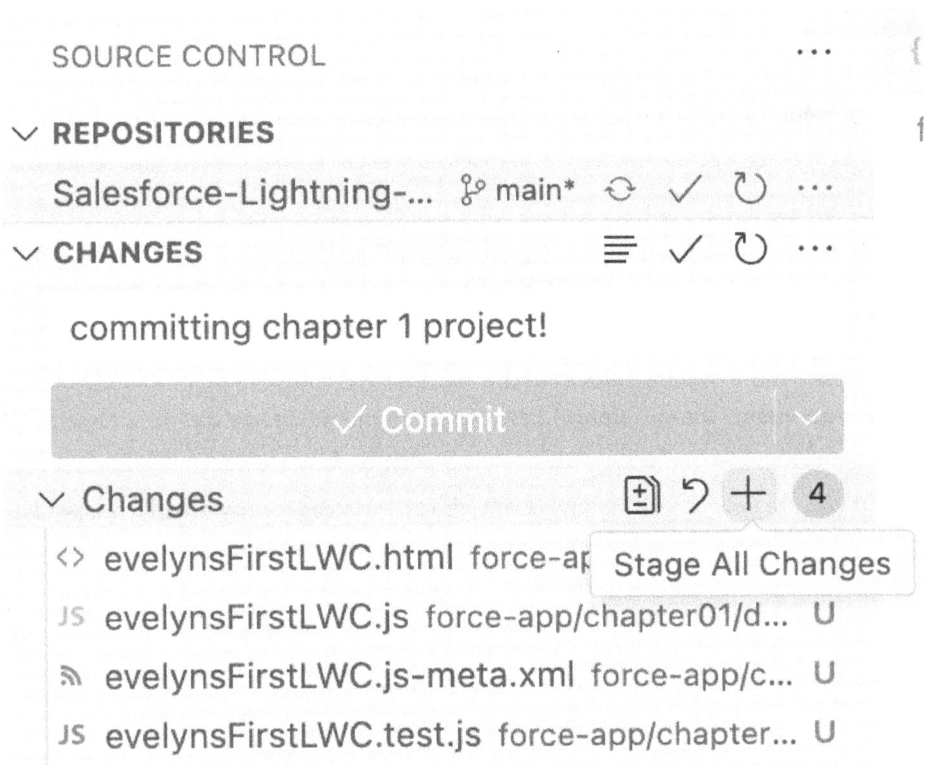

Figure 1.11: The SOURCE CONTROL tab in VSCode showing that we are getting ready to stage the files for evelynsFirstLWC to the main branch of our forked repository.

40. Once you have committed your changes, you can sync to the **remote repository**, which is your fork on GitHub. While this cookbook is not meant to be a comprehensive lesson in Git and GitHub, we want to try to get familiar with source control, as this is a growing skill requirement for Salesforce developers.

There's more

After building and deploying the `MyFirstLWC` component, other features can be added to this base. For example, native JavaScript functionality can be utilized to grab the current time rather than the date, or an **Apex controller class** can be built to extend the functionality to include interaction with the database to show related sObjects on the user record page via MyFirstLWC. We will be exploring how to write an Apex controller class in the next chapter.

See also

- The sample files for Chapter 1, Getting Ready for Lightning Web Components Development, are located at `https://github.com/PacktPublishing/Salesforce-Lightning-Web-Component-Cookbook/tree/main/force-app/chapter01/default/lwc/myFirstLWC`.
- If you are completely new to developing LWCs, the developer documentation can be found in the Lightning Web Components Developer Guide, located at `https://developer.salesforce.com/docs/platform/lwc/overview`.
- To add more building blocks to the MyFirstLWC component, or to build other components, the Salesforce Lightning Component Library can be accessed via `https://developer.salesforce.com/docs/component-library/overview/components`.
- If you are new to writing JavaScript, the MDN Web Docs by Mozilla are available at `https://developer.mozilla.org/en-US/docs/Web/JavaScript`.

Get this book's PDF version and more

Scan the QR code (or go to `packtpub.com/unlock`). Search for this book by name, confirm the edition, and then follow the steps on the page.

UNLOCK NOW

Note: Keep your invoice handy. Purchases made directly from Packt don't require an invoice

2

Writing Apex for Lightning Web Components

With three frontend frameworks, Salesforce is an infinitely extensible customer relationship management platform. Having read *Chapter 1, Getting Ready for Lightning Web Component Development*, you are now prepared to write code in the modern Lightning Web Components framework with an **Integrated Development Environment**, or **IDE**.

Not only are you ready for development in an IDE, but you are also prepared to catch errors and anti-patterns before they ship with the assistance of a **linter**. We will cover debugging common Apex and JavaScript errors in *Chapter 15, Debugging Lightning Web Components*, by which point you will already be an expert.

Additionally, you set up a Salesforce Developer Edition org to practice retrieving and deploying the sample code for this cookbook. You seeded your Developer Edition org with test data, as well as deployed some of the necessary components to complete the projects laid out in this cookbook.

Finally, you built a simple **Lightning Web Component** (**LWC**) utilizing native JavaScript functionality and learned a little bit about the parts that make up an LWC. We touched on the three main component files – `HTML`, `JavaScript`, and the `js-meta.xml` file – all of which are necessary for taking the LWC from prospect to production. One thing we did not touch on, however, was connecting the LWC to the database via Salesforce's proprietary programming language, Apex.

In this chapter, you will learn how to build a robust backend for your LWCs utilizing Apex, laying the foundation for the rest of this cookbook. We are going to be covering the following main recipes:

- Building your next LWC
- Writing Apex classes for LWCs
- Wrapper classes
- The @AuraEnabled annotation
- Importing methods, objects, and fields into LWCs
- Calling Apex methods from LWCs
- Throwing exceptions
- Bringing it all together

Technical requirements

The recipes for this book can be found at `https://github.com/PacktPublishing/Salesforce-Lightning-Web-Component-Cookbook`, where each chapter has its own folder under the `force-app` folder. This GitHub repository is structured in the form of a Salesforce DX project, which will allow you to easily fork the repository for deployment in a free Salesforce Developer Edition org. The code for *Chapter 2, Writing Apex for Lightning Web Components,* is located at `https://github.com/PacktPublishing/Salesforce-Lightning-Web-Component-Cookbook/tree/main/force-app/chapter02`.

The components in this book require the use of an integrated development environment (**IDE**), such as **Visual Studio Code** (**VSCode**) or **Salesforce Code Builder**. Detailed instructions for setting up an IDE are located in *Chapter 1, Getting Ready for Lightning Web Component Development*, in the *Setting up your IDE* section.

If you are building the projects in this cookbook as written, you will need to seed your Salesforce Developer Edition org with test data. Detailed instructions for seeding your org are in *Chapter 1, Getting Ready for Lightning Web Component Development*, in the *Setting up the Salesforce Lightning Web Components cookbook org* recipe.

Lastly, the edition of Salesforce required to implement the recipes in this book is Developer, Performance, Unlimited, Enterprise, or Database.com. You can sign up for a free Salesforce Developer Edition org at `https://developer.salesforce.com/signup`.

Building your next LWC

In *Chapter 1, Getting Ready for Lightning Web Component Development*, you built a simple LWC where you imported two built-in Apex methods, `getRecord` and `getFieldValue`, to connect your frontend to the Salesforce database to display the name of a user record. We also used native JavaScript functionality to grab and display the current date. What does this process look like if you want to build more robust functionality? Let's look at some business requirements.

Imagine you are a Salesforce developer for an art broker tasked with building a solution that allows end users to transfer artworks (**assets**) between different museums (**accounts**). Because the art broker has thousands of accounts spanning the globe, you want to enable end users to filter accounts based on the country and city where the account is located.

Additionally, there is a requirement to document the history of each asset's residencies (**asset residencies**). These are created and updated by a record-triggered flow upon insertion or update of an asset record. This flow is included in the cookbook repository under the `force-app/chapter00/default/flows` directory and does not need to be constructed. For end users, you want to display the geolocation of the account associated with each of the last 10 asset residencies on a map so that an end user can easily see where each artwork has been.

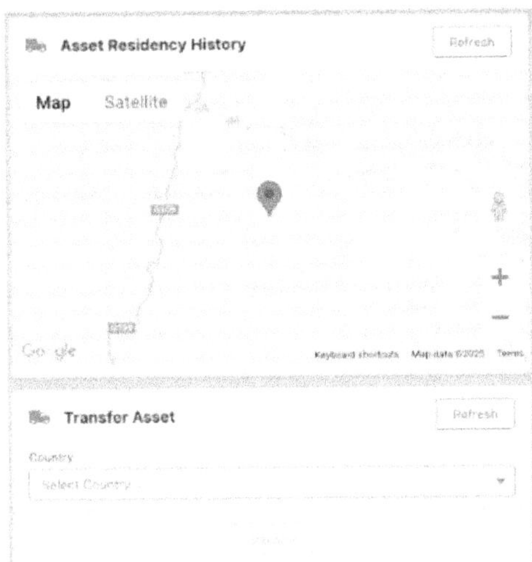

Figure 2.1: A screenshot of the functionality we will be building, showing an Asset Residency History component and a Transfer Asset component.

Let's look at the simplified **entity relationship diagram** (**ERD**) for this use case to understand the business requirements further. Each account can have one or more assets associated with it, and for historical tracking reasons, there is an asset residency **junction object** record, which is a record that is used to create a many-to-many relationship in Salesforce every time an asset is associated with an account.

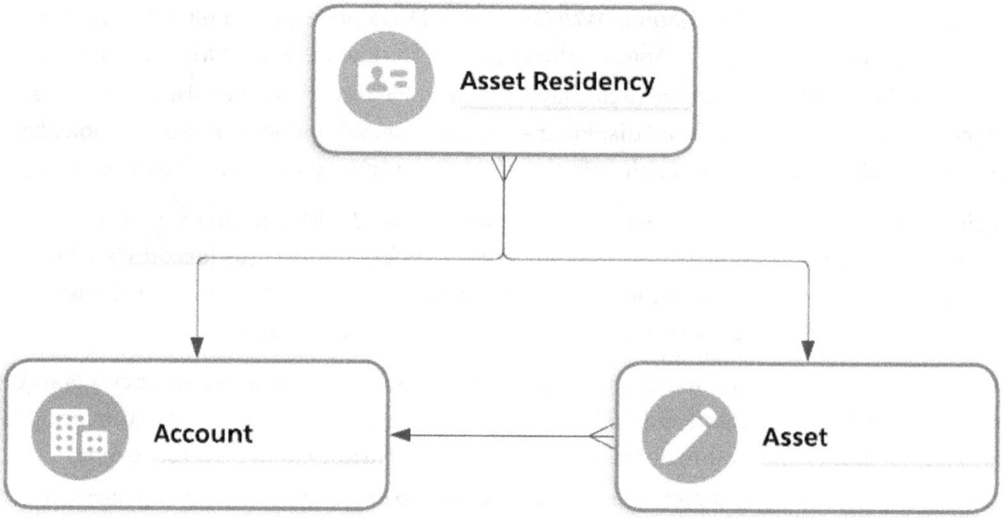

Figure 2.2: A simplified view of the ERD for the business use case

With the test data you set up in the *Setting up the Salesforce Lightning Web Components cookbook org* recipe of *Chapter 1, Getting Ready for Lightning Web Component Development*, you have at least 25 accounts with corresponding contacts and at least 10 assets in the Salesforce Developer Edition org. If you are building the cookbook project as written and have not yet completed these steps, take a moment to do so now. To ensure that the flow required for this project is deployed, deploy the *force-app/chapter00* folder in its entirety to your org.

When I am building a new LWC, I often like to start by building out my component's **user interface** (**UI**), which is controlled by the HTML file. Not only does building the HTML file help me visualize the **user experience** (**UX**) and allow me to test as I go, but I am able to define the data structure required of my related Apex controller class. Having defined the data structure, I can then build my Apex controller to suit the needs of my component. To demonstrate this, let's start by building out the `transferAsset` LWC.

How to do it...

You have been tasked with building a solution that allows end users to transfer artworks between different museums based on the country and city in which the museum is located. Simply put, you are going to update the `AccountId` field on the **Asset** object. The business has also called out that they want to make the end users' lives easier by allowing them to filter the accounts that the end user can select from by country and city.

This is a perfect use case for a custom LWC with two of the most used elements: **lightning-combobox** and **lightning-datatable**. The **lightning-combobox** element represents a drop-down menu, while the **lightning-datatable** element represents a table that displays data. We will become intimately familiar with these two components throughout the course of this cookbook.

Let's get started, shall we?

1. Start by creating a new LWC. This is most easily achieved by utilizing the SFDX extension pack that you installed in *Chapter 1*. Press *Ctrl* + *Shift* + *P* (*Cmd* + *Shift* + *P* on macOS) and select **SFDX: Create Lightning Web Component**. Enter the filename `transferAsset` and select the default directory (`force-app/main/default/lwc`). This will create a new LWC in a separate folder from the example code in `force-app/chapter02`.

   > **Note**
   >
   > While different companies and organizations have different standard naming conventions, we are going to be using descriptive names for our components that describe what the components do. These descriptive names will be in **camelCase**, which is a naming convention that capitalizes the first letter of each word in a phrase except for the first word and removes spaces. If you have deployed the cookbook repository in its entirety, you will find that there is already a component named `transferAsset`. You can differentiate your component from mine by prefacing your component with `yourName`, such as `yourNameTransferAsset`.

2. We are going to want to put this component on the **Asset** record page, so first let's update the `.js-meta.xml` file to reflect this. Enter `transferAsset.js-meta.xml` and update it to the following to expose the LWC to the **Lightning Record Page** for the **Asset** object:

```
<?xml version="1.0" encoding="UTF-8"?>
<LightningComponentBundle xmlns="http://soap.sforce.com/2006/04/metadata">
    <apiVersion>63.0</apiVersion>
    <isExposed>true</isExposed>
    <targets>
        <target>lightning__RecordPage</target>
    </targets>
```

```
    <targetConfigs>
        <targetConfig targets="lightning__RecordPage">
            <objects>
                <object>Asset</object>
            </objects>
        </targetConfig>
    </targetConfigs>
</LightningComponentBundle>
```

3. The highlighted lines of code represent our deviation from the originally provided `.js-meta.xml` file.

> **Note**
>
> If you are unfamiliar with the file structure of LWCs or a `.js-meta.xml` file, there is a description of the base file types we will be utilizing in the *How it works* section of the *Retrieving and deploying metadata from Salesforce* recipe in *Chapter 1, Getting Ready for Lightning Web Component Development*.

Because you are placing this component on a Lightning record page, you are going to want to put the component elements in a visual container to keep the component looking clean. For this purpose, it is common to utilize a **lightning-card** element with a descriptive title. Let's take a look at the documentation for the `lightning-card`, located at `https://developer.salesforce.com/docs/component-library/bundle/lightning-card`. Keep this documentation open throughout the exercise. A `lightning-card` element has four main slots: `title`, `actions`, `footer`, and body. For example, this `.html` file yields the user interface seen in *Figure 2.3*:

```
<template>
    <lightning-card icon-name="utility:animal_and_nature" variant="base">
        <div slot="title">
            My Cool Title
        </div>
        <lightning-button label="Action Button" slot="actions"></lightning-
button>
        <lightning-button label="Footer Button" slot="footer"></lightning-
button>
        <!-- Body Goes Here -->
        <p class="slds-p-around_medium">I am the body!</p>
```

```
    </lightning-card>
</template>
```

This file will render a `lightning-card` element that has a title, an icon, and buttons in the actions and footer slots.

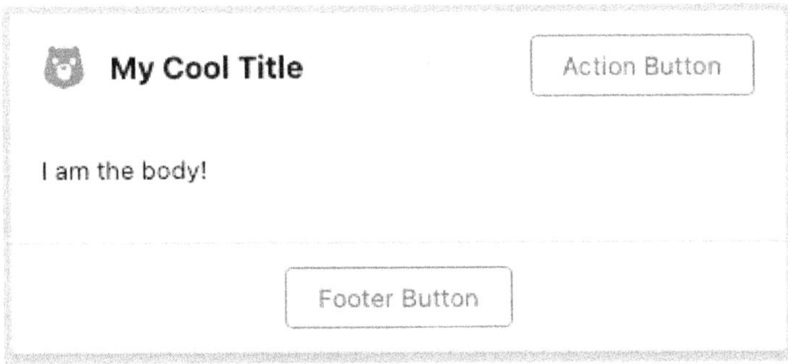

Figure 2.3: A basic lightning-card with labeled features

4. Now that you know a little bit about the `lightning-card` element, let's add one to the `transferAsset.html` file. In between the `template` tags, type `lwc-card`, and select the `lwc-card` option without the wrench in the dropdown, pictured in *Figure 2.4*. This autocomplete feature is part of the expanded **Salesforce extension pack** that you installed in *Chapter 1, Getting Ready for Lightning Web Component Development*.

Figure 2.4: A screenshot illustrating the autocomplete feature included in the Salesforce extension pack.

5. Once you have selected the `lwc-card` option without the wrench, your `transferAsset.html` file will look something like this:

```
<template>
   <lightning-card icon-name="standard:account" variant="base">
      <div slot="title">
         Card Title
      </div>
      <div slot="actions">
      </div>
      <div slot="footer">
```

```
        </div>
        <div>
            <!-- Card Body -->
        </div>
    </lightning-card>
</template>
```

6. Let's start by picking an icon from the **SLDS icon library**, located at `https://www.lightningdesignsystem.com/2e1ef8501/p/83309d-iconography`. It can also easily be found if you search for `SLDS icon library` in your favorite search engine. Replace the `icon-name` attribute value with the type and name of your chosen icon in the format of `type:name`, such as `utility:activity`. Let's also add a descriptive title, replacing `Card Title` with `Transfer Asset`.
7. Save and deploy your updated `transferAsset` component to your developer org and place it on the **Asset** Lightning record page on the upper right-hand side of the page, directly above the **Activity** module. Because you have set `isExposed` to `true` and therefore exposed the LWC to **Lightning Record Pages** in the `.js-meta.xml` file, `transferAsset` will appear under the **Custom Components** dropdown in **Lightning App Builder**. For now, the component will be an empty `lightning-card` with a title and an icon that you will be able to refresh as you fill it out.

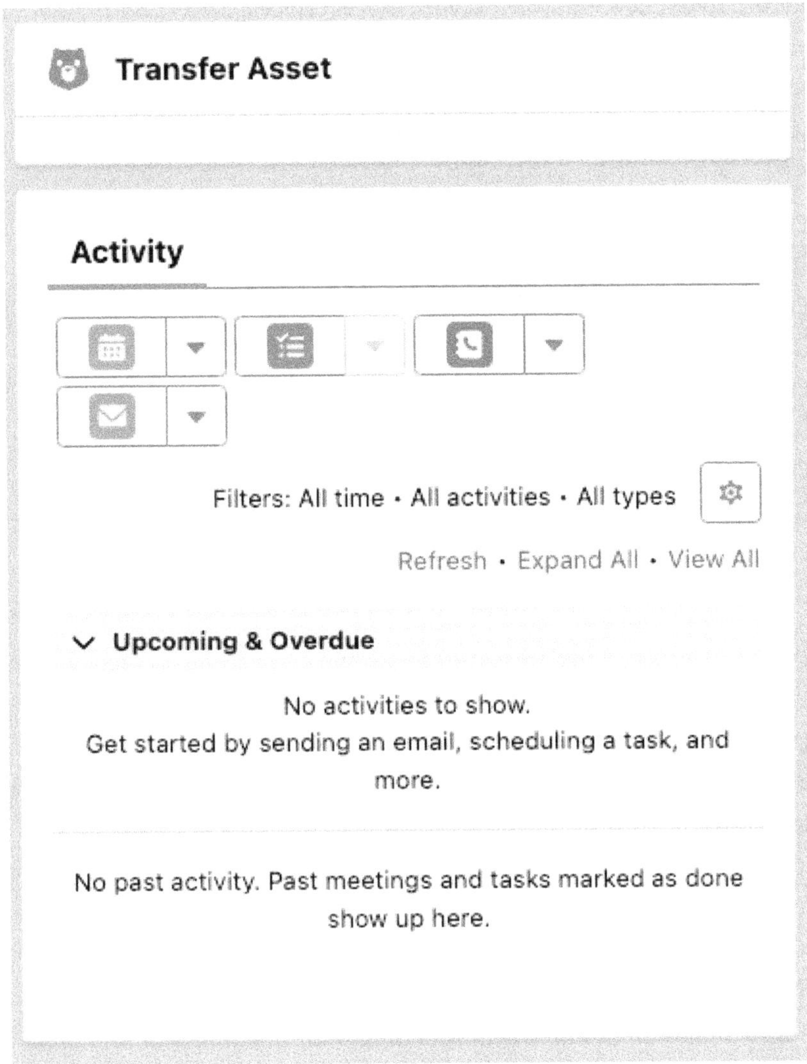

Figure 2.5: The transferAsset LWC placed on the record page above the Activity module

8. Next, you will need to fill out the LWC. Pull up the documentation for **lightning-button**, which can be accessed at `https://developer.salesforce.com/docs/component-library/bundle/lightning-button`, or by traversing the **Components** menu on the left-hand side of the `lightning-card` documentation you pulled up earlier. Notice that there are several variations of buttons. There are UX considerations for each style of button, which we will discuss in *Chapter 11, Writing Accessible Lightning Web Components*, but for now, pick your favorite.

9. Return to VSCode, and add a `lightning-button` element to both the `actions` and `footer` slots of your `lightning-card`. Like the `lightning-card`, you can utilize the Salesforce Extensions Pack autocompletion tool and type `lwc-button`, which will give you the option to add a button template.

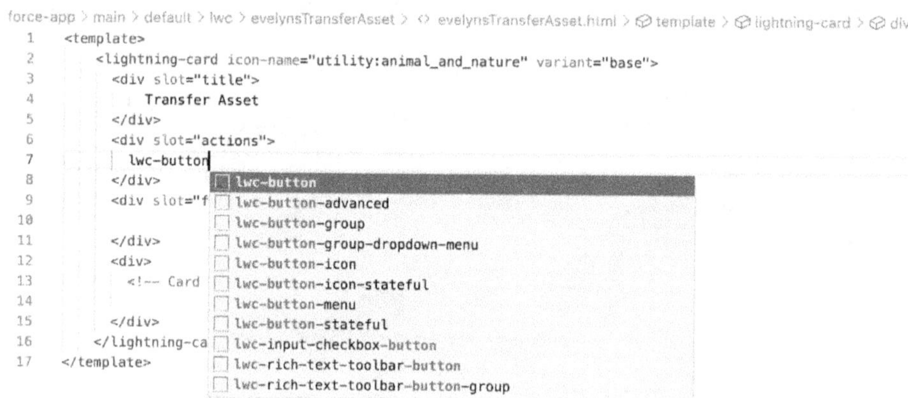

Figure 2.6: A screenshot showing the autocomplete options for the lwc-button command

10. Utilizing the autocomplete feature yields the `<lightning-button variant="base" label="Button Label" onclick={handleClick}></lightning-button>` tag, which you can modify for our purposes. Edit the `variant` attribute to your favorite variant of button from the documentation, and change each `lightning-button` tag label to something descriptive. For our use case, you are going to set the `actions` slotted button to *Refresh*, and the footer slotted button to *Transfer*. Lastly, change the `onclick` attributes for each button to a descriptive function name, such as `handleRefresh` and `handleTransfer`, respectively. Make note of these function names, as we will be building the functions in the related JavaScript file. In the *Transfer* button, let's additionally add a `disabled` attribute, which you will set equal to a variable you will create in the JavaScript file called `transferDisabled`.

11. In all, our `lightning-button` tag will look similar to the following:

```
<lightning-button label="Transfer" onclick={handleTransfer}
disabled={transferDisabled} slot="footer"></lightning-button>
```

12. Deploy your updated LWC to your Developer Edition org and refresh your **Asset** record page to see the changes. You may have to open your browser's **Developer Tools** and

issue a hard refresh to see the changes. Your updated LWC should look something like this:

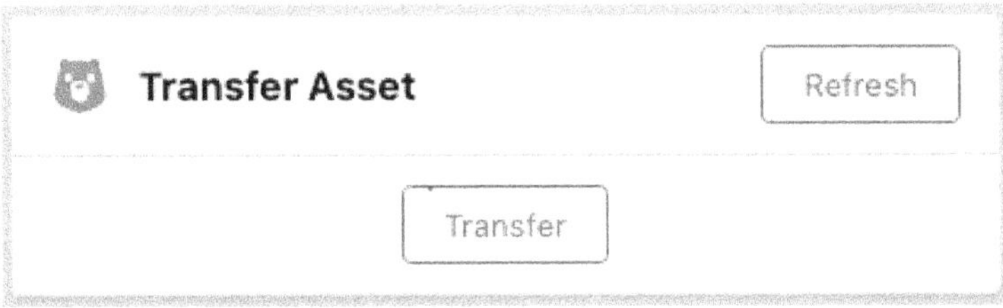

Figure 2.7: The updated transferAsset LWC with the utility:animal_and_nature icon from the SLDS icon library

> **Note**
>
> In order to be able to see your changes right away without a hard refresh, you can go to **Setup** > **Session Settings** and deselect the **Enable secure and persistent browser caching to improve performance** checkbox. This should typically only be done in a Developer Edition org or sandbox.

Notice that if you click on the buttons, nothing happens, and the **Transfer** button is not yet disabled. This is because you have not defined the `handleRefresh` and `handleTransfer` functions and the `transferDisabled` variable in the JavaScript file yet. We will come back to these items once you have written the Apex.

1. Continuing in our HTML file, you are going to fill out the body slot. Looking back at the business requirements, you know that you must filter the museum account records that art assets can be transferred to by country and by city and then present the end user with the resulting accounts. Typically, this would be done with a dropdown that presents the country, a dependent dropdown that presents the city, and a resulting table of some sort that displays the resulting account information. Pull up the documentation for `lightning-combobox` and `lightning-datatable`, which will work nicely for our purposes.
2. Once you have reviewed the relevant documentation, add two `lightning-combobox` elements and a `lightning-datatable` element below the `<!-- Card Body -->` comment in your HTML file. As you can probably guess, the shorthand notation for these elements will be lwc-`combobox` and lwc-`datatable`.
3. For your first `lightning-combobox` element, set the following attributes:
   - `name="transferCountry"`

- `label="Country"`
- `value={countryValue}`, which represents a function we will write called `countryValue`
- `placeholder="Select Country..."`
- `options={countryOptions}`, which represents a variable we will define called `countryOptions`
- `onchange={handleCountryChange}`, which represents a function we will write called `handleCountryChange`
- The values in quotations represent text literals, while the curly brackets denote that you will be accessing a variable or function in the JavaScript file.

4. Repeat step 14 for your second `lightning-combobox` element, replacing instances of *Country* with *City* to yield the following:

```
<lightning-combobox name="transferCity" label="Cities" value={cityValue}
placeholder="Select City..." options={cityOptions}
onchange={handleCityChange}></lightning-combobox>
```

5. Enter the following for your `lightning-datatable` tag:

```
<lightning-datatable key-field="accountId" data={accountData}
columns={columns} max-row-selection="1" onrowselection={setAccountId}></
lightning-datatable>
```

6. These attributes, in order, will set the primary key for `lightning-datatable` to a variable called `accountId`, set the contents to a variable called `accountData`, set the column values to a variable called `columns`, limit the end user to selecting one account at a time, and call a `setAccountId` function when a row is selected.
7. Deploy your changes one more time and refresh the asset record page. You should see something similar to the following:

Figure 2.8: An updated view of the transferAsset LWC with lightning-combobox elements

That looks kind of goofy, doesn't it? We are missing some styling elements that could make this look cleaner. We definitely need some space between the edge of the `lightning-card` and the dropdowns of the `lightning-combobox` elements. In HTML, this is called **padding**. We can additionally use **margins**, which will add some space outside of our padding.

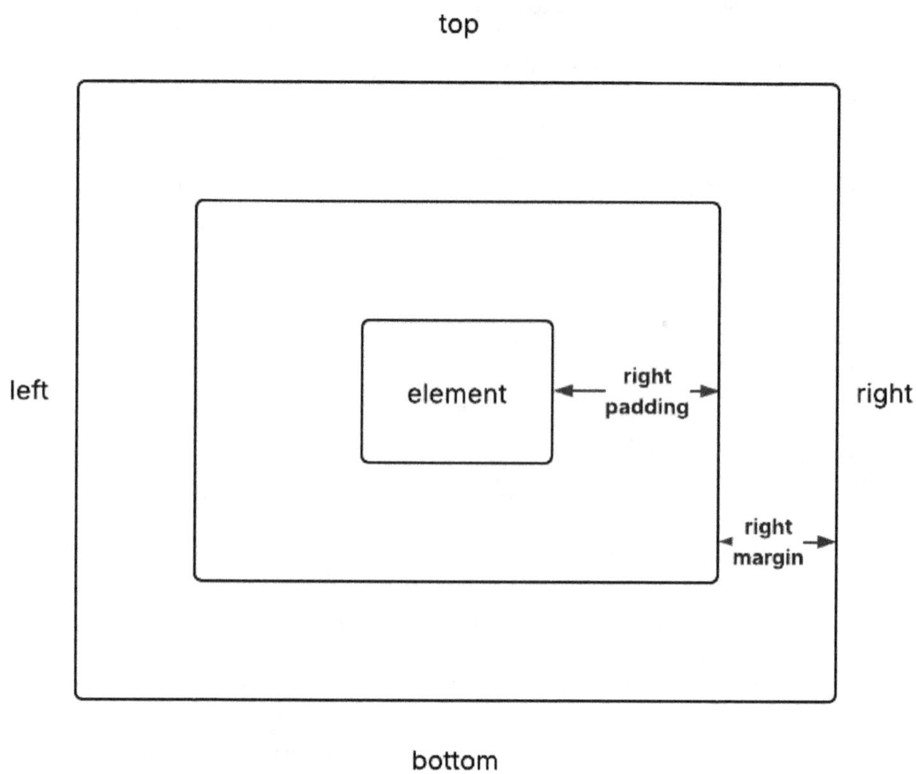

Figure 2.9: A diagram representing padding and margins, showing a right padding and a right margin

Let's pull up the Lightning Design System documentation on padding, located at `https://www.lightningdesignsystem.com/utilities/padding`. To add padding to the sides of the elements, add the following **class attribute** to each of your `lightning-combobox` tags and your `lightning-datatable` tag: `class="slds-p-horizontal_medium"`. This class attribute adds padding to both the right and left sides of the elements within the tag. Your `lightning-combobox` tag will now look like the following:

```
<lightning-combobox
    name="transferCountry"
    class="slds-p-horizontal_medium"
    label="Country"
    value={countryValue}
    placeholder="Select Country..."
    options={countryOptions}
```

```
    onchange={handleCountryChange}
></lightning-combobox>
```

Redeploy your LWC to your org and refresh the page one more time. Much better!

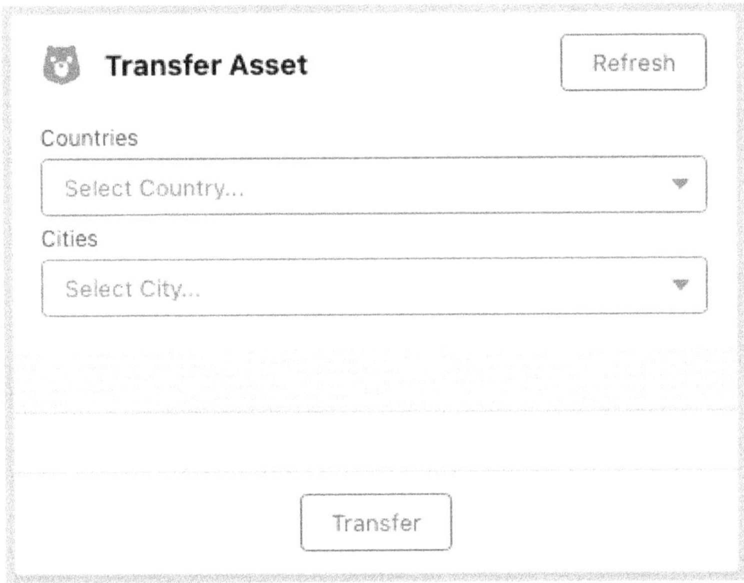

Figure 2.10: An updated view of the transferAsset LWC with appropriately padded lightning-combobox elements

8. Click on each of the dropdowns in your LWC on the **Asset** record page. Notice that nothing happens. This is because you have not yet queried the database. We are not quite there yet, but soon! For now, it makes sense to hide the elements if they are not populated so that it does not confuse the end user. Remember, the **Accounts** data table is going to be dependent on the selected value in the **Cities** combobox, and the **Cities** combobox is going to be dependent on the selected value in the **Countries** combobox. Therefore, let's hide these elements when they are empty. We can render parts of the **Document Object Model** (**DOM**) conditionally utilizing the template **directive tags** supplied at `https://developer.salesforce.com/docs/platform/lwc/guide/create-conditional.html`. We will learn more about the DOM in *Chapter 6*, *Composing Lightning Web Components*, but for now, know that the DOM is what contains our components. The tag you will be adding to the HTML file will be the `<template lwc:if={myCoolProperty}></template>` tag, which will display the inner tags if the value of `myCoolProperty` is **truthy**, meaning that it is `true` or it exists. The opposite of truthy is **falsy**, where the value is either `false`, `undefined`, or `null`. We are going to want

one surrounding the city `lightning-combobox`, and one surrounding the account `lightning-datatable`.

9. Add the template tag around your `transferCity` `lightning-combobox` element, like so:

```
<template lwc:if={cityOptions}>
    <lightning-combobox
        name="transferCity"
        class="slds-p-horizontal_medium"
        label="City"
        value={cityValue}
        placeholder="Select City..."
        options={cityOptions}
        onchange={handleCityChange}
    ></lightning-combobox>
</template>
```

This will display the `transferCity` `lightning-combobox` only if the value of the `cityOptions` variable is truthy.

10. Add the template tag with the `lwc:if` directive around your `lightning-datatable` element, like so:

```
<template lwc:if={accountData}>
    <lightning-datatable
        class="slds-p-horizontal_medium"
        key-field="accountId"
        data={accountData}
        columns={columns}
        max-row-selection="1"
        onrowselection={setAccountId}
    ></lightning-datatable>
</template>
```

This will display the **Account** `lightning-datatable` only if the value of the `accountData` variable is true.

11. Save your LWC and deploy one more time. We now see just the *transferCountry* combobox, and you are ready to start building the Apex to populate it.

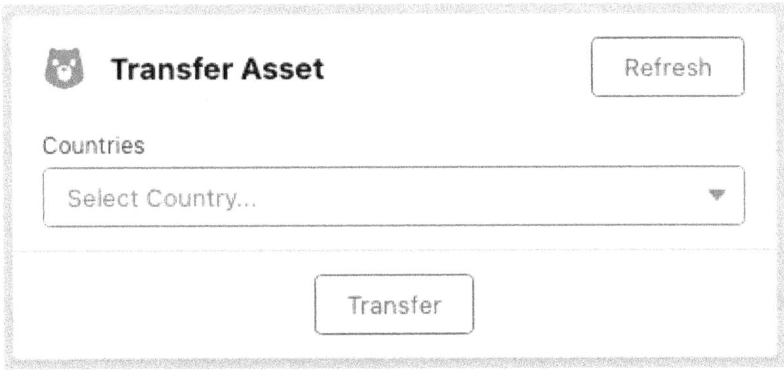

Figure 2.11: An updated view of the transferAsset LWC with elements conditionally hidden by template if:true tags.

See also

- The sample HTML file for the `transferAsset` LWC is located under the `force-app/chapter02/default/lwc/transferAsset/transferAsset.html` directory in your forked repository for comparison. This file is located at `https://github.com/PacktPublishing/Salesforce-Lightning-Web-Component-Cookbook/tree/main/force-app/chapter02/default/lwc/transferAsset/transferAsset.html` in the cookbook repository.
- The Salesforce Developers Component Library is available at `https://developer.salesforce.com/docs/component-library`.
- The Salesforce Lightning Design System guide is available at `https://www.lightningdesignsystem.com`.
- The Salesforce Lightning Web Components Developer Guide is available at `https://developer.salesforce.com/docs/platform/lwc/overview`.
- The Salesforce documentation for Enabling Secure Browser Caching is available at `https://developer.salesforce.com/docs/atlas.en-us.lightning.meta/lightning/perf_secure_browser_caching.htm`.

Writing Apex classes for LWCs

The LWC that you built in the previous recipe looks great, but it is functionally useless because you have not connected it to the database yet. That is where **Apex** comes in. Apex is Salesforce's proprietary programming language, which is based on Java. Apex is a strongly typed, object-oriented programming language.

> **Note**
>
> The classes in the following recipes are named in accordance with how Salesforce describes its classes in Trailhead and its documentation to help visualize where each class sits and what logic, if any, is being performed. We will introduce a more formal naming convention in *Chapter 3, Working with a Selector Class.*

How to do it...

Let's look back at our business use case of transferring assets between accounts. We know that we are going to change the `AccountId` field on the **Asset** object record that the LWC resides on in order to reparent it, and that we are going to select the account to reparent under from a filtered list. Let's start by creating an Apex class to interact with the **Account** table in our database. This will allow us to query for the specified account records that we need to populate the `lightning-combobox` and `lightning-datatable` elements from earlier, and ultimately update the asset with the selected account record's ID.

1. Start by creating a new Apex class. Press *Ctrl* + *Shift* + *P* (*Command* + *Shift* + *P* on macOS) and select **SFDX: Create Apex Class**. Enter the filename `TransferAssetPersistence`, and select the default directory (`force-app/main/default/classes`). This will create a new Apex class in a separate folder from the example code in `force-app/chapter02`.
2. Modify the class definition to `without sharing` and delete the constructor. The reason you are defining `TransferAssetPersistence` as `without sharing` is so that any end user can transfer their asset to any account, regardless of who owns the account. Your initial class definition should now look like this:

```
public without sharing class TransferAssetPersistence { ... }
```

3. Let's go back to the requirements. We want the two `lightning-combobox` elements to contain a list of *countries* and a list of *cities* that correspond to the selected *country* from the first combobox, and we only want to show the *countries* that have accounts in them. This is a perfect use case for two **aggregate queries**. An aggregate query allows us to aggregate data about the results of our query, such as a sum of a given number field or a count of the total number of IDs across our query results. Build two `static` methods that return a `List<AggregateResult>`, one called `getCountries` with no parameters,

and the other called `getCities` that takes a `String` parameter of `selectedCountry`. These will look like the following to start with:

```
public static List<AggregateResult> getCountries() { ... }
public static List<AggregateResult> getCities(String selectedCountry)
{ ... }
```

4. Your queries here will look similar. We are going to build two aggregate queries on the **Account** object, the first with `COUNT` on the `Id` field and grouped by `BillingCountry`, and the second with `COUNT` on the `Id` field and grouped by `BillingCity`. In the `getCities` method, you will also utilize the `selectedCountry` parameter as a bind variable with which you filter the aggregate query results by the user-selected *country*. Let's also alphabetize both sets of results with `NULLS FIRST`. In all, the two aggregate query methods will look like the following:

```
public static List<AggregateResult> getCountries() {
   return [SELECT COUNT(Id), BillingCountry FROM Account GROUP BY
BillingCountry ORDER BY BillingCountry NULLS FIRST];
}
public static List<AggregateResult> getCities(String selectedCountry) {
   return [SELECT COUNT(Id), BillingCity FROM Account WHERE BillingCountry
= :selectedCountry GROUP BY BillingCity ORDER BY BillingCity NULLS FIRST];
}
```

5. Next, let's create a method to `getAccountsByCity`. We will accept one parameter, a `String` called `selectedCity`. The fields you want to grab with this query are `Id`, `Name`, `BillingCity`, and `BillingState`, and you are going to filter on `BillingCity`.
6. In all, the `getAccountsByCity` method will look like the following:

```
public static List<Account> getAccountsByCity(String selectedCity) {
   return [SELECT Name, BillingCity, BillingState FROM Account WHERE
BillingCity = :selectedCity];
}
```

7. Lastly, you want one `static void` method to update the database. This is going to be the simplest method, where you accept a parameter of an asset and then update it. This will look like this:

```
public static void updateAsset(Asset ast) {
    update ast;
}
```

8. Save and deploy your class to your Developer Edition org.
9. Now you can build the **service layer class**, which we will call `TransferAssetService`, that will hold our business logic. We are going to use this class to access the methods of the **persistence layer** class that we just wrote, `TransferAssetPersistence`.

See also

- The sample file for the `TransferAssetPersistence` class is located under the `force-app/chapter02/default/classes/TransferAssetPersistence.cls` directory in your forked repository for comparison. This file is located at `https://github.com/PacktPublishing/Salesforce-Lightning-Web-Component-Cookbook/tree/main/force-app/chapter02/default/classes/TransferAssetPersistence.cls` in the cookbook repository.
- The full Salesforce **Apex Developer Guide** can be found at `https://developer.salesforce.com/docs/atlas.en-you.apexcode.meta/apexcode/apex_dev_guide.htm`.

Wrapper classes

To make the query data easily digestible by an LWC, we are going to introduce the concept of **wrapper classes**. Like an `sObject`, a wrapper class holds information. Unlike an `sObject`, the wrapper class does not hit the database directly. Your wrapper classes are going to allow you to transform `sObject` records into a format that is easily parsed into and out of **JavaScript Object Notation (JSON)**, meaning it is easily parsed into JavaScript objects that can be consumed by the frontend.

How to do it...

1. Start by creating a new Apex class named `TransferAssetService`, and select the default directory (`force-app/main/default/classes`).

2. Think about the data types you are going to need for our use case. Hopefully, you still have your documentation pulled up! We will start with the comboboxes. Look at the example for **Basic Combobox** in the **Salesforce Lightning Component Reference** at `https://developer.salesforce.com/docs/component-library/bundle/lightning-combobox/example`. If you look at the `options` getter in the `basic.js` file, you see that the `options` variables should be formatted as a list of JavaScript objects with the properties of `label` and `value`. For the wrapper class, this means that you will define variables for `label` and `value`—case sensitive. The property names of the wrapper class must exactly match the property names of the JavaScript object depicted by the JSON being ingested.
3. Inside the `TransferAssetService` file, define an **inner class** called `LocaleWrapper`. This is going to be the wrapper for both countries and cities. Your inner class is going to have two `@AuraEnabled public String` instance variables: `label` and `value`. We will touch on what the `@AuraEnabled` annotation means in the next recipe. For now, know that it exposes the variables to the LWC.
4. Build a constructor for your inner class that accepts a `String` parameter called `locale`. We are going to use the constructor to construct an instance of `LocaleWrapper` from our `locale` string. In all, the wrapper class will look like this:

```
public class LocaleWrapper {
   @AuraEnabled public String label;
   @AuraEnabled public String value;
   public LocaleWrapper(String locale) {
      this.label = locale == null ? 'No Locale Specified' : locale;
      this.value = locale;
   }
}
```

Let's go ahead and break this down line by line:

- The declaration of an inner class, `LocaleWrapper`.
- The declaration of the inner class's instance variables, `label` and `value`.
- A constructor that accepts a `String` parameter for `locale`.
- The `this` keyword is used to access the instance variables of the inner class.
- A **ternary operator** is used to define the `label` variable if the `locale` parameter is equal to `null`. If the supplied `locale` parameter is equal to `null`, the `label` will

be `No Locale Specified`. If `locale` is not `null`, we will use the supplied value for `locale`.

- A variable definition sets our instance variable, `this.value`, to `locale`.

> **Note**
>
> By utilizing without sharing in the `TransferAssetPersistence` class in conjunction with `LocaleWrapper`, you can display a limited amount of information about an account to a user who does not have read access to the record, such as an account record that is owned by a user in a different department.

5. Build a similar inner `AccountWrapper` class with the `String` type instance variables of `accountId`, `accountName`, `accountCity`, and `accountState`. These variables will also be exposed to the LWC via the `@AuraEnabled` annotation. Just like the `LocaleWrapper` class, you want a constructor that accepts an account record and assigns the instance variables based on information from that account:

```
public class AccountWrapper {
   @AuraEnabled public String accountId;
   @AuraEnabled public String accountName;
   @AuraEnabled public String accountCity;
   @AuraEnabled public String accountState;
   public AccountWrapper(Account acc) {
      this.accountId = acc.Id;
      this.accountName = acc.Name;
      this.accountCity = acc.BillingCity;
      this.accountState = acc.BillingState;
   }
}
```

6. Next, you will build a wrapper class for the asset record that you are inserting in the `TransferAssetPersistence` class. This one will look a little bit different, as you are going to be accepting values from the LWC rather than passing values to the LWC. Thus,

the class variables, `assetId` and `accountId`, do not have to be annotated with `@AuraEnabled`. Your `AssetWrapper` inner class will look like this:

```
public class AssetWrapper {
    public String assetId;
    public String accountId;
    public AssetWrapper(String assetId, String accountId) {
        this.assetId = assetId;
        this.accountId = accountId;
    }
}
```

7. Now that you have the wrapper classes defined, let's start building out the methods. We are going to have four methods:
    - `getComboboxCountries`, which accepts no parameters and returns a list of `LocaleWrappers`
    - `getComboboxCities`, which accepts a parameter of type `String`, `countryName`, and returns a list of `LocaleWrappers`
    - `getAccountWrappers`, which accepts a parameter of type `String`, `selectedCity`, and returns a list of `AccountWrappers`
    - `transferAssetWrapper`, a void method that accepts a parameter of type `AssetWrapper`, `wrap`, and calls the `updateAsset` method of the `TransferAssetPersistence` class

   Each of these methods will be `static`, meaning that you do not have to create an instance of the class to access them.

8. Your `getComboboxCountries` and `getComboboxCities` methods will look remarkably similar. For each, you are going to declare a new `List<LocaleWrapper>` variable, `countries` and `cities`, respectively. From there, you will iterate over the results of the relevant `TransferAssetPersistence` methods and add a new `LocaleWrapper` to the `List<LocaleWrapper>` for each `AggregateResult` returned by the `TransferAssetPersistence` method. When you are through writing these methods, they will look like this:

```
public static List<LocaleWrapper> getComboboxCountries() {
    List<LocaleWrapper> countries = new List<LocaleWrapper>();
    for(AggregateResult ar : TransferAssetPersistence.getCountries()) {
```

```
        countries.add(new
LocaleWrapper(String.valueOf(ar.get('BillingCountry'))));
    }
    return countries;
}
public static List<LocaleWrapper> getComboboxCities(String countryName) {
    List<LocaleWrapper> cities = new List<LocaleWrapper>();
    for(AggregateResult ar : TransferAssetPersistence.getCities(countryName))
{
        cities.add(new LocaleWrapper(String.valueOf(ar.get('BillingCity'))));
    }
    return cities;
}
```

9. Your `getAccountWrappers` method will also bear a striking resemblance to the previous methods, with a few key changes. We will be returning a `List<AccountWrapper>`, and you will be iterating over the list of **Account** sObject records returned by the `getAccountsByCity` method of the `TransferAssetPersistence` class, yielding a method that looks like this:

```
public static List<AccountWrapper> getAccountWrappers(String selectedCity) {
    List<AccountWrapper> accounts = new List<AccountWrapper>();
    for(Account acc :
TransferAssetPersistence.getAccountsByCity(selectedCity)) {
        accounts.add(new AccountWrapper(acc));
    }
    return accounts;
}
```

10. Finally, you will build the `transferWrap` method, which accepts an `AssetWrapper` and constructs an **Asset** sObject record from that wrapper. We will then use the `updateAsset` method of the `TransferAssetPersistence` class to update the constructed asset. Your method will look like the following:

```
public static void transferWrap(AssetWrapper wrap) {
    Asset ast = new Asset(Id = wrap.assetId, AccountId = wrap.accountId);
    TransferAssetPersistence.updateAsset(ast);
}
```

11. Save and deploy your class to your Developer Edition org.

Now that you have the `TransferAssetService` class, you can expose the methods to the LWC in a **presentation-layer class**.

See also

The sample file for the `TransferAssetService` class is located under the `force-app/chapter02/default/classes/TransferAssetService.cls` directory in your forked repository for comparison. This file is located at `https://github.com/PacktPublishing/Salesforce-Lightning-Web-Component-Cookbook/tree/main/force-app/chapter02/default/classes/TransferAssetPersistence.cls` in the cookbook repository.

The @AuraEnabled annotation

We saw the **@AuraEnabled** annotation while building the wrapper classes in the previous recipe. So far, you know that utilizing this annotation can expose the wrapper class instance variables to an LWC. In this recipe, you are going to utilize the `@AuraEnabled` annotation to expose the methods of a **presentation layer class** to the `TransferAsset` component.

> Note
>
> It should be assumed that all methods and variables exposed by the `@AuraEnabled` annotation can be called by a bad actor with any parameters, regardless of whether the parameters are sanitized. These methods should be treated as a web service interface.

How to do it...

1. Create the final Apex class for this component, named `TransferAssetPresentation`, and select the default directory (`force-app/main/default/classes`). This class will contain four methods:
    - `returnCountries`, a static method that accepts no parameters, returns a `String` derived from the `TransferAssetService.getComboboxCountries()` method, and is annotated with `@AuraEnabled(cacheable=true)`.
    - `returnCities`, a static method that accepts a `String` type parameter, `countryName`, returns a `String` derived from the `TransferAssetService.getComboboxCities(...)` method, and is annotated with `@AuraEnabled`.
    - `returnAccounts`, a static method that accepts a `String` type parameter, `cityName`, returns a `String` derived from the

`TransferAssetService.getAccountWrappers(...)` method, and is annotated with `@AuraEnabled`.

  - `setAssetWrapper`, a static void method that accepts two `String` type parameters, `assetId` and `accountId`, wraps these parameters into an `AssetWrapper`, and calls the `transferAssetWrapper` method of the `TransferAssetService` class.

2. The first method you will be writing will be our simplest: `returnCountries`. You may notice that only the `returnCountries` method is annotated as `cacheable=true`, and you will discover why as you connect this method to the user interface. The addition of the **cacheable=true** keyword to the `@AuraEnabled` annotation allows you to improve runtime performance by caching the method's returned results in client-side storage. Because you are storing the list of countries throughout the duration of a user transaction, it makes sense to cache them. Additionally, you can refresh the cache on command from an LWC, which you will see in the final recipe of this chapter.
3. For the return statement, you are going to use the static `serialize` method of the `JSON` class to **serialize** the list of `LocaleWrappers` from the `TransferAssetService.getComboboxCountries()` method. For now, the `returnCountries` method will look like this:

```
@AuraEnabled(cacheable=true)
public static String returnCountries(){
    return JSON.serialize(TransferAssetService.getComboboxCountries());
}
```

4. Next, you are going to build similar methods, `returnCities` and `returnAccounts`. Each of these methods will be annotated with `@AuraEnabled` with no need for caching. The reason for this will be evident once you connect it to the frontend, as each of the elements that pull their data from these methods is rendered in a way that is dependent on other elements. We will once again utilize the static `serialize` method of the `JSON` class to serialize the respective wrappers. These two methods will end up as the following for now:

```
@AuraEnabled
public static String returnCities(String countryName){
    return
JSON.serialize(TransferAssetService.getComboboxCities(countryName));
}
@AuraEnabled
```

```
public static String returnAccounts(String cityName){
    return JSON.serialize(TransferAssetService.getAccountWrappers(cityName));
}
```

5. Rounding out the apex for the `TransferAsset` component, you must take the two `String` parameters, `assetId` and `accountId`, and serialize them into an `AssetWrapper` object for use in the `TransferAssetService.transferAssetWrapper(...)` method:

```
@AuraEnabled
public static void setAssetWrapper(String assetId, String accountId){
    TransferAssetService.transferAssetWrapper(new
TransferAssetService.AssetWrapper(assetId, accountId));
}
```

> **Note**
>
> You may be wondering why you are using a wrapper class instead of just instantiating an asset and updating it right in the `@AuraEnabled` method. Remember the `TransferAssetPersistence` class, which was defined as `without sharing`? The `TransferAssetPersistence` class grants users who do not have edit access on the asset `sObject`, such as a customer service representative who is scheduling the transportation of an artwork from museum to museum, the ability to update the `AccountId` field on the specified **Asset** sObject record without respect to sharing rules. We have to be careful with the classes that we mark as `without sharing` for this reason.

6. Save and deploy your class to your Developer Edition org.

Having completed the Apex classes for the `transferAsset` LWC, you are ready to import them into the component.

See also

- The sample file for the `TransferAssetPresentation` class is located under the `force-app/chapter02/default/classes/TransferAssetPresentation.cls` directory in your forked repository for comparison. This file is located at `https://github.com/PacktPublishing/Salesforce-Lightning-Web-Component-Cookbook/tree/main/`

`force-app/chapter02/default/classes/TransferAssetPresentation.cls` in the cookbook repository.

- The full documentation for **Calling Apex Methods** is located at `https://developer.salesforce.com/docs/platform/lwc/guide/apex.html`. To read the documentation for the `@AuraEnabled` annotation, navigate to the **Expose Apex Methods to Lightning Web Components** section.

Importing methods, objects, and fields into LWCs

Your methods are exposed. Now what? Let's return to the LWC files and open the `transferAsset.js` JavaScript file. For now, your file should look like the following:

```
import { LightningElement } from 'lwc';
export default class TransferAsset extends LightningElement {}
```

We are going to build this file out and modify it to accept the results of the methods of the `TransferAssetPresentation` class over the next three recipes.

How to do it...

Before you can call the Apex methods in the `TransferAssetPresentation` class, you need to import them. And before you can import the methods, you need to import some **decorators**:

1. In the first line of your file, add the `api` and `wire` decorators to the `import` statement ending in `from` 'lwc'. Note that JavaScript is case-sensitive, so `api` and `wire` must be in all lowercase.
   The `@api` decorator allows you to expose a public method or property to the JavaScript file and makes a component aware of its record context, while `@wire` allows you to provision Salesforce data with a **wire adapter**.

   > **Note**
   >
   > In older LWC files, you may see the `@track` decorator, which was previously required to make fields, such as JavaScript objects and arrays, reactive. As of the Spring '20 update, the `@track` decorator is no longer necessary and can be removed.

Once you have the decorators added, the first `import` statement will look like the following:

```
import { LightningElement, api, wire } from 'lwc';
```

2. Next, you must import the Apex methods that you exposed via the `@AuraEnabled` annotation. You must have a separate `import` statement for each method in the following format:

```
import methodName from '@salesforce/apex/ClassName.methodName';
```

If there is a namespace, as would be the case if an Apex class were contained in a **managed package**, the import format would be as follows:

```
import methodName from '@salesforce/apex/namespace.ClassName.methodName';
```

As it stands, you are not using a managed package for the contents of this book, so the next four import statements will look like this:

```
import returnCountries from '@salesforce/apex/
TransferAssetPresentation.returnCountries';
import returnCities from '@salesforce/apex/
TransferAssetPresentation.returnCities';
import returnAccountWrappers from '@salesforce/apex/
TransferAssetPresentation.returnAccounts;
import setAssetWrapper from '@salesforce/apex/
TransferAssetPresentation.setAssetWrapper';
```

3. Lastly, you are going to import two types of **event** from the `lightning` service. We will cover events and how to dispatch them in depth in *Chapter 6, Composing Lightning Web Components*, but for now, all you need to know is that you are going to import `RefreshEvent` and `ShowToastEvent`, which will allow you to refresh the record page and show a toast notification, respectively. These two `import` statements will look like the following:

```
import { RefreshEvent } from 'lightning/refresh';
import { ShowToastEvent } from 'lightning/platformShowToastEvent';
```

4. Next, you will define a constant, `columns`, right before the JavaScript class definition. The variable will be a list of JavaScript objects with the properties of `label` and `fieldName`, per the documentation for a simple `lightning-datatable`. We know from `AccountWrapper` that we want to display `accountName`, `accountCity`, and `accountState`, so these will populate the value of the `fieldName` key-value pairs. For the `label` values, let's use `Account`, `City`, and `State`. This will yield the following for the constant:

```
const columns = [
    { label: 'Account', fieldName: 'accountName' },
    { label: 'City', fieldName: 'accountCity' },
    { label: 'State', fieldName: 'accountState' }
];
```

5. Let's begin the `TransferAsset` class definition. Based on the values in the `transferAsset.html` file, you know that you are going to need the following class variables:
    - `countryOptions;`
    - `countryValue;`
    - `cityOptions;`
    - `cityValue;`
    - `accountData;`
    - `accountValue;`
    - `columns = columns;`
    - `transferDisabled = true;`
6. These variables will be placed right below our class definition in the JavaScript file.
7. We also know that you are going to need the ID of the **Asset** sObject record that the LWC resides on, which you can access using the imported `@api` decorator, like so:
    - `@api recordId;`

    This is a built-in function of Salesforce that allows the LWC to be context-aware, and the variable name must be exactly `recordId`. Similarly, you can get the `sObject` API name by creating an `@api objectApiName` variable—case sensitive. To use this built-in functionality, your LWC must be invoked in a **record context** in Lightning Experience, and the variable names must exactly match. This is a good place for a reminder that JavaScript is extremely case sensitive!

8. For the final variable, you will declare an `error` variable to track any errors that you encounter in the execution of the component.

    - `error;`

   We will define our functions in the next recipe.

See also

The Call Apex Methods documentation can be found at `https://developer.salesforce.com/docs/platform/lwc/guide/apex.html`.

Calling Apex methods from LWCs

Now that we have our variables declared, let's assign their values. Several of our values will be assigned directly from the Apex methods in our `import` statements, which is possible because we have formatted our method return values into suitable data types with the help of our wrapper classes.

How to do it...

1. Let's start by calling the imported Apex methods. We want the list of countries to be populated when the page loads, so you are going to use the `@wire` decorator to wire the method to either a property or a function. Because you are receiving the `LocaleWrapper` serialized into JSON, you want to parse the result of the method before assigning it to the `countryOptions` variable. You will be wiring a JavaScript function to process the Apex method results.
2. Because the `returnCountries` method accepts no parameters, you are going to start off the wire function like so:

```
@wire(returnCountries)
wiredCountries({error, data}) {
   if (data) {...}
   else if (error) {...}
}
```

   Breaking this down line by line, you have the following:

    - The `@wire` decorator allows you to invoke the Apex method, `returnCountries`, through the wire service.

   - A JavaScript function, `wiredCountries`, that receives the data from the wire service in the form of a JavaScript object with either an `error` property or a `data` property.
   - An `if-else` statement that performs some action if the `data` property is truthy, or else performs some action if the `error` property is truthy.

   We will take a look at a `@wire` function with parameters and a slightly different format toward the end of the chapter.

3. In the event that the `data` value is truthy, you want to set the value of the `countryOptions` class variable to `JSON.parse(data)`, which is a built-in static method under the `JSON` namespace that parses the JSON object that was returned from the Apex method. We also want to set the `error` class variable to `undefined` so that you are not sending false positives.
4. If, however, the `data` value is falsy and the `error` value is truthy, you want to do some type of error handling. We will set the `error` class value to the value of `error`, set `countryOptions` to `undefined`, and, for testing purposes, you will use the `console.error()` method to display the received error message. Your resulting wire function will look like this:

```
@wire(returnCountries)
wiredCountries({error, data}) {
    if (data) {
        this.countryOptions = JSON.parse(data);
        this.error = undefined;
    } else if (error) {
        this.error = error;
        this.countryOptions = undefined;
        console.error(error.message);
    }
}
```

> **Note**
>
> While it is common to see console messages in code, it is not best practice! Console outputs in JavaScript, similar to `System.debug()` statements in Apex, can slow down application performance. Not only that, but logged comments can potentially reveal sensitive information or otherwise grant bad actors access

> to parts of your code base. Because of this, you will be removing the `console.error()` statements before the chapter is through.

5. Save and deploy the `transferAsset` component. Now, when you click on the **Countries** dropdown, you should see something similar to the following, where each drop-down option corresponds to a `LocaleWrapper` object with the properties `label` and `value`, and the label is displayed:

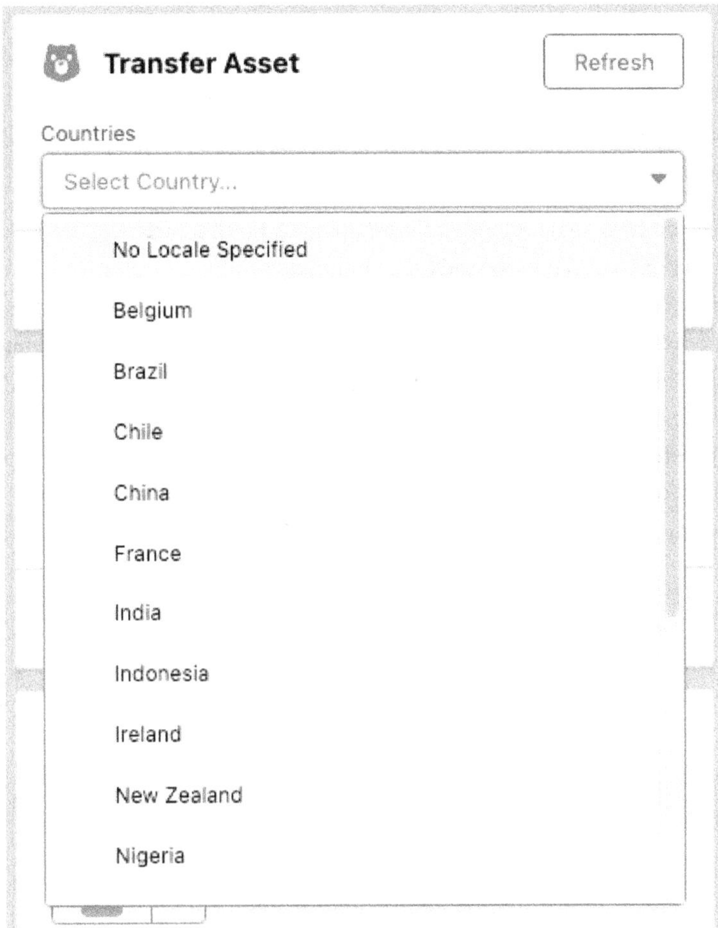

Figure 2.12: A list of countries returned by the aggregate query in our Apex.

Next, you are going to account for what happens when a country is selected.

6. Return to the `transferAsset.js` file and enter the following function below your wire function:

```
handleCountryChange(event) {
    this.countryValue = event.target.value;
    this.cityOptions = undefined;
    this.accountData = undefined;
    this.getCities(this.countryValue);
}
```

This function sets the value of `countryValue` to the `value` property that corresponds to the label of the `LocaleWrapper` that you passed in through the wired Apex method, clears the `cityOptions` and `accountData` variables, and then calls the next function you are going to write, `getCities`.

7. So far, you have learned how to wire an Apex method on page load, but what do you do if you want to pull data based on a changed variable or a click of a button? This is where **imperative Apex calls** come in. There are two ways to call Apex methods imperatively, both of which we will explore in *Chapter 4, Synchronous and Asynchronous Processing in Components*, but for now, we are going to look at the **Async/Await** pattern. Utilizing an **async** function declaration, you can cleanly enable asynchronous, **promise**-based behavior from the Apex method, where the transaction is paused until you get the results. For our use case, the JavaScript function of `getCities` is going to look like the following:

```
async getCities(countryValue) {
    try {
        const cities = await returnCities({countryName : countryValue});
        this.cityOptions = JSON.parse(cities);
        this.error = undefined;
    } catch (error) {
        this.error = error;
        this.cityOptions = undefined;
        console.error(error.message)
    }
}
```

We want the **await** keyworded function to be inside of a `try-catch` block in case there is an unexpected error during the processing of the asynchronous function. Similar to earlier, you set `cityOptions` to a parsed version of the list of `LocaleWrapper` object string and set the `error` variable to `undefined` in the event that the data is retrieved successfully. If an error is caught by the `try, catch` block, you display an error message in the console and set the `cityOptions` variable to undefined.

Try saving and deploying the `transferAsset` LWC. Now, you can utilize the **Cities** dropdown, although if you select a city in the dropdown, you will receive an error. This is because we still have a few more functions to define.

Figure 2.13: The transferAsset LWC with both dropdowns populated

Note

The test data, generated by the open source solution `https://generatedata.com`, is completely random, so the cities and geolocations on the accounts may not be geographically accurate. This is why you are seeing Shanghai listed as a city in Belgium. This is expected behavior.

1. To mitigate the error you see when you click on a city in the dropdown, you must define the `handleCityChange` function. On city change, you want to update `cityValue` to the newly selected city, and you want to pass that value into a function you are going to write called `getAccounts`. We will be covering events in depth in *Chapter 6, Composing*

Lightning Web Components, but for now, know that we will be retrieving the value of the target event utilizing **dot notation**. Your `handleCityChange` function will look like this:

```
handleCityChange(event) {
    this.cityValue = event.target.value;
    this.getAccounts(this.cityValue);
}
```

2. Like the `getCities` function, you are going to use an asynchronous imperative Apex call. Your `getAccounts` function will look like this:

```
async getAccounts(cityValue) {

    try {
        const accounts = await returnAccounts({cityName : cityValue});
        this.accountData = JSON.parse(accounts);
        this.error = undefined;
    } catch(error) {
        this.accountData = undefined;
        this.error = error;
        console.error(error.message);
    }
}
```

3. Once again, you must define a function for when you select an account. We already named this function in the `transferAsset.html` file as `setAccountId`. We also want to enable the **Transfer** button when an account is selected, so you will set the `transferDisabled` variable to `false`:

```
setAccountId(event) {
    this.accountValue = event.detail.selectedRows[0].accountId;
    this.transferDisabled = false;
}
```

> **Note**
>
> We will be covering **change events** in *Chapter 6, Composing Lightning Web Components*, but for now, all you need to know is that you access the `accountId` value from the `AccountWrapper` object.

4. Save and deploy the component. Now, you can select a country, city, and account, and all you have to do is finish the functionality of the buttons.

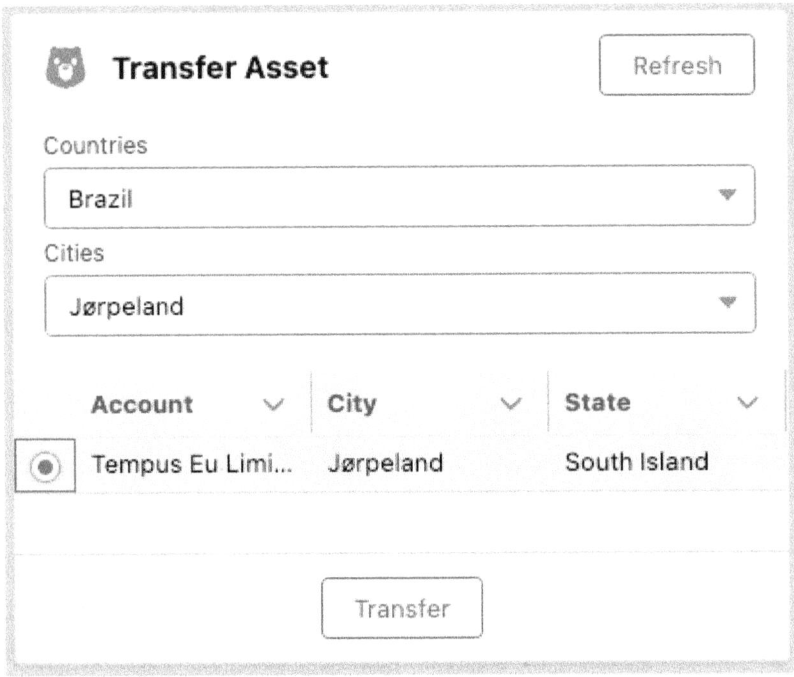

Figure 2.14: Progress on the transferAsset component, showing sample data for country, city, and account

5. Returning to the `transferAsset.js` file, add the following function:

```
handleRefresh() {
    this.countryValue = undefined;
    this.cityOptions = undefined;
    this.accountData = undefined;
    this.dispatchEvent(new RefreshEvent());
}
```

Line by line, you are clearing the variables and dispatching a `RefreshEvent`, which is a built-in event type that allows you to refresh the Lightning record page. Save and deploy your changes, and try selecting a country, city, and account, and then select the **Refresh** button. Notice that the **Transfer Asset** form is reset.

6. Now that you have a function setting `accountValue` and a function resetting the form, you are ready to build the `handleTransfer` function. Again, this is going to be an

asynchronous, **imperative Apex** call on the `setAssetWrapper` method so that the method is executed when a certain set of criteria is met. This method accepts two parameters, so the imperative call will look a little different:

```
async handleTransfer() {
    try {
        await setAssetWrapper({assetId : this.recordId, accountId :
this.accountValue});
        this.handleRefresh();
    } catch(error) {
        this.error = error;
        console.error(error.message);
    }
}
```

Save and deploy your changes. We now have a functioning LWC! The only thing you are missing is robust **error handling**, which you will cover in the next recipe.

See also

- The sample JavaScript file for the `transferAsset` LWC is located under the `force-app/chapter02/default/lwc/transferAsset/transferAsset.js` directory in your forked repository for comparison. This file is located at `https://github.com/PacktPublishing/Salesforce-Lightning-Web-Component-Cookbook/tree/main/force-app/chapter02/default/lwc/transferAsset/transferAsset.js` in the cookbook repository.
- The full documentation for **Wire Apex Methods to Lightning Web Components** is located at `https://developer.salesforce.com/docs/platform/lwc/guide/apex-wire-method.html`.
- The documentation for **Call Apex Methods Imperatively** is located at `https://developer.salesforce.com/docs/platform/lwc/guide/apex-call-imperative.html`.
- The Mozilla **mdn web docs** reference has detailed documentation of JavaScript functionality, including the Async/Await pattern, here: `https://developer.mozilla.org/en-US/docs/Web/JavaScript/Reference/Statements/async_function`.

Throwing exceptions

Now that you have tested the code and verified that we are ready to move on to the final steps, you can take the console statements out. We do not want to just remove them without replacing them, however, as this would cause a **quiet failure** in the event of a database error. Generally, when there is an error in code, you want to make sure that it is noticeable, or **loud**, so that it does not have downstream impacts.

How to do it...

Salesforce allows you to expose any errors as **exceptions**, which tell you when something has gone wrong. These exceptions can be system namespaced, or they can be custom, but all exceptions provide methods for returning an error message and exception type. We will take a look at custom exceptions later in the book, but first, let's look at the built-in `AuraHandledException`.

1. Return to the `TransferAssetPresentation.cls` file and notice how you are simply returning the results of a method call or calling a method. If you were to have a failure when calling one of the methods, or while you are serializing the wrapper classes into JSON, the code would fail, and you would likely struggle to pinpoint where.
2. Start by adding a try-catch block that catches an `AuraHandledException`, `e`, around each return statement. For example, the `returnCountries` method goes from the following:

```
@AuraEnabled(cacheable=true)
public static String returnCountries(){
    return JSON.serialize(TransferAssetService.getComboboxCountries());
}
```

3. And it becomes the following:

```
@AuraEnabled(cacheable=true)
public static String returnCountries(){
    try {
        return JSON.serialize(TransferAssetService.getComboboxCountries());
    } catch(Exception e) {
        throw new AuraHandledException(e.getMessage());
    }
}
```

4. Copy this pattern for each of the four methods in the `TransferAssetPresentation` class, and then save and deploy your updated class.
5. Return to the `transferAsset.js` file, and add one final function, `showNotif`, which accepts three parameters: `title`, `msg`, and `variant`:

```
showNotif(title, msg, variant) {
    const evt = new ShowToastEvent({
        title: title,
        message: msg,
        variant: variant,
    });
    this.dispatchEvent(evt);
}
```

Your parameters will allow you to set a custom title, message, and variant for the toast notification. Look up the **Toast Notifications** documentation in the **Lightning Web Components Developer Guide** (linked in the *See also* section for this recipe) to see that the variant options are as follows:

- `Info`: (default) a gray box with an info icon
- `success`: a green box with a checkmark icon
- `warning`: a yellow box with a warning icon
- `error`: a red box with an error icon

We can show a toast notification for any number of reasons, which I encourage you to explore in your **Transfer Asset** component. For now, you will just be adding a toast that shows when you get a server-side error.

6. Where you have placed the `console.error(error.message)` code, replace these lines with the following:

```
this.showNotif('There has been an error!', error.message, 'error');
```

This line of code dispatches a `ShowToastEvent` with the title **"There has been an error!"** and the contents of the error message, in the red error variant. This will look something like the following:

Figure 2.15: A toast message with the title "There has been an error!" and the message "This is a bad error!"

Try playing around and adding a success variant toast when your country or city data loads.

See also

- The official Salesforce Developers guide to **Exception Class and** built-in exceptions is located at `https://developer.salesforce.com/docs/atlas.en-you.apexref.meta/apexref/apex_classes_exception_methods.html`.
- The Lightning Web Components Developer Guide documentation on toast notifications is located at `https://developer.salesforce.com/docs/platform/lwc/guide/use-toast.html`.

Bringing it all together

Having built the second LWC and learned about important concepts in Apex development for LWCs, you are ready to build a more complicated component. Hopefully, by now, you have played with your **Transfer Asset** component a bit, which will have generated **Asset Residency** junction object records for each transfer. If you are not seeing **Asset Residency** junction objects, be sure you have deployed the `force-app/chapter00` directory. Looking back at the business requirements, you remember that you want to display each of these **Asset Residency** records on a map on the **Asset** record page.

How to do it...

This example LWC is shorter, but more complicated, than the `transferAsset` component. Let's dive in.

1. Start by creating a new LWC named `assetMap`, and select the default directory (`force-app/main/default/lwc`).
2. Add a `lightning-card` tag with your favorite SLDS icon, a title of `Asset Residency History`, and a `Refresh` button in the `actions` slot with an `onclick` function of `{refreshMap}`.

3. In between the `div` tags labeled as `<!-- Card Body -->`, add a `lightning-map` tag (shorthand: `lwc-map`), and remove all the attributes except for `map-markers={mapMarkers}` and `list-view="hidden"`. The `lightning-map` tag will allow you to use the **Google Maps API** to display a map with markers of your choosing on the Salesforce record page. Your HTML file should now look something like this:

```
<template>
   <lightning-card icon-name="utility:transport_heavy_truck" variant="base">
      <div slot="title">
         Asset Residency History
      </div>
      <lightning-button label="Refresh" onclick={refreshMap}
slot="actions"></lightning-button>
      <div>
         <lightning-map map-markers={mapMarkers} list-view="hidden"> </
lightning-map>
      </div>
   </lightning-card>
</template>
```

4. Update the `assetMap.js-meta.xml` file to the following to expose your LWC to the Lightning record page for the **Asset** object:

```
<?xml version="1.0" encoding="UTF-8"?>
<LightningComponentBundle xmlns="http://soap.sforce.com/2006/04/metadata">
    <apiVersion>63.0</apiVersion>
    <isExposed>true</isExposed>
    <targets>
        <target>lightning__RecordPage</target>
    </targets>
    <targetConfigs>
        <targetConfig targets="lightning__RecordPage">
            <objects>
                <object>Asset</object>
            </objects>
        </targetConfig>
    </targetConfigs>
</LightningComponentBundle>
```

5. Save and deploy the component, and drag it to the top-right corner of your Lightning record page, above the **Transfer Asset** component that you just built. Your page should now look something like this:

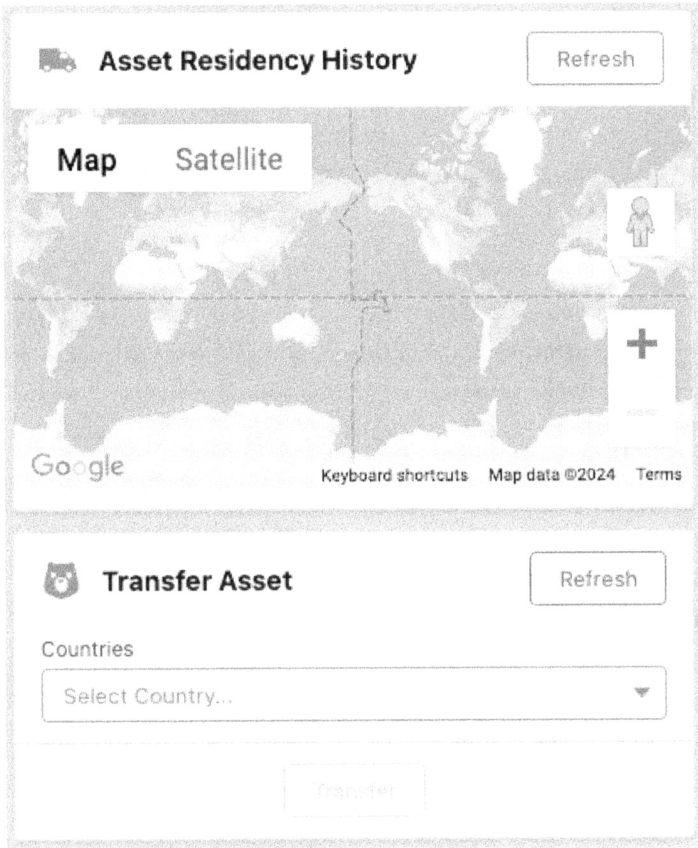

Figure 2.16: The updated user interface containing both the Asset Residency History component and the Transfer Asset component

We will be adding `mapMarkers` in the next few steps, which means now is a good time to review the `lightning-map` component documentation at `https://developer.salesforce.com/docs/component-library/bundle/lightning-map/documentation`.

6. Notice that there is an example of the `mapMarkers` list that accepts **Latitude** and **Longitude**, two fields that happen to be populated on the test data that you imported to your Salesforce Developer Edition org under the `Account.Museum_Office__c` geolocation field. Note that the JavaScript array structure is slightly different from the

structure you utilized in the last several recipes – this array is an array of JavaScript objects with a `location` property that holds two key-value pairs for `Latitude` and `Longitude`. Based on this, the wrapper class is going to have to be nested. Having created the LWC and placed it on the page, you are once again ready to build out the Apex classes. Create a new Apex class named `assetMapPersistence` and select the default directory (`force-app/main/default/classes`). Again, because this is the persistence layer class, and we want all users to be able to access our queried asset residencies, you are going to want to change the class definition to `without sharing` and delete the default constructor.

> **Note**
>
> The persistence layer class will not always be without sharing, and it is important to respect the sharing model of your org and the sharing requirements for your use case. In this instance, you want the end user to be able to see all the asset residency junction object records for a given asset, regardless of owner.

7. This class will have one static method that accepts a parameter of type `Id`, `assetId`, and returns a `List<Asset_Residency__c> sObject` record. We will need to traverse the `Resident_Account__r` master-detail relationship to get the `Name`, `Museum_Office__Latitude__s`, and `Museum_Office__Longitude__s` fields from the parent account record for the specified asset. We also want to limit the query to the 10 most recent asset residency records to improve the performance of the map. In all, the class will look like this:

```
public without sharing class AssetMapPersistence {
   public static List<Asset_Residency__c> getResidencies(Id assetId) {
      return [SELECT Id, Name, Resident_Account__r.Name,
Resident_Account__r.Museum_Office__Latitude__s,
Resident_Account__r.Museum_Office__Longitude__s FROM Asset_Residency__c
WHERE Asset__c = :assetId ORDER BY CreatedDate DESC LIMIT 10];
   }
}
```

8. Create a second Apex class named `assetMapService` and select the default directory (`force-app/main/default/classes`). Return to the documentation and note the

structure of the `mapMarkers` array that you will be building with the wrapper classes. This structure will look like this:

```
mapMarkers = [
   {
      location: {
         Latitude: 'LAT',
         Longitude: 'LONG',
      },
      value: 'VAL',
      title: 'TITLE'
   },
];
```

So, how can you achieve this structure with wrapper classes? Here's the simple answer: you are going to nest them.

9. We will start by building the simpler wrapper class, `MarkerWrapper`, which has two `String` properties: `Latitude` and `Longitude`. In the constructor, you want to accept an `Asset_Residency__c` parameter, `residency`, and use this parameter to get the `String` value of the residency's latitude and longitude fields. This will end up looking like this:

```
public class MarkerWrapper {
   @AuraEnabled public String Latitude;
   @AuraEnabled public String Longitude;
   public MarkerWrapper(Asset_Residency__c residency) {
      this.Latitude =
String.valueOf(residency.Resident_Account__r.Museum_Office__Latitude__s);
      this.Longitude =
String.valueOf(residency.Resident_Account__r.Museum_Office__Longitude__s);
   }
}
```

10. Now, you must build the `LocationWrapper`, which will have a `MarkerWrapper` property called `location`. We must name this property to match the JSON structure that you are going to serialize into. We are also going to add `value` and `title` properties. Similarly to

MarkerWrapper, you are going to pass a parameter of Asset_Residency__c residency into the constructor to populate these values. Your wrapper class will look like this:

```
public class LocationWrapper {
    @AuraEnabled public MarkerWrapper location;
    @AuraEnabled public String value;
    @AuraEnabled public String title;
    public LocationWrapper(Asset_Residency__c residency) {
        this.location = new MarkerWrapper(residency);
        this.title = residency.Resident_Account__r.Name;
        this.value = residency.Name;
    }
}
```

11. Lastly, for this class, you are going to create the getLocationWrappers method. This will accept an Id type parameter of assetId, which will be passed into the AssetMapPersistence.getResidencies(assetId) method. We will then iterate over the results of this method and transform each asset residency into a LocationWrapper object, like so:

```
public static List<LocationWrapper> getLocationWrappers(Id assetId) {
    List<LocationWrapper> mapMarkers = new List<LocationWrapper>();
    List<Asset_Residency__c> residencyList =
AssetMapPersistence.getResidencies(assetId);
    for(Asset_Residency__c residency : residencyList) {
        mapMarkers.add(new LocationWrapper(residency));
    }
    return mapMarkers;
}
```

12. Finally, you will wrap up with the AssetMapPresentation Apex class. Remember, you want any errors to be loud, so you should throw AuraHandledException in the event of failure:

```
public with sharing class AssetMapPresentation {
    @AuraEnabled(cacheable=true)
    public static String getMapMarkers(String assetId) {
        try {
            return
```

```
JSON.serialize(AssetMapService.getLocationWrappers(assetId));
        } catch(Exception e) {
            throw new AuraHandledException(e.getMessage());
        }
    }
}
```

Notice how you are utilizing the `@AuraEnabled(cacheable=true)` annotation here. This will allow you to wire a function in the JavaScript file, as well as refresh the cached data at the click of a button.

13. Similarly to the `transferAsset.js` file, you are going to start the JavaScript file by importing the things you need. Open the `assetMap.js` file and import the following:

```
import { LightningElement, api, wire } from 'lwc';
import getMapMarkers from '@salesforce/apex/
AssetMapPresentation.getMapMarkers'
import{ refreshApex } from '@salesforce/apex';
import { ShowToastEvent } from "lightning/platformShowToastEvent";
```

Notice that you are importing the `getMapMarkers` method with the same decorators and the same `ShowToastEvent` as last time, but you have a new import: `refreshApex`. The `refreshApex` method will allow you to refresh the client-side `cacheable=true` data from the `assetMapPresentation` class.

14. Next, you will declare the class variables. As before, you want to grab the Id of the asset record on which the map resides, so the first variable will be `@api recordId`.
15. We are then going to declare a private variable, denoted with an underscore before the variable name: `_wiredMarkers`. This variable will store the result of the wired function, which you will build in a moment.

> **Note**
>
> Technically, there are no **private variables** in JavaScript versions earlier than ES2022, just **class-scoped** and **function-scoped** variables. The underscore denotes that the `_wiredMarkers` variable should not be exposed and should only be used in the class for which it is currently scoped. After ES2022, private variables are denoted using a hash sign, such as `#wiredMarkers`.

16. Your last variable will be `mapMarkers`, which will hold the array of `LocationWrappers` once they have been serialized into a JSON string and parsed into a JavaScript object.
17. Now that you have the variables declared, you can wire the `getMapMarkers` method to a function. This wire function is going to look different than the wire function that you wrote for `transferAsset.js`, however. For starters, the `getMapMarkers` method accepts a parameter of `assetId`, which will be stored as a **key-value pair** in curly brackets:

```
@wire(getMapMarkers, {assetId : '$recordId'})
```

The next difference is that, instead of wiring a function that produces an object with `{error, data}` properties, you are going to have one property – `result`:

```
wiredMapMarkers(result) {...}
```

18. This difference is required to utilize the built-in `refreshApex` method that Salesforce provides. Next, you are going to assign the full value of `result` to the `_wiredMarkers` variable, like so:

```
{
    this._wiredMarkers = result;
    ...
}
```

We will then access the `data` and `error` properties of the `result` object to parse the wrapper class and provide error handling:

```
{
    ...
    if (result.data) {
        this.mapMarkers = JSON.parse(result.data);
        this.error = undefined;
    } else if(result.error) {
        this.error = result.error;
        this.mapMarkers = undefined;
        this.showNotif('There has been an error!', this.error, 'error');
    }
}
```

In all, the wire function will look like this:

```
@wire(getMapMarkers, {assetId : '$recordId'})
wiredMapMarkers(result) {
   this._wiredMarkers = result;
   if (result.data) {
      this.mapMarkers = JSON.parse(result.data);
      this.error = undefined;
   } else if(result.error) {
      this.error = result.error;
      this.mapMarkers = undefined;
      this.showNotif('There has been an error!', this.error, 'error');
   }
}
```

19. Next, you can create the `refreshMap` function, which will simply return the value of `refreshApex(this._wiredMarkers)`:

```
refreshMap() {
   return refreshApex(this._wiredMarkers);
}
```

A detailed explanation of how to refresh the client-side cache with the `refreshApex` method can be found at `https://developer.salesforce.com/docs/platform/lwc/guide/apex-result-caching.html`.

20. Lastly, you are going to use the same `showNotif` function you used in the `transferAsset.js` file to enable loud error handling. We can optionally put this in a utility JavaScript file so that you do not have the same code in two places, which we will cover in *Chapter 4, Synchronous and Asynchronous Processing in Components*. For now, you will just paste the same function into the `transferAsset.js` file:

```
showNotif(title, msg, variant) {
   const evt = new ShowToastEvent({
      title: title,
      message: msg,
      variant: variant,
   });
```

```
    this.dispatchEvent(evt);
}
```

21. Now that you have built all the files, you can save and deploy the full map. Because you were having fun playing with the Transfer Asset component, you can see several map markers on the map.

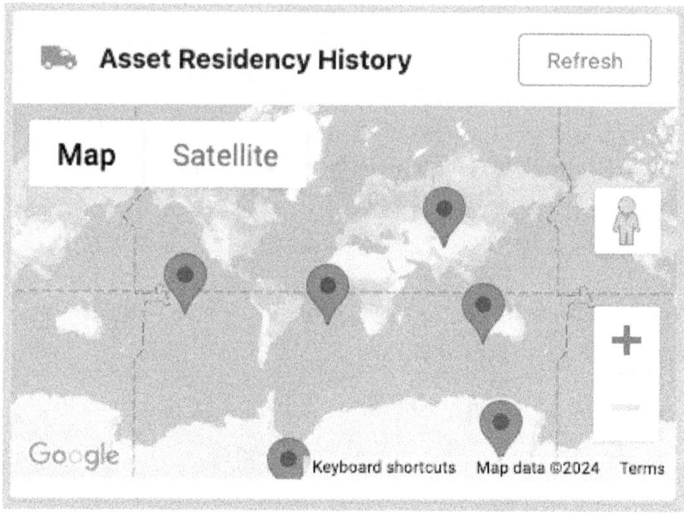

Figure 2.17: The Asset Residency History map with six markers placed according to the sample data

> **Note**
>
> The test data, generated by the open source solution `https://generatedata.com`, is completely random, so the cities and geolocations on the accounts may not be geographically accurate. This is why you are seeing two account records located in Antarctica and three in the middle of the ocean. This is expected.

See also

- The sample files for the `assetMap` LWC are located under the `force-app/chapter02/default/lwc/assetMap` directory in your forked repository for comparison, with the classes under the `force-app/chapter02/default/classes` directory. The `assetMap` files can be found at `https://github.com/PacktPublishing/Salesforce-Lightning-Web-`

`Component-Cookbook/tree/main/force-app/chapter02/default/lwc/assetMap` in the cookbook repository.

- The full Salesforce-provided **lwc-recipes** GitHub Repository is located at `https://github.com/trailheadapps/lwc-recipes`. This repository is full of examples of diverse types of LWCs.

3

Working with a Selector Class

Now that you have gotten a few **Lightning Web Components** (**LWCs**) under your belt, you can see the importance of a well-built backend. In *Chapter 2, Writing Apex for Lightning Web Components*, you built a component utilizing a three-class pattern that allows end users limited, view-only access to **Account** records to transfer **Assets** between **Accounts** with different owners, utilizing the concept of **wrapper classes**. You also expanded your knowledge of wrapper classes and utilized the built-in Google Maps API to display historical **Asset Residencies** on a map.

While this three-class pattern is useful as a jumping-off point and achievable in most small- to mid-sized orgs, those who work in larger Salesforce orgs may notice some pain points with this methodology. Although we have implemented a modest example of the **separation of concerns** by separating our functions into a **persistence layer**, a **presentation layer**, and a **service layer**, there will end up being a lot of code repetition if this pattern is followed, and our test classes will be slow to run. Enter the selector class.

The selector class is going to serve as storage for any and all queries related to a given **Salesforce object** (**sObject**). This allows for one centralized location for queries with similar return types and fields, which provides an easy way to add security checks to verify the sharing settings of a user before performing database operations. We will cover the following main recipes in this chapter:

- Building a SOQL and SOSL utility class
- Connecting to the database with a selector class
- Performing business logic with a service class
- Exposing a wrapper with a controller class
- Building a selector-friendly LWC

Technical requirements

The recipes for this book can be found at `https://github.com/PacktPublishing/Salesforce-Lightning-Web-Component-Cookbook`, where each chapter has its own folder under the `force-app` folder. This GitHub repository is structured in the form of a Salesforce DX project, which will allow you to easily fork the repository for deployment in a free Salesforce Developer Edition org. The code for *Chapter 3*, *Working with a Selector Class*, is located at `https://github.com/PacktPublishing/Salesforce-Lightning-Web-Component-Cookbook/tree/main/force-app/chapter03`.

The components in this book require the use of an **integrated development environment** (**IDE**), such as **Visual Studio Code** (**VS Code**) or **Salesforce Code Builder**. Detailed instructions for setting up an IDE are located in *Chapter 1*, *Getting Ready for Lightning Web Component Development*, in the *Setting up your IDE* section.

If you are joining us in this chapter and are planning on building the project as written, be sure that you have completed the steps in the *Setting up the Salesforce Lightning Web Components Cookbook org* recipe, located within *Chapter 1*, *Getting Ready for Lightning Web Component Development*. This will entail forking the *Cookbook* repository and deploying the folder at `force-app/chapter00` to ensure that you have all the necessary sObjects, custom fields, and automations required to complete the recipes in this book. Additionally, the *Setting up the Salesforce Lightning Web Components Cookbook org* recipe will walk you through creating the test data necessary to test this recipe.

Lastly, the edition of Salesforce required to implement the recipes in this book must be Developer, Performance, Unlimited, Enterprise, or Database.com. You can sign up for a free Salesforce Developer Edition org at `https://developer.salesforce.com/signup`.

Building a SOQL and SOSL utility class

In *Chapter 2*, *Writing Apex for Lightning Web Components*, we saw that we can build a **persistence layer** class that holds our queries separately from our business logic using a strategy known as **decoupling**. However, what if we have more than one sObject that we want to query for, or what if we want to reuse our queries in other contexts? This is a situation where we would not want our queries to be tied to a specific LWC, and instead, would want our queries grouped by sObject for ease of navigation and for maximum reusability. So, how do we achieve this?

Getting ready

To write our Apex, let's first look at the query methods of the `Database` and `Search` classes. We are going to want to utilize **dynamic SOQL** and **dynamic SOSL** so that our queries can be built and executed at runtime, allowing us to tailor each query result to business needs. The specific methods we want to look at are the `Database.query` and `Search.query` methods. Notice that each method accepts a `String` parameter, with `Database.query` accepting a SOQL query, and `Search.query` accepting a SOSL query. Optionally, we can add a parameter for the level of access we want to grant with our queries. As we saw in *Chapter 2, Writing Apex for Lightning Web Components*, we can achieve similar functionality using the Apex `with` and `without sharing` keywords. It is important to note, however, that these keywords are applied at the class level, rendering all query results contained within the class subject to the keyword specifications. Lastly, if we need to specify a bind variable in our SOQL query, we can use the `Database.queryWithBinds` method. For now, we will create an Apex method in a new class for each of these three system methods.

How to do it...

1. Start by creating a new Apex class called `Util_Query`, and annotate the class with the `virtual` definition modifier. The `virtual` modifier tells our code that we can `extend` this class and override its methods. After writing our class definition, we will write the following three methods:

```
public virtual class Util_Query {
   public List<SObject> query(String queryString, AccessLevel level) {
      return Database.query(String.escapeSingleQuotes(queryString), level);
   }
   public List<SObject> queryWithBinds(String queryString, Map<String,
Object> bindMap, AccessLevel level) {
      return Database.queryWithBinds(String.escapeSingleQuotes(queryString),
bindMap, level);
   }
   public List<List<SObject>> search(String searchString, AccessLevel level)
{
      return Search.query(String.escapeSingleQuotes(searchString), level);
   }
}
```

2. We will see exactly why we are writing a utility class for our queries in *Chapter 14, Testing Apex with Mocking and Stubbing*, but for now, know that it will allow us to unit test our code easily.
3. For each Apex method, you will accept a `String` parameter of an appropriate query called `searchString` and an `AccessLevel` object called `level`, and return the `sObject`

result of the respective system provided method, either `Database.query`, `Database.queryWithBinds`, or `Search.query`.

4. For our `queryWithBinds` method, we will also include a parameter of the `Map<String, Object>` type so that we can include any bind variables necessary in our query. Because we are utilizing dynamic SOQL and SOSL, we must additionally utilize the `escapeSingleQuotes` method of the `String` class around our `searchString` input to prevent **injection attacks** from bad user input.

See also

- The sample file for the `Util_Query` class is located under the `force-app/chapter03/default/classes/Util_Query.cls` directory in your forked repository for comparison. This file is located at `https://github.com/PacktPublishing/Salesforce-Lightning-Web-Component-Cookbook/tree/main/force-app/chapter03/default/classes/Util_Query.cls`.
- The documentation for the system-provided `Database` class can be found at `https://developer.salesforce.com/docs/atlas.en-us.apexref.meta/apexref/apex_methods_system_database.htm`.
- The documentation for the system-provided `Search` class can be found at `https://developer.salesforce.com/docs/atlas.en-us.apexref.meta/apexref/apex_methods_system_search.htm`.
- The full documentation for writing Apex classes can be found at `https://developer.salesforce.com/docs/atlas.en-us.apexcode.meta/apexcode/apex_classes.htm`.
- The documentation for extending a class in Apex can be found at `https://developer.salesforce.com/docs/atlas.en-us.apexcode.meta/apexcode/apex_classes_extending.htm`.
- An example of an extended class can be found at `https://developer.salesforce.com/docs/atlas.en-us.apexcode.meta/apexcode/apex_classes_example.htm`.
- The documentation for interfaces can be found at `https://developer.salesforce.com/docs/atlas.en-us.apexcode.meta/apexcode/apex_classes_interfaces.htm`.

Connecting to the database with a selector class

Once we have a thorough understanding of our `Util_Query` class, we can use it to build a selector class for our `Account` sObject. This class will house all the queries that we use for the `Account` sObject across multiple LWCs and all Apex classes that require querying **Account** records. This allows us to reuse our queries in multiple places while following the **DRY principle**: **Don't Repeat Yourself**.

> **Note**
>
> This selector class model differs from the model provided by Andrew Fawcett in *Chapter 7, Application Selector Layer*, of Packt's *Salesforce Platform Enterprise Architecture*, and in the **Common Apex Library** (**fflib**). This model is similar but can be implemented without the overhead of factory classes. When should you use advanced topics like these? Trailhead lays out a good reference in the **Separation of Concerns** module, linked in the *See also* section for this recipe. When deciding whether to implement an architectural model based on the *Separation of Concerns* module, org size, the complexity of solutions required, and the number of developers should all be taken into consideration. The examples provided in this chapter fall into the mid-size org category, whereas the code presented in *Chapter 2, Writing Apex for Lightning Web Components*, may fall under the qualifications presented for small-size orgs. We will cover more advanced use cases in later chapters.

How to do it...

Let's go through the following steps:

1. Start by creating a new Apex class, `AccountSelector`. Denote the class with the `inherited` sharing keyword, which will enforce the sharing settings of any class that calls our `AccountSelector` class. It is important to make sure that this code is secure, as it can be run in the `without sharing` mode quite easily, potentially granting view access to records that should not be viewed. We included a parameter that accepts an `AccessLevel` object in our SOQL utility class methods, so this is a concern that we have already mitigated.
2. After the class name, extend the class by adding `extends Util_Query` to the end of your class definition. It is important to note that the `Util_Query` class must be deployed to

your org before we can deploy our `AccountSelector` class due to this dependency. Your class shell will look like this:

```
public inherited sharing class AccountSelector extends Util_Query { ... }
```

3. Next, we are going to define a `@TestVisible private` class constant, `TOP_TEN_ACOUNTS_QUERY`. We do this by defining a `@TestVisible private static final String` variable before our first method. The annotation of `@TestVisible` enables us to access this variable in our test classes, while reserving use of the variable to the class that it is defined in. The value we are going to assign to our constant will be the text of a SOQL query that selects the following fields from the first ten `Account` sObject records returned in order of descending annual revenue, with `null` values appearing at the end of the resulting list:
   - `Id`
   - `Name`
   - `Phone`
   - `BillingCity`
   - `BillingState`
   - `BillingCountry`
   - `Museum_Office__latitude__s`
   - `Museum_Office__longitude__s`
   - `AnnualRevenue`
4. We also want to exclude any of the Developer Edition default accounts provided by Salesforce upon creation of a new Dev org, so we will add a **null check** on the `Museum_Office_latitude__s` field, which will exclude any records that do not have their **Museum Office** geolocation field populated. In all, our constant will look like this:

```
@TestVisible private static final String TOP_TEN_ACCOUNTS_QUERY = 'SELECT
Id, Name, Phone, BillingCity, BillingState, BillingCountry,
Museum_Office__latitude__s, Museum_Office__longitude__s, AnnualRevenue FROM
Account WHERE Museum_Office__latitude__s != null ORDER BY AnnualRevenue DESC
NULLS LAST LIMIT 10';
```

> **Note**
>
> By utilizing `Museum_Office__latitude__s != null` in our query, we are making this query **non-performant.** This is a trade-off that we are making so that we can filter out the default **Account** records that Salesforce provides in their Developer Edition orgs.

5. Finally, we are going to write a method that calls the `query` method of the `Util_Query` virtual class. Let's take a look, shall we?

```
public List<Account> topTenAccountsByRevenue() {
   List<Account> queryResult = (List<Account>) query(TOP_TEN_ACCOUNTS_QUERY,
AccessLevel.SYSTEM_MODE);
   return queryResult;
}
```

This looks a little bit different than the methods that we have seen before. Let's break it down line by line. First, let's look at the method signature. This is a **non-static method**, which we have not seen yet in this cookbook. This means that the method is an instance method of the `AccountSelector` class, where an instance of the `AccountSelector` class needs to be instantiated before we can access it and other class methods.

Another important feature of this declaration is that non-static methods can only be called directly by other non-static methods, which will help us later in the cookbook when we cover **stubbing** and **mocking** in *Chapter 14, Testing Apex with Mocking and Stubbing*. To call a non-static method from a static method, there must be an instance of the class that the non-static method resides in, as in the preceding example. We will also see this in action later in this chapter.

Next, moving left to right on the first line of our method definition, we notice that our list of query results, `queryResult`, is being cast as a type of `(List<Account>)`, denoted by the parentheses, before the value is assigned to our variable. When we look back at the `query` method of the `Util_Query` class, we see that it returns a `List<sObject>` collection rather than a `List<Account>` collection. Because of this, we need to use a strategy called **casting** to transform the list of generic sObject records into a list of `Account` records. We can confidently do so because we have defined our query to return a list of accounts. We will look at a more complex form of casting in *Chapter 5, Accessing External Data Sources via Lightning Web Component.*

Lastly, we see our query method being called. Notice that because we have **extended** the virtual Util_Query class, we have access to all its methods, and they can be called as though they were within the same file. When we receive the returned list of accounts from the query method, we check to see whether the list is empty. If it is empty, we return null; otherwise, we return the list of results. For this example, we want to make sure we return null rather than an empty list, as these two values are different in JavaScript, although this can be handled in several different ways.

This wraps up our AccountSelector class (for now!). As we grow our org and add more LWCs and Apex, we can easily add new methods for querying **Account** records to this selector class so that they may be reused.

See also

- The sample file for the AccountSelector class is located under the force-app/chapter03/default/classes/AccountSelector.cls directory in your forked repository for comparison. This file is located at https://github.com/PacktPublishing/Salesforce-Lightning-Web-Component-Cookbook/tree/main/force-app/chapter03/default/classes/AccountSelector.cls.
- To learn more about the separation of concerns, see the Separation of Concerns module on Trailhead at https://trailhead.salesforce.com/content/learn/modules/apex_patterns_sl/apex_patterns_sl_soc.
- The Salesforce documentation for the sharing keywords in Apex is located at https://developer.salesforce.com/docs/atlas.en-us.apexcode.meta/apexcode/apex_classes_keywords_sharing.htm.
- The article on extending a class is located at https://developer.salesforce.com/docs/atlas.en-us.apexcode.meta/apexcode/apex_classes_extending.htm.
- The Salesforce documentation on classes and casting is located at https://developer.salesforce.com/docs/atlas.en-us.apexcode.meta/apexcode/apex_classes_casting.htm.
- The documentation on static and instance methods, variables, and initialization code is located at https://developer.salesforce.com/docs/atlas.en-us.apexcode.meta/apexcode/apex_classes_static.htm.
- To learn more about **selector layer principles**, check out Andrew Fawcett's book, *Salesforce Platform Enterprise Architecture*, published by Packt.

Performing business logic with a service class

Now that we have the results of our query, we need to prepare these results to be served to an LWC. If we were just displaying **Account** record information, we would be able to directly pass our `List<Account>` into our LWC for client-side processing and display, which we will see an example of in *Chapter 4, Synchronous and Asynchronous Processing in Components,* but our data structure is a little bit more complicated. Because we are once again utilizing the `lightning-map` component in our LWC, we know that we need a wrapper to contain the geolocation of the **Museum Office** so that we can display a marker on our map at that location. We can largely copy our wrapper classes from our `AssetMapService` class that we built in *Chapter 2, Writing Apex for Lightning Web Components,* with a few minor changes. We will also need to build a similar wrapper class for our `Account` record that holds a list of marker wrappers.

How to do it...

Let's take a look at the following steps:

1. Create a new `public with sharing` Apex class called `AccountService`. Within this class, create an inner class named `AccountWrapper`.
2. To start off, our `AccountWrapper` class will need to have an `@AuraEnabled public` property for each of the fields that we queried for, as well as a list of location wrappers, in the form of `@AuraEnabled public List<LocationWrapper>`, called `markers`. Based on what we know from *Chapter 2, Writing Apex for Lightning Web Components,* we know that our `LocationWrapper` class will have an `@AuraEnabled public MarkerWrapper` called `location`, as well as two `@AuraEnabled public String` type properties called `value` and `title`. Here, we will define these wrapper classes as **subclasses** of the `AccountService` class, although we could reuse the wrappers from *Chapter 2, Writing Apex for Lightning Web Components.* We are not reusing these wrappers for clarity.
3. Once we have our wrapper classes defined, we will write a constructor for `AccountWrapper` that accepts a parameter of an `Account` record, `acct`. This will look like the following:

```
public AccountWrapper(Account acct) {
   this.Id = acct.Id;
   this.Name = acct.Name;
   this.Phone = acct.Phone;
   this.BillingCity = acct.BillingCity;
   this.BillingState = acct.BillingState;
```

```
        this.BillingCountry = acct.BillingCountry;
        this.AnnualRevenue = acct.AnnualRevenue;
        this.markers = new List<LocationWrapper>();
        MarkerWrapper marker = new MarkerWrapper();
        marker.Latitude = String.valueOf(acct.Museum_Office__Latitude__s);
        marker.Longitude = String.valueOf(acct.Museum_Office__Longitude__s);
        LocationWrapper location = new LocationWrapper();
        location.location = marker;
        location.title = acct.Name;
        location.value = acct.Id;
        this.markers.add(location);
    }
```

4. Having written our wrapper classes, we are ready to build out the rest of the `AccountService` class.
5. The first thing we are going to do is declare an instance of the `AccountSelector` class as a `@TestVisible private` instance variable. Remember, an instance variable is a non-static variable. Our declaration at the top of the class will look like this:

```
    @TestVisible private AccountSelector accountSelect = new AccountSelector();
```

   We instantiate a class in much the same way we instantiate a new sObject record, as each sObject is roughly an instance of a class.
6. After we have defined our class variable, `accountSelect`, we can write our method, `getTopAccountWrappers`, in which we will call the `topTenAccountsByRevenue` method of the `AccountSelector` class and parse the results as members of our `AccountWrapper` class. We can do this by iterating over a variable of the `List<Account>` type, `queryResult`, constructing a new `AccountWrapper` class for each iterable, and returning the `AccountWrappers` list. In all, our method will look like this:

```
    public List<AccountWrapper> getTopAccountWrappers() {
        List<Account> queryResult = accountSelect.topTenAccountsByRevenue();
        List<AccountWrapper> queriedWrappers = new List<AccountWrapper>();
        for(Account acct : queryResult) {
            queriedWrappers.add(new AccountWrapper(acct));
        }
        return queriedWrappers;
    }
```

As you can see, we call the `topTenAccountsByRevenue` method of the `AccountSelector` class by using **dot notation** with the instance of the `AccountSelector` class, `accountSelect`, and the method name. If we call the method directly by using `AccountSelector.topTenAccountsByRevenue()`, we will receive the following error:

```
Non static method cannot be referenced from a static context: List<Account>
AccountSelector.topTenAccountsByRevenue()
```

Therefore, we must call the method in a non-static context, as shown in the highlighted line in the previous code block.

See also

- The sample file for the `AccountService` class is located under the `force-app/chapter03/default/classes/AccountService.cls` directory in your forked repository for comparison. This file is located at `https://github.com/PacktPublishing/Salesforce-Lightning-Web-Component-Cookbook/tree/main/force-app/chapter03/default/classes/AccountService.cls`.
- The Component Library documentation for the `lightning-map` component is located at `https://developer.salesforce.com/docs/component-library/bundle/lightning-map/documentation`.

Exposing a wrapper with a controller class

The last thing we need to do to send data to an LWC is expose our wrapper with a **controller class**. Create one more Apex class titled `TopAccountsController`, and designate the sharing for the class as `public with sharing`.

How to do it...

Let's go through the following steps:

1. Much like we saw in *Chapter 2, Writing Apex for Lightning Web Components*, we are going to want to start by annotating our method, `returnAccountWrapperList`, which returns a `String` value, with `@AuraEnabled(cacheable=true)`. The reason for this is that we want to cache our `AccountWrapper` results on the client side so that only one server trip will be made, resulting in faster load times for our end users.
2. After we have defined the signature for our method, we are going to add a `try-catch` block to its body. In the `try` portion, we will declare a variable of the

`List<AccountService.AccountWrapper>` type called `wrapsToStringify`, which we will set equal to the results of the `getTopAccountWrappers` method of the `AccountService` class. Because `getTopAccountWrappers` is a non-static method, we must instantiate a member of the `AccountService` class, which we can do in one line:

```
List<AccountService.AccountWrapper> wrapsToStringify = new
AccountService().getTopAccountWrappers();
```

3. Following the declaration and instantiation of the `wrapsToStringify` variable, we can return the result of a **ternary operator**:

```
return wrapsToStringify == null ? null : JSON.serialize(wrapsToStringify);
```

   This ternary operator returns `null` if `wrapsToStringify` is equal to `null`; otherwise, it serializes and returns `wrapsToStringify`. Again, we want to do this because `null` is not equal to an empty list—the two are completely different objects in JavaScript!

4. Within our `catch` block, we will throw an `AuraHandledException` error to display on our frontend:

```
throw new AuraHandledException(e.getMessage());
```

Now that we have completed our `TopAccountsController` class, we are ready to start building our LWC.

See also

The sample file for the `TopAccountsController` class is located under the `force-app/chapter03/default/classes/TopAccountsController.cls` directory in your forked repository for comparison. This file is located at `https://github.com/PacktPublishing/Salesforce-Lightning-Web-Component-Cookbook/tree/main/force-app/chapter03/default/classes/TopAccountsController.cls`.

Building a selector-friendly LWC

Following our business use case from the previous chapters, take a second to imagine you are a Salesforce developer for an art broker who has been tasked with building a solution that allows end users to view the artworks (**Assets**) at different museums (accounts). In *Chapter 2*, you built a component that allows end users to easily transfer an **Asset** from one account to another, as well as a Google Map that updates to show the geolocation of each of the last 10 accounts that each asset has been associated with. Now that we have accounted for individual **Asset** movement between accounts, we want to start building out a component that displays information about each of the top 10 accounts by annual revenue, so that we can ensure that our top clients get first pick when new artwork becomes available.

Depending on your team's structure, you may have a **user experience (UX)** designer who provides a basic layout for the finished component. Our art brokering business is well staffed, so we have been given the following mockup to help us visualize what we are building:

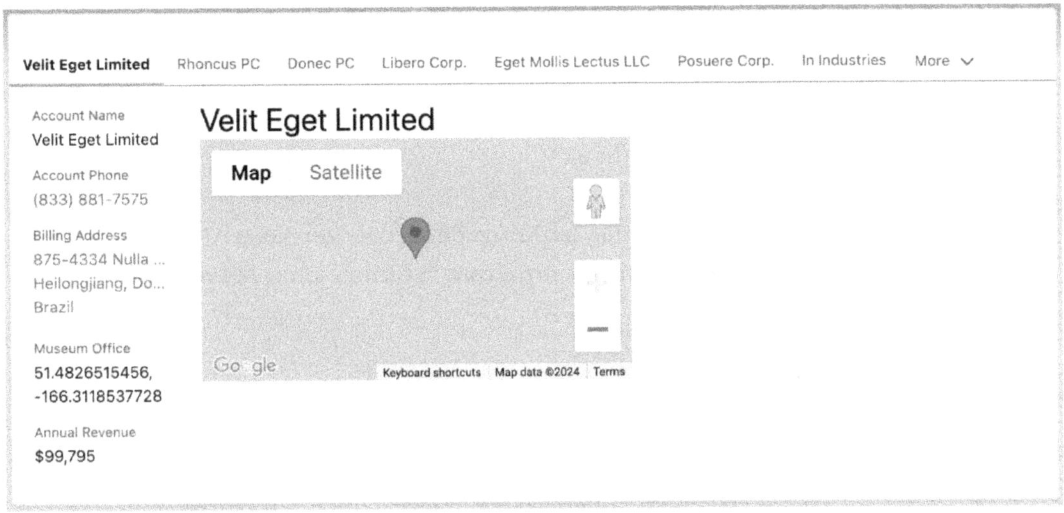

Figure 3.1: The sample provided by our UX designer shows a Lightning tabset with three columns of 1/6 width, 1/3 width, and 1/2 width.

As we see, we have a tab for each of our top accounts, with each tab hosting key information about the account, such as name, address, and annual revenue in a column, which takes up 1/6 of the width of our screen. We also have a map with the location of our account in a second column, taking up 1/3 of our screen. Lastly, we notice that half of our layout is blank, which is intentional, as we will be building the components for this column in *Chapter 4, Synchronous and Asynchronous Processing in Components.*

How to do it...

Let's take a look at the following steps:

1. Pull up the **LWC Component Reference** and navigate to VS Code to create a new LWC. We are going to call this LWC `topTenAccountTabset`. Edit your `js-meta.xml` file to expose the component to the `lightning__AppPage` and `lightning__HomePage` targets. This will allow us to place this component on either a **Lightning app page** or a

Lightning home page, allowing our end users to easily see information about our top 10 accounts. Your `js-meta.xml` file will look like the following:

```
<?xml version="1.0" encoding="UTF-8"?>
<LightningComponentBundle xmlns="http://soap.sforce.com/2006/04/metadata">
    <apiVersion>64.0</apiVersion>
    <isExposed>true</isExposed>
    <targets>
        <target>lightning__AppPage</target>
        <target>lightning__Tab</target>
    </targets>
</LightningComponentBundle>
```

Note

The API version in this book may be different from the most recent API version provided by Salesforce, and therefore the code in GitHub, as the API version updates with each release.

2. Open your `topTenAccountTabset.html` file and add two conditional `lwc:if|else` directives between the opening and closing `template` tags, with the `if` tag set to render if a variable called `accounts`, to be defined in our JavaScript file, is **truthy**. Your HTML file should now look like the following:

```
<template>
    <template lwc:if={accounts}>
    </template>
    <template lwc:else>
    </template>
</template>
```

3. Within the `lwc:else` tags, we are going to add a **lightning-spinner** component. Remember, this tag can be added via the autocomplete feature provided by the **Salesforce Extensions Pack** by typing `lwc-spinner` in your HTML file and pressing *Enter*. This component will display an animated spinner while our accounts are loading and hide the spinner when loading has been completed. This is a common pattern that is used to indicate to the end user that data is still being processed.

4. Next, add a **lightning-card** tag with no attributes between the `lwc:if` tags. This `lightning-card` tag will hold a new-to-us component called **lightning-tabset**. We will use this component to iterate over our list of accounts returned by our Apex method, `returnAccountWrapper`, with a `for:each` directive to show a tab for each of our top 10 accounts, which we will discuss in a moment. For now, to start our opening `lightning-tabset` tag, add the attributes `active-tab-value={activeAccountId}`, which will be equal to the value provided by the open tab, and `variant="standard"`, which sets the styling for our tab to the standard styling. So far, our file will look like this:

```
<template>
    <template lwc:if={accounts}>
        <lightning-card>
            <lightning-tabset active-tab-value={activeAccountId}
variant="standard">
            </lightning-tabset>
        </lightning-card>
    </template>
    <template lwc:else>
        <lightning-spinner alternative-text="Loading" size="large"></
lightning-spinner>
    </template>
</template>
```

5. Inside our opening and closing `lightning-tabset` tags, add a `template` tag with a `for:each` directive. Like our `lwc:if`, `lwc:elseif`, and `lwc:else` directives, we are going to specify a variable for the `for:each` directive to add dynamic behavior to our LWC. In this case, the variable we will be using will once again be our array of `Account` records, `for:each={accounts}`, and each item in our array will be an account.
6. To specify our iterable item, we use `for:item="account"`. These two attributes will allow us to iterate over our array accounts as though we were utilizing a `for each` loop in Apex, with each item being labeled as `account`. To visualize this, let's look at some pseudocode for an Apex for each loop:

```
for(Account account : List<Account> accounts) {
    System.debug('My account's name is: ' + account.Name);
}
```

In this example, we are iterating over each account in a list of accounts that is returned from a SOQL query or defined elsewhere in our method. Knowing this, our `template` tag, which has similar functionality, will look like the following:

```
<template for:each={accounts} for:item="account">
   My account's name is: {account.Name}
</template>
```

Like our previous Apex `for each` loop pseudocode, everything in between these two tags will be able to access the fields of the `Account` variable in the order it appears in our list of accounts, yielding a tab for each index in our list. We can access the fields in the specified account using dot notation, such as `{account.Name}` to grab the name of our **Account** record.

7. Inside our `template for:each` directive tags, we are going to add another new-to-us component, **lightning-tab**. The attributes for this tag will be `label`, `value`, and `key`, where `label` is the verbiage displayed on the tab, `value` is the value that is passed to `active-tab-value` when each tab is selected, and `key` is a unique computed value to distinguish each tab from the others.
8. For our use case, use `label={account.Name}` to display the **Name** field of the specified **Account** record, where both `value=` and `key=` will be `{account.Id}`. The 15- or 18-digit Salesforce ID is a unique, computed value that we will not only use as our key, but we will also want to pass our `Id` value to the nested component that we will be building in *Chapter 6, Composing Lightning Web Components*. Our `lightning-tab` tags will look like this:

```
<lightning-tab label={account.Name} value={account.Id} key={account.Id}>
   // columns markup goes here...
</lightning-tab>
```

9. Now, we need to add our columns. We are going to do this using the `slds-grid` system. Add a `div` tag between your `lightning-tab` tags with the class attribute of `"slds-grid slds-gutters"`, which will initialize a grid container (`slds-grid`) and add Salesforce's default horizontal padding between columns (`slds-gutters`). The benefit of utilizing `slds-gutters` rather than specifying a specific pixel width to pad with is that if Salesforce changes the default level of padding applied to components, your columns

will automatically be updated to the same default level of padding. In between your `lightning-tab` tags, you will have the following:

```
<div class="slds-grid slds-gutters">
</div>
```

10. Next, let's add some content to our columns. From the documentation, linked in the *See also* section for this recipe, we know that there can be up to 12 columns (denoted by the `slds-col` class) in our grid. From our ticket, we know that we want 3 columns with respective widths of 1/6 (2/12), 1/3 (4/12), and 1/2 (6/12), where the full set of columns takes up the width of our LWC. To build out these three columns, we will have three `div` tags, each with a class attribute containing the `slds-col` class, as well as an `slds-size_SIZE` class corresponding to the desired size of the column as a fraction.
11. As we called out, our sizes will be `1-of-6`, `1-of-3`, and `1-of-2`, where `1` represents the numerator of a fraction, and the number after `of` represents the denominator. You can reduce your fraction, as I have, or, if you prefer, you can use a fraction of `12` to make the column width math a little easier, yielding `2-of-12`, `4-of-12`, and `6-of-12`. Both methods yield the same result.
It is important to note that there do not have to be 12 columns, and columns need not have an even denominator. For example, `slds-size_1-of-5` will yield a column that takes up 20%, or 1/5, of the page. This can be seen in the diagram here:

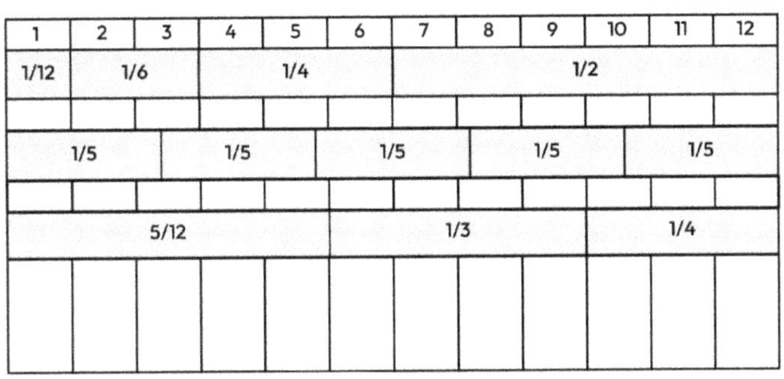

Figure 3.2: A diagram showing different examples of slds-grid layouts.

12. After building our columns, our `div` tags will look like the following:

```
<div class="slds-col slds-size_1-of-6">
  <!-- our account info goes here -->
</div>
```

```
<div class="slds-col slds-size_1-of-3">
    <!-- our map goes here -->
</div>
<div class="slds-col slds-size_1-of-2">
    <!-- our Chapter 4 code goes here -->
</div>
```

13. Let's take a look at our first column. We are going to replace `<!-- our account info goes here -->` with a **lightning-record-view-form**, which will allow us to display read-only values with their field labels from our **Account** record in the form of a series of `lightning-output-field` components using the **Lightning Data Service**. We are going to start with our `lightning-record-view-form`.
14. First, we'll need to specify a `record-id` attribute, which will be `{account.Id}`. Remember, `account` is the **Account** record that we are accessing in the order it appears in our `accounts` list.
15. Next, we will fill our `lightning-record-view-form` with a series of `lightning-output-field` tags, each with a `field-name` attribute representing the **Account** record's field label and value displayed. The fields specified in our ticket are `Name`, `Phone`, `BillingAddress`, `Museum_Office__c`, and `AnnualRevenue`. In all, our first `div class="slds-col slds-size_1-of-6"` tag will look like the following:

```
<div class="slds-col slds-size_1-of-6">
    <lightning-record-view-form
        record-id={account.Id}
        object-api-name="Account"}
    >
        <lightning-output-field
            field-name="Name">
        </lightning-output-field>
        <lightning-output-field
            field-name="Phone">
        </lightning-output-field>
        <lightning-output-field
            field-name="BillingAddress">
        </lightning-output-field>
        <lightning-output-field
            field-name="Museum_Office__c">
        </lightning-output-field>
```

```
        <lightning-output-field
            field-name="AnnualRevenue">
        </lightning-output-field>
    </lightning-record-view-form>
</div>
```

16. In our next column, denoted by `<div class="slds-col slds-size_1-of-3">`, we are going to nest another `div` tag, this time with the attribute `class="slds-text-heading_large"`, which will enclose the `{account.Name}` variable as a plain text output:

```
<div class="slds-text-heading_large">
    {account.Name}
</div>
```

Because our plain text output is wrapped in this `div` tag, it will be displayed with Salesforce's Lightning Design System (SLDS) heading styling in a large size.

17. After our heading, we will add a new `lightning-map` component, which we first saw in *Chapter 2, Writing Apex for Lightning Web Components,* to the second `div class="slds-col ..."` tag. Our title will be `{account.Name}`, `map-markers` will be `{account.markers}`, and `markers-title` will also be `{account.Name}`. Like our map component in *Chapter 2, Writing Apex for Lightning Web Components,* we will be using our wrapper class to pass our `marker` information to our LWC. In all, our second `slds-col` classed `div` tag will look like this:

```
<div class="slds-col slds-size_1-of-3">
    <div class="slds-text-heading_large">
        {account.Name}
    </div>
    <lightning-map
        title={account.Name}
        map-markers={account.markers}
        markers-title={account.Name}>
    </lightning-map>
</div>
```

18. Remember, we are leaving our third `div` tag and the second half of our screen blank for *Chapter 4, Synchronous and Asynchronous Processing in Components,* so we will leave the

third column, denoted by the `<div class="slds-col slds-size_1-of-2">` tag, untouched for now.

19. Having built out our Apex and HTML files, we can deploy them and connect them by building our JavaScript file. First, let's import our necessary **decorators** and methods. Our first two imports will be as follows:

```
import { LightningElement, wire } from 'lwc';
import returnAccountWrapperList from '@salesforce/apex/
TopAccountsController.returnAccountWrapperList';
```

Remember, to import a method from Apex, we import `methodName` from `'@salesforce/apex/[namespace].ClassName.methodName'`.

20. Our last import will be the following:

```
import { ShowToastEvent } from "lightning/platformShowToastEvent";
```

This will ensure that we can once again have a `showNotif` function in our JavaScript file that shows a toast message when called. We will be learning how to build utility JavaScript files in *Chapter 4*, so don't worry! You will only have to write this function twice more: once now, and once for our utility.

21. At the bottom of your class, add the following function:

```
showNotif(title, msg, variant) {
    const evt = new ShowToastEvent({
        title: title,
        message: msg,
        variant: variant,
    });
    this.dispatchEvent(evt);
}
```

We'll be examining **event dispatching** further in *Chapter 6, Composing Lightning Web Components*.

22. Next, let's define an empty variable, `accounts`, at the top of our JavaScript class. This corresponds to the list of **Account** records that we are iterating over in our HTML file.

We will also define an empty variable, `error`, to store any error messages we receive while running our code.

23. Lastly, to populate our accounts, we will wire our `returnAccountWrapperList` method. In this particular `wire` function, we will have three cases: `if (data)`, where there is a result returned by our `wire` function; `else if (error)`, for if there is an error that occurs while we are receiving the data stream; and `else`, which will be called if `data` and `error` are both `null`, meaning that we successfully called our `wire` function, but no data was returned. This will occur if you are directly following this tutorial and have not completed the *Setting up the Salesforce Lightning Web Components Cookbook org* recipe in *Chapter 1, Getting Ready for Lightning Web Component Development*. Our `wire` function will look like this:

```
@wire(returnAccountWrapperList)
wiredAccounts({error, data}) {
   if(data) {
      this.accounts = JSON.parse(data);
      this.error = undefined;
   } else if(error) {
      this.error = error;
      this.accounts = undefined;
      this.showNotif('There has been an error!', this.error, 'error');
      } else {
      this.error = undefined;
      this.accounts = undefined;
      this.showNotif('Please complete Chapter 1 org setup!', 'You have no 
accounts with geolocations to query, which is why you are seeing this 
notification. Please review Chapter 1.', 'warning');
   }
}
```

Line by line, we are provisioning a wire service and configuring our adapter (`returnAccountWrapperList`), defining a function (`wiredAccounts`) to receive the stream of data from the wire service, and setting our `accounts` and `error` variables based on the results of the data stream. Additionally, we are showing an error toast if there is an error, and a warning toast if nothing is returned.

There's more...

In this section, we learned about the `for:each` directive. A related directive that can be used is the `iterator` directive, which allows you to iterate over an array by index rather than by object. If we were to utilize the `iterator` directive for this use case, our `template` tag may look like the following:

```
<template iterator:account={accounts}>
    <div lwc:if={account.first}>
        This is the first value in the list.
    </div>
    <div lwc:ifelse={account.last}>
        This is the last value in the list.
    </div>
    <div lwc:else>
        This account, {account.value.Name}, is the {account.index}th account in the
list.
    </div>
</template>
```

In this example, our `account` iterator represents the account at the index specified. We can use the built-in `value`, `index`, `first`, and `last` properties to grab information about each account in our `accounts` array. This pattern allows us to apply special formatting to the `first`, `last`, and ith items in our list, for example, highlighting even rows in a table. To access the properties of the item at the specified index, use `{iteratorName}.value.{propertyName}`, in this case, `{account.value.Name}`, to access the `Name` field of our specified `account`.

To visualize this as a `for` loop, let's look at the following pseudocode:

```
for(Integer ii = 0; ii < List<Account> accounts.size(); ii++) {
    if(ii == 0) {
        System.debug('This is the first value in the list.');
    } else if (ii == accounts.size() - 1) {
        System.debug('This is the last value in the list.');
    } else {
        System.debug('This account, ' + accounts[ii].Name + ', is the ' + ii + 'th
account in the list.');
    }
}
```

Instead of accessing our **Account** records directly, we must access them using the index at which they appear in the `accounts` list.

> **Note**
>
> You may have noticed that I used two `i` characters, `ii`, to define my `for` loop's `index` variable. This is a helpful practice because `ii` is much more searchable in code than `i`. While most variables should have descriptive names dictated by company coding standards, such as `index`, this double-character variable definition in place of a single character is a practice that I would selfishly like to see adopted.

See also

- The sample HTML, JavaScript, and `js-meta.xml` files for the `topTenAccountTabset` LWC are located under the `force-app/chapter03/default/lwc/topTenAccountTabset` directory in your forked repository for comparison. This file is located at `https://github.com/PacktPublishing/Salesforce-Lightning-Web-Component-Cookbook/tree/main/force-app/chapter03/default/lwc/topTenAccountTabset/` in the cookbook repository.
- The full *Lightning Web Components Component Reference* can be found at `https://developer.salesforce.com/docs/component-library/overview/components`.
- Documentation on spinners and their uses can be found at `https://lightningdesignsystem.com/components/spinners/`.
- The *Lightning Web Components Developer Guide* page on HTML template directives is available at `https://developer.salesforce.com/docs/platform/lwc/guide/reference-directives.html`.
- The documentation for the SLDS grid system is available at `https://lightningdesignsystem.com/utilities/grid/`.
- The *Lightning Web Components Developer Guide* page on understanding the wire service is located at `https://developer.salesforce.com/docs/platform/lwc/guide/data-wire-service-about.html`.

Get this book's PDF version and more

Scan the QR code (or go to `packtpub.com/unlock`). Search for this book by name, confirm the edition, and then follow the steps on the page.

Part 2

Intermediate JavaScript Topics in LWC Development

Now that you have mastered the basics of Lightning Web Component development, you are ready to begin tackling harder problems in JavaScript. You will learn how to translate between legacy and modern JavaScript patterns and when to use each, as well as how Salesforce distorts our JavaScript within the **Shadow Document Object Model** (**Shadow DOM**) for security. We will also go in-depth on the dos and don'ts of JavaScript eventing. In mastering these topics, you will be preparing yourself to build fully custom components.

This part has the following chapters:

4

Synchronous and Asynchronous Processing in Components

In *Chapter 3, Working with a Selector Class,* we learned how to build a robust backend for our **Lightning Web Components** (**LWCs**), complete with a **query utility**. Now that we know some backend best practices, let's look at how we can build a frontend to match.

Previously, in *Chapter 2, Writing Apex for Lightning Web Components,* we introduced the concept of **wrapper classes** to build a strong foundation for passing data from our Apex into our LWCs with the use of a JSON string. In this chapter, we will be examining two other ways to pass data from Apex to an LWC: passing a wrapper class directly into our JavaScript via **imperative Apex**, and passings Objects directly into our JavaScript via imperative Apex. These patterns are arguably easier to work with, although both come with their own quirks.

Finally, the main purpose of this chapter is to learn about the two types of **asynchronous processing** in LWCs. Like learning a spoken language, I find that seeing a "translation" of code helps me to understand the nuances of different methods of accomplishing the same task, so we are going to do the same thing in several ways so that we can see an example of how to translate legacy **promise chains** into **async/await functionality**, as well as know when promise chains can still be useful.

We are going to be covering the following main recipes:

- Returning `@AuraEnabled` sObjects
- Asynchronous processing in LWCs
- Synchronous processing in LWCs
- Reusable utility components

Technical requirements

The recipes for this book can be found at `https://github.com/PacktPublishing/Salesforce-Lightning-Web-Component-Cookbook`, where each chapter has its own folder under the `force-app` folder. This GitHub repository is structured in the form of a Salesforce DX project, which will allow you to easily fork the repository for deployment in a free Salesforce Developer Edition org. The code for *Chapter 4, Synchronous and Asynchronous Processing in Components*, is located at `https://github.com/PacktPublishing/Salesforce-Lightning-Web-Component-Cookbook/tree/main/force-app/chapter04`.

The components in this book require the use of an **integrated development environment** (**IDE**), such as **Visual Studio Code** (**VS Code**) or **Salesforce Code Builder**. Detailed instructions for setting up an IDE are located in *Chapter 1, Getting Ready for Lightning Web Components*, in the *Setting up your IDE* section.

If you are building the projects in this cookbook as written, you will need to seed your Salesforce Developer Edition org with test data. Detailed instructions for seeding your org are located in *Chapter 1, Getting Ready for Lightning Web Components*, in the *Setting up the Salesforce Lightning Web Components Cookbook org* section.

Lastly, the edition of Salesforce required to implement the recipes in this book must be Developer, Performance, Unlimited, Enterprise, or Database.com. You can sign up for a free Salesforce Developer Edition org at `https://developer.salesforce.com/signup`.

Returning @AuraEnabled sObjects

Early in the book, we learned about passing wrapper classes into JavaScript as a JSON string, which is a commonly used pattern. Another commonly used pattern, and arguably an easier pattern to follow, is utilizing the **@AuraEnabled** tag to directly serialize sObjects into JSON for ingestion by our frontend. We started with serializing and deserializing our wrapper classes into JSON objects so that we could get familiar with some of the JSON methods and `String` manipulation as we build our LWC repertoire. Now that we are familiar with these methods, we can build on this foundation and serialize sObjects directly.

Getting ready

Following our business use case, we are going to continue building out our **Top Accounts** page, started in *Chapter 3, Working with a Selector Class*, which will allow us to view our top 10 accounts by annual revenue, as well as some of the art that they currently have on display. The recipes in this chapter will guide you through building a component that shows the artworks (**assets**) that each museum (**account**) has on display, grouped together by the artwork's related **tag**.

How to do it...

1. Start by creating a new `public with sharing` Apex class, `TagSelector`. Like our previous **selector classes**, this class will extend the `Util_Query` utility class that we built in *Chapter 3, Working with a Selector Class*:

```
public with sharing class TagSelector extends Util_Query {...}
```

2. Create a `@TestVisible private static final String` class variable, `TAGS_WITH_ASSETS_BY_ACCOUNT_QUERY`, that will be equal to the following query text:

```
'SELECT Id, Name, (SELECT Id, Name, Department__c, Description,
Is_Public_Domain__c, Object_Id__c, Primary_Image__c FROM Assets__r WHERE
AccountId = :accountId) FROM Tag__c'
```

3. This query retrieves a **tag** and its child `Asset` records, or `Asset` records that have the specified **tag** as a **lookup relationship** value.
4. has on display, grouped together by the artwork'sThis method will return a list of `Tag` object records:

```
public List<Tag__c> tagsWithAssetsByAccount(Id accountId) {...}
```

5. Because we have a **bind variable** in our query of `accountId`, we need to use the `queryWithBinds` method of our `Util_Query` class to get our query results. To do this, we will need to create a `Map<String, Object>` called `bindMap` that "binds" our parameters to the bind variables in our query:

```
Map<String, Object> bindMap = new Map<String, Object>{
    'accountId' => accountId
};
```

6. If we had additional bind variables, we would separate them with a comma, like so:

```
Map<String, Object> bindMap = new Map<String, Object>{
    'firstField' => firstValue,
    'secondField' => secondValue,
    'thirdField' => thirdValue // ...and so on
};
```

7. This follows the format required to construct a map in one line, as described in the *Apex Map Class* documentation.
8. Now that we have our `bindMap`, we can get our list of `tag` object records that meet the criteria for a given account. Don't forget to add an `AccessLevel` value of `SYSTEM_MODE`, which will allow us to see records that aren't necessarily owned by us. This will allow end users to be able to tell which artworks (assets) belong to which museum (account), regardless of who owns the `Asset` records:

```
List<Tag__c> queryResult = (List<Tag__c>)
queryWithBinds(TAGS_WITH_ASSETS_BY_ACCOUNT_QUERY, bindMap,
AccessLevel.SYSTEM_MODE);
return queryResult;
```

9. Having written our selector class, we can build out our **service class**. For learning purposes, this class will have two methods: one that will parse queried records into a wrapper class, and one that will pass sObject records directly into our controller class. We will write each of these methods to learn how to translate between the two. Start by creating a new `public with sharing` class, `AssetsByTagService`.
10. In our first method, `getTagsWithAssetsByAccount`, we will accept one parameter of `Id accountId`, and we will simply return the results of the non-static method from our `TagSelector` class:

```
public List<Tag__c> getTagsWithAssetsByAccount(Id accountId){
   return new TagSelector().tagsWithAssetsByAccount(accountId);
}
```

11. We are going to simply pass our `Tag` sObject records into our controller class. Note that this will require more processing on the front end.
12. For our second method, `getTagsWithAssetsWrappersByAccount`, we're going to accept the same parameters, and we are also going to call the non-static method of our `TagSelector` account, but in addition, we are going to process the result into `@AuraEnabled` wrapper classes to pass to our controller class. Because we are using a parent-to-child SOQL query, we will need to create a wrapper for each of our objects queried. Go ahead and create two wrapper classes, `TagWrapperCh04` and `AssetWrapperCh04`. We already have existing wrappers for both sObjects, `TagWrapper` in the `force-app/chater00` directory for the Cookbook setup we completed in *Chapter 1*,

Getting Ready for Lightning Web Component Development, and `AssetWrapper`, which we wrote in *Chapter 2, Writing Apex for Lightning Web Components*, but to keep everything clear, we are going to do some duplication of efforts here.

13. In your `TagWrapperCh04` class, create the following class variable with the `@AuraEnabled` tag:

```
@AuraEnabled public List<AssetWrapperCh04> assets;
```

14. Next, create your `TagWrapperCh04` constructor, which will accept a parameter of a `Tag__c` sObject record, `tagToWrap`:

```
public TagWrapperCh04(Tag__c tagToWrap) {
   this.assets = new List<AssetWrapperCh04>();
   for(Asset ast : tagToWrap.Assets__r) {
      AssetWrapperCh04 assetWrapper = new AssetWrapperCh04(ast);
      assetWrapper.tagId = tagToWrap.Id;
      assetWrapper.tagName = tagToWrap.Name;
      this.assets.add(assetWrapper);
   }
}
```

15. Now that we've created our `TagWrapperCh04` constructor, let's create `AssetWrapperCh04` to populate it with. This wrapper will have the following `@AuraEnabled` class variables, as well as a constructor that accepts an `Asset` record and initializes our class variables:

```
@AuraEnabled public String tagId;
@AuraEnabled public String tagName;
@AuraEnabled public String assetId;
@AuraEnabled public String assetName;
@AuraEnabled public String assetDepartment;
@AuraEnabled public String assetDescription;
@AuraEnabled public String assetObjectId;
@AuraEnabled public Boolean assetIsPublicDomain;
@AuraEnabled public String assetPrimaryImage;
public AssetWrapperCh04(Asset ast) {
   this.assetId = ast.Id;
   this.assetName = ast.Name;
   this.assetDepartment = ast.Department__c;
   this.assetDescription = ast.Description;
```

```
        this.assetIsPublicDomain = ast.Is_Public_Domain__c;
        this.assetObjectId = ast.Object_Id__c;
        this.assetPrimaryImage = ast.Primary_Image__c;
    }
```

16. Once we have written our wrapper classes and their constructors, we can write the method to process our query results into the wrappers. This will end up looking like the following:

```
public List<AssetWrapperCh04> getTagsWithAssetsWrappersByAccount(Id
accountId){
    List<Tag__c> tagList = new
TagSelector().tagsWithAssetsByAccount(accountId);
    List<AssetWrapperCh04> assetWrapperList = new List<AssetWrapperCh04>();
    for(Tag__c tag : tagList) {
        TagWrapperCh04 wrappedTag = new TagWrapperCh04(tag);
        assetWrapperList.addAll(wrappedTag.assets);
    }
    return assetWrapperList;
}
```

17. Finally, we can write our controller class. Create the final Apex class of the chapter, `AssetsByTagController`, and create two `@AuraEnabled(cacheable=true)` public static methods: one returning a `List<Tag__c>` called `returnTagsWithAssetsByAccount`, and one returning a `List<AssetsByTagService.AssetWrapperCh04>` called `returnTagsWithAssetsWrappersByAccount`. Each method will accept our familiar parameter of `String accountIdString`. These two methods will look remarkably similar, with the only difference between the two being the different service class methods called by each controller method.
18. In each method, start by making sure that our `accountIdString` is, in fact, an Id value. This is a simple way to validate our front-end input.

```
Id accountId = Id.valueOf(accountIdString);
```

19. Next, return the result of our non-static service methods, `getTagsWithAssetsByAccount` and `getTagsWithAssetsWrappersByAccount`, in the appropriately named controller method.
20. This will give us the following for each method:

returnTagsWithAssetsByAccount

```
@AuraEnabled(cacheable=true)
public static List<Tag__c> returnTagsWithAssetsByAccount(String
accountIdString){
   try {
      Id accountId = Id.valueOf(accountIdString);
      return assetsByTagService
         .getTagsWithAssetsByAccount(
            accountId
         );
   } catch (Exception e) {
      throw new AuraHandledException(e.getMessage());
   }
}
```

returnTagsWithAssetsWrappersByAccount

```
@AuraEnabled(cacheable=true)
public static List<AssetsByTagService.AssetWrapperCh04>
returnTagsWithAssetsWrappersByAccount(String accountIdString){
   try {
      Id accountId = Id.valueOf(accountIdString);
      return assetsByTagService
         .getTagsWithAssetsWrappersByAccount(
            accountId
         );
   } catch (Exception e) {
      throw new AuraHandledException(e.getMessage());
   }
}
```

21. To reiterate, each of these methods passes our data to the frontend in a different way: `returnTagsWithAssetsByAccount` returns the sObjects directly, and `returnTagsWithAssetsWrappersByAccount` returns the wrappers for each sObject. The former will require more processing on the frontend, while the latter handles our processing on the backend. How you proceed in a production environment is only limited by your company standards, the processing time required, and your level of familiarity with JavaScript!

See also

The sample files for *Chapter 4, Synchronous and Asynchronous Processing in Components*, classes are located under the `force-app/chapter04/default/classes` directory in your forked repository for comparison. These files are located at `https://github.com/PacktPublishing/Salesforce-Lightning-Web-Component-Cookbook/tree/main/force-app/chapter04/default/classes`.

Asynchronous processing in LWCs

Now that we have built the backend to accommodate two different data structures, let's see what these data structures look like and how we can use asynchronous processing to view them. But first, what is asynchronous processing? A better starting question may be, what is synchronous processing?

Synchronous processing in computing refers to a computer reading code line by line, operating on the code it encounters in the order that it is encountered. Everything happens in sequential order, one after the other, in a single thread of execution. Vanilla JavaScript is generally a synchronous programming language, as in, it usually operates in a single thread of execution. What this means in practice is that if we have a long-running function in a block of code, we must wait for it to be completed to move on to the next set of instructions.

Asynchronous processing occurs when a task, usually long-running, such as a callout, occurs outside of the main thread of execution. In Apex, this can happen with a `@future(callout=true)` annotated method, where we send a callout to an external system while our code is running. In JavaScript, these tasks are usually browser functions such as `fetch()`, which is, well, a callout! Because JavaScript runs synchronously, we need a way to handle asynchronous browser functions in a synchronous manner. We will explore two ways to do this: the `async/await` pattern and promise chaining, each of which is explored in this recipe.

Now that we know a little about asynchronous processing and that we must execute our asynchronous code synchronously, we can create our latest LWC to see how it works.

How to do it...

1. Create a new LWC, `assetsByTag`. For now, place a **lightning-spinner** component within an `lwc:if` directive in the HTML file as a placeholder. If an `isLoaded` variable is **falsy**, we will display the spinner. This will allow us to verify that we have placed our component correctly in the next steps:

```
<template>
    <template lwc:if={isLoaded}>
        <!-- cool stuff coming here! -->
```

```
    </template>
    <template lwc:else>
        <lightning-spinner
            alternative-text="Loading..."
            size="large"
            variant="base"
        ></lightning-spinner>
    </template>
</template>
```

2. In the JavaScript file for `assetsByTag`, instantiate an `@api accountId` variable. We will also create three private variables, denoted by an underscore (_) in front of the variable name. These variables will be called `_tagsWithAssetsResult`, `_tagsWithAssetsPromiseResult`, and `_tagsWithAssetsWrappersResult`. Be sure to import the `api` decorator at the top of your JavaScript file:

```
import { LightningElement, api } from 'lwc';
export default class AssetsByTag extends LightningElement {
    @api accountId;
    _tagsWithAssetsResult;
    _tagsWithAssetsPromiseResult;
    _tagsWithAssetsWrappersResult;
}
```

> **Note**
>
> JavaScript added support for private properties in its classes in **ES2022**. This is denoted in vanilla JavaScript using the pound (#) symbol, such as `#myPrivateProperty`. As of the writing of this book, this is not available to Salesforce developers, so we use an underscore (_) to denote that a property should not be used outside of its current context.

3. Navigate to the HTML file of the `topTenAccountTabset` component that we created in *Chapter 3, Working with a Selector Class*. If you haven't completed the code in that chapter, you can find this code in the `force-app/chapter03` directory for deployment to your Salesforce developer org. In the third column of our **lightning-tab**, between the `<!-- Chapter 4 Code Here -->` comments, add a reference to our `assetsByTag` component. In order to do this, we will add `c-` to the front of our component name and

convert from camel case to kebab case, where we use hyphens instead of capital letters to separate the words in our component name.

For example, if our component name is `myCoolComponent`, our component reference will look like this:

```
<c-my-cool-component></c-my-cool-component>
```

4. Note that we must have a closing tag here.
5. Our `topTenAccountTabset` file will now have the following:

```
<!-- Chapter 4 Code Here -->
   <c-assets-by-tag account-id={account.Id}></c-assets-by-tag>
<!-- Chapter 4 Code Here -->
```

6. Notice that we have taken our `@api`-decorated variable, `accountId`, and converted it to its kebab case variant to indicate that we are passing in an `account.Id` variable, which is the `Id` value of our iterated-over account, into our child component. We will dive into this further in *Chapter 6, Composing Lightning Web Components*, but for now, note that in order to pass variables from parent to child LWC, we must have the `@api` variable decorated in our child component, and we must take the variable name in its kebab case variant and place it as a property of our child component's tag in the parent component.
7. Deploy all changes, including the changes to `topTenAccountTabset`, and navigate to your **Top Accounts** page via the **App Launcher**. If you have added the `assetsByTag` component tag into `topTenAccountTabset` correctly, you should see our spinner over the page. We will remove this in due time, don't worry! Your **Top Accounts** page should look like the following:

Figure 4.1: The updated Top Accounts page showing a lightning-spinner element.

8. Return to your `assetsByTag.js` JavaScript file, where we will be building out the bulk of the rest of the functionality for the chapter. Now that we have the shell of our LWC built, we are going to explore the two different forms of asynchronous processing available to us in JavaScript.

How it works...

Async and await functions

The first method for asynchronous processing that we are going to explore is the `async/await` pattern. This pattern has been widely available since April 2017, and is the preferred method for asynchronous processing in modern LWC development.

The `async` function allows us to bind the result of an asynchronous call to a variable in a clean and concise way, which allows us to avoid promise chaining, which we will explore in the next section of this recipe. There are some scenarios in which promise chaining is still preferred, which we will explore in *Chapter 5, Accessing External Data Sources via Lightning Web Components*, but for now, we will be doing a direct comparison of the two methods to perform the same functionality so that we can understand how each pattern works, and, hopefully, how to translate between the two. Let's get started!

1. Recall that we have two methods in our `AssetsByTagController` class. Return to your `getTagsWithAssets.js` file, and import these two Apex methods:

```
import returnTagsWithAssetsByAccount from '@salesforce/apex/
AssetsByTagController.returnTagsWithAssetsByAccount';
import returnTagsWithAssetsWrappersByAccount from '@salesforce/apex/
AssetsByTagController.returnTagsWithAssetsWrappersByAccount';
```

2. For our first function, `getTagsWithAssets`, we are going to create an `async` function. This means that we will use the `async` keyword in our function definition, as shown here:

```
async getTagsWithAssets() { ... }
```

3. This designates our function as an asynchronous function, allowing us to resolve a promise with the return value of the specified `await` function—in our case, our chosen Apex method.
4. Next, let's add a `try-catch` block inside our asynchronous function. For now, we will leave our `catch` block empty, as we will be coming back to it in the *Reusable utility components* recipe. Within our `try` block, however, let's define a `const` variable, `tagsWithAssets`, and set it equal to the value returned by our Apex method. We use a `const` declaration here so that we prevent ourselves from operating directly on the results of our imperative Apex call, as this will result in an error. We will also log the result to our console so we can see what our data structure looks like. Our `try-catch` block will look like the following:

```
try{
   const tagsWithAssets = await
returnTagsWithAssetsByAccount({ accountIdString : this.accountId });
   console.log('tagsWithAssets: ' + JSON.stringify(tagsWithAssets));
} catch(error) {
   //error processing here...
}
```

5. Notice that we use the `await` expression before our imperative Apex call. Each `async` function can have zero or more `await` expressions, meaning multiple promises can be resolved in a single function, but each `await` expression must be within an `async` function.
6. The neat thing about the `await` expression is that it effectively pauses our code's execution until we get a response back from our Apex method. This allows us to process the resolved promise **semi-synchronously**. If we did not have the `await` expression, our code would continue running, meaning we might not have the results we need to continue our processing.

7. For our second function, `getTagsWithAssetsWrappers`, we are going to use the `async/await` pattern on our `returnTagsWithAssetsWrappersByAccount` method. This will look remarkably similar to our `getTagsWithAssets` function:

```
async getTagsWithAssetsWrappers() {
    try{
        const tagsWithAssetsWrappers = await
returnTagsWithAssetsWrappersByAccount({ accountIdString : this.accountId });
        console.log('tagsWithAssetsWrappers: ' +
JSON.stringify(tagsWithAssetWrappers));
    } catch(error) {
        //error processing here...
    }
}
```

8. Once we have these functions, let's add them to a `connectedCallback` function so that our tags are pulled on component render:

```
connectedCallback() {
    this.getTagsWithAssets();
    this.getTagsWithAssetsWrappers();
}
```

9. Deploy your changes to your org and open your **console log** within **Dev Tools** to see what our two different Apex methods return. Recall that `getTagsWithAssets` is returning `@AuraEnabled` sObject records and will therefore need processing on the frontend, while `getTagsWithAssetsWrappers` is returning our wrapper classes that were defined in our Apex to simplify our frontend processing.
10. Open your **Top Accounts** page to **Ultricies PC**, and let's look at the output for the `Birds` tag, first from our `tagsWithAssets` function, which will look similar to the following:

```
{"Id":"a02bm000005CLdhAAG","Name":"Birds","Assets__r":
[{"Tag__c":"a02bm000005CLdhAAG","Id":"02ibm000000B8ThAAK","Name":"Easy
Chair","Department__c":"The American
Wing","Is_Public_Domain__c":true,"Object_ID__c":"3497","Primary_Image__c":"h
ttps://images.metmuseum.org/CRDImages/ad/original/DP108634.jpg"}]}
```

11. We see that we have our tag Id and name, followed by an array of `Asset` records defined by the `Assets__r` relationship. This is a good starting point, but we will need to do some more processing to get our data usable by the component we are going to be adding. We will look at this in the *Synchronous processing in LWCs* recipe.
12. Now, let's look at the same output for the `Birds` tag from our `tagsWithAssetWrappers` function:

```
{"assetDepartment":"The American
Wing","assetId":"02ibm000000B8ThAAK","assetIsPublicDomain":true,"assetName":
"Easy Chair","assetObjectId":"3497","assetPrimaryImage":"https://
images.metmuseum.org/CRDImages/ad/original/
DP108634.jpg","tagId":"a02bm000005CLdhAAG","tagName":"Birds"}
```

13. In this output, we see that we have an array of `Asset` records that have been formatted so that each has a `tagId` and `tagName` property. This is known as **flattening the data structure**, which will make our data easier to work with. Instead of having two object layers, we now only have one.
14. Whether we flatten the data structure on the frontend in our JavaScript file or on the backend with Apex is a matter of personal preference, balanced with component performance.

How it works...

Promise chain

One of the best ways to learn a language, whether spoken or typed, is to see a translation for comparison. Now that we understand `async/await` patterning, let's look at how to do the same thing with a **promise chain**. We will see an advanced use case for a promise chain in *Chapter 5, Accessing External Data Sources via Lightning Web Components*, and you may see promise chains in legacy code, so it's important we cover them! Because `getTagsWithAssetsWrappers` provides us with already flattened data, let's take a look at our `getTagsWithAssets` function:

1. Below your `getTagsWithAssets` function, create a third function, `getTagsWithAssetsPromise`. Unlike our previous asynchronous functions, this function will not carry the `async` designation, as we do not want to mix the `async/await` and promise patterns in LWCs!

```
getTagsWithAssetsPromise() { ... }
```

It is important that you do not mix async functions with promise chain functions, as it can have unexpected consequences, colloquially referred to as callback hell. Callback hell occurs when multiple nested functions make code harder to read and debug by obscuring the single thread of execution.

JS callbackhell.js ×

Users > evelynmaguire > Documents > Book Drafts > JS callbackhell.js > ...

```
getHungry(function(cookbook) {
    readRecipe(cookbook, function(recipe) {
        buyGroceries(recipe, function(ingredients) {
            makeCookies(ingredients, function(cookieDough) {
                bakeCookies(cookieDough, function(heat) {
                    console.log("cookies baked at: " + heat);
                });
            });
        });
    });
});
```

Figure 4.2: A visual representation of callback hell, where a series of nested functions for baking cookies makes it hard to follow what is going on!

To write this in a way that makes it easier to follow, we would give each function a place at the top level of the program and use either async/await patterning or promise chaining to ensure that the single thread of execution is easy to follow, as we are doing in this recipe.

2. Next, add your imperative Apex call. We will not be setting it equal to a variable at this juncture, but we will be processing it further in a moment! Do not end this line with a semicolon:

```
returnTagsWithAssetsByAccount({ accountIdString : this.accountId })
```

3. Now that we have our imperative Apex call, we are going to add our promise chain. On the line immediately following your imperative Apex, tab in once, and add the following, starting with a period:

```
    .then(tagsWithAssets => {
        console.log('tagsWithAssetsPromise: ' +
JSON.stringify(tagsWithAssets));
    })
    .catch(error => {
```

```
        //error processing here...
    })
```

4. What we are doing here is creating a **promise**, which is an object that represents the completion or failure of our imperative Apex call. If our Apex succeeds, we pass the value into our callback, denoted by the `then` function, and if it fails, we `catch` the error.
5. Where we have our console log, we would be able to take the result of our imperative Apex call, `tagsWithAssets`, and apply the additional processing we need to flatten the data structure.
6. Now that we have our `getTagsWithAssetsPromise` function, we can verify visually that its output is the same as `getTagsWithAssets` by adding our promise function into `connectedCallback`:


```
{"Id":"a02bm000005CLdhAAG","Name":"Birds","Assets__r":
[{"Tag__c":"a02bm000005CLdhAAG","Id":"02ibm000000B8ThAAK","Name":"Easy
Chair","Department__c":"The American
Wing","Is_Public_Domain__c":true,"Object_ID__c":"3497","Primary_Image__c":"h
ttps://images.metmuseum.org/CRDImages/ad/original/DP108634.jpg"}]}
```


7. Having visually verified the outputs, we can flatten our data for our `getTagsWithAssets` and `getTagsWithAssetsPromise` functions. This will be done using synchronous processing. No further processing is needed for `getTagsWithAssetsWrappers`.

See also

- The sample files for the `assetsByTag` LWC are located under the `force-app/chapter04/default/lwc/assetsByTag` directory in your forked repository for comparison. These files are located at `https://github.com/PacktPublishing/Salesforce-Lightning-Web-Component-Cookbook/tree/main/force-app/chapter04/default/lwc/assetsByTag`.
- The *Mozilla MDN Web Docs* documentation for asynchronous JavaScript can be found at `https://developer.mozilla.org/en-US/docs/Learn_web_development/Extensions/Async_JS`.
- The *Mozilla MDN Web Docs* documentation for the `async` function is available at `https://developer.mozilla.org/en-US/docs/Web/JavaScript/Reference/Statements/async_function`.

- The *Mozilla MDN Web Docs* documentation on using promises is available at `https://developer.mozilla.org/en-US/docs/Web/JavaScript/Guide/Using_promises`.
- *Callback Hell: Taming JavaScript's Async Complexity*, a cheeky reader with some great information on preventing callback hell, is available at `https://callbackhell.com`.

Synchronous processing in LWCs

Having learned about methods of asynchronous processing in LWCs, what does that mean for synchronous processing? We know that by utilizing the `async/await` and promise chain patterns, we can execute code semi-synchronously, but what does that look like? Remember, synchronous code is code that runs from top to bottom. By practicing our synchronous code writing, we can learn a lot about manipulating data with vanilla JavaScript.

How to do it...

1. We know that we have to flatten the data structure of our `getTagsWithAssets` and `getTagsWithAssetsPromise` functions, so let's start there. Create a new function, `tagFlattener`. We will use `tagFlattener` in both functions so that we can see how each type of asynchronous function fits into our JavaScript file. This function will accept one parameter, `tagsWithAssets`, which will represent the return from our imperative Apex call:

```
tagFlattener(dataToFlatten) { ... }
```

2. In the first line of our `tagFlattener` function, declare a new empty array, `flattenedData`:

```
let flattenedData = [];
```

3. We will be adding our flattened `Tag` and `Asset` combination objects to this array.
4. Now, let's go back to our `Birds` tag provided by `getTagsWithAssets` and `getTagsWithAssetsPromise`. Let's beautify our JSON output a little bit so we can more easily view the data structure:

```
{
    "Id": "a02bm000005CLdhAAG",
    "Name": "Birds",
    "Assets__r": [
        {
```

```
            "Tag__c": "a02bm000005CLdhAAG",
            "Id": "02ibm000000B8ThAAK",
            "Name": "Easy Chair",
            "Department__c": "The American Wing",
            "Is_Public_Domain__c": true,
            "Object_ID__c": "3497",
            "Primary_Image__c": "https://images.metmuseum.org/CRDImages/ad/
original/DP108634.jpg"
        }
    ]
}
```

5. Remember that this is a single `tag` object in an array of similar `tag` objects. We want to take each `tag` object and flatten it so that our `tag` information appears on each of the **assets** associated with it, and place each of those transformed **assets** into a separate array. Because we have two layers of objects, we are going to need to loop through twice. This can be achieved with a `for` loop and the JavaScript `map` function.
6. Create a `for` loop that iterates over the tags in `tagsToFlatten` and use the `map` function to get the assets for each tag. Within the `map` function, return a new JavaScript object that matches each sObject field with its requisite wrapper class attribute name. (Hint: We are aiming to create the same data structure as is returned by our `getTagsWithAssetsWrappers` function.) In order to return the same data structure, we will use the following:

```
for(let tag of tagsToFlatten) {
    let assets = tag.Assets__r;
    let flattenedAssets = assets.map((asset) => {
        return ({
            assetDepartment : asset.Department__c,
            assetId : asset.Id,
            assetIsPublicDomain : asset.Is_Public_Domain__c,
            assetName : asset.Name,
            assetObjectId : asset.Object_ID__c,
            assetPrimaryImage : asset.Primary_Image__c,
            tagId : tag.Id,
            tagName: tag.Name
        })
    });
```

```
        flattenedData = [...flattenedData, ...flattenedAssets];
    }
```

7. In the last line of the previous snippet, notice that we use two ellipses, or two **spread operators**, to merge two arrays into one. We go into a deeper explanation of this operator in *Chapter 5, Accessing External Data Sources in Lightning Web Components,* but for now, think of it as though we are spreading out our `flattenedData` and `flattenedAssets` arrays like cards on a table to combine them into a single hand. Finally, sort and return your `flattenedData` array at the end of your `tagFlattener` function:

```
flattenedData.sort((a, b) => {
        return (a.assetName > b.assetName) ? 1 : -1;
    }
);
return flattenedData;
```

8. Place the resulting `tagFlattener` function within the `getTagsWithAssets` and `getTagsWithAssetsPromise` functions. We will do this by removing our `console.log()` statements and setting our respective `private` variables to the result, as shown here:

```
async getTagsWithAssets() {
    try{
        const tagsWithAssets = await
returnTagsWithAssetsByAccount({ accountIdString : this.accountId });
        this._tagsWithAssetsResult = this.tagFlattener(tagsWithAssets);
    } catch(error) {
        //error processing here...
    }
}
getTagsWithAssetsPromise() {
    returnTagsWithAssetsByAccount({ accountIdString : this.accountId })
        .then(tagsWithAssets => {
            this._tagsWithAssetsPromiseResult =
this.tagFlattener(tagsWithAssets);
        })
        .catch(error => {
            //error processing here...
```

```
        })
}
```

9. We will also remove the `console.log()` statement from `getTagsWithAssetsWrappers` and set our respective `private` variable, like so:

```
async getTagsWithAssetsWrappers() {
    try{
        const tagsWithAssetWrappers = await
returnTagsWithAssetsWrappersByAccount({ accountIdString : this.accountId });
        let wrappersToSort = [...tagsWithAssetWrappers];
        let sortedWrappers = wrappersToSort.sort((a, b) => {
                return (a.assetName > b.assetName) ? 1 : -1;
            }
        );
        this._tagsWithAssetsWrappersResult = sortedWrappers;
    } catch(error) {
        //error processing here...
    }
}
```

10. Line by line, we are imperatively calling our Apex and assigning the results to a constant, cloning that constant to sort so that we don't operate on it, sorting our clone, and setting our `private` variable to the result of the sorted clone.
11. To verify that our outputs are all the same, let's add a **getter function** called `isLoaded`. Our getter will update the value of the `isLoaded` variable based on the results of the return value, allowing us to update our variable value in real time. To test, we will turn off `lightning-spinner` when `isLoaded` is `true`. We can do this by temporarily setting our getter to the following:

```
get isLoaded() {
    return JSON.stringify(this._tagsWithAssetsResult)
== JSON.stringify(this._tagsWithAssetsPromiseResult) &&
JSON.stringify(this._tagsWithAssetsResult) ==
JSON.stringify(this._tagsWithAssetsWrappersResult);
}
```

12. The reason we are sorting our wrappers and stringifying them is so that we can see that the results of our three functions are equal, regardless of the output type in the console.

> **Note**
>
> Remember, JavaScript is case-sensitive! If you have deployed all of your changes and are still seeing the spinner, be sure to check your capitalization.

13. Finally, now that we know that our data is outputting the same values for our three functions, let's format the outputs for use in **lightning-tree-grid**. Similar to `lightning-data-table`, `lightning-tree-grid` allows us to view data in a tabular format. The key difference is that `lightning-tree-grid` allows us to group objects by similar characteristics. In this case, we are going to be grouping our `Asset` records by the tag to which they are assigned. Another common use case for `lightning-tree-grid` is showing hierarchical relationships, such as parent accounts and child accounts. Let's start by building our `columns` file in the next recipe.

See also

- The sample files for the `assetsByTag` LWC are located under the `force-app/chapter04/default/lwc/assetsByTag` directory in your forked repository for comparison. These files are located at `https://github.com/PacktPublishing/Salesforce-Lightning-Web-Component-Cookbook/tree/main/force-app/chapter04/default/lwc/assetsByTag`.
- The *Mozilla MDN Web Docs* documentation for the `spread` operator is available at `https://developer.mozilla.org/en-US/docs/Web/JavaScript/Reference/Operators/Spread_syntax`.
- The *Mozilla MDN Web Docs* documentation for the `map` function is available at `https://developer.mozilla.org/en-US/docs/Web/JavaScript/Reference/Global_Objects/Array/map`.

Reusable utility components

The first reusable utility component we will build is an export file for our columns. This serves as an example of when a JavaScript file can be broken up into smaller pieces, which will provide the knowledge foundation for the notifications utility component we will build toward the end of the chapter.

How to do it...

1. Within your `assetsByTag` folder, create a new JavaScript file by right-clicking on the `assetsByTag` folder and selecting **New File...**. Name this file `assetsByTagColumns.js`, and be sure to include the `.js`!
2. Populate the `assetsByTagColumns.js` file with the following columns definition:

```
export const COLUMNS_DEFINITION = [
    {
        type: 'text',
        fieldName: 'tagName',
        label: 'Tag'
    },
    {
        type: 'text',
        fieldName: 'assetName',
        label: 'Asset Name'
    },
    {
        type: 'text',
        fieldName: 'assetObjectId',
        label: 'Asset Id'
    },
    {
        type: 'text',
        fieldName: 'assetIsPublicDomain',
        label: 'Public Domain?'
    }
];
```

3. These are the columns we will be aligning to, and we will restructure our flattened data to match this output.
4. To import our `COLUMNS_DEFINITION` constant into our main `assetsByTag.js` file, we will use the following:

```
import { COLUMNS_DEFINITION } from './assetsByTagColumns';
```

5. This will import our JavaScript file, `assetsByTagColumns`, from the same folder.

6. Initialize two more class variables: `gridColumns`, which we will set equal to our imported `COLUMNS_DEFINITION`, and `gridData`, which we will leave undefined:

```
gridColumns = COLUMNS_DEFINITION;
gridData;
```

7. We will be using these variables in our `lightning-tree-grid` component, which we will need to add to our `assetsByTag.html` file. As we recall, we left a space within our `lwc:if` directive. Add the following `lightning-tree-grid` component within your `lwc:if` directive tags:

```
<template lwc:if={isLoaded}>
    <lightning-tree-grid
        columns={gridColumns}
        data={gridData}
        key-field="tagName"
        hide-checkbox-column
    ></lightning-tree-grid>
</template>
```

8. Now that we have our columns definition imported, we can format the outputs of our imperative Apex calls. To format all three of our outputs from our `getTagsWithAssets` function, the `getTagsWithAssetsPromise` function, and the `getTagsWithAssetsWrappers` function, let's create one final function in the `assetsByTag.js` file called `treeGridFormatter`. This function will accept one parameter of an array, `dataToFormat`:

```
treeGridFormatter(dataToFormat) { ... }
```

9. In the next line, create an empty array, `tagArray`:

```
let tagArray = [];
```

10. Next, iterate over the `dataToFormat` array using a `for` loop. Construct a new JavaScript object like so:

```
for(let asset of dataToFormat) {
    let tagObject = {
        "tagName" : asset.tagName,
```

```
        "assetName" : '',
        "assetObjectId" : '',
        "assetIsPublicDomain" : '',
        "_children" : []
    }
    if(tagArray.find((objectToFind) => (objectToFind.tagName ===
tagObject.tagName)) === undefined) {
        tagArray.push(tagObject)
    }
    tagArray.find((objectToFind) => (objectToFind.tagName ===
tagObject.tagName))._children.push(asset);
}
```

11. Line by line, we are iterating over our flattened `Asset` records in the `dataToFormat` array, constructing a new `tagObject` that will hold `_children`, or assets that will fit under each `Tag` tree, and checking to see whether `tagArray` already contains a tag with the specified `tagName` value. We do this using the `.find()` method, which iterates over every object in `tagArray` and designates the current iterated-over object as `objectToFind`. If `tagArray` does not already have that tag, we add it. Once we have verified that `tagArray` contains the specified tag, either through adding it or finding it, we find the object that matches the specified `tagName` value and add the asset to its `_children` array.
12. Now that we have our `treeGridFormatter` function, we can add it to each of our imperative Apex functions. Note that in each of the following code snippets, the line with our `treeGridFormatter` function is highlighted.
13. This will look like the following for the `async/await` patterned `getTagsWithAssets` function:

```
async getTagsWithAssets() {
    try{
        const tagsWithAssets = await
returnTagsWithAssetsByAccount({ accountIdString : this.accountId });
        this._tagsWithAssetsResult =
        this.tagFlattener(tagsWithAssets);
        this.treeGridFormatter( this._tagsWithAssetsResult);
    } catch(error) {
        //error processing...
```

```
    }
}
```

14. And it will look like the following for the `getTagsWithAssetsPromise` function, which is structured as a promise-based function:

```
getTagsWithAssetsPromise() {
    returnTagsWithAssetsByAccount({ accountIdString : this.accountId })
        .then(tagsWithAssets => {
            this._tagsWithAssetsPromiseResult =
this.tagFlattener(tagsWithAssets);
            this.treeGridFormatter( this._tagsWithAssetsPromiseResult);
        })
        .catch(error => {
            //error processing...
        })
}
```

15. Finally, for our wrapper class-based `getTagsWithAssetsWrappers` function, we will have the following:

getTagsWithAssetsWrappers():

```
async getTagsWithAssetsWrappers() {
    try{
        const tagsWithAssetWrappers = await
returnTagsWithAssetsWrappersByAccount({ accountIdString : this.accountId });
        let wrappersToSort = [...tagsWithAssetWrappers];
        let sortedWrappers = wrappersToSort.sort((a, b) => {
                return (a.assetName > b.assetName) ? 1 : -1;
            }
        );
        this._tagsWithAssetsWrappersResult = sortedWrappers;
        this.treeGridFormatter( this.tagsWithAssetsWrappersResult);
    } catch(error) {
        //error processing...
    }
}
```

16. Finally, we will add our error notification utility. This will replace our `//error processing...` comments and will be reusable in later chapters. Within the `lwc` folder

you are working in, create a new folder, `notifUtils`. In this folder, we will be creating three files: `notifUtils.js`, `notifUtils.js-meta.xml`, and `toastCSS.css`. This folder structure will look like the following:

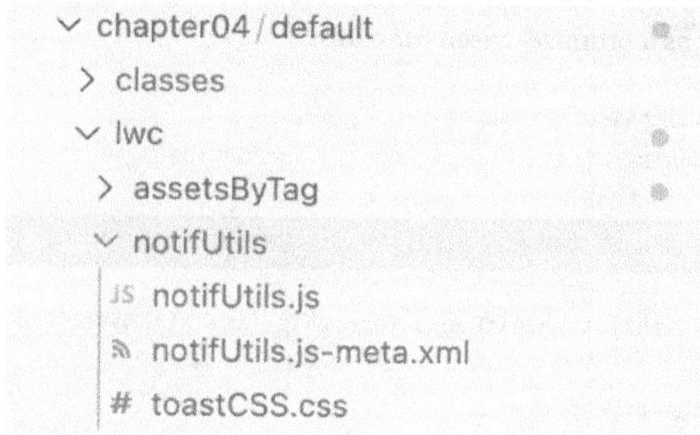

Figure 4.3: A screenshot showing the desired folder structure and required files

17. Let's start by building our `toastCSS.css` file, as we will need to import it as a **static resource**. Our **Cascading Style Sheets (CSS)** file will contain the following, which will allow us to display multiple lines in our **toast notifications**:

```
.toastMessage {
    white-space: break-spaces !important;
}
```

18. Create your static resource, either in the Salesforce user interface in **Setup**, or by deploying the following files in VS Code:

Figure 4.4: A screenshot showing the structure of the staticresources folder.

19. To create your static resource, create a folder, `staticresources`, under the `force-app/default` directory, and move your `toastCSS.css` file into it. Create a file, `toastCSS.resource-meta.xml`, and populate it with the following:

```
<?xml version="1.0" encoding="UTF-8"?>
<StaticResource xmlns="http://soap.sforce.com/2006/04/metadata">
   <cacheControl>Public</cacheControl>
   <contentType>text/css</contentType>
</StaticResource>
```

20. Deploy this folder to your Salesforce org. If you created the static resource in **Setup**, you can create shells of these files and retrieve the metadata for them by right-clicking on the `staticresources` folder and selecting **SFDX: Retrieve This Source from Org**, or retrieve them from your org directly by using the **Org Browser** tool.
21. Next, returning to our `notifUtils` folder, we are going to copy our `notifUtils.js-meta.xml` file from another, existing `.js-meta.xml` file:

```
<?xml version="1.0" encoding="UTF-8"?>
<LightningComponentBundle xmlns="http://soap.sforce.com/2006/04/metadata">
   <apiVersion>61.0</apiVersion>
   <isExposed>false</isExposed>
</LightningComponentBundle>
```

22. Finally, let's build our `notifUtils.js` file. The first thing we are going to do is import the items necessary. As we saw in *Chapter 2, Writing Apex for Lightning Web Components*, and *Chapter 3, Working with a Selector Class*, we will need to import `ShowToastEvent`:

```
import { ShowToastEvent } from 'lightning/platformShowToastEvent';
```

23. Our next two imports will be the `loadStyle` module from `'lightning/platformResourceLoader'`, which will allow us to import and apply our custom CSS file, `toastCSS`:

```
import { loadStyle } from 'lightning/platformResourceLoader';
import customCSS from '@salesforce/resourceUrl/toastCSS';
```

24. Finally, before the class definition, instantiate a `mainObject` variable:

```
let mainObject;
```

25. We will use this variable to load our CSS and accept values for our constructor.
26. Within the class definition for `NotifUtils`, start by adding a JavaScript constructor with a parameter of `superMain`. This constructor will set the value of `mainObject` to `superMain`, which will be the JavaScript class we are calling our utility from, and we will also be utilizing `loadStyle` to load our `customCSS` file:

```
export default class NotifUtils {
    constructor(superMain) {
        mainObject = superMain;
        loadStyle(mainObject, customCSS);
    }
    // rest of code here...
}
```

27. Lastly, let's create a function, `showNotif`. This will be the function we call from the JavaScript classes that import `notifUtils`. This will be similar to what we saw in *Chapter 2, Writing Apex for Lightning Web Components*, and *Chapter 3, Working with a Selector Class*, but we won't have to type it all out every time!

```
    showNotif(title, msg, variant) {
    const evt = new ShowToastEvent({
```

```
        title: title,
        message: msg,
        variant: variant
    });
    mainObject.dispatchEvent(evt);
}
```

28. We are accepting a parameter for the title of the toast notification, the message body, and the variant of toast we want to display. We then dispatch our event through the `mainObject`, which is the JavaScript file we passed in via our constructor. Remember, we will be learning more about dispatching events in *Chapter 6*, *Composing Lightning Web Components*, but for now, all we need to know is that this tells the toast notification to send.
29. In order to use our toast utility, let's return to our `assetsByTag.js` file. The first thing we will need to do is import our utility. Before the class definition, add the following:

```
import Utilities from 'c/notifUtils';
let utility;
```

30. At the beginning of our `connectedCallback` function, add the following line:

```
utility = new Utilities(this);
```

31. This will set our `mainObject` in our utilities class as the global `this` of our `assetsByTag` JavaScript file.
32. Now that we have the basics, navigate to where we have an `//error processing...` comment in our `catch` blocks, and add the following:

```
utility.showNotif('There has been an error in [FUNCTION_NAME]!',
error.message, 'error');
```

33. Replace [FUNCTION_NAME] with the name of the function that the catch block is in so that we can tell where we're getting an error. Here is an example:

```
utility.showNotif('There has been an error in getTagsWithAssets!',
error.message, 'error');
```

34. Deploy your changes, and feel free to play around with the placement of the showNotif function call to test different toast variants.

See also

- The sample files for the notifUtils utility are located under the force-app/chapter04/default/lwc/notifUtils directory in your forked repository for comparison. These files are located at https://github.com/PacktPublishing/Salesforce-Lightning-Web-Component-Cookbook/tree/main/force-app/chapter04/default/lwc/notifUtils.
- The sample files for the static resource required for the utility are located under the force-app/chapter04/default/staticresources directory in your forked repository for comparison. These files are located at https://github.com/PacktPublishing/Salesforce-Lightning-Web-Component-Cookbook/tree/main/force-app/chapter04/default/staticresources.
- The Salesforce documentation on utilizing custom CSS is available at https://developer.salesforce.com/docs/platform/lwc/guide/create-components-css.html.

Get this book's PDF version and more

Scan the QR code (or go to `packtpub.com/unlock`). Search for this book by name, confirm the edition, and then follow the steps on the page.

UNLOCK NOW

Note: Keep your invoice handy. Purchases made directly from Packt don't require an invoice.

5

Accessing External Data Sources via Lightning Web Components

Now that we know how to write **asynchronous JavaScript** through the **async/await** pattern and with **promise chains**, let's look at a common use case for this method of processing: retrieving data from an external source. We will do this through a **REST API** callout in Apex and with the **Fetch API** in JavaScript.

We are going to be covering the following main recipes:

- Writing REST APIs in Apex
- Deserializing JSON results into wrappers
- Serializing wrappers into JSON
- Displaying retrieved data
- Parsing JSON into JavaScript objects
- Utilizing the fetch API in JavaScript

Technical requirements

The recipes in this book can be found at `https://github.com/PacktPublishing/Salesforce-Lightning-Web-Component-Cookbook`, where each chapter has its own folder under the `force-app` folder. This GitHub repository is structured in the form of a Salesforce DX project, which will allow you to easily fork the repository for deployment in a free Salesforce Developer Edition org. The code for *Chapter 5, Accessing External Data Sources via Lightning Web Components*, is located at `https://github.com/PacktPublishing/Salesforce-Lightning-Web-Component-Cookbook/tree/main/force-app/chapter05`.

The components in this book require the use of an **Integrated Development Environment (IDE)**, such as **Visual Studio Code (VSCode)** or **Salesforce Code Builder**. Detailed instructions for setting up an IDE are located in *Chapter 1, Getting Ready for Lightning Web Component Development*, in the *Setting up your IDE* section.

If you are building the projects in this cookbook as written, you will need to seed your Salesforce Developer Edition org with test data. Detailed instructions for seeding your org are located in *Chapter 1, Getting Ready for Lightning Web Component Development*, in the *Setting up the Salesforce Lightning Web Components Cookbook org* section.

Lastly, the edition of Salesforce required to implement the recipes in this book must be Developer, Performance, Unlimited, Enterprise, or Database.com. You can sign up for a free Salesforce Developer Edition org at `https://developer.salesforce.com/signup`.

Writing REST APIs in Apex

In *Chapter 4, Synchronous and Asynchronous Processing in Components*, we learned about the **async/await pattern** and **promise chaining** in JavaScript, which allows us to handle our asynchronous code **semi-synchronously**. A common use case for this pattern is calling out to an external API. Let's start with building a **REST callout** in Apex.

How to do it...

1. To write our API class, we must first create a new `public with sharing class AddAssetAPI`.
2. Create three `public static String` methods in your class: `getDepartments`, `searchByTerm`, and `getSearchedAssetInfo`.
3. The first method we will take a look at is `getDepartments`. This method will not contain any parameters. Pull up the Salesforce *Invoking Callouts Using Apex* documentation, which is linked in the *See also* section of this recipe.
4. The basic structure of a REST callout in Apex is the following:

```
Http http = new Http();
HttpRequest request = new HttpRequest();
request.setEndpoint(/*endpoint*/);
request.setMethod(/*method*/);
HttpResponse response = http.send(request);
if(response.getStatusCode == 200) {
    //do something on success
} else {
```

```
    //do something on error
}
```

There are other options we can add to our callout, such as setting the request header or body, but for now, this will be fine.

5. Replace the endpoint comment with a reference to the included **named credential**, `The_Met_Named`. This named credential is included in the setup components for the org, located in the `force-app/chapter00` directory. We are going to extend our endpoint by adding a subdirectory of `departments`, which will end up looking like this:

```
request.setEndpoint('callout:The_Met_Named/
  departments');
```

6. Next, we need to set our HTTP method. Because we are retrieving data from an external source, we will use the `GET` HTTP method:

```
request.setMethod('GET');
```

7. In our `if-else` block, we are simply going to return our response body using `response.getBody()` if our status code is `200`, meaning our endpoint was successfully reached, and `return null` in any other case. This will look as follows:

```
if(response.getStatusCode() == 200) {
   return response.getBody();
} else {
   return null;
}
```

8. For our next two methods, all that is going to change from this first `getDepartments` method is our parameters, which will dictate our endpoint subdirectory. Start with `searchByTerm`, which will accept a `String` parameter of `searchTerm` and an `Integer` parameter of `departmentId`. The idea is that we will be passing in a department ID selected from our first API results into a different endpoint, along with a search term to grab searched items from a given department.
9. After adding our method parameters, we are going to set our endpoint. Our endpoint subdirectory will be `search`, and we will add a query to our endpoint with a parameter for an escaped `searchTerm` and a parameter for our department ID. These requirements

come from the Open Access API documentation, linked in the *See also* section for this recipe. This will look as follows:

```
request.setEndpoint('callout:The_Met_Named/search?
q='+String.escapeSingleQuotes(searchTerm)+'&departmentId='+departmentId);
```

10. Lastly, we will build our `getSearchedAssetInfo` method. The idea here is to take an asset ID, retrieved from the `searchByTerm` method and selected from within a datatable by the end user, and return all info about the selected asset. This method will take an `Integer` parameter, `objectId`, and we will add a subdirectory to our endpoint of `objects`, followed by `objectId`. These requirements come from the Open Access API documentation. Our endpoint will look as follows:

```
request.setEndpoint('callout:The_Met_Named/objects/' + objectId);
```

See also

- The sample file for the `AddAssetAPI` class is located under the `force-app/chapter05/default/classes/AddAssetAPI.cls` directory in your forked repository for comparison. This file is located at `https://github.com/PacktPublishing/Salesforce-Lightning-Web-Component-Cookbook/blob/main/force-app/chapter05/default/classes/AddAssetAPI.cls`.
- The Salesforce *Invoking Callouts Using Apex* documentation is available at `https://developer.salesforce.com/docs/atlas.en-us.apexcode.meta/apexcode/apex_callouts.htm`.
- The documentation for The Metropolitan Museum of Art's Open Access API is located at `https://metmuseum.github.io`.

Deserializing JSON results into wrappers

Now that we are successfully returning a JSON string in each of our `addAssetAPI` methods, let's process them for use in an LWC.

How to do it...

1. Start by creating a new `public with sharing class AddAssetService`.
2. In your `AddAssetService` class, add three shell wrapper classes: `SearchWrapper`, `DepartmentWrapper`, and `DepartmentsWrapper`.

3. Starting with `SearchWrapper`, add two properties, the first being `public Integer total`, and the second being `public<List>Integer objectIds`. Your wrapper class will look as follows:

```
public class SearchWrapper {
  public Integer total;
  public List<Integer> objectIds;
}
```

4. In your `DepartmentWrapper` class, add two properties: `public Integer departmentId` and `public String displayName`.
5. Lastly, for the `DepartmentsWrapper` class, add the `public List<DepartmentWrapper> departments` property.
6. Once we have built the three wrapper classes, we are ready to start working with our JSON. Write a non-static `public` method, `getDepartmentWrappers`, that returns an instance of the `DepartmentsWrapper` class. This will look like the following:

```
public DepartmentsWrapper getDepartmentWrappers() {
   return (DepartmentsWrapper)
JSON.deserialize(AddAssetAPI.getDepartments(), DepartmentsWrapper.Class);
```

7. Let's take a deeper look at our `return` statement. As we saw in *Chapter 3, Working with a Selector Class*, we are using **casting** to transform the result of the static `deserialize` method of the `JSON` class. This method accepts two parameters: a string called `jsonString` and a `System.Type` object called `apexType`. Simply, this method takes a string of JSON and converts it into an instance of the given `System.Type`. In this instance, our JSON string is returned by `AddAssetAPI`, and it is converted into a `DepartmentsWrapper` type in Apex by mapping the property values in the JSON string to record fields on a given object, or in our case, matching the property values to the property values in our wrapper class. We then cast these `DepartmentsWrapper.Class` objects as a `DepartmentsWrapper`.

> **Note**
>
> For our JSON to be properly deserialized, we must ensure that our **wrapper classes** fit the requirements given to us by the JSON structure. This means that the cases of the property names we define in our wrapper classes must exactly

> match the cases of the names of the properties output by our API callout, as it is case sensitive.

8. Now that we have a list of departments, we're going to add the search functionality to our **service class**. I have to warn you, we are going to break some best-practice rules here! Later in this chapter, we will refactor this to follow best practices, but for now, we are going to practice our **JSON deserializing**.
9. Create another public, non-static method, `getSearchedAssets`, that accepts two parameters, `String searchTerm` and `Integer departmentId`. Have your new method return a `List<ObjectWrappers.AssetWrapper>`. Wait, what is `ObjectWrappers`?! This is a utility class that was included when you set up your org following the instructions in *Chapter 1, Getting Ready for Lightning Web Component Development*. This class is wholly made up of wrapper classes for use in multiple classes, which serves to illustrate how we can reuse code. Your method definition should look like this:

```
public List<ObjectWrappers.AssetWrapper> getSearchedAssets(String
searchTerm, Integer departmentID){...}
```

10. Now that we have the method definition for `getSearchedAssets`, let's build our `SearchWrapper`, which we will be generating using the `searchByTerm` method of our `AddAssetAPI` class. Similar to the preceding, we will be using the static `deserialize` method of the `JSON` class to do so. The first line of your method will look something like this:

```
SearchWrapper searchWrap = (SearchWrapper)
JSON.deserialize(AddAssetAPI.searchByTerm(searchTerm, departmentId),
SearchWrapper.Class);
```

11. Next, we are going to declare and initialize a list of our `AssetWrappers`. Remember, the `AssetWrapper` subclass belongs to the `ObjectWrappers` class:

```
List<ObjectWrappers.AssetWrapper> assetWrapperList = new
List<ObjectWrappers.AssetWrapper>();
```

12. Let's go ahead and populate our `assetWrapperList`. But first, let's recall that an **empty list** and **null** are two different objects in JavaScript, so we need to check to see whether our `SearchWrapper searchWrap` is populated. Build out an `if-else` block that checks to

see whether our `searchWrap.objectIds` list is populated. If it is, we will do some processing to populate our `assetWrapperList`; if not, we will return `null`, like so:

```
if(searchWrap.objectIDs != null) {
    //populate assetWrapperList here
    return assetWrapperList;
} else {
   return null;
}
```

13. Now we can go ahead with our list population. Write a `for` loop that iterates over the list of `searchWrap.objectIDs` using an `Integer` type iterator, `objId`, representing each object ID in a list of integer object IDs. Inside the `for` loop, we are going to create another `AssetWrapper`, which will be the deserialized result of the `getSearchedAssetInfo` method of the `AddAssetAPI` class. Here is where I must call out our **governor limits**! Placing a callout inside a `for` loop is *not a best practice*. Only 100 callouts can be made per transaction, and this is an easy way to exceed that hard-coded limit. Fortunately, we are filtering our results by department and a search term, so our limits shouldn't be hit, but we will still refactor this in the *Utilizing the fetch API in JavaScript* recipe to adhere to best practices.

> **Note**
>
> Part of being a good developer is weighing best practices against what is required of the solution. Because the Open Access API that we are using does not allow a `GET` request on multiple object IDs at the same time, as of the time of writing, adherence to best practices must be weighed against a number of things, including, but not limited to, endpoint requirements, org-specific limits, Salesforce's governor limits, development time required, and development resources available. Try not to judge the writers of legacy code too harshly; they likely weighed these considerations (and more!) to come up with the solution that they wrote.

14. After taking into consideration the needs of our org, our `for` loop inside our `if` block will end up looking something like this:

```
for(Integer objId : searchWrap.objectIDs) {
   ObjectWrappers.AssetWrapper assetWrapper =
```

```
        (ObjectWrappers.AssetWrapper) JSON.deserialize(
            AddAssetAPI.getSearchedAssetInfo(objId),
            ObjectWrappers.AssetWrapper.Class
        );
    assetWrapperList.add(assetWrapper);
}
```

15. Lastly, we are going to grab the wrapper for a selected asset in a `public` non-static method called `getSearchedAssetWrapper`. This method will accept a parameter of an `Integer objectId`, and return an `ObjectWrappers.AssetWrapper` object. The method signature will look like the following:

```
public ObjectWrappers.AssetWrapper getSearchedAssetWrapper(Integer object
Id) {
    //return statement here...
}
```

16. The `return` statement in our method will, once again, be the result of the `deserialize` method of the `JSON` class, this time against the `getSearchedAssetInfo` method of the `AddAssetAPI` class:

```
return (ObjectWrappers.AssetWrapper)
JSON.deserialize(AddAssetAPI.getSearchedAssetInfo(objectId),
ObjectWrappers.AssetWrapper.Class);
```

17. This return statement will make up the body of our method. We will revisit this functionality later, but for now, we have what we need to start building our LWC. Don't forget to deploy your Apex to ensure it compiles!

See also

- The sample file for the `AddAssetService` class is located under the `force-app/chapter05/default/classes/AddAssetService.cls` directory in your forked repository for comparison. This file is located at `https://github.com/PacktPublishing/Salesforce-Lightning-Web-Component-Cookbook/blob/main/force-app/chapter05/default/classes/AddAssetService.cls`.

- The Salesforce documentation for the system-provided JSON class is available at `https://developer.salesforce.com/docs/atlas.en-us.apexref.meta/apexref/apex_class_System_Json.htm`.
- The Salesforce documentation for classes and casting can be found at `https://developer.salesforce.com/docs/atlas.en-us.apexcode.meta/apexcode/apex_classes_casting.htm`.

Serializing wrappers into JSON

Now that we have parsed our API results, let's get ready to pass them to our eventual LWC with a controller class.

How to do it...

1. First, create a new `public with sharing class AddAssetController`. This class will start with two `@AuraEnabled(cacheable=true)` methods, `returnDepartmentsWrapper` and `searchAssetWrappers`. In order to access the return values for these methods, we will need to create a static instance of the `AddAssetService` class:

```
public with sharing class AddAssetController {
    @TestVisible private static AddAssetService addAssetService = new
AddAssetService();
    //methods go here...
}
```

   Declaring and initializing a static instance of a class is similar to the concept of the **singleton pattern** in Java. This pattern allows us to use our instance methods in a static context, which will help us with the testing we will be doing in *Chapter 14, Testing Apex with Mocking and Stubbing*. We will also be able to ensure that our controller class has only one instance of the service class, and all interactions with the service class will flow through this instance.

2. Start by writing your `returnDepartmentsWrapper` method. Because the method is designated as `@AuraEnabled`, we know that the method definition must be `public static`, and we know we will be returning a string based on our methods in the `AddAssetService` class. Your method definition should look as follows:

```
@AuraEnabled(cacheable=true)
public static String returnDepartmentsWrapper(){...}
```

3. Inside the method body, add a `try-catch` block that catches an `Exception e` and throws a `new AuraHandledException(e.getmessage)` so that we can expose our error message on the frontend:

```
try{
    //return values here
} catch (Exception e) {
    throw new AuraHandledException(e.getMessage);
}
```

4. Within our `try` block, we will grab our `DepartmentsWrapper` object result from the *non-static* `getDepartmentWrappers` method of the `AddAssetService` class. Because this method is non-static, we access it using dot notation from our static instance of the `AddAssetService` class:

```
AddAssetService.DepartmentsWrapper retrievedDepartments =
addAssetService.getDepartmentWrappers();
```

5. In the last step of this method, we will write a **ternary operator** that returns `null` or the serialized wrapper object as a JSON string. The opposite of deserializing, **serializing** takes an object and transforms it into a JSON string. This ternary will look as follows:

```
return retrievedDepartments == null ? null :
JSON.serialize(retrievedDepartments);
```

6. Next, we are going to write a similar method called `searchAssetWrappers`, this time using the non-static `getSearchedAssets` method of the `AddAssetService` class. Remember: we are using **dot notation** with the static instance of our `AddAssetService` class, `addAssetService`, to call this method. Recall that this method, written in the last recipe, accepts a `String` parameter of a search term and an `Integer` parameter of a departmental ID. We will also accept these parameters in our `searchAssetWrappers` method definition so that we can pass them to our service class:

```
@AuraEnabled(cacheable=true)
public static String searchAssetWrappers(String search, Integer
departmentId) {
    try {
        List<ObjectWrappers.assetWrapper> searchResults =
```

```
addAssetService.getSearchedAssets(search, departmentId);
      return searchResults == null ? null : JSON.serialize(searchResults);
   } catch(Exception e) {
      throw new AuraHandledException(e.getMessage());
   }
}
```

7. This looks great, but there's something missing. Because we are accepting user input, we need to escape our `String search` for single quotes. Additionally, because we are searching for single words, we want to escape any whitespace or non-alphabetical characters. This can be handled with a **regular expression**.
8. At the top of your class, add two `String` constants, `REGEXP` and `REPLACE`. To declare a class constant, which can be used in any method of the class, we will place the following outside of our first method:

```
public static final String REGEXP = '[^a-zA-Z]';
public static final String REPLACE = '';
```

9. The first constant represents a regular expression that checks for any characters that are not in the range of all letters in either lowercase or uppercase. The second is an empty string, which is what we will replace all non-alphabet characters with. These two strings will help us sanitize our inputs in our search method.
10. In the first line of your `try-catch` block for the `searchAssetWrappers` method, declare a new string variable, `searchTerm`, and set it equal to the non-static `replaceAll` method of the `String` class being called on your `search` parameter. The `replaceAll` method accepts two parameters: a string to match our regular expression and a string to replace the matched text with, or our empty `REPLACE` value. This will look like the following:

```
String searchTerm = search.replaceAll(
   REGEXP, REPLACE
);
```

11. Now, substitute the `searchTerm` variable for the `search` parameter in the `getSearchedAssets` method on the next line:

```
List<ObjectWrappers.AssetWrapper> searchResults = new
AddAssetService().getSearchedAssets(searchTerm, departmentId);
```

12. This concludes our work on the `AddAssetController` class, and we are ready to build our LWC.

See also

- The sample file for the `AddAssetController` class is located under the `force-app/chapter05/default/classes/AddAssetController.cls` directory in your forked repository for comparison. This file is located at `https://github.com/PacktPublishing/Salesforce-Lightning-Web-Component-Cookbook/blob/main/force-app/chapter05/default/classes/AddAssetController.cls`.
- An essay on singletons, *When is a Singleton not a Singleton?*, is available at `https://oracle.com/technical-resources/articles/java/singleton.html`.
- If you are new to regular expressions, there are many helpful tools available for use to learn them. One of my favorites is located at `https://regex101.com`.
- The Salesforce documentation for the `String` class is located at `https://developer.salesforce.com/docs/atlas.en-us.apexref.meta/apexref/apex_methods_system_string.htm`.

Displaying retrieved data

Now that we have our backend built to retrieve data, let's build out our frontend. So far, we have built LWCs to place on record pages and app pages, but let's look at another use case: a **screen flow**.

How to do it...

1. Create a new LWC called `addAssetDepartment`. In the `.js-meta.xml` file, set the `isExposed` property to `true`, and add a target of `lightning__FlowScreen`. Additionally, we will add a `targetConfig` tag for an `outputOnly` property called `departmentId`. Your `.js-meta.xml` file will look as follows:

```
<?xml version="1.0" encoding="UTF-8"?>
<LightningComponentBundle xmlns="http://soap.sforce.com/2006/04/metadata">
```

```
    <apiVersion>61.0</apiVersion>
    <isExposed>true</isExposed>
    <targets>
       <target>lightning__FlowScreen</target>
    </targets>
    <targetConfigs>
       <targetConfig targets="lightning__FlowScreen">
          <property name="departmentId" label="Department Id" type="Integer"
role="outputOnly"/>
       </targetConfig>
    </targetConfigs>
</LightningComponentBundle>
```

2. We will be using the `targetConfigs` tag throughout this recipe, but for now, know that we have created a variable that can be output from the LWC into the context of a screen flow called `departmentId`.
3. In your HTML file for `addAssetDepartment`, build a **lightning-card** element. Start by setting the `icon-name` property of the `lightning-card` tag to `"utility:new"`, which will show an icon indicating that we are creating records:

```
<lightning-card icon-name="utility:new" variant="base">
   ...
</lightning-card>
In the "title" slot of your lightning-card, add the text Select
Department:
<div slot="title">
   Select Department
</div>
```

4. Within the `"actions"` slot, add a reset button. A reset button will typically use the `brand-outline` styling and have a label of `Reset`. We want to have this button disabled when there is nothing selected and erase selections when this button is clicked, so we will build two functions, `resetDisabled` and `handleReset`. Your actions `div` will look as follows:

```
<div slot="actions">
   <lightning-button
      <lightning-button
         variant="brand-outline"
```

```
        label="Reset"
        disabled={resetDisabled}
        onclick={handleReset}
    ></lightning-buton>
</div>
```

5. Next, in the "body" slot, we are going to add an `lwc:if` directive based on whether the department wrappers have been loaded, determined by a Boolean variable, `departmentsLoaded`.
6. Within our `lwc:if` tag, we will place a `lightning-combobox` with the following attributes:

```
name="departmentGroup"
label="Departments"
placeholder="Select a department..."
options={options}
onChange={handleDeptSelect}
value={departmentId}
required
```

7. We will place this **lightning-combobox** within a `div` tag with a class of `"slds-p-horizontal_medium"` to add adequate horizontal padding.
8. Finally, we will add a large **lightning-spinner** within our `lwc:else` tag to indicate that our departments are still loading.
9. Now that we have our frontend for the `addAssetDepartment` LWC, let's look at our JavaScript file. We need to import our `returnDepartmentsWrapper` method from the `AddAssetController` class, as well as our `Utilities` from `'c/notifUtils'`, to display the **toast utility** that we built in *Chapter 4, Synchronous and Asynchronous Processing in Components*. We will define a variable of utility before our class definition, which we will initialize in a `connectedCallback` function to make use of our toast utility. We must not forget to import the `api` decorator so that we can expose our `departmentId` variable to the **screen flow** that this LWC will reside in. Our class definition will look as follows:

```
import { LightningElement, api } from 'lwc';
import returnDepartmentsWrapper from '@salesforce/apex/
AddAssetController.returnDepartmentsWrapper';
import Utilities from 'c/notifUtils';
```

```
let utility;
export default class AddAssetDepartment extends LightningElement { ... }
```

10. At the top of our JavaScript class, we need to define our class variables. We already know from our HTML file that we need a `departmentsLoaded` Boolean, which we will set to `false` until the departments have loaded, and an empty array of department wrappers called `options` that we will populate with our `returnDepartmentsWrapper` Apex method. From our `.js-meta.xml` file, we also know that we need an exposed variable, `departmentId`, which will be set upon the selection of a department in our `lightning-combobox`. Our class variable definitions will look like the following:

```
@api departmentId;
departmentsLoaded = false;
options = [];
```

11. We also know that we need a `resetDisabled` Boolean. Because this variable is dependent on whether there is a selected department, we can use a **getter** to define this automatically:

```
get resetDisabled() {
    return this.departmentId === undefined;
}
```

12. This will set our reset button's `disabled` property to `true` when `departmentId` is undefined, and `false` when it has a value, meaning that a value has been selected in our `combobox`.
13. Having defined all the variables present in our HTML file, we can define a **connectedCallback** function. In our `connectedCallback` function, we want to initialize the `utility` variable so that we can use our toast utility, and we also want to call an **asynchronous function** that grabs our department wrappers from Apex. We want to do this in our `connectedCallback` function because this will allow us to load and cache our data before we are able to with a wire function, per the LWC order of operations. Our `connectedCallback` will end up looking like so:

```
connectedCallback() {
    utility = new Utilities(this);
```

```
        this.loadDepartments();
    }
```

14. We have yet to define the `loadDepartments` function, so we will take a look at this function next. As we recall from *Chapter 4, Synchronous and Asynchronous Processing in Components*, we can make an asynchronous function act synchronously using an `async/await` pattern:

```
async loadDepartments() {
    try {
        const data = await returnDepartmentsWrapper();
        if (data) {
            let temp = JSON.parse(data);
            let departments = [];
temp.departments.map((tmp) => {
                let tmpClone =
                    {
                        ...tmp,
                        label:tmp.displayName,
                        value:tmp.departmentId
                    };
                departments.push(tmpClone);
            });
            departments.sort (
                (a, b) =>
                    (a.label - b.label) ? 1 : -1
            );
            this.options = departments;
        }
        this.departmentsLoaded = true;
    }
    catch(error) {
        this.options = undefined;
        utility.showNotif('There has been an error loading departments!',
error, 'error');
    }
}
```

Let's break this down line by line. Note that some of the lines have been expanded to accommodate spacing:

15. First, we resolve the promise implied by the `async` designation on our function signature by returning the department values from our API callout.
16. Next, we verify whether we have any values returned. If we do, we parse our returned JSON string into a temporary variable, `temp`, and designate an empty array, `departments`, to hold our department objects.
17. To prepare our department objects for display by our LWC, we access and iterate over the list of departments, `temp.departments`, which follows the JSON structure dictated by the Open Access API documentation. We complete this iteration using the JavaScript `map` method.
18. As we iterate over these values, we use a **spread operator** to assign new properties to a **shallow copy** of our iterator. These properties, `label` and `value`, allow us to nicely display our `departmentWrapper` results in our `combobox`. We then add our copied object, `tmpClone`, to the end of our `departments` array.
19. After all our `departments` have been added, we use the JavaScript `sort` method to sort our objects in place. We then set our `options` variable equal to the sorted `departments` array. We do this so that we are not operating on a value that our LWC depends on.
20. Once our options are set, we set `departmentsLoaded` to `true` so that our `lightning-spinner` stops, and our user can select a department.
21. After we have populated our `lightning-combobox`, we need to add selection handling. Per our HTML file, our function will be called `handleDeptSelect`, and it will need to receive an `event` as a parameter:

```
handleDeptSelect(event) {
    this.departmentId = +event.detail.value;
}
```

22. We will dive into events in the next chapter, so we won't spend too much time on them here, but there is something important to point out: the plus sign (`+`). No, it's not a typo! The result of `event.detail.value` is a string, and adding the + sign converts it to an integer. This is what is called **type conversion**, and it is similar to what we have seen with casting in Apex. This is known as type conversion rather than **type coercion** because we have explicitly required a conversion from a string type to an integer with the use of a + sign. This can also be achieved using the `Number` function, as follows:

```
this.departmentId = Number(event.detail.value);
```

23. Lastly, for this LWC, we need to write our `handleReset` function. In this function, we will simply set the value of `departmentId` to `undefined`:

```
handleReset() {
    this.departmentId = undefined;
}
```

This will prevent us from having to reload our cached `departments` for our `combobox` but will clear any selected value.

24. Once we have completed and deployed this LWC, we can place it into a screen flow. Navigate to **Flows** in **Setup** and create a new screen flow called `Add Assets To Account`.

25. Now that your flow is created, add a screen that contains your `addAssetDepartment` LWC, and add an appropriate label and API name for the screen. A variable for `departmentId` will automatically be created for your flow based on the `targetconfigs` we implemented in our `.js-meta.xml` file.

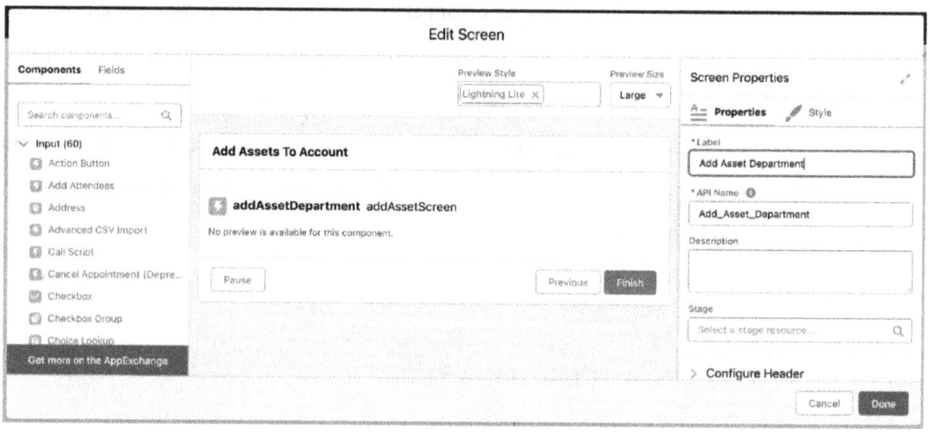

Figure 5.1: A screenshot of the Edit Screen modal in Flow Builder

26. Save and activate your screen flow and create an **action button** on the **Account** object called **Add Assets** that launches the screen flow to test the beginnings of your functionality. Be sure to add this button to your **Account** record page.

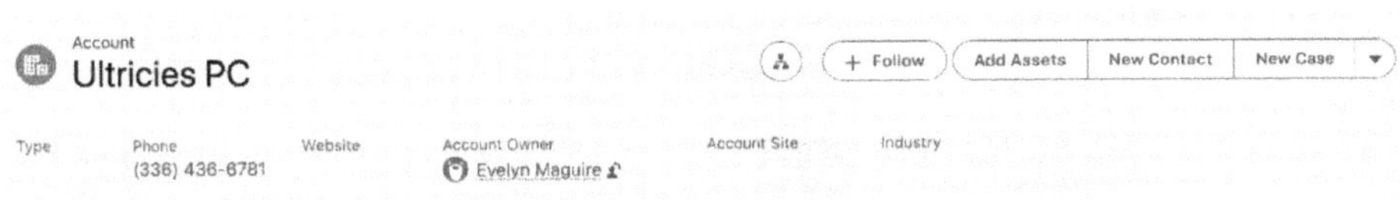

Figure 5.2: A screenshot of the Account record for A Aliquet Incorporated showing that the Add Assets action button has been added to the page layout

27. Once we click on the **Add Assets** button, we should see our first screen, which will have a number of departments pulled directly from The Metropolitan Museum of Art's Open Access API. Note that your departments may differ slightly, as the data is being pulled from a real API, and the exhibits may change.

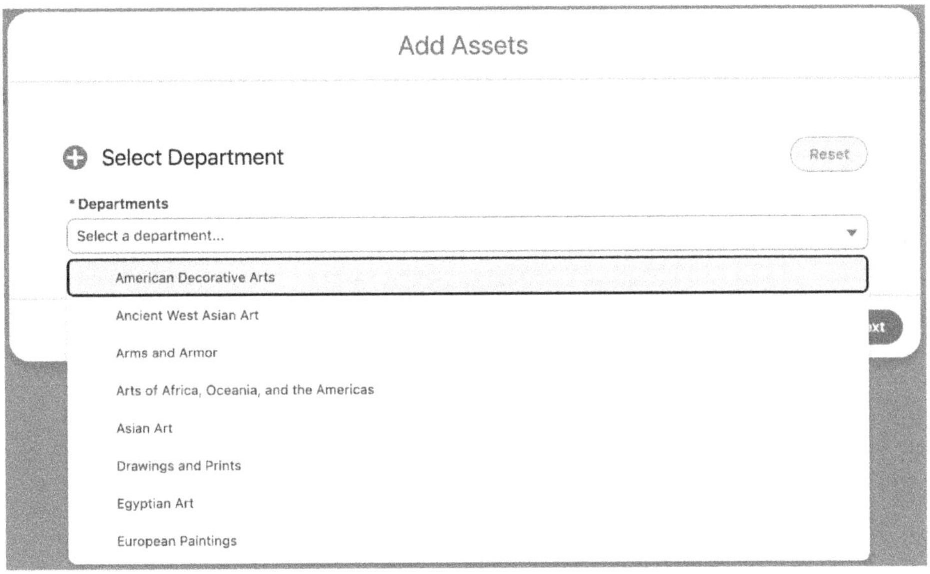

Figure 5.3: A screenshot of the first screen of the Add Assets screen flow, which shows a dropdown of departments pulled from The Metropolitan Museum of Art's Open Access API

28. After testing your `lightning-combobox`, create another LWC, this time called `addAssetSearch`. This LWC will be the next screen in our screen flow, so our `.js-meta.xml` file will look similar to our `addAssetDepartment.js-meta.xml` file, with one key difference. Copy your `addAssetDepartment.js-meta.xml` file into your `addAssetSearch.js-meta.xml` file, and change your `property` tag to the following:

```
<property name="searchTerm" label="Search Term" type="String"
role="outputOnly"/>
```

This will allow us to take an input from our end user in our LWC and pass it as an output into our flow and into our third and final LWC of the chapter.

29. In your HTML file for the `addAssetSearch` LWC, add another `lightning-card` with a title of `Enter Search Term` and a `lightning-input` component with a type of `text`, a label of `Enter a search term...`, and an onchange property of a `{handleChange}` function. To make our `lightning-input` look nice, we will wrap it in a `div` with `class="slds-p-horizontal_medium"` to add padding around it. All in all, our HTML file will look like the following:

```
<template>
    <lightning-card icon-name="utility:new" variant="base">
        <div slot="title">
            Enter Search Term
        </div>
        <div>
            <div class="slds-p-horizontal_medium">
                <lightning-input
                    type="text"
                    label="Enter a search term..."
                    onchange={handleChange}
                >
                </lightning-input>
            </div>
        </div>
    </lightning-card>
</template>
```

30. To round out this LWC, open your JavaScript file. Add the `api` keyword to the default `import`:

```
import { LightningElement, api } from 'lwc';
```

31. Use the `@api` decorator to declare a class variable of `searchTerm`, which will allow us to utilize this variable outside of the LWC and pass it into our flow:

```
@api searchTerm;
```

32. Lastly, define the `handleChange` function that we call in the HTML file on the `combobox` value change. Once again, this function will accept an `event` as a parameter, and we will set our `searchTerm` variable equal to that event's `event.detail.value`:

```
handleChange(event) {
   this.searchTerm = event.detail.value;
}
```

> **Note**
>
> Notice that we have used the JavaScript `this` keyword several times in this chapter. While in Apex, `this` refers to an **instance of a class**, the `this` keyword in JavaScript has to do with **variable scoping**, which can be a tricky topic for new JavaScript developers. In the context of a standalone function, the `this` keyword refers to a **global object**, in "this" case, the JavaScript class representing our Lightning Web Component.

33. Add your `addAssetSearch` LWC to your screen flow as a second screen, add an appropriate label and API name for your screen, and save your flow as a new version to test this functionality.
34. For our last LWC of the chapter, we are going to select the assets we want to add from the results of our search. Create a new LWC called `addAssetPicker`. Copy the `.js-meta.xml` file from one of your previous LWCs and paste it into your `addAssetPicker.js-meta.xml` file.
35. Add your `targetConfig` properties. Whereas in our previous `addAsset` LWCs, we were declaring `outputOnly` properties, this time, we will be passing in variables as `inputOnly`. Create two `property` tags of types `String`, `recordId` and `searchTerm`, and one of type `Integer`, `departmentId`:

```
<property name="recordId" label="Account Record Id" type="String"
role="inputOnly"/>
<property name="searchTerm" label="Search Term" type="String"
role="inputOnly"/>
<property name="departmentId" label="Department Id" type="Integer"
role="inputOnly"/>
```

36. We are going to add one more property, this time an `outputOnly` variable of type `Integer[]` called `selectedAssets`:

```
<property name="selectedAssets" label="Selected Asset Ids" type="Integer[]"
role="outputOnly"/>
```

> **Note**
>
> Remember that in Apex, arrays and lists are interchangeable data structures, with an array being denoted by a given data type and square brackets ([ ]), such as `Integer[]` or `Asset[]`, while the same lists would be represented by `List<Integer>` and `List<Asset>`, respectively. Because angled brackets (<>) are **protected characters** in HTML, we must use an array here.

37. Now that our `.js-meta.xml` file is built, let's look at our HTML file. Once again, place a `lightning-card` element between the two `template` tags in the `assetPicker.html` file.
38. In the `title` slot, add the text `Select Assets`.
39. In the `actions` slot, add two **lightning-button** components, the first with a `Save` label and the second with the `Reset` label. Both buttons will be disabled when the `buttonsDisabled` variable is equal to `true`, and each will have its own `onclick` function, `handleSave` and `handleReset`, respectively.
40. Lastly, for our HTML file, we will add an `lwc:if|elseif|else` directive tag. This tag will have the following elements:

```
<template lwc:if={assetsLoaded}>
    <lightning-dual-listbox name="assets"
        label="Select Assets to Import"
        source-label="Available"
        selected-label="Selected"
        field-level-help="Select Assets to Import"
        disabled={listDisabled}
        options={options}
        value={selectedAssets}
        onchange={handleChange}
    ><lightning-dual-listbox>
</template>
<template lwc:elseif={searchIsNull}>
```

```
    Please enter another search term! The term "{searchTerm}" yielded no
results.
</template>
<template lwc:else>
    <lightning-spinner
        alternative-text="Loading..."
        size="large"
        variant="base"
    ></lightning-spinner>
</template>
```

41. Now that we have some of our variables, we can begin our JavaScript file. At the top of your `addAssetPicker.js` file, import the `api` decorator, the `searchAssetWrappers` method of the `AddAssetController` method, and `Utilities` from `'c/notifUtils'`. Declare a `utility` variable using the `let` keyword to round out our class definition.
42. For your first class variable, declare a `recordId` (case-sensitive) variable with the `@api` designation. In conjunction with our variable declaration in the `.js-meta.xml` file, this designation will allow us to grab the ID of the record that our screen flow is launched from.
43. We are going to declare three more `@api` decorated variables: `searchTerm`, `departmentId`, and `selectedAssets`. Note that each of these corresponds to a declaration in our `.js-meta.xml` file, as this is necessary for passing variables between our screen flow and our LWC. We will investigate other uses of the `api` decorator in *Chapter 6, Composing Lightning Web Components.*
44. Define the following additional variables:

```
searchResults = []; //to hold all results of our search
options; //to hold the options for our dual listbox
isLoaded = false; //to denote whether our search is loaded
searchIsNull = false; //to denote if our search returns null
savePressed = false; //to denote whether our Save button has been pressed
buttonsDisabled = true; //to track whether our buttons are disabled
```

45. We will also have two variables that are dependent on these variables that we have defined, which will be defined using getters. The first getter will be a Boolean, `assetsLoaded`, which will be written as follows:

```
get assetsLoaded() {
returnthis.isLoaded&&!this.searchIsNull;
}
```

    This will return `true` when the assets are loaded and the value is not equal to `null`.

46. Our second getter function will be called `listDisabled` and will return the same value as the `savePressed` variable, meaning that when the **Save** button is pressed, our list will be disabled in the UI so that changes cannot be made after pressing the button:

```
get listDisabled() {
   return this.savePressed;
}
```

    These are examples of two simple getter functions. We will take a look at more advanced use cases in later chapters.

47. Build your `connectedCallback` function as such:

```
connectedCallback() {
   utility = new Utilities(this);
   this.sendSearch();
}
```

Like the previous LWCs in this chapter, the first line of our function initializes a new instance of our toast utility that we built in *Chapter 4, Synchronous and Asynchronous Processing in Components*, while the second line calls a function that we will write in the next recipe.

See also

- The sample files for the `addAssetDepartment` LWC are located under the `force-app/chapter05/default/lwc/addAssetDepartment` directory in your forked repository for comparison. These files are located at `https://github.com/PacktPublishing/Salesforce-Lightning-Web-Component-Cookbook/tree/main/force-app/chapter05/default/lwc/addAssetDepartment`.

- The sample files for the `addAssetSearch` LWC are located under the `force-app/chapter05/default/lwc/addAssetSearch` directory in your forked repository for comparison. These files are located at `https://github.com/PacktPublishing/Salesforce-Lightning-Web-Component-Cookbook/tree/main/force-app/chapter05/default/lwc/addAssetSearch`.
- The sample files for the `addAssetPicker` LWC are located under the `force-app/chapter05/default/lwc/addAssetPicker` directory in your forked repository for comparison. These files are located at `https://github.com/PacktPublishing/Salesforce-Lightning-Web-Component-Cookbook/tree/main/force-app/chapter05/default/lwc/addAssetPicker`.
- The documentation for the JavaScript `.sort()` function is available at `https://developer.mozilla.org/en-US/docs/Web/JavaScript/Reference/Global_Objects/Array/sort`.
- The sample file for the *Add Asset To Account* screen flow is located under the `force-app/chapter05/default/flows/Add_Asset_To_Account.flow-meta.xml` directory in your forked repository for comparison. This file is located at `https://github.com/PacktPublishing/Salesforce-Lightning-Web-Component-Cookbook/blob/main/force-app/chapter05/default/flows/Add_Asset_To_Account.flow-meta.xml`.
- For more information on screen flows, see *What Is a Screen Flow?* from the Salesforce Admins blog at `https://admin.salesforce.com/blog/2023/what-is-a-screen-flow`.
- To read more about configuring LWCs for screen flows, see `https://developer.salesforce.com/docs/platform/lwc/guide/use-config-for-flow-screens.html`.

Parsing JSON into JavaScript objects

In the last recipe, we built out the first half of our `addAssetPicker.js` file. In this recipe, we will be adding our search and save functionality and revisiting our Apex to tie everything together. Recall our `connectedCallback` function in the previous recipe? This is where we will start.

How to do it...

1. The first thing we will do is write our function declaration. We will be writing an asynchronous function that calls our `searchAssetWrappers` method of our `AddAssetController` Apex class:

```
async sendSearch() {
    try {
        const searchResultsJSON = await searchAssetWrappers( {search :
this.searchTerm, departmentId : this.departmentId} );
        //processing here...
    } catch(error) {
        //error handling here...
    }
}
```

2. Remember, it is best practice to have a `try-catch` block surrounding our Apex function in case there is an error on the backend, including any `AuraHandledExceptions` that we have thrown.
3. Next, let's continue with our error handling, as it will be quick. When we receive an error, we want to set our `options` variable to `undefined` and call our `showNotif` function from our imported `notifUtils`. Recall that we defined our utility variable in our `connectedCallback`, so we will do this as follows:

```
this.options = undefined;
utility.showNotif('There has been an error searching for assets!', error,
'error');
```

4. As the parameters for our `showNotif` function, recall that we have our error title, our message, and the type of toast notification to show. It is helpful to add a descriptive title and message here.
5. Now, let's do our data processing. Our `searchAssetWrappers` Apex method returns a JSON string or `null`, depending on whether any results are returned. If `null` is returned,

we want to set `searchIsNull` to `true`, and if `else` is returned, we want to do some additional processing. We'll start by writing out the shell for our `if-else` block:

```
if(searchResultsJSON == null) {
   this.searchIsNull = true;
} else { ... }
```

> **Note**
>
> Remember that because **falsy** values exist in JavaScript, we can also write our `if` block as follows: `if(!searchResultsJSON) {...}`. This is largely going to depend on your company's coding standards. The **bang operator**, or `!`, must first coerce whatever variable you present it with into a **truthy** or **falsy** value, which can have unintended consequences. It can also be harder to read quickly, leading to misinterpretation of code. For these reasons, you will often see me use `foo === true` rather than `!bar`.

6. Now that we have our `null` case handling, let's do our actual JSON processing. In our first line, let's parse our data into JavaScript objects, as promised in the recipe's title:

```
let searchResults = JSON.parse(searchResultsJSON);
```

7. To allow our search results to be displayed properly in our `lightning-dual-listbox`, we must transform them into objects that have a `value` property and a `label` property. We can do this by iterating over our `searchResults` array of objects and utilizing a **spread operator** on each item:

```
searchResults.map((sr) => {
   let srClone = {...sr, label:sr.title, value:sr.objectId};
   this.searchResults.push(srClone);
});
```

8. Let's look at our spread operator in line 2 of this code section and think about it for a moment. The way I like to remember spread operator notation on JavaScript objects is that if each object is a card cataloging system, we are essentially *spreading out* our cards on a table and inserting two more cards, a `label` property with a value of `sr.title` and a `value` property with a value of `sr.objectId`.

> **Note**
>
> Conversely, we can use our spread operator on the other end of our curly brackets, like so: `{label:_, value:_, ...srClone} = sr;`.
>
> Using the spread operator in this way, we can remove the `label` and `value` properties from our original `sr` object, yielding our `srClone`. We can set the `label` and `value` properties equal to an underscore character (_) to show that they will be unused elsewhere in our code.

9. After our `map` method has added each of our rearranged `srClone` objects to our class `searchResults` variable, let's sort in place and set our `options` equal to the result. Once we have done that, we can set our component to loaded:

```
this.searchResults.sort(
    (a, b) =>
        (a.label - b.label) ? 1 : -1
);
this.options = this.searchResults;
this.isLoaded = true;
```

10. Now that we have built our record display processing, let's begin to build our save functionality. To save our newly acquired artworks as **Asset** records, we must first define our selections. Recall that we are using a function called `handleChange` in our `addAssetPicker.html` file. Let's start here. First, define a function, `handleChange`, that accepts an `event` as a parameter:

```
handleChange(event) { ... }
```

11. Next, we will set our declared `selectedAssets` variable to the `detail value` of the passed-in `event`:

```
this.selectedAssets = event.detail.value;
```

12. In addition to setting our `selectedAssets` value, we want to disable our buttons if there are no selected assets to limit what the end user can do through the UI. We will do this

by setting our `buttonsDisabled` variable to `true` if there are no selected assets, and `false` otherwise:

```
if(this.selectedAssets === false || this.selectedAssets.length === 0) {
   this.buttonsDisabled = true;
} else {
   this.buttonsDisabled = false;
}
```

> **Note**
>
> Again, there are a couple of different ways that you could write this code block. I am a fan of ternary operators in a lot of cases, which would look as follows: `this.buttonsDisabled = (!this.selectedAssets || this.selectedAssets.length === 0) ? true : false;`. This is a lot sleeker, but the trade-off is that it is harder to read for those who might not be as familiar with JavaScript.

13. While we are building our buttons, let's define our `handleReset` function, which is called when we press the **Reset** button defined in our `addAssetPicker.html` file. We want to clear any selected values and disable our buttons, like so:

```
handleReset() {
   this.selectedAssets = undefined;
   this.buttonsDisabled = true;
}
```

14. Let's return to our Apex files, where we will be creating **persistence layer classes** for the **Asset**, **Constituent**, and **Tag** objects. Recall that a persistence layer class interacts with our database. We are going to start by creating a *public with sharing Apex* class called `Tags`:

```
public with sharing class Tags extends Util_DML {
  public List<Database.UpsertResult> upsertTags(List<Tag__c> tagsToUpsert) {
     try {
        return upsertRecords(tagsToUpsert, 'AAT__c');
     } catch (Exception e) {
        throw new AuraHandledException(e.getMessage());
     }
```

```
    }
}
```

15. Notice that we are extending a `Util_DML` class, which is located in the `force-app/chapter00` directory that was deployed in *Chapter 1, Getting Ready for Lightning Web Component Development*. If you haven't deployed this class, do so now. We will be doing a deep dive into this class in *Chapter 14, Testing Apex with Mocking and Stubbing*, but for now, know that it helps us perform **DML operations** on sObjects.
16. We will create a similar class, `Constituents`:

```
public with sharing class Constituents extends Util_DML{
  public List<Database.UpsertResult> upsertConstituents(List<Constituent__c>
constituentsToUpsert) {
     try{
        return upsertRecords(constituentsToUpsert, 'Constituent_Id__c');
     } catch (Exception e) {
        throw new AuraHandledException(e.getMessage());
     }
  }
}
```

17. Finally, we will create our `Assets` class. This will also be `public with sharing class extends Util_DML`:

```
public with sharing class Assets extends Util_DML
{ ... }
```

18. For our method, we want to upsert our **Asset** records and return information that we can pass to our LWC:

```
public Map<Integer, String> upsertAssetsAndReturnInfoMap(List<Asset>
assetsToUpsert) {
  Map<Integer, String> assetInfoMap = new Map<Integer, String>();
  try{
     List<Database.upsertResult> upsertResults =
upsertRecords(assetsToUpsert, 'Object_ID__c');
     List<Id> idList = new List<Id>();
     for(Database.upsertResult ur : upsertResults) {
        if(ur.isCreated() && ur.isSuccess()) {
```

```
                idList.add(ur.getId());
            }
        }
        if(idList.size() > 0) {
            for(Asset ast : [SELECT Id, Name, Object_ID__c FROM Asset WHERE Id
IN :idList]) {
                assetInfoMap.put(
                    Integer.valueOf(ast.Object_ID__c),
                    ast.Name
                );
            }
        } else {
            return null;
        }
    } catch (Exception e) {
        //error processing
    }
    return assetInfoMap;
}
```

This method upserts our `assetsToUpsert` with our `Object_Id__c` field as our upsert field and then iterates over the upsert results and grabs key information about the upserted records.

19. Once we have created our persistence layer classes, it's time to return to `AddAssetController` and `AddAssetService` and add one more method to each. We need to have a controller class method that accepts a JSON `String` from our LWC, and a service class method that processes this data to upsert a list of **Asset** records and any related **Constituent** and **Tag** records via persistence layer classes.

20. Let's start with our `upsertAssetsAndReturnInfoMap` method within the `AddAssetService` class. This method will receive a list of `AssetWrapper` objects and an `AccountId` as parameters, iterate over the wrappers, and generate any **Asset**, **Constituent**, and **Tag** records that need to be upserted. I won't be walking you through building this entire method, as it would take up several pages, but let's give ourselves a good start. The full method, as well as the persistence layer classes and a series of DML

utility classes, can be found linked in the *See also* section for this recipe. Let's start with the method signature:

```
public Map<Integer, String>
upsertAssetsAndReturnInfoMap(List<ObjectWrappers.AssetWrapper>
assetWrappers, Id accountId) { ... }
```

21. Next, we will declare and initialize the variables needed to process our wrappers:

```
List<Asset> assetsToUpsert = new List<Asset>();
List<Constituent__c> constituentsToUpsert = new List<Constituent__c>();
List<Tag__c> tagsToUpsert = new List<Tag__c>();
Map<String, String> assetIdToConstituentIdMap = new Map<String, String>();
Map<String, String> assetIdToTagIdMap = new Map<String, String>();
```

22. We will then iterate over our `assetWrappers` parameter:

```
for(ObjectWrappers.AssetWrapper assetWrapper : assetWrappers) { ... }
```

23. Within our `for` loop, we will define a `Constituent__c` record, a `Tag__c` record, and an `Asset` record that we will use to store the data contained within our wrappers:

```
Constituent__c constituentToUpsert = new Constituent__c();
Tag__c tagToUpsert = new Tag__c();
Asset assetToUpsert = new Asset();
```

24. Once we have defined our shell records, we are going to check whether the `assetWrapper` we are currently looking at in our loop-through has any items in the `constituents` property, and if it does, we grab the first `constituent` from our `assetWrapper` and populate our **Constituent** shell, `constituentToUpsert`, with this information:

```
if(assetWrapper.constituents != null) {
    constituentToUpsert.Name = nullCheck(assetWrapper.constituents[0].name);
    //continue assigning fields...
    constituentsToUpsert.add(constituentToUpsert);
}
```

Note

You'll notice that I have a **helper method** called `nullCheck` on each line. This is to avoid repetitive ternary operators on each line of code. This method is `static`, accepts a `String` value as a parameter, and returns either the value, if not `null`, or `Not Provided`:

```
public static String nullCheck(String value) {
return value == null ? 'Not Provided' : value;
}
```

This method is defined at the bottom of my Apex class, `AddAssetService`, above my **wrapper classes**. Because it is defined in the same class, we do not need to use dot notation to access it.

25. Next, we will do the same thing with our tags. Note that we want all **Asset** records to have an associated **Tag** record, so in the event that there isn't a tag associated with a given `assetWrapper`, we define one with an `AAT__c` value of `99999`:

```
if(assetWrapper.tags != null) {
   tagToUpsert.Name = nullCheck(assetWrapper.tags[0].term);
   tagToUpsert.AAT__c =
nullCheck(assetWrapper.tags[0].AAT_URL).removeStart(AAT_URL_STRING);
   //continue assigning fields...
   tagsToUpsert.add(tagToUpsert);
} else {
   tagToUpsert.Name = 'No Tag Given';
   tagToUpsert.AAT__c = '99999';
   tagsToUpsert.add(tagToUpsert);
}
```

Note

To define the `AAT__c` field, we are grabbing the `AAT` number off the end of the `AAT_URL` for the tag. To do this, we are using the `removeStart` method of the `String` class with a constant, `AAT_URL_STRING`, that we will define as a class variable at the top of our `AddAssetService` class:

> @TestVisible private static final String AAT_URL_STRING = 'http://vocab.getty.edu/page/aat/';

26. After populating our **Constituent** and **Tag** shells, we can populate the values on our `assetToUpsert`. I'll list the first few here for reference:

```
assetToUpsert.Accession_Number__c = assetWrapper.accessionNumber;
assetToUpsert.Accession_Year__c = assetWrapper.accessionYear == '' ? null :
Integer.valueOf(assetWrapper.accessionYear);
assetToUpsert.Is_Public_Domain__c = assetWrapper.isPublicDomain;
assetToUpsert.AccountId = Id.valueOf(accountId);
//continue assigning fields...
```

> **Note**
>
> For our `Accession_Year__c` field, which is a `Number` field, we must ensure that the value is an integer, so if our `accessionYear` property of our wrapper is an empty string (`''`), we assign `null`, or if it's a string, we convert it to an integer. Similarly, we get the `Id.valueOf(accountId)` to ensure that our `accountId` is an ID and not a string.

27. Once all our fields have been assigned to the values of their respective wrapper properties, we are going to prepare some `Map` magic and add our `assetToUpsert` to our `assetsToUpsert` list:

```
assetIdToConstituentIdMap.put(assetToUpsert.Object_ID__c,
constituentToUpsert?.Constituent_Id__c);
assetIdToTagIdMap.put(assetToUpsert.Object_ID__c, tagToUpsert?.AAT__c);
assetsToUpsert.add(assetToUpsert);
```

This concludes our `for` loop.

28. Outside of our `for` loop, we will start by upserting our **Constituent** and **Tag** records if there are any:

```
if(constituentsToUpsert.size() > 0) {
   constituents.upsertConstituents(
      constituentsToUpsert
```

```
    );
}
if(tagsToUpsert.size() > 0) {
    tags.upsertTags(tagsToUpsert);
}
```

29. Next, we are going to use our `Map` magic to *rehydrate* our **Constituent** and **Tag** records, or re-query the records to grab their IDs that have been set through our DML operations. Let's start with our **Constituent** records:

```
List<String> constituentIdsToRehydrate = assetIdToConstituentIdMap.values();
List<Constituent__c> rehydratedConstituents = [SELECT Id, Constituent_Id__c
FROM Constituent__c WHERE Constituent_Id__c IN :constituentIdsToRehydrate];
Map<String, Id> constituentIdWithIdMap = new Map<String, Id>();
for(Constituent__c cnst : rehydratedConstituents) {
    constituentIdWithIdMap.put(cnst.Constituent_Id__c, cnst.Id);
}
```

30. Line by line, we grab the values of our `assetIdToConstituentIdMap`, representing our `Constituent__c.Constituent_Id__c` field, query for the **Constituent** records that have those external IDs, declare and instantiate a new `Map` called `constituentIdWithIdMap`, and iterate through our rehydrated list of **Constituent** records to pair our `Constituent_Id__c` with the Salesforce ID of the **Constituent** record. We will do the same thing for the **Tag** sObject:

```
List<String> tagIdsToRehydrate = assetIdToTagIdMap.values();
List<Tag__c> rehydratedTags = [SELECT Id, AAT__c FROM Tag__c WHERE AAT__c
IN :tagIdsToRehydrate];
Map<String, Id> tagIdWithIdMap = new Map<String, Id>();
for(Tag__c tag : rehydratedTags) {
    tagIdWithIdMap.put(tag.AAT__c, tag.Id);
}
```

31. Once we have our `Maps` populated, it's time for the magic! We know that we want to associate our **Asset** record with the **Constituent** and **Tag** records, so we use the external

ID fields we paired off earlier to retrieve the newly populated Salesforce IDs of our **Constituent** and **Tag** records if they exist:

```
for(Asset ast : assetsToUpsert) {
    String assetConstituent =
assetIdToConstituentIdMap.get(ast.Object_ID__c);
    String assetTag = assetIdToTagIdMap.get(ast.Object_ID__c);
    ast.Primary_Constituent__c =
constituentIdWithIdMap.get(assetConstituent);
    ast.Tag__c = tagIdWithIdMap.get(assetTag);
}
```

32. To wrap up this method, if there are **Asset** records to upsert, we return the result of our service class method; if not, we return `null`:

```
if(assetsToUpsert.size() > 0) {
    return assets.upsertAssetsAndReturnInfoMap(assetsToUpsert);
}
return null;
```

33. To end our Apex adventures with the `AddAssetController` class in this chapter, add the following method that uses the JSON methods we have learned about so far:

```
@AuraEnabled
public static Map<Integer, String> saveAssetWrappers(String jsonToParse, Id
accountId) {
    try {
        List<ObjectWrappers.AssetWrapper> assetWrappers =
(List<ObjectWrappers.AssetWrapper>) JSON.deserialize(jsonToParse,
List<ObjectWrappers.AssetWrapper>.Class);
        Map<Integer, String> saveResults = new
AddAssetService().upsertAssetsAndReturnInfoMap(assetWrappers, accountId);
        return saveResults == null ? null : saveResults;
    } catch (Exception e) {
        throw new AuraHandledException(e.getMessage());
    }
}
```

34. Finally, we can build the save functionality into our LWC. Return to your `addAssetPicker.js` file and start by defining an asynchronous function called

`handleSave`. For now, we will leave out the `try-catch` block we used in the `sendSearch` function:

```
async handleSave() { ... }
```

35. Recall that we are activating our save functionality via a button in our `addAssetPicker.html` file. When this button is pressed, we want to deactivate our `lightning-dual-listbox` so that no more selections can be made, and we want to disable our buttons. Let's start by setting our variables for whether the button is pressed and whether the buttons are disabled to `true`:

```
this.savePressed = true;
this.buttonsDisabled = true;
```

36. Now, we must prepare a variable, `recordsToSave`, which will be the selected assets from our `lightning-dual-listbox`. To determine which of our `searchResult` objects have been selected from our options, we can utilize the `filter` method in JavaScript:

```
let recordsToSave = this.searchResults.filter(asset =>
this.selectedAssets.includes(asset.objectId));
```

The `filter` method provides a shallow copy of an array with only the items that pass the test given by the parameter function—in this case, any assets where `asset.objectId` is included in `this.selectedAssets`.

37. In order to pass this into our Apex function, we are going to transform our JavaScript objects into a JSON string. In our last line, before we implement a `try-catch` block, we will assign a `jsonToParse` variable like so:

```
let jsonToParse = JSON.stringify(recordsToSave);
```

38. Now let's take a look at the `try-catch` block. We know from the sample Apex file that we will be upserting our **Asset** records, and we will want to notify the end user if a duplicate **Asset** record has been found. We can do this with our toast utility:

```
const saveResult = await saveAssetWrappers({ jsonToParse : jsonToParse,
accountId : this.recordId});
let savedMessage = '', unsavedMessage = '';
let unsavedRecords;
```

```
if(saveResult) {
    let propertyList = Object.getOwnPropertyNames(saveResult);
    for(let property of propertyList) {
        savedMessage += saveResult[property] + ', item number ' + property +
'.\n';
    }
    utility.showNotif('You have successfully inserted the following
record(s):', savedMessage, 'success');
    unsavedRecords = recordsToSave.filter(unsavedAsset => !
propertyList.includes(unsavedAsset.objectId));
}
if(unsavedRecords && unsavedRecords.length != 0) {
    for(let record of unsavedRecords) {
        unsavedMessage += record.title + ', item number ' + record.objectId +
'.\n';
    }
    utility.showNotif('The following duplicate record(s) were not saved: ',
unsavedMessage, 'info');
}
if(!saveResult && !unsavedRecords) {
    for(let duplicate of recordsToSave) {
        unsavedMessage += duplicate.title + ', item number ' +
duplicate.objectId + '.\n';
    }
    utility.showNotif('The following duplicate records were not saved: ',
unsavedMessage, 'info');
}
```

39. Finally, our `catch` block will be as follows:

```
catch(error) {
    utility.showNotif('There has been an error!', error, 'error');
}
```

40. Now that we have completed our LWCs, we can add them all to our screen flow. Return to Flow Builder, and ensure there are three screens in your *Add Assets to Account* screen flow, one for each LWC, in the order of `addAssetDepartment`, `addAssetSearch`, and `addAssetPicker`:

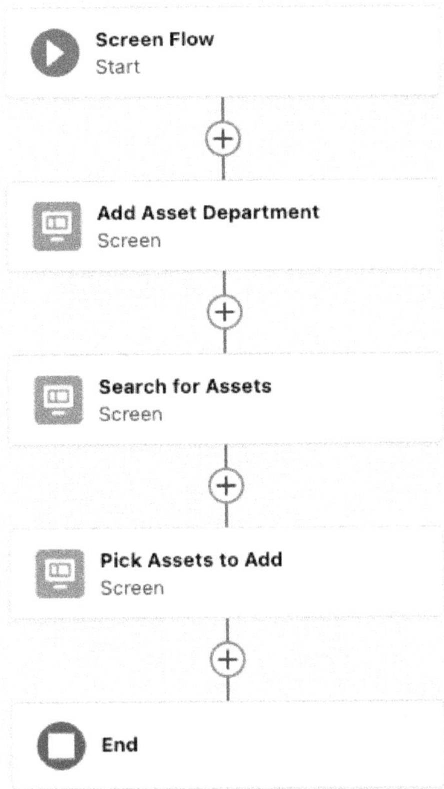

Figure 5.4: A screenshot of the final screen flow in Flow Builder

41. We can now activate our flow and try adding new assets to our **Account** records. If you need a few suggestions, try searching in the **Arms and Armor** department for `sword`, the **Asian Art** or **European Art** department for `dragon`, or **Islamic Art** for `tile`!

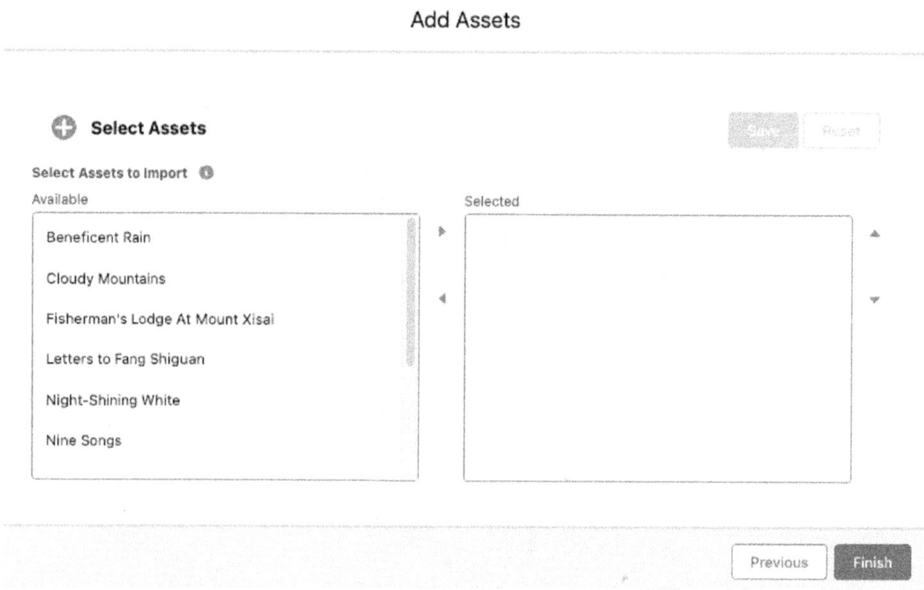

Figure 5.5: A screenshot of the Add Assets screen in the screen flow, with a selection of fine dragon art!

See also

- The sample files for the `addAssetDepartment` LWC are located under the `force-app/chapter05/default/lwc/addAssetDepartment` directory in your forked repository for comparison. These files are located at `https://github.com/PacktPublishing/Salesforce-Lightning-Web-Component-Cookbook/tree/main/force-app/chapter05/default/lwc/addAssetDepartment`.
- The sample files for the `addAssetSearch` LWC are located under the `force-app/chapter05/default/lwc/addAssetSearch` directory in your forked repository for comparison. These files are located at `https://github.com/PacktPublishing/Salesforce-Lightning-Web-Component-Cookbook/tree/main/force-app/chapter05/default/lwc/addAssetSearch`.
- The sample files for the `addAssetPicker` LWC are located under the `force-app/chapter05/default/lwc/addAssetPicker` directory in your forked repository for comparison. These files are located at `https://github.com/PacktPublishing/Salesforce-Lightning-Web-Component-Cookbook/tree/main/force-app/chapter05/default/lwc/addAssetPicker`.

- The sample file for the *Add Asset To Account* screen flow is located under the `force-app/chapter05/default/flows/Add_Asset_To_Account.flow-meta.xml` directory in your forked repository for comparison. This file is located at `https://github.com/PacktPublishing/Salesforce-Lightning-Web-Component-Cookbook/blob/main/force-app/chapter05/default/flows/Add_Asset_To_Account.flow-meta.xml`.
- The sample files for the Apex persistence layer classes and utility classes are located under the `force-app/chapter05/default/classes` directory in your forked repository. These files are located at `https://github.com/PacktPublishing/Salesforce-Lightning-Web-Component-Cookbook/tree/main/force-app/chapter05/default/classes`.

Utilizing the fetch API in JavaScript

You may remember that earlier in the chapter, we introduced some code that does not follow Salesforce best practices. Don't worry, we're going to fix that! Recall that we have an API call in a `for` loop, which is a surefire way of hitting governor limits. Let's take a look at the Fetch API in JavaScript and how we can utilize it to avoid hitting these limits.

How to do it...

1. First, start by creating a new **Remote Site setting** in your Salesforce Developer Edition org. This is a necessity, as we will be accessing our external API via JavaScript. If you followed the org setup instructions in *Chapter 1, Getting Ready for Lightning Web Component Development*, you may already have the necessary settings.

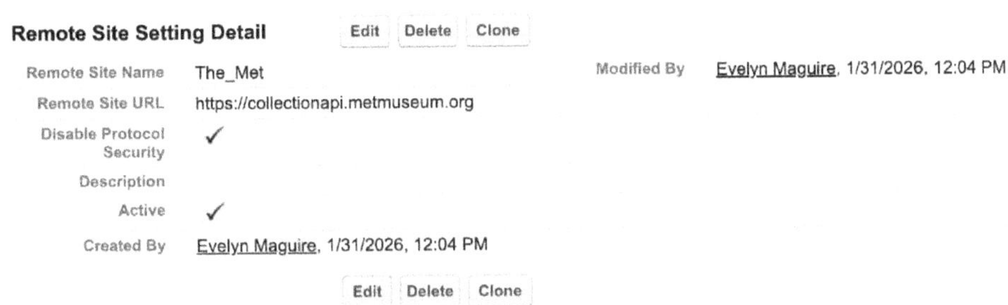

Figure 5.6: A screenshot of the necessary Remote Site setting

   Remote Site Name will be `The_Met`, and **Remote Site URL** will be `https://collectionapi.metmuseum.org`.

2. You must also add this URL to the trusted URLs in **Setup**. Ensure all boxes are checked in the **CSP Directives** section.

3. Next, return to your `addAssetPicker.js` file. First, we are going to create a function, `getObject`, that accepts a parameter of `objectId`. This function is going to utilize the JavaScript **fetch API** in a **promise chain** to retrieve and transform an `objectId`'s returned JSON value:

```
getObject(objectId) {
    return fetch('https://collectionapi.metmuseum.org/public/collection/v1/
objects/' + objectId)
        .then(objectFetch => {
            return objectFetch.json();
        })
        .then(objectJSON => {
            let objectClone = {...objectJSON, label:objectJSON.title,
value:objectJSON.objectID.toString()};
            return objectClone;
        })
        .catch(error => {
            utility.showNotif('There has been an error in getObject!!',
error.message, 'error');
        });
}
```

4. Note that we are using a promise chain with the fetch API to easily visualize the steps that are occurring. As an additional challenge, try converting this into an `async`/`await` function!
5. Now that we have a function to return an `objectId`'s JSON value in a format that is usable, we need to create a function to iterate over a list of `objectIds`, that is, `searchObjects`:

```
searchObjects(objectIds) {
    return Promise.all(objectIds.map(objectId => {
        let object = this.getObject(objectId)
            .then(returnedObject => {
                return returnedObject;
            })
            .catch(error => {
                utility.showNotif('There has been an error in searchObjects!',
error.message, 'error');
            });
```

```
        return object;
    }));
}
```

Let's take a look at this function from the inside out:

6. Let's start by looking at the third line, where we see that we are declaring a variable, `object`, which is the result of the `getObject` function for a given `objectId`. We resolve the promise by returning our `returnedObject`, and catch any errors.
7. Returning to the second line of this function, we notice that we are using the `map()` function on our parameter, which would be an array of `objectIds`. The `map` function will iterate over the specified array and perform a function on each item, which we are dubbing `objectId`, and place the results into another array. In this case, our `map` function is creating an array of promises to return our `returnedObject`.
8. Finally, we return the result of our array of promises. We do this using `Promise.all()`, which takes an array of promises and waits until they are all resolved to return the result. Altogether, this function returns an array of JavaScript objects representing our assets.
9. Now that we are successfully returning an array of assets, let's wrap this function inside a search function, `sendSearchFetchAPI`. Recall that we are passing in our search parameters from our screen flow, so this function will not take any parameters, but instead will use our `@api` decorated class variables. Add a `fetch()` function to the specified API endpoint. In the first chained element of our `fetch()` function, we will return the JSON value of the result of our API call:

```
fetch('https://collectionapi.metmuseum.org/public/collection/v1/search?q=' +
JSON.stringify(this.searchTerm).slice(1, -1) + '&departmentId=' +
this.departmentId)
    .then(sendSearchFetch => {
        return sendSearchFetch.json();
    })
```

10. Next, we will check whether our return value has a property of an array of `objectIDs`, as defined by the Open Access documentation. If there are no `objectIDs`, we will resolve

the promise and set our class variable, `searchIsNull`, to `true`; otherwise, we will send our `objectIDs` for processing by our `searchObjects` function:

```
.then(sendSearchResponse => {
   if(sendSearchResponse.objectIDs == null) {
      Promise.resolve(this.searchIsNull = true);
   }
   return this.searchObjects(sendSearchResponse.objectIDs);
})
```

11. After returning our array of searched objects, `searchResults`, we can sort our `searchResults`, set them as the options for our `lightning-dual-listbox`, and set our `isLoaded` variable to `true`:

```
.then(searchResults => {
   this.searchResults = searchResults;
   this.searchResults.sort((a, b) => (a.label - b.label) ? 1 : -1);
   this.options = this.searchResults;
   this.isLoaded = true;
})
```

12. Finally, we can catch any errors and display our notifications utility if necessary:

```
.catch(error => {
   utility.showNotif('There has been an error!', error.message, 'error');
});
```

13. You can test this functionality by changing the `connectedCallback` function in `addAssetPicker.js` from `this.sendSearchApex()` to `this.sendSearchFetchAPI()`.

See also

- The sample files for the `addAssetPicker` LWC are located under the `force-app/chapter05/default/lwc/addAssetPicker` directory in your forked repository for comparison. These files are located at `https://github.com/PacktPublishing/Salesforce-Lightning-Web-Component-Cookbook/tree/main/force-app/chapter05/default/lwc/addAssetPicker`.

- The Salesforce *Call APIs from JavaScript* documentation is located at `https://developer.salesforce.com/docs/platform/lwc/guide/js-api-calls.html`.
- The Salesforce *Manage Trusted URLs* documentation is located at `https://help.salesforce.com/s/articleView?id=sf.security_trusted_urls_manage.htm&type=5`.

Get this book's PDF version and more

Scan the QR code (or go to `packtpub.com/unlock`). Search for this book by name, confirm the edition, and then follow the steps on the page.

Note: Keep your invoice handy. Purchases made directly from Packt don't require an invoice.

6

Composing Lightning Web Components

Now that we have a good understanding of how to build a frontend and backend for our LWCs, let's make them talk to each other.

In *Chapter 3, Working with a Selector Class*, we began working with a component called `topTenAccountTabset`. This component houses information about each of the top 10 accounts in order of decreasing annual revenue. In *Chapter 4, Synchronous and Asynchronous Processing in Components*, we added the `assetsByTag` component, which displays the artworks (assets) for each museum (account), arranged by the category of art they fall under (tag). We saw a very simple example of parent-to-child component communication, and built a **utility component** called `notifUtils` to house our toast notifications.

In this chapter, we will be adding our final component to the **Top Accounts** page by inserting it into our `topTenAccountTabset` component. To do this, we will be looking at the `flattenedViewContacts` component, housed on the **Account record** FlexiPage included with the code from the book. This component is fairly simple, but we can break it into smaller components to encourage code reuse and to use it as an example for the different types of events we can propagate. These recipes will give you a solid foundation in event propagation, which will allow our components to communicate with each other.

We are going to be covering the following main recipes:

- Working with the shadow DOM
- Building child components
- Building parent components
- Communication from parent to child
- Communication from child to parent through events
- Handling events in the parent component
- Configuring event propagation from child to parent
- Sibling component communication

Technical requirements

The recipes for this book can be found at `https://github.com/PacktPublishing/Salesforce-Lightning-Web-Component-Cookbook`, where each chapter has its own folder under the `force-app` folder. This GitHub repository is structured in the form of a Salesforce DX project, which will allow you to easily fork the repository for deployment in a free Salesforce Developer Edition org. The sample code for *Chapter 6, Composing Lightning Web Components*, is located at `https://github.com/PacktPublishing/Salesforce-Lightning-Web-Component-Cookbook/tree/main/force-app/chapter06`, while the setup code for this chapter is located at `https://github.com/PacktPublishing/Salesforce-Lightning-Web-Component-Cookbook/tree/main/force-app/chapter06_setup`.

The components in this book require the use of an **Integrated Development Environment** (**IDE**), such as **Visual Studio Code** (**VSCode**) or **Salesforce Code Builder**. Detailed instructions for setting up an IDE are located in *Chapter 1, Getting Ready for Lightning Web Component*, in the *Setting up your IDE* section.

If you are building the projects in this cookbook as written, you will need to seed your Salesforce Developer Edition org with test data. Detailed instructions for seeding your org are located in *Chapter 1, Getting Ready for Lightning Web Component*, in the *Setting up the Salesforce Lightning Web Components Cookbook org* section.

Lastly, the edition of Salesforce required to implement the recipes in this book must be Developer, Performance, Unlimited, Enterprise, or Database.com. You can sign up for a free Salesforce Developer Edition org at `https://developer.salesforce.com/signup`.

Working with the shadow DOM

In this recipe, we will be experimenting with deconstructing a flattened version of the code we are going to write to solidify the concepts needed for this chapter. If you have not already, deploy the *Chapter 4, Synchronous and Asynchronous Processing in Components,* `force-app/chapter04` directory, as well as the *Chapter 6, Composing Lightning Web Components,* setup folder, located within the `force-app/chapter06_setup` directory, to a new Salesforce Developer Edition org. This project, unlike many other projects in the book, stands on its own, with no dependencies on custom objects or data. It is written this way as this is such an important topic to visualize, and likely a chapter where many of you are starting your *Lightning Web Components Cookbook* journey.

If you are starting your journey with me here, if needed, there are detailed instructions on how to set up GitHub and VSCode in *Chapter 1, Getting Ready for Lightning Web Component Development.*

Once you have deployed the code, navigate to the **Account record** page for the **Burlington Textiles Corp of America** record, which is included in every Developer Edition org, and assign the **Chapter 06** FlexiPage for the **Account** sObject to your user's profile. If you have deployed the `Chapter04` and `Chapter06_setup` directories and assigned the appropriate **Lightning record page**, you will see the following module in the top-right corner:

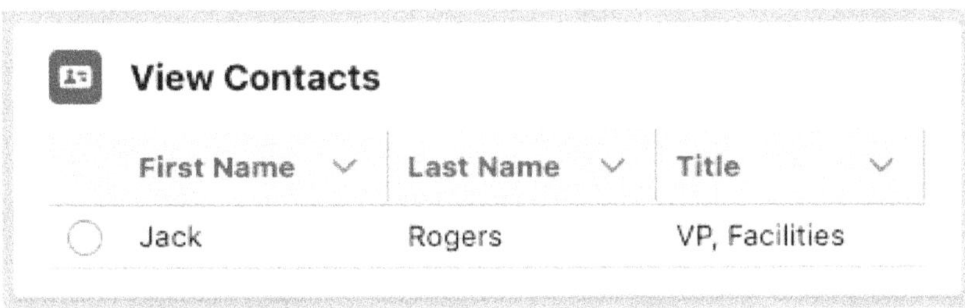

Figure 6.1: The completed flattenedViewContacts component

This component allows us to select a contact for a given account and uses a **screen flow** to add an **Event** sObject record for the selected contact. Once we have added the **Event** record, the component refreshes, as does the record page. The screen flow is available for inspection in the `force-app/chapter06_setup/default/flows` directory and is called **Create Event For Contact From LWC** in **Flow Explorer**. In summation, we will be using **JavaScript events** to create **Event** sObject records with a **screen flow** embedded in an LWC – neat!

Once you see this component, open VSCode. We are ready to begin.

How to do it...

1. Navigate to the `force-app/chapter06_setup/default/lwc/flattenedViewContacts.html` file, where we will be examining the flattened structure of the component we will be building.
2. Notice that we have several layers of tags, which can be represented by the following diagram:

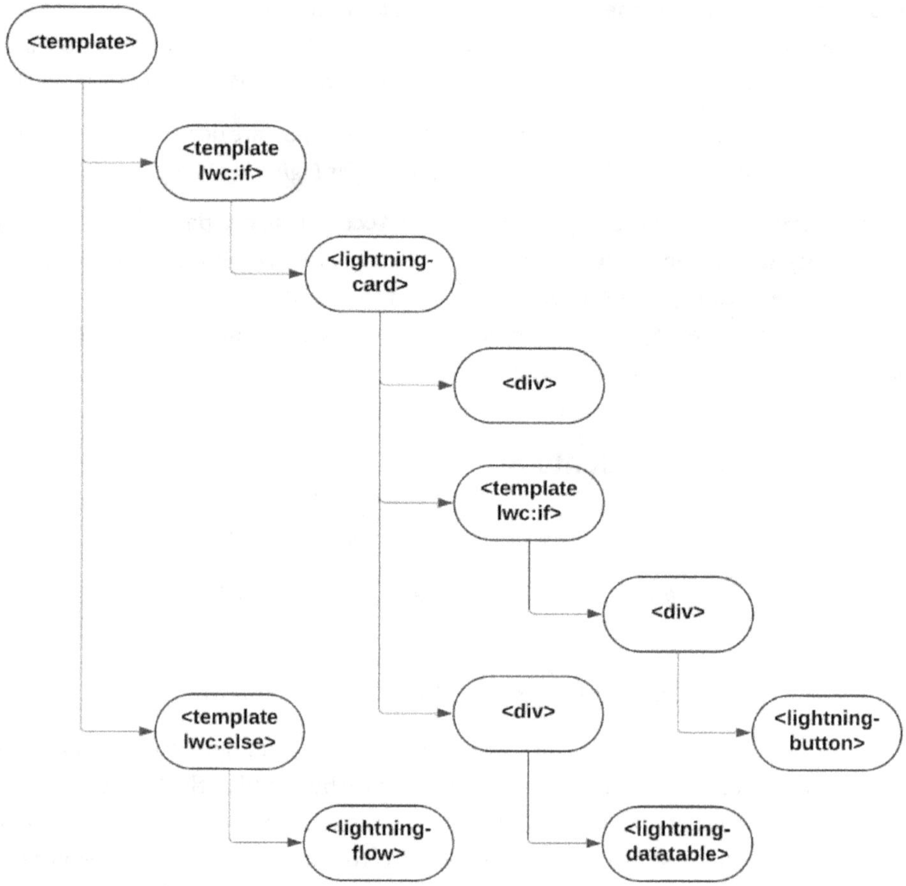

Figure 6.2: A diagram illustrating the structure of the tags in the flattenedViewContacts component

3. As we can see, there are six layers of nested tags in the `flattenedViewContacts.html` file, which represents our **shadow DOM**, or **Document Object Model**. This shadow DOM is implemented by Salesforce to prevent an LWC from being manipulated in arbitrary ways, either intentionally by a bad actor or unintentionally by a developer. In

many ways, it is like the **JavaScript DOM**, but it does have some limitations that are predicated by whether your org uses **Lightning Locker** or **Lightning Web Security** (**LWS**), which we will be discussing further in *Chapter 7, Building Secure Components with Lightning Locker and Lightning Web Security.*

4. Now, this is a project-based cookbook, so we won't be spending too much time here, as we'll be too busy breaking down this one component into five to practice our **JavaScript event handling**. That being said, I encourage you to read the links in the *See also* section of this recipe to build a good foundation for the rest of this chapter.

See also

- The sample code for the `flattenedViewContacts` LWC is available at `https://github.com/PacktPublishing/Salesforce-Lightning-Web-Component-Cookbook/tree/main/force-app/chapter06_setup/default/lwc/flattenedViewContacts`.
- JavaScript Document Object Model (DOM) reference guide from the MDN Web Docs: `https://developer.mozilla.org/en-US/docs/Web/API/Document_Object_Model`
- Introduction to the DOM from the MDN Web Docs: `https://developer.mozilla.org/en-US/docs/Web/API/Document_Object_Model/Introduction`
- Salesforce documentation on the Shadow DOM, located here: `https://developer.salesforce.com/docs/platform/lwc/guide/create-dom.html`

Building child components

Look at the diagram in the *Working with the shadow DOM* recipe one more time. We are going to spend the next two recipes separating this one component into five components that will be nestled together. This will serve as an exercise in breaking down a large component, as well as practice in getting these components to talk to each other.

How to do it...

1. We are going to start by breaking down our diagram so we can visualize what we are doing. We are going to start from the bottom, with our grandchild component, and work our way up until we reach our top-level child components.

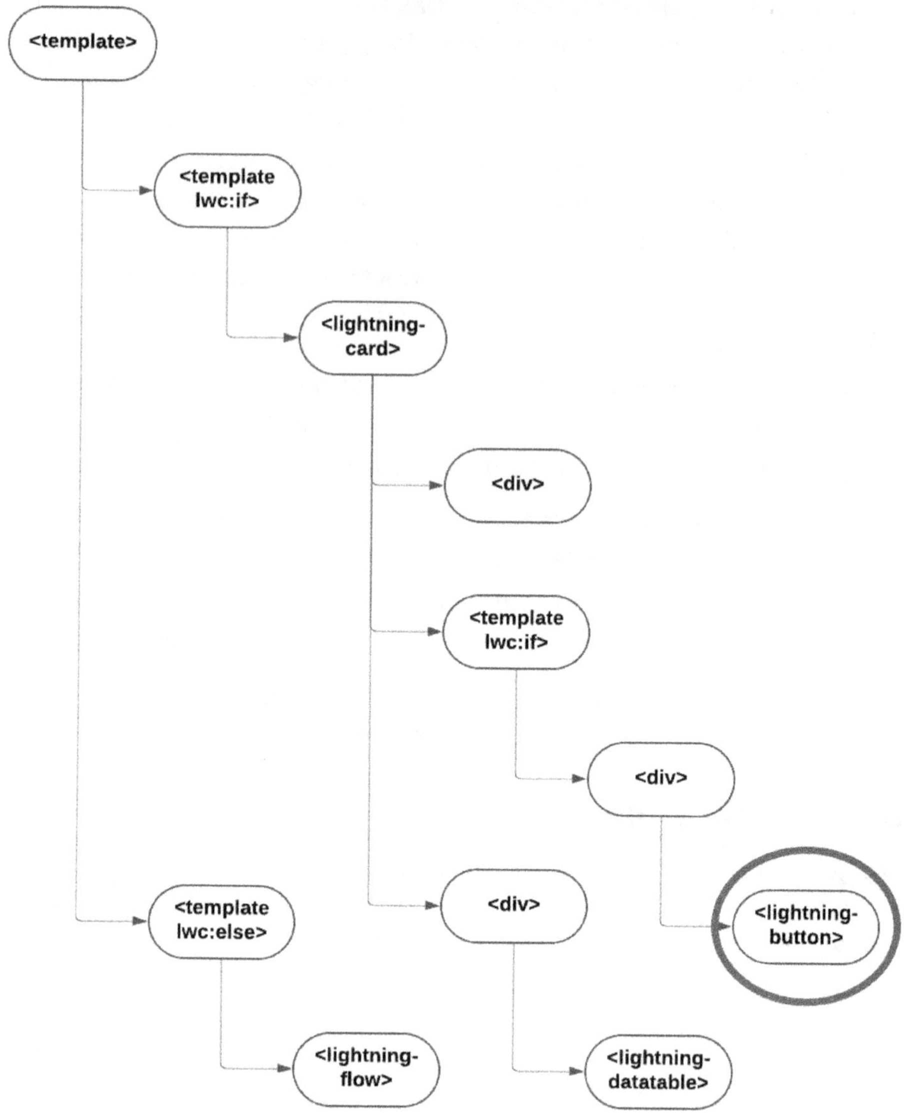

Figure 6.3: A diagram we will become quite familiar with, illustrating the element that we will be working on – the <lightning-button> grandchild component is highlighted

2. Taking a look at our deepest component, we see that we are going to build a component with a single **lightning-button**. While it may not make sense to get this granular in a real-world org, we are doing this so that we can visualize how JavaScript events propagate through different layers of the shadow DOM in Salesforce. It will all come together soon!

3. Start by creating a new LWC called `viewContactsAddEventButton`. For now, we are just going to put a `lightning-button` component in between the two `template` tags in our `.html` file, as shown here:

```
<lightning-button
   class="slds-var-p-horizontal_medium"
   variant="brand"
   label="Add Event"
   onclick={handleAddEvent}
></lightning-button>
```

4. That's it! Not only will this illustrate our JavaScript event handling in detail, but we are also working on building our LWC confidence. On to the next!
5. Create a second LWC called `viewContactsContactDatatable`. Again, we are going to focus on the `.html` file first. In between your `template` tags, add a `lightning-datatable` component with the following attributes, remembering that we will be building our JavaScript file soon:

```
<lightning-datatable
   key-field="Id"
   data={contactsToView}
   columns={contactColumnsDatatable}
   onrowselection={handleContactSelect}
   max-row-selection="1"
></lightning-datatable>
```

6. Once we have created this LWC, enter the `viewContactsContactDatatable.js` file and begin it with the following definition for our `contactColumnsDatatable` variable:

```
import { LightningElement, api } from 'lwc';
export default class ViewContactsContactDatatable extends LightningElement {
   contactColumnsDatatable = [
      {label: 'First Name', fieldName: 'FirstName'},
      {label: 'Last Name', fieldName: 'LastName'},
      {label: 'Title', fieldName: 'Title'},
      {label: 'Email', fieldName: 'Email'},
      {label: 'Phone', fieldName: 'Phone'}
   ];
```

```
    @api contactsToView;
}
```

7. Line by line, we are adding the `api` decorator to our imports, defining our `ViewContactsContactDatatable` class, setting the values for our `lightning-datatable` columns, and inheriting the `contactsToView` variable from our parent component.

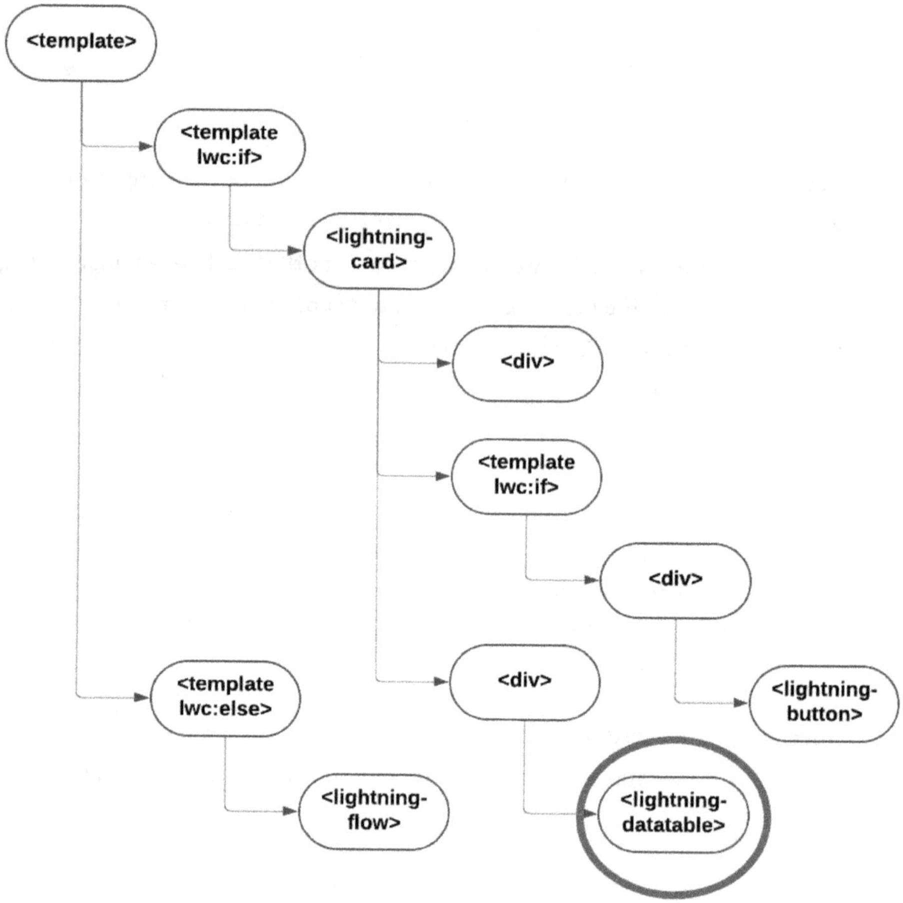

Figure 6.4: Our flattened DOM diagram, illustrating that the element we just added is the <lightning-datatable> component

8. Next, we are going to build a component to embed a **screen flow** into our LWC. This flow, `Create_Event_For_Contact_From_LWC`, has been created for you as part of the `chapter06_setup` folder deployment. Create a new LWC called

`viewContactsLightningFlow`, and enter the following **lightning-flow** tag with the specified attributes:

```
<lightning-flow
   flow-api-name="Create_Event_For_Contact_From_LWC"
   flow-input-variables={flowInputVariables}
   flow-finish-behavior="NONE"
   onstatuschange={handleFlowStatusChange}
></lightning-flow>
```

9. We will see how to build `input-variables` when we build our JavaScript file in the *Sibling component communication* recipe, but for now, all we need to know is how to embed the flow.

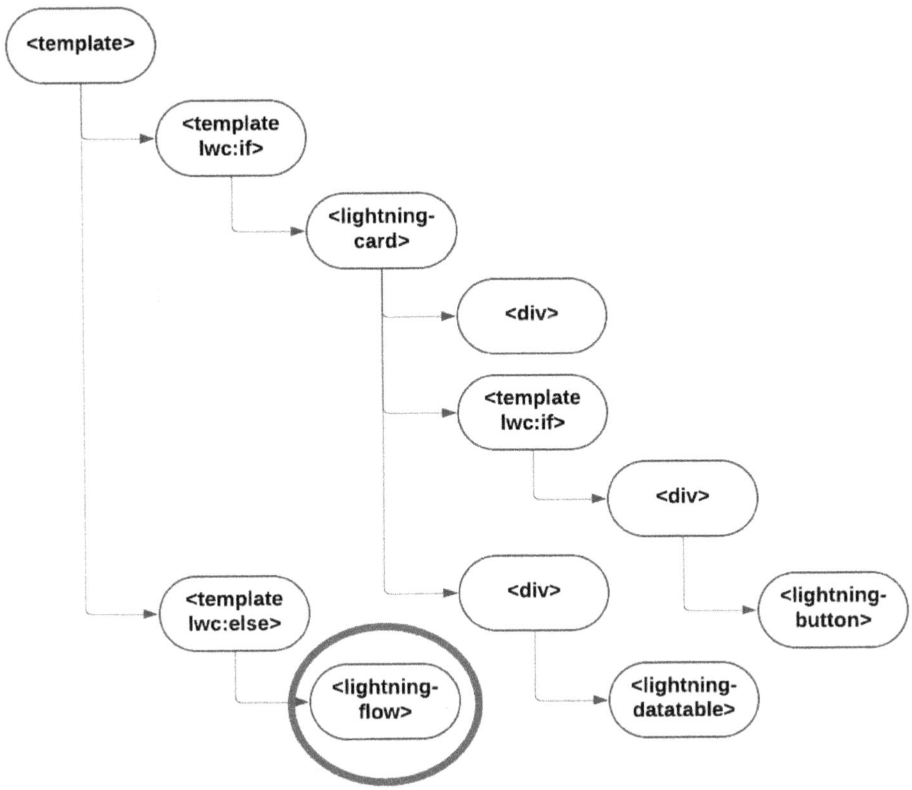

Figure 6.5: Once again, our flattened DOM diagram, illustrating that we have added the <lightning-flow> component where it sits in the DOM tree

See also

- The sample code for the LWCs we are writing in this chapter is available at `https://github.com/PacktPublishing/Salesforce-Lightning-Web-Component-Cookbook/tree/main/force-app/chapter06/default/lwc`
- The Lightning Web Components Component Reference page for `lightning-button`: `https://developer.salesforce.com/docs/component-library/bundle/lightning-button/example`
- The Lightning Web Components Component Reference page for `lightning-datatable`: `https://developer.salesforce.com/docs/component-library/bundle/lightning-datatable/example`
- The Lightning Web Components Developer Guide article on embedding a flow in an LWC: `https://developer.salesforce.com/docs/platform/lwc/guide/use-flow-embed-component.html`
- A Salesforce Developers Blog post entitled *Embed Screen Flows in Your Lightning Web Components*: `https://developer.salesforce.com/blogs/2022/12/embed-screen-flows-in-your-lightning-web-components`
- A Trailhead module titled *Build a Bear-Tracking App with Lightning Web Components*: `https://trailhead.salesforce.com/content/learn/projects/lwc-build-flexible-apps`

Building parent components

Now that we have built most of our child and grandchild components, we are going to build a **lightning-card** component and a shell component that will occupy dual roles as the parents of our other three components, and, optionally, as a child of the `topTenAccountTabset` component from *Chapter 3, Working with a Selector Class*. Let's dive in!

How to do it...

1. After building our flow component, the next component is `lightning-card`. Create a new LWC called `viewContactsLightningCard`, and note where it will sit within our DOM tree. We notice in our trusty diagram that this component will sit within our top `lwc:if` directive, and will serve as a parent to two `div` tags and another `lwc:if` directive:

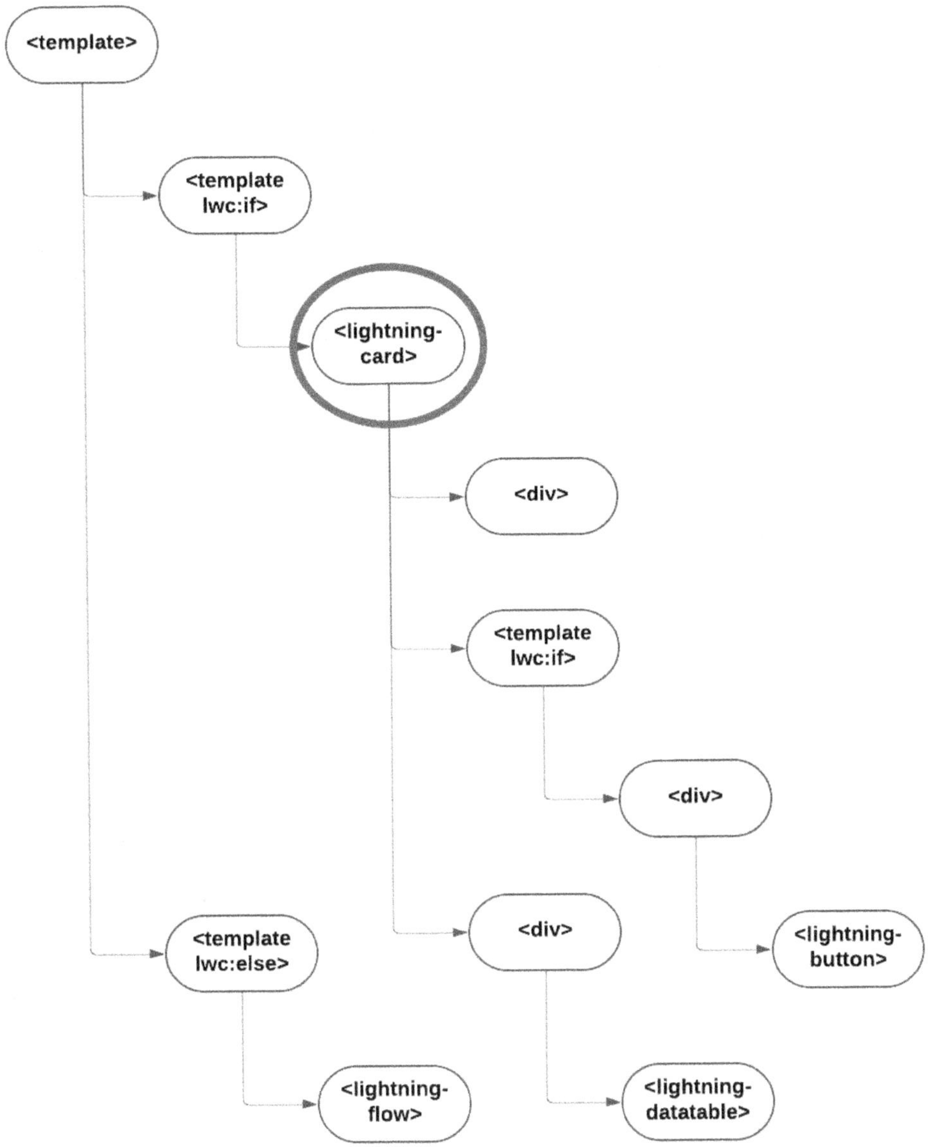

Figure 6.6: The final rendition of this diagram, illustrating where our <lightning-card> element will sit

2. Place the following between your `template` tags:

```
<lightning-card icon-name="standard:contact" variant="base">
  <div slot="title">
    View Contacts
```

```
    </div>
    <template lwc:if={contactIsSelected}>
        <div slot="actions">
            <c-view-contacts-add-event-button></c-view-contacts-add-event-
button>
        </div>
    </template>
    <div class="slds-var-p-horizontal_medium">
        <c-view-contacts-contact-datatable></c-view-contacts-contact-
datatable>
    </div>
</lightning-card>
```

3. Note the highlighted lines in the code. These are our child components, denoted by adding a `c-` to the front of our component name, and converting from **camel case** to **kebab case**, where instead of capitalizing each word, we use hyphens to separate them. For example, if our component name is `myCoolComponent`, our component reference will look like this:

```
<c-my-cool-component></c-my-cool-component>
```

4. Note that we must have a closing tag here.
5. We will be adding some attributes to our `c-view-contacts-contact-datatable` tag in due time, but otherwise, this is good to go! You have built a modest parent component that hosts two children. We'll be building a more robust parent component in the next step.
6. Create a new LWC called `viewContactsShell`. This LWC will house an `lwc:if|else` directive that depends on whether an expression, in this case a **Boolean** called `addEventInactive`, is **truthy** or **falsy**. Within our set of template `lwc:if|else` directive tags, we will place the `viewContactsLightningCard` and `viewContactsLightningFlow` child components, respectively. This will look like the following:

```
<template lwc:if={addEventInactive}>
    <c-view-contacts-lightning-card></c-view-contacts-lightning-card>
</template>
<template lwc:else>
    <c-view-contacts-lightning-flow></c-view-contacts-lightning-flow>
</template>
```

7. We will again be adding attributes to these tags when we start building our JavaScript files over the next few recipes, but for now, we just want to place our modest parent `lightning-card` component and our `lightning-flow` child components in our shell.
8. Optionally, if you would like to add the `viewContactsShell` component to the `topTenAccountTabset` component from *Chapter 3, Working with a Selector Class,* add the following between the `<!-- Chapter 6 Code Here -->` comments, or before the closing `</lightning-tab>` tag:

```
<c-view-contacts-shell record-id={account.Id}></c-view-contacts-shell>
```

9. This will insert an instance of the `viewContactsShell` component into the shadow DOM and pass in the ID of the Account record that is contained in the **Top 10 Accounts** iterator, denoted by the `for:each` directive operating on our `accounts` collection. We know that this will be stored in a variable called `recordId` in our `viewContactsShell.js` file, denoted by the `record-id` property within the tag using kebab case.
10. Now that we have placed our components, we have an HTML document structure that can be visualized by the following diagram:

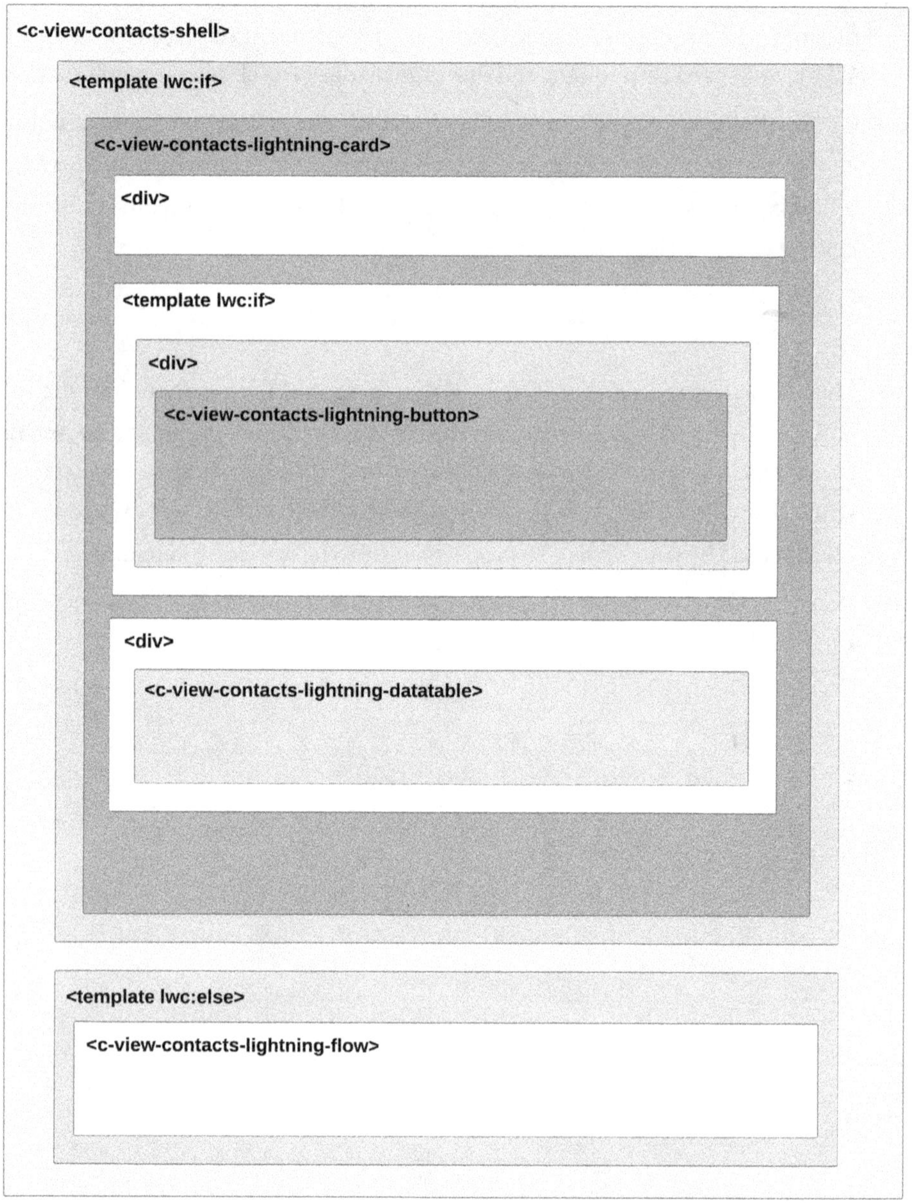

Figure 6.7: A diagram showing the approximate location of each HTML element located within our shadow DOM, starting with viewContactsShell as the outermost component

11. We will be iterating over this diagram through the next several recipes to help us visualize our event composition.

See also

- The sample code for the LWCs we are writing in this chapter is available at `https://github.com/PacktPublishing/Salesforce-Lightning-Web-Component-Cookbook/tree/main/force-app/chapter06/default/lwc`
- The code for the `topTenAccountTabset` LWC files from *Chapter 3, Working with a Selector Class* are located at `https://github.com/PacktPublishing/Salesforce-Lightning-Web-Component-Cookbook/tree/main/force-app/chapter03/default/lwc/topTenAccountTabset`
- The Salesforce Developer Docs article titled *Define a Component* is located at `https://developer.salesforce.com/docs/platform/lwc/guide/create-components-define.html`
- The Lightning Web Components Component Reference page for `lightning-card`: `https://developer.salesforce.com/docs/component-library/bundle/lightning-card/example`

Communication from parent to child

As we saw in the last recipe, we can pass variables from parent to child by creating an **attribute** in the child tag within the parent `.html` file. How do we access that variable? And what do we do when we want to pass more information in? Let's start from the top and work our way down as we split out our original JavaScript file.

How to do it...

1. Enter the newly created `viewContactsShell.js` file and open the `flattenedViewContacts.js` file as well. Our goal is to break out the JavaScript that corresponds to our child and grandchild components. Remember, our shell file holds the `lightning-card` and `lightning-flow` containing components, and the `lightning-card` component holds the `lightning-datatable` and `lightning-button` components. We are going to be passing values from the `viewContactsShell` component into the `viewContactsLightningCard` and `viewContactsLightningFlow` components.
2. To start, look at the `flattenedViewContacts.js` file. We know that to make a component aware of its record context, we utilize the `@api recordId` variable to pull the `recordId` from the Lightning record page that the component is hosted on. We are going to use a similar process to make our component aware of its context within another

component. Remember the tag for `viewContactsShell` within `topTenAccountsTabset`? We utilized the `record-id` attribute, which is the familiar kebab case variant of the `recordId` variable, to pass the ID of an iterated-over **Account** record into our shell component. This is where these two concepts meet. Note that we use `@api recordId` in the `viewContactsShell.js` file so that we can place it within our `topTenAccountTabset` component from *Chapter 3, Working with a Selector Class*, or directly on an **Account record** page, as we have done with the `flattenedViewContacts` component.

3. Don't forget to add the `api` decorator to your imports:

```
import { LightningElement, api } from 'lwc';
export default class ViewContactsShell extends
NavigationMixin(LightningElement) {
   @api recordId;
   ...
}
```

4. Now that we have connected these dots, let's import our `c/notifUtils` notification utility component from *Chapter 4, Synchronous and Asynchronous Processing in Components*. Add the following import and variable above the class definition in the `viewContactsShell.js` file:

```
import Utilities from 'c/notifUtils';
let utility;
```

5. This will import our component as `Utilities`, and define a `utility` variable, which we will define in our `connectedCallback` function:

```
connectedCallback() {
   utility = new Utilities(this);
}
```

6. This will allow us to utilize the `utility.showNotif(title, message, variant)` function elsewhere in our component.
7. Next, we will **wire** a function, `returnContactsPerAccount`, which is in the `ViewContactController` Apex class, provided in the `chapter06_setup` folder that you deployed at the start of this chapter.

> **Note**
>
> We have spent a lot of this book so far focusing on building **selector classes**, **service classes**, and **controller classes** in Apex, so we will not be building them in this chapter to save some time. I encourage you to read through the files on GitHub or in VSCode to familiarize yourself with them. If you are not yet familiar with this pattern, refer to *Chapter 3, Working with a Selector Class*.

Remember, we must also import our `wire` decorator, meaning our first line of the document will look like the following:

```
import { LightningElement, api, wire } from 'lwc';
```

8. To wire our function, we will need to pass in a variable, `accountIdString`, and we will be returning a list of contact records per our Apex class. Let's build this so we can future-proof our code for the use of `refreshApex` at a later date, which, as you will recall from *Chapter 2, Writing Apex for Lightning Web Components*, requires passing in the entirety of a wired function into a single `result` variable and assigning it to a variable such as `_wiredContacts`. If the `wire` function call is successful, we will assign the `data` property of the `result` variable to a variable we will declare called `contactsToView`. Upon error, we will use the `utility.showNotif(title, message, variant)` function. Within the JavaScript class definition, add the following:

```
_wiredContacts;
contactsToView;
@wire(returnContactsPerAccount, {accountIdString : '$recordId'})
wiredContacts(result) {
   this._wiredContacts = result;
   if (result.data) {
      this.contactsToView = result.data;
   } else if(result.error) {
      this.contactsToView = undefined;
      utility.showNotif('There has been an error returning contacts!',
result.error, 'error');
   }
}
```

9. This function is also available to copy from the `flattenedViewContacts.js` file, which is in the GitHub repository for this chapter.
10. Lastly, we know from the `flattenedVewContacts.html` file that we will need two variables defined for the `lwc:if` directives: `selectedContact` and `addEventInactive`. Let's add these below our other class variables:

```
selectedContact = '';
addEventInactive = true;
```

11. We know that `selectedContact` must be equal to an empty `String` variable because we will be passing it into an embedded flow, and `addEventInactive` will be a Boolean that will initially be `true`.
12. Return to the `viewContactsShell.html` file and add a `contacts-to-view={contactsToView}` attribute to the `c-view-contacts-lightning-card` tag to pass the `contactsToView` variable into the `lightning-card` carrying component:

```
<c-view-contacts-lightning-card
    contacts-to-view={contactsToView}>
</c-view-contacts-lightning-card>
```

13. For now, we are done with this component! We will be adding some JavaScript event handling in the *Communication from child to parent* recipe.
14. Returning to our nested parent component, `viewContactsLightningCard`, we know we need to accept the passed-in variable of `contactsToView` using the `api` decorator, as we outlined in the previous step, and a variable of `contactIsSelected`, which will be set to `true` when we know that a contact record has been selected from the `lightning-datatable` component:

```
import { LightningElement, api } from 'lwc';
export default class ViewContactsLightningCard extends LightningElement {
    @api contactsToView;
    contactIsSelected = false;
}
```

15. For now, this completes our JavaScript file. Let's pass this variable down one more time into the `viewContactsContactDatatable.js` file via the `viewContactsLightningCard.html` file:

```
<c-view-contacts-contact-datatable
   contacts-to-view={contactsToView}>
</c-view-contacts-contact-datatable>
```

16. Again, we must accept this variable with our `api` decorator in the `viewContactsContactDatatable.js` file:

```
import { LightningElement, api } from 'lwc';
export default class ViewContactsContactDatatable extends LightningElement {
   @api contactsToView;
}
```

There are a few more complex examples of parent-child communication that we will see in later chapters, such as a parent component calling a method from a child component, but for now, we will tamp down the complexity so that we can focus on JavaScript event propagation.

See also

- The code for the `notifUtils` notification utility files from *Chapter 4, Synchronous and Asynchronous Processing in Components* is located at `https://github.com/PacktPublishing/Salesforce-Lightning-Web-Component-Cookbook/tree/main/force-app/chapter04/default/lwc/notifUtils`
- The Apex files for *Chapter 6, Composing Lightning Web Components*, are located at `https://github.com/PacktPublishing/Salesforce-Lightning-Web-Component-Cookbook/tree/main/force-app/chapter06/default/classes`
- A helpful tutorial, *Communicate Between Lightning Web Components* on Trailhead, is located at `https://trailhead.salesforce.com/content/learn/projects/communicate-between-lightning-web-components`
- Another Trailhead module, titled *Communicate from Parent to Child*, is located at: `https://trailhead.salesforce.com/content/learn/projects/communicate-between-lightning-web-components/communicate-from-parent-to-child`

Communication from child to parent through events

Now that we have passed our data down into our child and grandchild components, we need to find a way to send information back up the shadow DOM and into our top-level components. We will be doing this using **JavaScript events**.

To start, let's describe what a JavaScript event is. Simply, an event is a communication sent by the browser when the end user takes some sort of action on a web page. We can react to these events in response by **handling the event**. For now, we are going to build our JavaScript events, which we will be configuring in the next recipe, and handling in the *Handling events in the parent component* recipe. We are going to be starting at the innermost layer of our DOM, our grandchild component, `viewContactsAddEventButton`.

Let's get started.

How to do it...

1. Open the `viewContactsAddEventButton.html` file and note the declarative `onclick` listener. The **click event** (with a listener of `onclick`) is a built-in JavaScript event that registers a **mousedown event** (which has a listener of `onmousedown`) and **mouseup event** (with its own listener of `onmouseup`) by the end user. This is one type of JavaScript eventing, where we define a custom `on[jsevent]` listener attribute in our LWC tag and create a handler function, `handle[JsEvent]`. In this case, we define a custom JavaScript event, `addevent`, where the event we are adding is an **Event** sObject record in Salesforce.
2. Open the `viewContactsAddEventButton.js` file, where we will be building our JavaScript event.
3. Create a new function, `handleAddEvent`:

```
handleAddEvent() {
    let updateAddEventInactive = false;
    const addEventEvent = new CustomEvent('addevent', {
        detail: {
            addEventInactive : updateAddEventInactive
        }
    });
    this.dispatchEvent(addEventEvent);
}
```

4. Line by line, within this section of code, we are doing the following:

5. Defining the **handler function**, `handleAddEvent`
6. Initializing and defining a variable, `updateAddEventInactive`
7. Initializing a new event for dispatch, `addEventEvent`, of type `CustomEvent`, which will be propagated when a **click event** is called as defined in our `.html` file
8. Note that the name of the JavaScript event defined is `addevent`, which means that the **listener** we will use in our parent component `.html` file is `onaddevent`
9. Setting the `detail` property for our event so that we can pass the values of necessary variables up the shadow DOM
10. Dispatching the event using the **bubbling phase** of the event lifecycle

> **Note**
>
> The events used in LWCs only use the bubbling phase of the JavaScript event lifecycle, meaning that the event is passed from the innermost member of the shadow DOM to the outermost. In JavaScript documentation, there is also the **capture phase**, in which the event travels from the outermost element of the DOM to the innermost, and the **target phase**, where the event reaches the **target** element. We don't have to worry about these two phases, but they are helpful to know about when reading JavaScript documentation.

11. We will add some more properties to `CustomEvent` in the next recipe, but for now, we will move on to the `viewContactsContactDatatable` files.
12. Open the `viewContactsContactDatatable.html` file. Notice we have one built-in event defined – `onrowselection` – which we will handle with the `handleContactSelect` function.
13. Open the `viewContactsContactDatatable.js` file next. This is where we will define `handleContactSelect`. This function is going to look a little bit different, as we are also receiving data from the built-in `onrowselection` event handler:

```
handleContactSelect(event) {
   let updatedSelectedContact = event.detail.selectedRows[0].Id;
   const selectContactEvent = new CustomEvent('selectcontact', {
      detail: {
         selectedContact : updatedSelectedContact
      }
   });
```

```
        this.dispatchEvent(selectContactEvent);
    }
```

Notice the function parameter of `event`. This is the event we are receiving upon `onrowselection`, or when a row is selected by the radio button. Because the `rowselection` event can handle multiple rows at the same time, we know that the value received will be an array. Because we are only selecting one row, or one contact record, as defined in our `.html` file, we must get the zeroth index of the array returned by `event.detail.selectedRows`. We then grab the `Id` property of this object, utilizing dot notation so that we can pass `updatedSelectedContact` as an `Id` string up through the shadow DOM.

14. Now that we have events propagating from our innermost components, we can handle them in their respective parent components.

See also

- An MDN Web Docs article titled *Introduction to Events*: `https://developer.mozilla.org/en-US/docs/Learn_web_development/Core/Scripting/Events`
- An MDN Web Docs article titled *Element: click event*: `https://developer.mozilla.org/en-US/docs/Web/API/Element/click_event`
- The Salesforce documentation for `lightning-datatable`: `https://developer.salesforce.com/docs/component-library/bundle/lightning-datatable/documentation`
- *Communicate Between Lightning Web Components* module on Trailhead: `https://trailhead.salesforce.com/content/learn/projects/communicate-between-lightning-web-components`
- A Trailhead module titled *Communicate from Child to Parent*: `https://trailhead.salesforce.com/content/learn/projects/communicate-between-lightning-web-components/communicate-from-child-to-parent`

Handling events in the parent component

As you will recall, the `viewContactsShell` component is a parent to the `viewContactsLightningCard` component and the `viewContactsLightningFlow` component. We will be discussing the `viewContactsLightningFlow` component in the final recipe of the chapter.

You will also recall that the `viewContactsLightningCard` component is parent to two sets of nested components, one containing the `viewContactsAddEventButton` component and the other containing the `viewContactsContactDatatable` component. Now that we have these inner components firing JavaScript events, how do we handle them? First, we are going to visualize where these events are propagated from and where we are putting their listeners. The following diagram will allow us to visualize where our data is traveling to and from within our component:

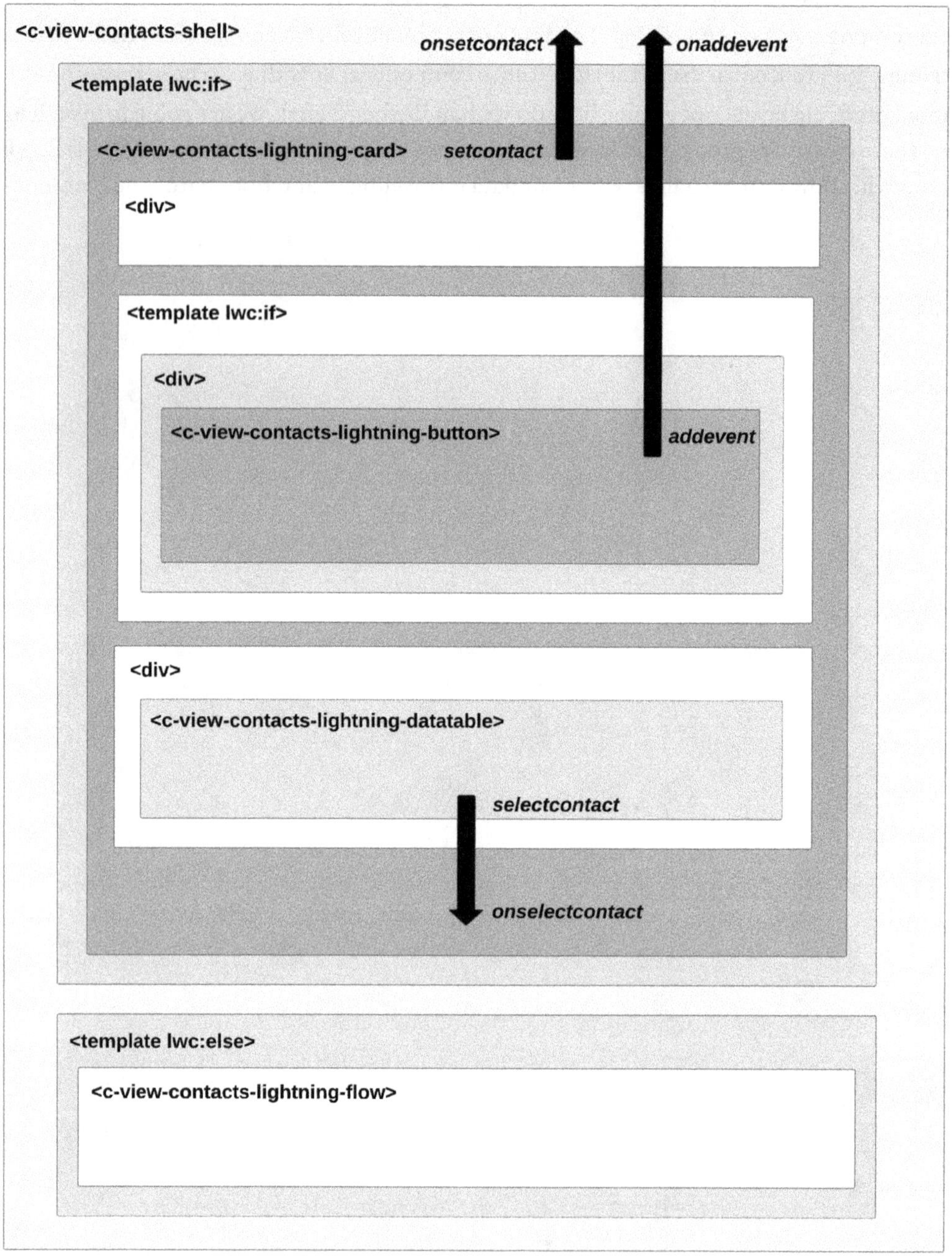

Figure 6.8: Shadow DOM diagram with arrows denoting where the events from each inner element are propagating to

Note

For illustrative purposes, I am showing the events traveling into the parent. This is not a highly technical illustration, as the events will be handled declaratively within the child tag that is located within the parent. This stylistic choice is made to make the diagram more concise and readable as the chapter progresses.

Note that we must make a stop with our contact record information en route to its final destination. This stop will be located within the `viewContactsLightningCard` component so that we can conditionally display the `viewContactsAddEventButton` component. Additionally, the `addevent` event skips straight from the `viewContactsLightningButton` component to the `viewContactsShell` component.

Now that we've got an idea of where everything is going, let's handle these events!

How to do it...

1. Starting from the `viewContactsShell` component, let's work our way back down the shadow DOM. We know that we need to add an event listener attribute to the tag that is emitting the event in the form of `oneventname`, so let's start in the `viewContactsShell.html` file.
2. Add the attributes of `onsetcontact={setContactToSelected}` and `onaddevent={triggerFlow}` to your opening `c-view-contacts-lightning-card` tag, as shown here:

```
<c-view-contacts-lightning-card
   contacts-to-view={contactsToView}
   onsetcontact={setContactToSelected}
   onaddevent={triggerFlow}>
</c-view-contacts-lightning-card>
```

3. Doing this defines the functions that will be called when an event listener detects that our events have been fired. For now, we will be using **declarative event listeners**, and we will look at more complex **programmatic event listeners** in later chapters.
4. Open the `viewContactsShell.js` file, where we will be defining the handler functions, `setContactToSelected` and `triggerFlow`.

5. Because of how we set up our events in the previous recipe, we know that we need to set the class variables that we defined at the start of the chapter, `selectedContact` and `addEventInactive`, to the new values that were bubbled up by our respective events:

```
setContactToSelected(event) {
    this.selectedContact = event.detail.setContactTo;
}
triggerFlow(event) {
    this.addEventInactive = event.detail.addEventInactive;
}
```

6. Simple enough. Setting these variables will pass `selectedContact` down to our embedded flow, as well as triggering the flow to start through the `lwc:if|else` directive on the `addEventInactive` variable.
7. Next, proceed to the `viewContactsLightningCard.html` file. Remember, we need `contactId` to stop over here to determine whether a contact record is selected in the `viewContactsContactDatatable` component, which will enable the viewing of the `viewContactsAddEventButton` component.
8. Add the `onselectcontact={handleSelectContact}` listener attribute to your opening `c-view-contacts-contact-datatable` tag:

```
<c-view-contacts-contact-datatable
    contacts-to-view={contactsToView}
    onselectcontact={handleSelectContact}>
</c-view-contacts-contact-datatable>
```

9. Let's go to the `.js` file and write the `handleSelectContact` function, which will include an event that bubbles up the contact record ID to the listener in the `c-view-contacts-contact-datatable` tag within the `viewContactsShell` component:

```
handleSelectContact(event) {
    let contactId = event.detail.selectedContact;
    this.contactIsSelected = true;
    const setContactEvent = new CustomEvent('setcontact', {
        detail: {
            setContactTo : contactId
        }
    });
```

```
        this.dispatchEvent(setContactEvent);
    }
```

This concludes our handling of events in the `viewContactsLightningCard` element! Go ahead and deploy your code if you haven't yet, and try playing with the component on the **Top Accounts** page.

See also

- The Salesforce Developer Documentation article entitled *Handle Events*: `https://developer.salesforce.com/docs/platform/lwc/guide/events-handling.html`
- A Trailhead module called *Handle Events in Lightning Web Components*: `https://trailhead.salesforce.com/content/learn/modules/lightning-web-components-basics/handle-events-in-lightning-web-components`

Configuring event propagation from child to parent

If you've deployed your code to your org and tried it, you might notice that it isn't yet working! This is because of two properties in the JavaScript `CustomEvent` object that we have been working with: `bubbles` and `composed`. What does this mean? Well, when an event **bubbles** (`bubbles: true`) up the shadow DOM, it won't cross a shadow DOM boundary unless it is **composed** (`composed: true`).

The default configuration for the `CustomEvent` object within an LWC is `bubbles: false, composed: false`. This is why we are not seeing our events propagating as expected. For me, the best way to remember how to do something is to break it and fix it. So, how can we fix it?

We'll start by defining the three acceptable uses of the `bubbles` and `composed` properties in our `CustomEvent` object:

- `bubbles: false, composed: false` (default)
- `bubbles: true, composed: false`
- `bubbles: true, composed: true`

> Note
>
> While it is possible to use `bubbles: false` and `composed: true` together, this is considered an **anti-pattern** in LWC development, as we are telling the JavaScript event to stay put in the shadow DOM and cross shadow DOM boundaries simultaneously! This can lead to unexpected behaviors.

Let's dive in and see an example of when to use each.

How to do it...

1. Let's look at our diagram in *Figure 6.8* one more time. We notice that our JavaScript events, `selectcontact` and `setcontact`, both emit an event from their respective child component, with the **declarative event listener** within the child component tag of its parent object `.html` file. The event does not **bubble** past the child that it is propagated from. As a result, the configuration will be `bubbles: false, composed: false`. It is notable that this is the default configuration for an event in Salesforce, so it is optional to add our properties to our events, but we will do so here for clarity. Let's take a look at the event being propagated from `lightning-datatable` first.

   viewContactsContactDatatable.js - handleContactSelect

```
const selectContactEvent = new CustomEvent('selectcontact', {
    bubbles : false,
    composed : false,
    detail: {
        selectedContact : updatedSelectedContact
    }
});
```

2. The event propagated by `lightning-datatable` is then handled within the `lightning-card` component, which we can see using the `event.detail.selectedContact` snippet:

   viewContactsLightningCard.js - handleSelectContact

```
handleSelectContact(event) {
let contactId = event.detail.selectedContact;
this.contactIsSelected = true;
const setContactEvent = new CustomEvent('setcontact', {
    bubbles : false,
    composed : false,
    detail: {
        setContactTo : contactId
    }
});
```

3. Next, we know that our `addevent` event passes shadow boundaries. As we see in *Figure 6.8*, we are passing our `updateAddEventInactive = false` variable up the shadow DOM so that it may be handled by placing its corresponding event listener, `onaddevent`,

in the tag of its parent component, `viewContactsLightningCard`, within the `viewContactsShell.html` file. Because this event is passing shadow boundaries, we are going to set its `bubbles` and `composed` properties to `true`:

viewContactsAddEventButton.js - handleAddEvent

```
const addEventEvent = new CustomEvent('addevent', {
   bubbles : true,
   composed : true,
   detail: {
      addEventInactive : updateAddEventInactive
   }
});
```

> **Note**
>
> Because this event configuration allows an event to pass **shadow DOM boundaries** in nested components, it is important to make sure that it is caught by a corresponding **event listener** so that there are no **memory leaks** in your component. Additionally, it is important to ensure that there aren't name clashes between components, as two nested components, each with an `addevent` event, could spell disaster!

4. So far, we've seen what it looks like when both the `bubbles` and `composed` properties are `true`, and when both are `false`, so what about our third acceptable configuration? We are going to do one more piece of building to visualize the `bubbles: true, composed: false` configuration, before we wrap up the chapter by enabling the embedded flow.
5. Navigate to the `viewContactsContactDatatable.js` file, and below the `selectcontact` event, add one more event:

```
const changeDivEvent = new CustomEvent('changediv', {
   bubbles : true,
   composed : false,
   detail: {
      newClass : 'slds-var-p-horizontal_medium slds-box slds-theme_warning'
   }
});
this.dispatchEvent(changeDivEvent);
```

6. This event configuration will allow the `changediv` event to be handled by the `div` element surrounding the `c-view-contacts-contact-datatable` tags in the `viewContactsLightningCard.html` file. In this configuration, the `changediv` JavaScript event travels until it finds a shadow root or the event gets cancelled. As a result, the `div` wrapper can react to the event.
7. Navigate to the `viewContactsLightningCard.html` file. In the `div` tag surrounding the `c-view-contacts-contact-datatable` tags, add an `lwc:ref` directive, and a declarative event listener called `onchangediv`:

```
<div lwc:ref="bodyDiv" class="slds-var-p-horizontal_medium"
onchangediv={changeBodyDivClass}>
    <c-view-contacts-contact-datatable
        contacts-to-view={contactsToView}
         onselectcontact={handleSelectContact}>
    </c-view-contacts-contact-datatable>
</div>
```

8. The `lwc:ref` directive, available in **Winter '23**, sets a reference, `bodyDiv`, that we can use to query our DOM elements easily using `this.refs.bodyDiv`. We will use this in the new function, `changeBodyDivClass`, within the `viewContactsLightningCard.js` file:

```
changeBodyDivClass(event) {
    let newClass = event.detail.newClass;
    this.refs.bodyDiv.className = newClass;
}
```

9. Deploy your changes, and notice that when a contact record is selected in `lightning-datatable`, we see the `div` surrounding it turn Salesforce warning yellow:

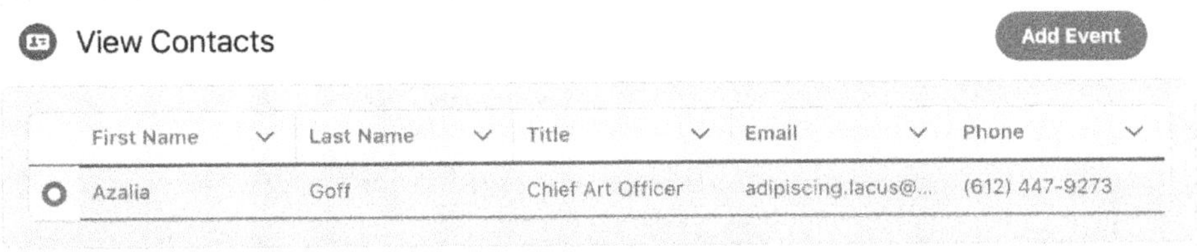

Figure 6.9: A screenshot of the View Contacts card on the Top Accounts page, showing that the outer div for the lightning-datatable has turned yellow

10. Now, we should have a good understanding of when to use each acceptable combination of the `bubbles` and `composed` properties on the `CustomEvent` JavaScript object. To sum up, let's take one more look at our diagram.

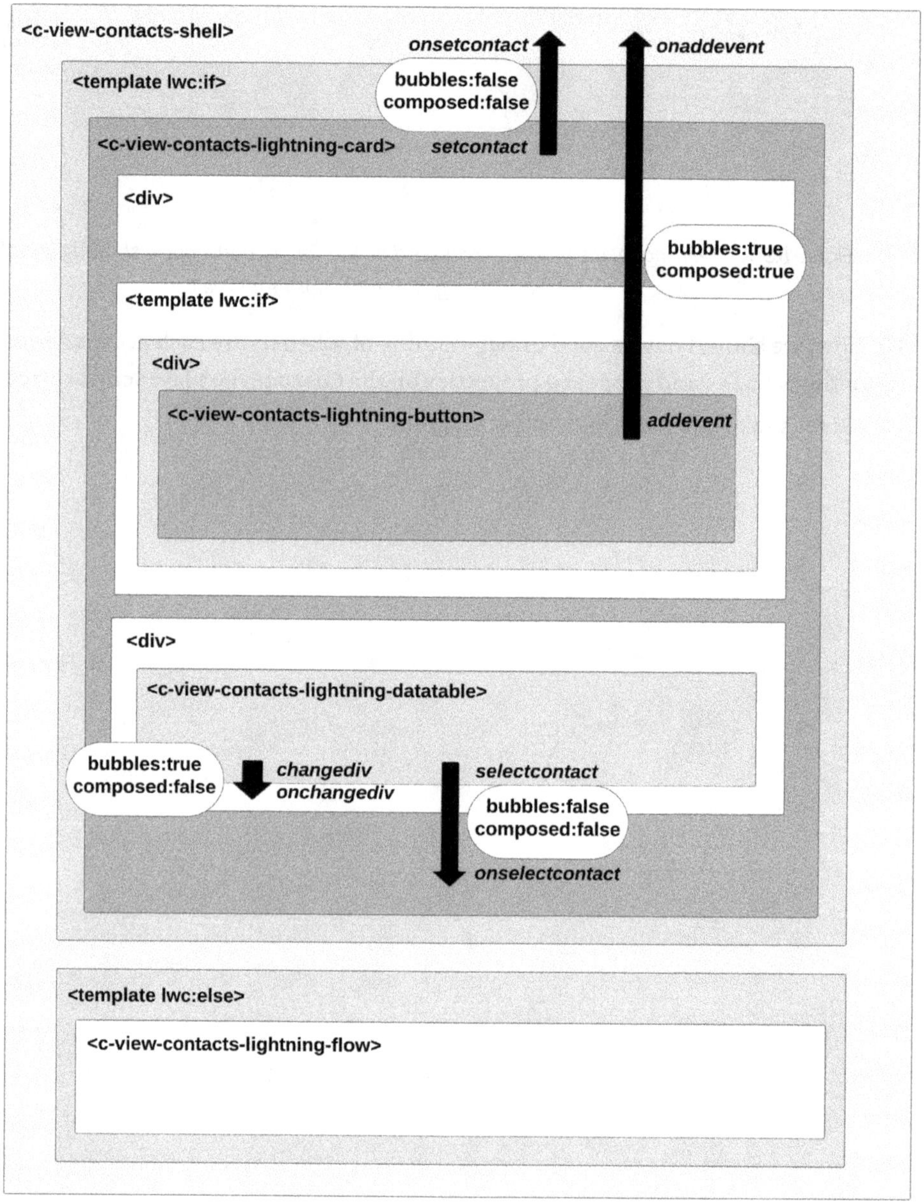

Figure 6.10: Our HTML elements diagram with an example of each of the three types of event composition that are permitted in Lightning Web Components

We see that our use of `bubbles` and `composed` dictates where our data can be read within the DOM.

See also

- A Salesforce Developers Blog post called *How Events Bubble in Lightning Web Components*: `https://developer.salesforce.com/blogs/2021/08/how-events-bubble-in-lightning-web-components`
- A Salesforce Developer documentation article called *Query DOM Elements with Refs*: `https://help.salesforce.com/s/articleView?id=release-notes.rn_lwc_templaterefs.htm&release=242&type=5`

Sibling component communication

Now that we have all the components communicating successfully in `viewContactsLightningCard`, let's make them communicate with its sibling component, `viewContactsLightningFlow`.

How to do it...

We are going to achieve this using a combination of the strategies we have learned so far in this chapter. Let's take a look one more time at our diagram to get an idea of what we are going to do.

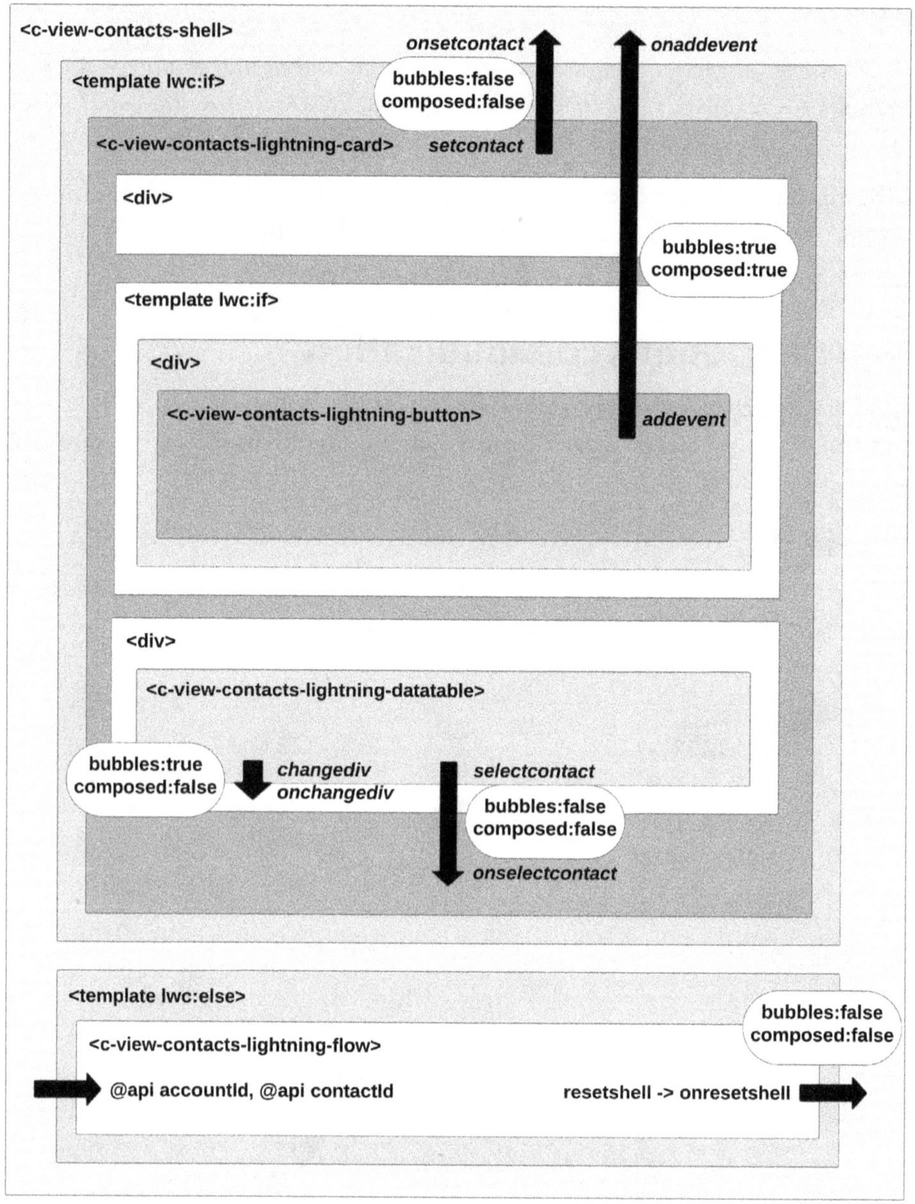

Figure 6.11: Our favorite diagram, illustrating how the broader component communicates with the viewContactsLightningFlow nested component

Now that we've had a refresher, let's begin:

1. Start by opening the `viewContactsLightningFlow.js` file. We know from the Salesforce documentation that we need to have a **getter** for `flowInputVariables`. Based on the pre-built flow, we need to pass in `AccountId` and `ContactId`. We also know that we have already passed these variables into `viewContactsShell` – `accountId` being passed down from `topTenAccountTabset`, and `contactId` being passed up from `viewContactsContactDatatable`. Let's combine this information to get the following:

```
@api accountId;
@api contactId;
get flowInputVariables() {
   return [
      {
         name: 'AccountId',
         type: 'String',
         value: this.accountId
      },
      {
         name: 'ContactId',
         type: 'String',
         value: this.contactId
      }
   ];
}
```

2. Additionally, we need to reset our shell component once our flow has completed. We already know, based on the `viewContactsLightningFlow.html` file, that this function is going to be called `handleFlowStatusChange`, so let's take a look:

```
handleFlowStatusChange(event) {
   if (event.detail.status === 'FINISHED') {
      let updateSelectedContact = '';
      let updateAddEventInactive = true;
      const resetShellEvent = new CustomEvent('resetshell', {
         bubbles : false,
         composed : false,
         detail : {
            selectedContact : updateSelectedContact,
            addEventInactive : updateAddEventInactive,
```

```
                outputVariables : event.detail.outputVariables[0].value
            }
        });
        this.dispatchEvent(resetShellEvent);
    }
}
```

3. Line by line, we are checking whether our flow finished successfully, resetting the `selectedContact` variable to an empty `String` value, setting `addEventInactive` back to `true`, and firing an event called `resetshell` that will not cross shadow DOM boundaries, but will pass up the updated info as well as `outputVariable` from our flow, which happens to be the ID of the Event sObject record that our flow will insert. Whew!
4. Return to the `viewContactsShell.html` file, where we will be adding attributes to pass `account-id` and `contact-id` into the JavaScript file, remembering that we need to use our snake case variant in the `c-view-contacts-lightning-flow` opening tag:

```
<c-view-contacts-lightning-flow
    account-id={accountId}
    contact-id={selectedContact}
    onresetshell={resetShell}>
</c-view-contacts-lightning-flow>
```

5. Finally, we will return one more time to the `viewContactsShell.js` file to add the event handler function:

```
resetShell(event) {
    this.addEventInactive = event.detail.addEventInactive;
    this.refreshPage();
    utility.showNotif('Your event has been inserted successfully!',
event.detail.outputVariables, 'success');
}
```

6. This will reset our shell and display a toast notification with the ID of the Event record that we created.
7. Deploy your code and pat yourself on the back for a job well done.

7

Building Secure Components with Lightning Locker and Lightning Web Security

Having learned the basics of how to emit and capture events within our Lightning Web Components, we can now talk about how Salesforce secures these events. In Salesforce orgs created after the Winter '23 updates, Salesforce Lightning Web Security is enabled for Aura and Lightning Web Components to enforce security best practices. We will spend the bulk of this chapter learning how **Lightning Web Security** (**LWS**) encapsulates and isolates JavaScript within our components to prevent them from accessing platform or package code. We will also take some time to discuss **Lightning Locker**, which is the previous security architecture. Because all new orgs come equipped with **Lightning Web Security**, we will touch on the key differences between **Lightning Locker** and **Lightning Web Security**, as well as how to prepare to upgrade a pre-**Winter '23** org to **LWS**.

We are going to be covering the following main recipes:

- Lightning security architecture basics
- Composing modal events with Lightning Locker
- Enforcing Lightning Web Security with ESLint
- Preparing to upgrade from Lightning Locker to Lightning Web Security

Technical requirements

The recipes for this book can be found at `https://github.com/PacktPublishing/Salesforce-Lightning-Web-Component-Cookbook`, where each chapter has its own folder under the **force-**

app folder. This GitHub repository is structured in the form of a Salesforce DX Project, which will allow you to easily fork the repository for deployment in a free Salesforce Developer Edition org. The code for *Chapter 7, Building Secure Components with Lightning Locker and Lightning Web Security*, is located at `https://github.com/PacktPublishing/Salesforce-Lightning-Web-Component-Cookbook/tree/main/force-app/chapter07`.

The components in this book require the use of an **Integrated Development Environment** (**IDE**), such as **Visual Studio Code** (**VSCode**) or **Salesforce Code Builder**. Detailed instructions for setting up an IDE are located in *Chapter 1, Getting Ready for Lightning Web Component Development*, in the *Setting up your IDE* section.

If you are building the projects in this cookbook as written, you will need to seed your Salesforce Developer Edition org with test data. Detailed instructions for seeding your org are located in *Chapter 1, Getting Ready for Lightning Web Component Development*, in the *Setting up the Salesforce Lightning Web Components Cookbook org* section.

Lastly, the edition of Salesforce required to implement the recipes in this book must be Developer, Performance, Unlimited, Enterprise, or Database.com. You can sign up for a free Salesforce Developer Edition org at `https://developer.salesforce.com/signup`.

Lightning security architecture basics

Think about your Salesforce org and the components within it. If you are in a large to mid-size org, there may be components built by multiple companies on the same page within your Salesforce org. These components may be comprised of native Salesforce functionality, third-party AppExchange components, open-source components, and homegrown solutions. These components must communicate with each other securely, without **passing along sensitive** information such as personally identifiable information (**PII**) that can be found on a record or within an end user's browser.

Enter **Lightning Locker**. **Lightning Locker** is a security architecture that isolates components from each other through **DOM access containment**. What this means, simply put, is that a given Lightning Web Component cannot reach into another LWC. This is also achieved using **secure wrappers** around global objects, such as **SecureWindow**, which intercepts calls to the **window** object. **Lightning Locker** is enabled for all Lightning components, meaning Aura and Lightning Web Components, that are built using API version 39.0 or later. To turn off **Lightning Locker**, the API version can be dropped to 38.0 or earlier.

In Spring '22, **Lightning Web Security** was introduced. **Lightning Web Security**, or **LWS**, is the most recent security architecture within Salesforce, and it is enforced as the default architecture for all orgs created after **Winter '23**. **LWS** is a client-side security architecture that enforces the use of **namespaces**. Simply put, to communicate with a component from another namespace, a homegrown component must **extend** or **compose** it. We will see what this looks like later in the chapter.

We will illustrate the difference between the two security architectures by building a **lightning-modal** component and passing an event within this component. Using the **LightningModal base component**, introduced in the Winter '23 release, capturing events composed by the modal is only possible with Lightning Web Security activated. Before we consume these events in **Lightning Web Security**, however, we will make a **Lightning Locker** compatible component. We will do this by placing the element that composes the `dispatchEvent` function in its own component and nesting that LWC within our **lightning-modal**.

Let's start by learning how to identify whether **LWS** is enabled in an org.

Getting started

To tell if you have Lightning Web Security enabled, navigate to *Setup > Session Settings*, where you can see if the **LWS Use Lightning Web Security for Lightning web components and Aura components** checkbox is checked.

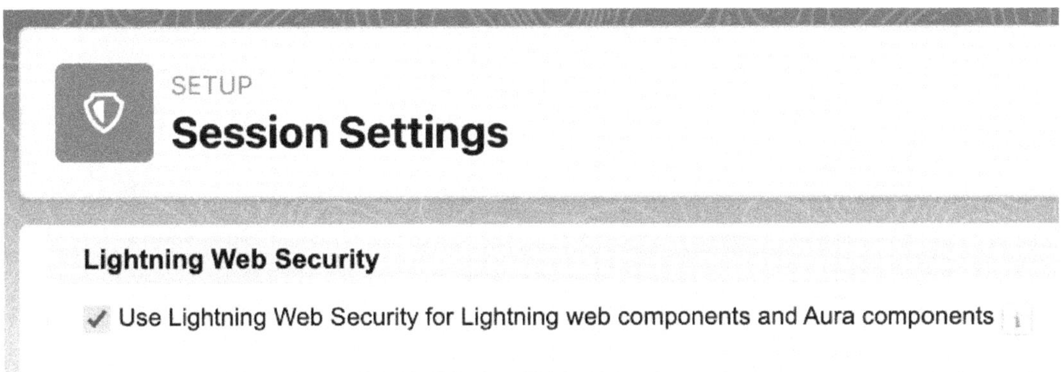

Figure 7.1: A screenshot of the Lightning Web Security checkbox in the Session Settings section of the Setup menu

We are going to uncheck this box, save our settings, and get ready to build a backwards-compatible component that will allow us to submit change requests. This component will look something like the following:

Figure 7.2: A screenshot of the New Change Request modal, which contains information pertaining to a sun-damaged painting

How to do it...

Returning to the business use case we have seen in previous chapters, imagine we are Salesforce developers at an art broker. In the unfortunate event that one of our artworks is damaged, we want to be able to use Salesforce's native **Service Cloud** capabilities to put in a **Change Request** to get it repaired or restored. In our ideal scenario, an end user would be able to navigate to an **Asset**'s record page and click a button to launch a **lightning-modal** that allows them to track information relating to the **Change Request**. Upon successful completion of the `lightning-record-form` inside the **lightning-modal**, we want to relate the **Asset** record to the created

Change Request record via a **Change Request Related Item** record and then navigate to the new **Change Request**'s record page.

1. Start by creating a new LWC called `changeRequestForm`. This form will build the body of our **lightning-modal**. Start by opening the `changeRequestForm.html` file and adding a **lightning-record-form** element between the default `template` tags:

```
<template>
    <lightning-record-form
        object-api-name={changeRequestApiName}
        fields={fields}
        onsuccess={handleSuccess}
    >
    </lightning-record-form>
</template>
```

2. We are using the **lightning-record-form** because it allows us to insert a record without the use of Apex for the given sObject via **Lightning Data Service**. When the save is successful, we will use the `handleSuccess` function to create one more record without Apex, which we will see in our JavaScript.
3. Open the `changeRequestForm.js` file and begin by importing our `api` decorator so that we can access the `recordId` that is passed in by our host LWC, which we will build momentarily:

```
import { LightningElement, api } from 'lwc';
export default class ChangeRequestForm extends LightningElement {
    @api recordId;
}
```

4. Once we have imported our decorator and declared our `recordId` variable, we will need to import the **Change Request** sObject and some of its fields into our JavaScript file. To import an sObject, we use the following format:

```
import SOBJECT_API_NAME from '@salesforce/schema/SOBJECT_API_NAME'
```

5. To import a field from that sObject, we use:

```
import FIELD_NAME from '@salesforce/schema/SOBJECT_API_NAME.FIELD_NAME'
```

6. So, for example, to import the **Change Request** sObject and its standard field **Business Justification**, we would use:

```
import CHANGE_REQUEST from '@salesforce/schema/ChangeRequest'
import BUSINESS_JUSTIFICATION from '@salesforce/schema/
ChangeRequest.BusinessJustification';
```

7. Import the **Change Request** sObject paired with the necessary field imports:
   - ChangeRequest sObject
   - BusinessJustification field
   - BusinessReason field
   - Category field
   - Description field
   - Subject field
   - RiskLevel field
   - Priority field
8. Import the **Change Request Related Item** sObject paired with the necessary field imports:
   - ChangeRequestRelatedItem sObject
   - ChangeRequestId (field)
   - AssetId (field)
   - Comment (field)
9. Next, add a class variable `changeRequestApiName` and set it equal to your imported **Change Request** variable:

```
changeRequestApiName = CHANGE_REQUEST;
```

10. Add one more class variable, an array called `fields`, that will carry your field imports for the **Change Request** sObject, ensuring that your variable names match the names you gave your field imports:

```
fields = [
    SUBJECT,
    CATEGORY,
    BUSINESS_REASON,
    BUSINESS_JUSTIFICATION,
```

```
    DESCRIPTION,
    RISK_LEVEL,
    PRIORITY
];
```

11. We need one more import before we can begin our `handleSuccess` function. Return to the top of your file and add the **createRecord** function, which is a function of the **uiRecordApi**:

```
import { createRecord } from 'lightning/uiRecordApi';
```

12. This function will allow us to create a record with specified inputs without Apex. Neat!
13. Now that we have all our imports, we can create the `handleSuccess` function outlined in our HTML file. This function is necessary to complete the action on our **lightning-record-form** and handle the creation of the **Change Request Related Item** record that will act as a junction object between the **Asset** and the **Change Request**. This function will be `asynchronous` and accept a parameter of an `event`:

```
async handleSuccess(event) { ... }
```

14. Looking at the documentation for the `createRecord` function, linked in the *See also* section of this recipe, we know that we need to pass in a `String` of `apiName` and a JavaScript object called `fields`. Within our `handleSuccess` function, instantiate a constant of an empty JavaScript object, `fields`:

```
const fields = {};
fields[CHANGE_REQUEST_ID.fieldApiName] = event.detail.id;
fields[ASSET_ID.fieldApiName] = this.recordId;
fields[COMMENT.fieldApiName] = event.detail.fields.BUSINESS_JUSTIFICATION;
```

15. Line by line, we are:
16. Adding a property for the **Change Request Id** field and setting it equal to the `id` of the **Change Request** we created in our **lightning-record-form**, which is passed in as part of the `onsuccess` event
17. Adding a property for the **Asset Id** field and setting it equal to our public `recordId` variable, which accepts the `recordId` from the record page that kicks off the **lightning-modal**

18. Adding a property for the **Comment** field and setting it equal to the value passed into our **Change Request** for the **Business Justification** field

> **Note**
>
> Notice that we have two variables called `fields` in our class, one as a **class variable** and one as a **function variable**. This is possible due to the nature of **variable scoping** in JavaScript. JavaScript has four main types of scope: **global**, **module**, **function**, and **block**. **Global variables** can be accessed anywhere within the code, and in our case, the **global variables** in Lightning Web Components are variables that are provided by Salesforce, such as `Aura` and `Sfdc`, both of which are blocked by **Lightning Locker** to prevent cross-framework dependencies. **Module variables**, or what I have been referring to in this book as **class variables**, are variables that are accessible in the module (in the case of Lightning Web Components, the class) that they are defined in. We access these variables within functions using `this`. **Function variables** are variables that are defined for use within a function using `let` or `const`, while **block variables** are defined in a block of code between curly braces, such as the code defined within the parameters of an iterable method like `.map({...})`. It is generally not recommended to use the same names for local variables and class properties, as this can understandably get quite confusing!

19. Now that we have the parameters for the `createRecord` function, we can build our `recordInput` and use it as a parameter in the `createRecord` function:

```
const recordInput = { apiName: CHANGE_REQUEST_ITEM.objectApiName, fields };
await createRecord(recordInput)
```

20. To round out this component, we will finish our `handleSuccess` function by adding an event that will bubble up to the parent component of the `changeRequestForm` LWC, which we will be building in the next recipe:

```
const successEvent = new CustomEvent('savesuccess', {
    bubbles: false,
    composed: false,
    detail: event.detail.id
```

```
});
this.dispatchEvent(successEvent);
```

21. Remember what we learned in *Chapter 6, Composing Lightning Web Components*: we do not need to specify `false` for `bubbles` and `composed`, as this is the default state for an LWC event, but we are doing so here for clarity.

How it works...

In our base component, we are using the **Lightning Data Service** to manipulate and add our **Change Request** record. The **Lightning Data Service** has built-in security features, such as maintaining **field-level security** across objects. This is an example of a Salesforce-provided component that can communicate with other components through composition of events, which we will see in the next recipe when we extend the **LightningModal** class.

See also

- The sample files for *Chapter 7, Building Secure Components with Lightning Locker and Lightning Web Security*, are available at `https://github.com/PacktPublishing/Salesforce-Lightning-Web-Component-Cookbook/tree/main/force-app/chapter07/default/lwc/changeRequestForm`.
- The Salesforce documentation for **Lightning Locker** is available at`https://developer.sale/sforce.com/docs/platform/lightning-components-security/guide/locker-intro.html`.
- The Salesforce documentation for **Lightning Web Security** is available at `https://developer.salesforce.com/docs/platform/lightning-components-security/guide/lws-intro.html`
- Salesforce provides a list of **LWS** FAQs at `https://help.salesforce.com/s/articleView?id=000392327&type=1`
- The Salesforce documentation for the **lightning-record-form** component can be viewed at `https://developer.salesforce.com/docs/component-library/bundle/lightning-record-form/documentation`
- The Salesforce documentation for the `createRecord` function is located at `https://developer.salesforce.com/docs/platform/lwc/guide/reference-create-record.html`

- More information about **Lightning Data Service** is available at `https://developer.salesforce.com/docs/platform/lwc/guide/data-ui-api.html`
- The MDN Developer Docs documentation on variable scoping in JavaScript is available at `https://developer.mozilla.org/en-US/docs/Glossary/Scope`

Composing modal events with Lightning Locker

Now that we know a little bit about how **Lightning Locker** and **Lightning Web Security** work to keep our data safe, how do we create a modal component with an event that is compatible with **Lightning Locker**?

How to do it...

1. We knew that we needed to wrap our element making the `dispatchEvent` call in its own component, which we accomplished in the last recipe. So how do we consume the events from the `changeRequestForm` component?
2. Create a new LWC, `changeRequestModal`. This LWC will house our `changeRequestForm` within a **lightning-modal.** Open the `changeRequestModal.html` file and add the following between the default template tags:

```
<template>
    <lightning-modal-header label="New Change Request"></lightning-modal-
header>
    <lightning-modal-body>
        <c-change-request-form record-id={content.recordId}
onsavesuccess={closeModal}></c-change-request-form>
    </lightning-modal-body>
</template>
```

3. The **lightning-modal-header** tag defines the header of our modal, while the **lightning-modal-body** tag houses our `changeRequestForm` LWC.
4. Next, enter the `changeRequestModal.js` file. This JavaScript file will look a little bit different than our standard LWC `.js` file. Instead of importing and extending the default `LightningElement`, we will be importing and extending the **LightningModal class**:

```
import { api } from 'lwc';
import LightningModal from 'lightning/modal';
export default class ChangeRequestModal extends LightningModal {
    @api content;
```

```
    closeModal(event) {
        this.close({navId : event.detail})
    }
}
```

5. All this JavaScript class does is accept an `api`-decorated variable of `content`, which we pass into our `changeRequestForm`. When our form saves successfully, denoted by the `savesuccess` event that is emitted by the form, we close the modal. Simple, right? The bulk of the code for our modal will be in our launcher component, which we will build next.
6. Create an LWC called `changeRequestLauncher`. This LWC will be the starting point for our modal flow, which will allow us to call the modal from a **Quick Action Button**. We will leave the HTML file in its default state.
7. Open the `changeRequestLauncher.js-meta.xml` file and modify it to the following:

```
<?xml version="1.0" encoding="UTF-8"?>
<LightningComponentBundle xmlns="http://soap.sforce.com/2006/04/metadata">
    <apiVersion>65.0</apiVersion>
    <isExposed>true</isExposed>
    <targets>
        <target>lightning__RecordAction</target>
    </targets>
    <targetConfigs>
        <targetConfig targets="lightning__RecordAction">
            <actionType>Action</actionType>
        </targetConfig>
    </targetConfigs>
</LightningComponentBundle>
```

8. We are exposing our LWC to be used in a **lightning__RecordAction**, and setting the LWC **actionType** to `Action`, which allows us to run custom code at the click of a button. We can also set an **actionType** of `ScreenAction`, which will open a modal by default. Because we want to build our modal from scratch to control exactly how it behaves, we will use the **actionType** of `Action`.

9. Open the `changeRequestLauncher.js` file, add the `api` decorator import, and add the public variable `recordId`, which will allow us to grab the `recordId` of the record page that launches the launcher:

```
import { LightningElement, api } from 'lwc';
export default class ChangeRequestLauncher extends LightningElement {
    @api recordId;
}
```

10. Additionally, we are going to import our `changeRequestModal` before our class definition:

```
import changeRequestModal from 'c/changeRequestModal';
```

11. Next, add an `api`-decorated function called `invoke`. This function will take no parameters. The `invoke` function is a Salesforce-provided function that kicks off our modal when paired with a **lightning__RecordAction**:

```
@api invoke() {
    changeRequestModal.open({
        size: 'large',
        description: 'A modal to insert a new Change Request for the specified
Asset.',
        content: {recordId : this.recordId}
    }).then((result) => {
        if(result) {
            this.handleSaveSuccess(result.navId);
        }
    })
}
```

12. The open function allows us to specify attributes for our modal, such as the `size`, a `description` for accessibility purposes, and the `content` that we are passing into the modal. As you'll notice in our `changeRequestModal.html` file, we are using `content.recordId` to access the `recordId` of the record page that kicked off the action, as the `recordId` is defined as a property of a JavaScript object and is thus accessible through **dot notation**.

13. Finally, recall that we want to navigate to the **Change Request** record that we created so that our end user can fill out any additional information. Add one more import to the top of your file: `NavigationMixin`. Recall that this changes our class signature:

```
import { NavigationMixin } from 'lightning/navigation';
export default class ChangeRequestLauncher extends
NavigationMixin(LightningElement) { ... }
```

14. Next, add the `handleSaveSuccess` function, called in our `invoke` function upon successful save of the `lightning-record-form`:

```
handleSaveSuccess(id) {
   this[NavigationMixin.Navigate]({
   type: 'standard__recordPage',
   attributes: {
      recordId: id,
      objectApiName: 'ChangeRequest',
      actionName: 'view'
   }
});
```

15. We are pulling the `navId` from the modal close event that was emitted by our `lightning-modal` component and using it to navigate to our desired location.

16. Now that we have completed our LWC, we can deploy it and add it to a button on the **Asset** object. Navigate to *Setup > Object Manager > Asset > Buttons, Links, and Actions*, and create a new **Action** with our `changeRequestLauncher` LWC:

Figure 7.3: A screenshot of the Change Request action button settings

17. If you do not see the option to add your `changeRequestLauncher`, make sure your `.js-meta.xml` file is configured appropriately for a **lightning__RecordAction**.
18. Once you have created this action, you can add it to the page layout for the **Asset** object.
19. Once you have added your button to the page layout, you can test it and see that not only is a **Change Request** record created, but the **Change Request** created is also associated with the appropriate **Asset** in the **Related Records** view.

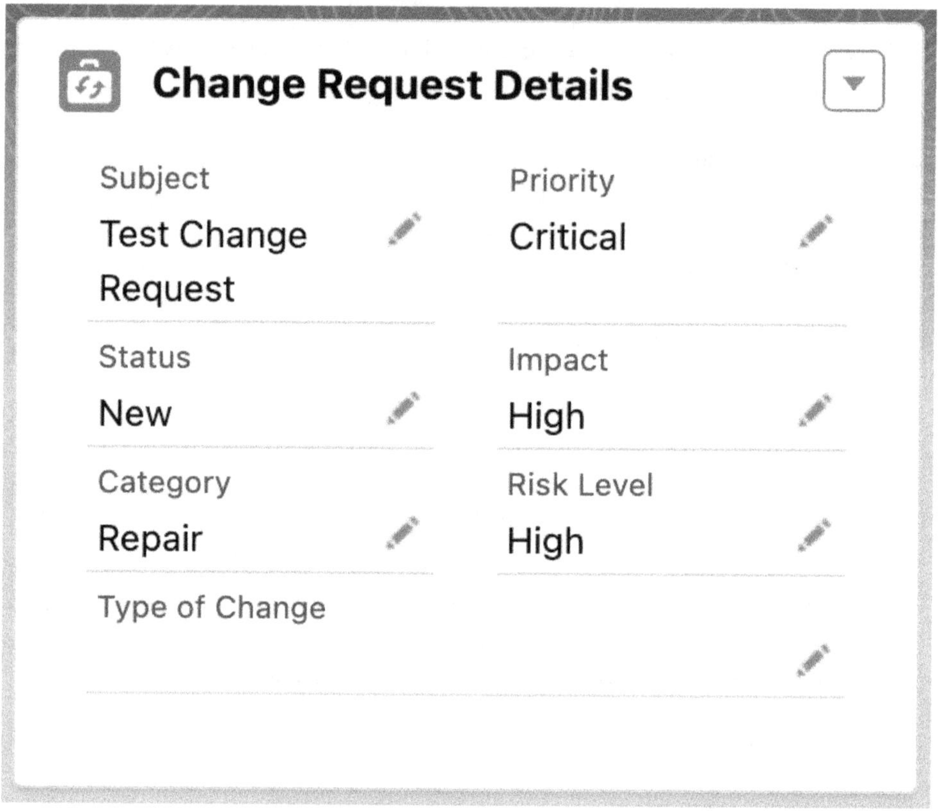

Figure 7.4: A screenshot of a test Change Request

20. To see the junction object relationship between the **Change Request** and **Asset** records, you will need to view the **Related** tab on the **Change Request** record page and scroll to **Related Assets**.

How it works...

Lightning Locker restricts access to certain DOM elements and JavaScript objects. This prevents event propagation outside of the modal. Therefore, we must wrap our event in its own component, `changeRequestForm`, to pass the event outside the modal.

See also

- The Salesforce documentation for the **lightning-modal** component is located at `https://developer.salesforce.com/docs/component-library/bundle/lightning-modal/documentation`.
- A Salesforce Developers Blog article titled A Deep Dive into the **LightningModal** Base Component is located at `https://developer.salesforce.com/blogs/2022/12/a-deep-dive-into-the-lightningmodal-base-component`.
- The V1 SLDS documentation for modals is available at `https://v1.lightningdesignsystem.com/components/modals`
- The V2 SLDS documentation for modals is available at `https://www.lightningdesignsystem.com/2e1ef8501/p/01c12a-modals`.

Enforcing Lightning web security with ESLint

In the event that you encounter a Salesforce org that predates 2023, which you likely will at some point in your career, there are several steps you should take to upgrade from **Lightning Locker** to **Lightning Web Security**. It is important to note that while most Aura and Lightning Web Components will successfully be upgraded to **LWS** from **Lightning Locker**, components must be tested to ensure compatibility. We will do this with **ESLint**, as well as a lot of manual testing.

How to do it...

If you don't already have **ESLint** installed and configured for your VSCode, there are detailed instructions on how to do so in *Chapter 1, Getting Ready for Lightning Web Component Development*, in the *Linting for Salesforce* recipe. Once these steps have been completed, we can install the rules needed to check for **API distortions** caused by **Lightning Web Security**.

1. Open a terminal in your *SALESFORCE-LIGHTNING-WEB-COMPONENT-COOKBOOK* directory in VSCode.
2. Use the following command to install the proper version of **ESLint**:

```
npm install --save-dev eslint @locker/eslint-config-locker --force
```

3. Note that we use the `--force` modifier to ensure that our previous versions are overwritten, so that we don't have broken dependencies.
4. Next, run the command:

```
npm run lint
```

5. This will run our linting rules. Note that we should not have errors, as so far, everything in our org has been compatible with **Lightning Web Security**. If there are issues that appear, you can use the following command to fix them:

```
npm audit fix
```

6. Running this command will automatically fix any simple errors found in your JavaScript
7. If there are any more complex errors, or if you are running **ESLint** for LWS on a pre-**LWS** production org, you will be able to test any errors using the **Lightning Web Security Console** and **API Distortion Viewer**, linked in the See also section for this recipe.

See also

- The guide for using **ESLint** with **Lightning Web Security** is located at: `https://developer.salesforce.com/docs/platform/lightning-components-security/guide/lws-tools-lint.html`.
- The step-by-step instructions for running the **ESLint** base rules against your org can be found at: `https://developer.salesforce.com/docs/platform/lightning-components-security/guide/lws-tools-lint.html#run-base-rules-against-your-project`.
- The **LWS Console** documentation and tool can be found at: `https://developer.salesforce.com/docs/component-library/tools/lws-console`.
- The rules for the **LWS ESLint** configuration are on GitHub at: `https://github.com/salesforce/lwsec-docs-mirror/tree/main/packages/%40locker/eslint-plugin-locker`.
- The LWS Distortion Viewer is located at: `https://developer.salesforce.com/docs/platform/lightning-components-security/guide/lws-tools-distortion-viewer.html`.

Preparing to upgrade from Lightning Locker to Lightning Web Security

Having checked to make sure our components are compatible with **Lightning Locker** and **Lightning Web Security**, we can turn our LWS back on. Return to *Setup > Session Settings*, where you can recheck the **LWS Use Lightning Web Security for Lightning web components and Aura components** checkbox. Try hard refreshing our **Asset** record page and verify that the **Change Request** button we implemented earlier in the chapter still works. If our component is compatible with **Lightning Locker** and **Lightning Web Security**, why would we want to upgrade? Well, we can actually reduce the number of child components in our parent modal by utilizing the eventing capabilities that **Lightning Web Security** grants us. Let's take a look.

How to do it...

The changes that we are going to make will be to flatten the `changeRequestModal` and `changeRequestForm` components into a single component called `changeRequestModalLws`.

1. Start by creating a new LWC called `changeRequestModalLws` and open the HTML file.
2. This file will be similar to the `changeRequestModal.html` file, but instead of using the `c-change-request-form` component in the `lightning-modal-body`, we are going to put our `lightning-record-form` directly into the component:

```
<template>
   <lightning-modal-header label="New Change Request">
   </lightning-modal-header>
   <lightning-modal-body>
      <lightning-record-form
         object-api-name={changeRequestApiName}
         fields={fields}
         onsuccess={handleSuccess}
      >
      </lightning-record-form>
   </lightning-modal-body>
</template>
```

3. Next, copy the code from your `changeRequestForm.js` file into the `changeRequestModalLws.js` file. We will make some slight tweaks, but this is a good starting point. To wrap our heads around what we are going to do, we are essentially going to take the `changeRequestForm.js` file and combine it with the `changeRequestModal.js` file to produce the `changeRequestModalLws.js` file.
4. Open your changeRequestModalLws.js file, which should have the previous file copied into it. Look at the imports. Because we are only going to have one flattened component, we need to extend the `LightningModal` class here. Add the `LightningModal` import statement to the top of your file, and extend it in your class definition:

```
import { api } from 'lwc';
import LightningModal from 'lightning/modal';
import { createRecord } from 'lightning/uiRecordApi';
```

```
...
export default class ChangeRequestModal extends LightningModal { ... }
```

5. Once you have your class definition changed, update the `@api recordId` class variable to `@api content`. This variable will represent the **content** passed in by our modal launcher, which we will define to carry our `recordId` later in the recipe, as opposed to carrying the `recordId` directly.
6. Next, let's look at the `handleSuccess` function. Instead of dispatching the event from `changeRequestForm` to our wrapper component, `changeRequestModal`, we are going to handle the entire event within `changeRequestModalLws`. Note the following highlighted changes, and make them in your copied code:

```
async handleSuccess(event) {
    const fields = {};
    fields[CHANGE_REQUEST_ID.fieldApiName] = event.detail.id;
    fields[ASSET_ID.fieldApiName] = this.content.recordId;
    fields[COMMENT.fieldApiName] =
event.detail.fields.BUSINESS_JUSTIFICATION;
    const recordInput = { apiName: CHANGE_REQUEST_ITEM.objectApiName,
fields };
    await createRecord(recordInput);
    const recordCreatedEvent = new CustomEvent("recordcreated", {
      detail: event.detail.id
    });
    this.dispatchEvent(recordCreatedEvent);
    this.close();
}
```

7. We notice that instead of accessing the `recordId` directly, we are accessing it via dot notation from the `content` class variable that we will pass in from our parent component.
8. We also have a slightly different event – we have renamed `savesuccess` to `recordcreated` for clarity, and we have removed the properties of `bubbles` and `composed` from our event definition because they default to `false`.
9. Finally, we use `this.close()` to close the modal in our `changeRequestModalLws.js` file.
10. Now that we have fixed up our `changeRequestModalLws` component, we can modify our `changeRequestLauncher` files to accommodate our LWS-ready component.

11. Navigate to your `changeRequestLauncher.js` file and refresh yourself on its contents. Rather than create a new request launcher file, we are going to edit the existing `invoke` function to fit our needs. We are going to use a **custom permissions** check to do so for easy testing. This way, we don't need to create a new button and action, and in a production org, we can test incrementally by rolling out to a certain number of users by use of a **feature flag** tool or a **custom permission** and **permission set** framework. We are going to use the latter, allowing us to manually assign a permission set to users for testing.
12. Open up your Salesforce developer org and navigate to *Setup > Custom Permissions*. Create a new **Custom Permission** called LWS Enabler. In a real production org, we would abide by our feature flagging and **Custom Permissions** naming conventions, but for now, we'll keep it simple. Leave all other defaults empty.

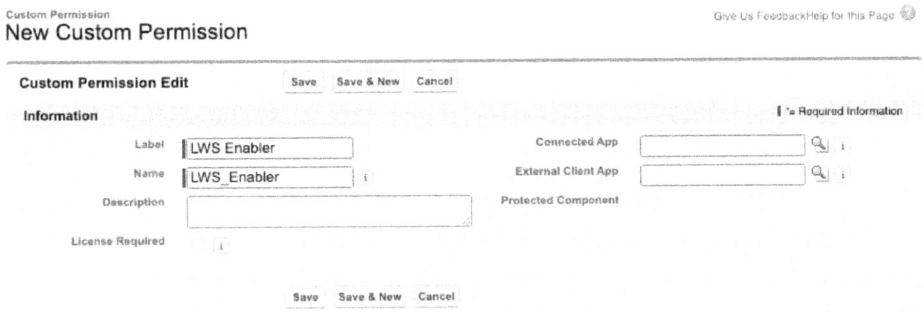

Figure 7.5: A screenshot of the Setup menu for creating a new Custom Permission

13. Once you have created the **Custom Permission**, create a new **Permission Set** by navigating to *Setup > Permission Sets*. Select **New** and name your **Permission Set** `Custom Permission: LWS Enabler`. Add the `LWS Enabler` **Custom Permission** to your **Permission Set** in the **Apps** menu of the **Permission Set** screen.
14. Go ahead and assign this **Permission Set** to yourself. We'll be adding a toggle to our LWC based on this permission. Navigate to your `changeRequestLauncher.js` file and update your imports to add this toggle:

```
import { LightningElement, api } from 'lwc';
import lwsEnabled from "@salesforce/customPermission/LWS_Enabler";
import changeRequestModal from 'c/changeRequestModal';
import changeRequestModalLws from 'c/changeRequestModalLws';
import { NavigationMixin } from 'lightning/navigation';
```

15. Go ahead and add an `if:else` block to the `@api invoke` function, with the `else` block around the existing code:

```
@api invoke() {
    if(lwsEnabled) { ... } else {
        console.log('Lightning Locker Compatible');
        changeRequestModal.open({
            size: 'large',
            description: 'A modal to insert a new Change Request for the
specified Asset.',
            content: {recordId : this.recordId}
        }).then((result) => {
            if(result) {
                this.handleSaveSuccess(result.navId);
            }
        })
    }
}
```

16. Note that we have also added a `console.log()` statement, which we wouldn't do in a production environment but will be helpful for us in testing this functionality.
17. Within the `if` block, add the following:

```
console.log('LWS Permission Set Assigned');
const result = changeRequestModalLws.open({
    size: 'large',
    description: 'An LWS only modal to insert a new Change Request for the
specified Asset.',
    content: {recordId : this.recordId},
    onrecordcreated: (event) => {
        event.stopPropagation();
        this.handleSaveSuccess(event.detail);
    }
})
```

18. This looks remarkably similar to the code in our `else` block, with a few key differences. The names of our events that we are capturing are different, for one, but we also handle the `onrecordcreated` and `onsuccess` events differently. This is due to the requirements of **Lightning Web Security**. Note that we can handle the `onrecordcreated` event

directly in the JavaScript, while the `onSuccess` event is bubbled from our `changeRequestForm` to our `changeRequestModal`, where we use `this.close()` to pass our event's `detail` property to the final step in `changeRequestLauncher` as the result of the promise returned by `this.open()`.

19. Like before, our `changeRequestLauncher.html` file will remain with two empty template tags.
20. Now we can test! Deploy your changes and do a hard refresh of the Asset record page.

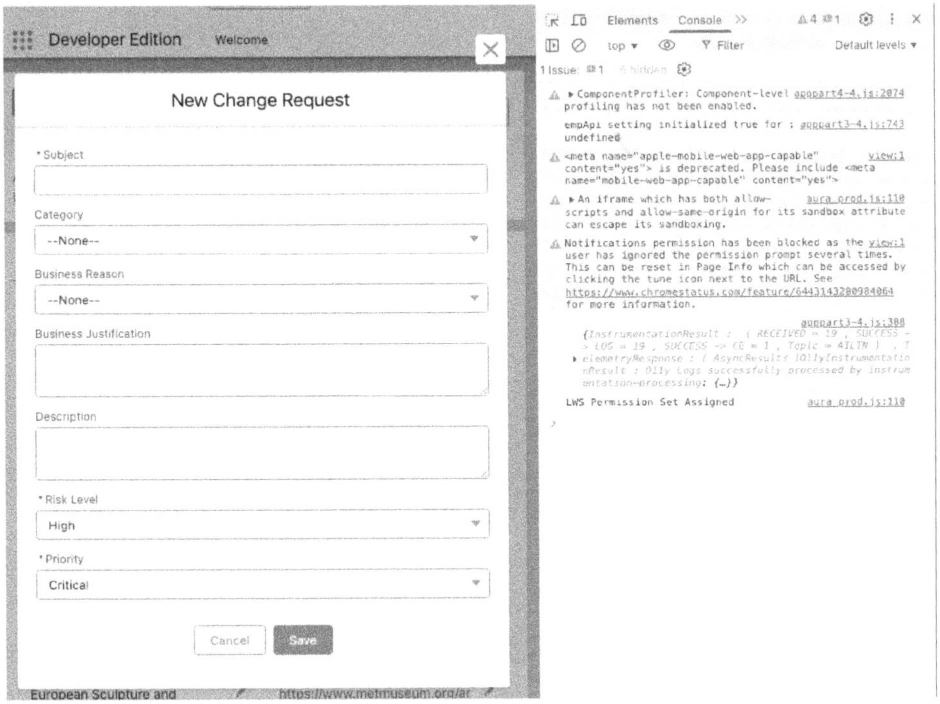

Figure 7.6: A screenshot of the New Change Request modal with the Developer Console showing the "LWS Permission Set Assigned" console log statement

21. If we have **LWS** turned on and the `Custom Permission: LWS Enabler` permission set assigned, we should see our console log telling us that we are in the appropriate chunk of code, and we will be able to go through the process as normal.
22. Once we have tested this, return to Setup and disable Lightning Web Security by unchecking the box at *Setup > Session Settings > LWS Use Lightning Web Security for Lightning web components and Aura components*. Keep the **Permission Set** assigned to yourself and keep the **developer console** open. Do a hard refresh on the **Asset** page and try running the process again.

23. Oh no! We get an error! Well, not really, oh no, this is expected! We see that there is an error of `Uncaught (in promise) TypeError: Failed to execute 'dispatchEvent' on 'EventTarget': parameter 1 is not of type 'Event'`. This is because we are trying to use a feature of **Lightning Web Security** without having it enabled.

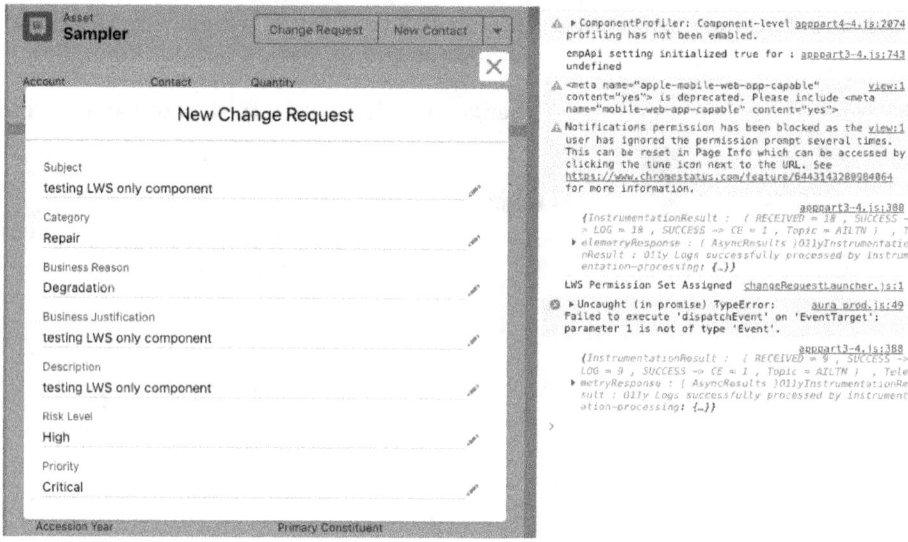

Figure 7.7: A screenshot of the New Change Request modal with the Developer Console showing the "LWS Permission Set Assigned" console log statement and a TypeError resulting from attempting to use a feature of LWS without having it enabled.

24. Now that we have proven that our changes are only compatible with **Lightning Web Security**, let's remove the `Custom Permission: LWS Enabler` **Permission Set** from ourselves and try one last time. Don't forget to hard refresh your page after removing the **Permission Set**!

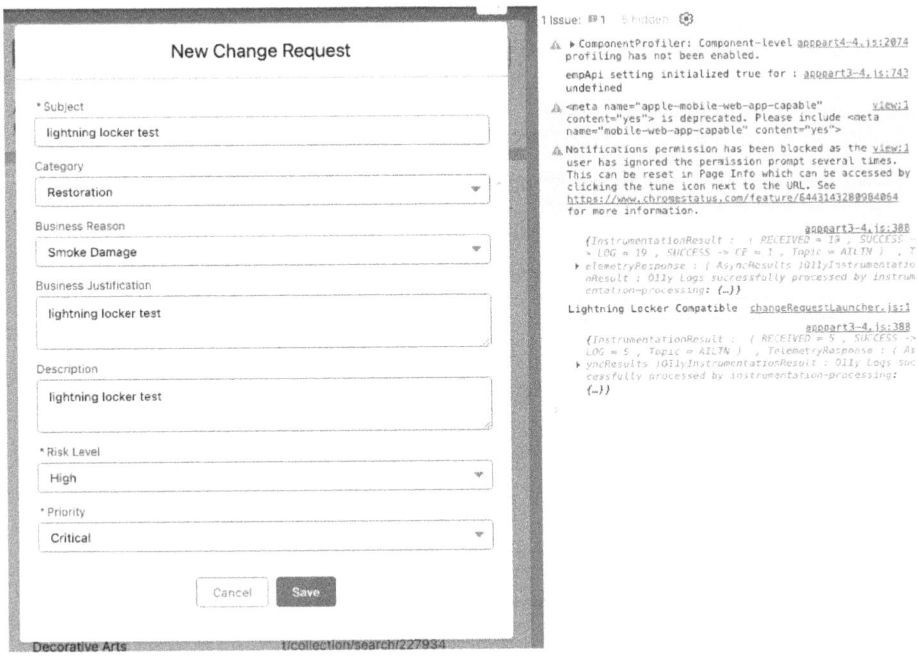

Figure 7.8: A screenshot of the New Change Request modal with the Developer Console showing the "Lightning Locker Compatible" console log statement.

How it works...

The reason that we are able to dispatch an event from the modal container in this example is that Lightning Web Security permits cross-namespace communication and event propagation. In the previous example, we found that the strict DOM encapsulation provided by Lightning Locker breaks this functionality. In order to secure the DOM in Lightning Locker, Locker enforces event retargeting, which necessitates the use of a wrapper component.

Now that we've learned how Lightning Locker and Lightning Web Security differ, we can venture into making our components accessible.

See also

- A comparison of the features of Lightning Locker and Lightning Web Security is located at: `https://developer.salesforce.com/docs/platform/lightning-components-security/guide/get-started-compare-lws-locker.html`.
- Documentation on enabling LWS in scratch orgs for testing is available at: `https://developer.salesforce.com/docs/platform/lightning-components-security/guide/lws-enable-scratch-orgs.html`.

- An example workflow for upgrading to LWS is available here: `https://developer.salesforce.com/docs/platform/lightning-components-security/guide/lws-test-workflow.html`.
- The guide on refactoring for LWS is available at: `https://developer.salesforce.com/docs/platform/lightning-components-security/guide/lws-refactor.html`.
- The documentation for Permissions within LWCs can be found: `https://developer.salesforce.com/docs/platform/lwc/guide/create-get-permissions.html`.

Part 3

Building Custom Lightning Web Components

What happens when the functionality requested goes beyond the scope of available components? Custom components can be built and reused throughout your Salesforce org. We will spend the first three chapters of this part building variations on a theme, exploring more advanced topics as we progress, ranging from CSS media queries and reactivity in components to extending base components with custom functionality, to building wholesale custom components from SLDS building blocks. Once we have built our custom components, we will learn about the whys and hows of accessibility in Salesforce by testing a custom component against an SLDS component.

This part has the following chapters:

8

Implementing Reactivity in Lightning Web Components

With *Chapter 7, Building Secure Components with Lightning Locker and Lightning Web Security,* behind us, we now know the basics of Salesforce security architectures, as well as how to utilize **Lightning Web Security** (**LWS**) to communicate between a modal and its host component. Now that we are very familiar with JavaScript events, we will be utilizing a new-to-us type of event to make a Lightning Web Components DOM reactive. Before we get there, we will be learning several ways to prepare a component for display on multiple device **form factors**, such as a desktop, tablet, or smartphone. Whether you are working in a legacy code base or developing in **Salesforce Code Builder** on the newest release, these recipes will help you to minimize your lines of code while maximizing your LWC functionality.

We are going to be covering the following main recipes:

- Writing Apex for lazy loading
- Configuring LWCs for different form factors
- Enabling lazy loading via infinite scroll
- Building a DOM reactive LWC
- Working with media queries

Technical requirements

The recipes for this book can be found at `https://github.com/PacktPublishing/Salesforce-Lightning-Web-Component-Cookbook`, where each chapter has its own folder under the `force-app` folder. This GitHub repository is structured in the form of a Salesforce DX project, which will allow you to easily fork the repository for deployment in a free Salesforce Developer Edition org.

The code for this chapter is located at `https://github.com/PacktPublishing/Salesforce-Lightning-Web-Component-Cookbook/tree/main/force-app/chapter08`.

The components in this book require the use of an **Integrated Development Environment (IDE)**, such as **Visual Studio Code (VSCode)** or **Salesforce Code Builder**. Detailed instructions for setting up an IDE are located in *Chapter 1, Getting Ready for Lightning Web Components*, in the *Setting up your IDE* section.

If you are building the projects in this cookbook as written, you will need to seed your Salesforce Developer Edition org with test data. Detailed instructions for seeding your org are located in *Chapter 1, Getting Ready for Lightning Web Components*, in the *Setting up the Salesforce Lightning Web Components Cookbook org* section.

In order to test some of the elements in this chapter, you will need to download the **Salesforce mobile app** or use the **developer tools** available in your browser.

Lastly, the edition of Salesforce required to implement the recipes in this book must be Developer, Performance, Unlimited, Enterprise, or Database.com. You can sign up for a free Salesforce Developer Edition org at `https://developer.salesforce.com/signup`.

Writing Apex for lazy loading

So far in this book, we have been utilizing **selector classes**, **service classes**, and **controller classes** to select what data we want to manipulate, determine how we are servicing the data, and effectively control how it is seen on the frontend. This chapter will be no different, although we will be adding a new trick to our repertoire.

When an LWC loads, there may be dozens, hundreds, or even millions of records that load with it. This can take a fair bit of processing time, and, depending on the number of sObject records returned, can even hit Salesforce's **SOQL query governor limits** if not done carefully. Enter **lazy loading**, which allows us to load a small segment of our data at a time. This technique is usually employed with an action taken by the end user, such as scrolling to the bottom of a component or clicking onto the next page of paginated results. To start this chapter, we are going to begin by laying the foundation for lazy loading via **infinite scroll** in a **lightning-datatable**.

Getting started

If you are joining us in this chapter and are planning on completing the project as written, there is a small amount of setup that will need to be completed. Detailed instructions for seeding your org are located in *Chapter 1, Getting Ready for Lightning Web Components*, in the *Setting up the Salesforce Lightning Web Components Cookbook org* section, with abbreviated instructions to follow.

The code we will need to deploy from the forked repository to complete the recipes in this chapter is contained within the `force-app/chapter00`, `force-app/chapter03/default/classes`, and `force-app/chapter04` directories. The permissions needed to complete this project are contained within the `force-app/chapter00` directory and are assigned via Apex Anonymous, while the `Util_Query` class we will be using is contained within `force-app/chapter03/default/classes`, and the `c/notifUtils` component is located in `force-app/chapter04`. If you have already completed this setup, you will not need to complete it again.

If you have not completed this setup, start by deploying the `force-app/chapter00` directory, and issue the following **Anonymous Apex** snippet, which will grant you the permissions necessary to complete this project:

```
OrgSetupClass.getPerms();
```

This snippet grants **permission set** access to a **named credential** that is contained within the `force-app/chapter00` setup files.

Next, we will insert 10 of my favorite pieces of public domain art from **The Metropolitan Museum of Art's Open Access Collection** into your Developer Edition org as **assets** and associate them with a new top **account** that will be inserted, **Ultricies PC**. To do this, issue the following snippet:

```
OrgSetupClass.dataSetup();
```

Now that you have completed these steps, you should have at least 25 accounts, 25 contacts, and 25 customers, as well as 10 asset records associated with the **Ultricies PC** account in your Developer Edition org.

Next, deploy the code in `force-app/chapter03/default/classes`. Note that you must drill down into the `classes` directory, as the example files for the component built in *Chapter 3, Working with a Selector Class,* contain components from other chapters. Drilling down into the `classes` directory prevents the need to deploy all of the dependencies at this time.

Finally, deploy the code in the `force-app/chapter04` directory. This will allow us to use the `c/notifUtils` component that we built in *Chapter 4, Synchronous and Asynchronous Processing in Components.*

How to do it...

Once we have completed the necessary setup, either by having deployed the required dependencies or by having written them in previous chapters, we are ready to begin.

1. Like previous chapters, we will begin by defining a **selector class**, called `AssetSelector`. This class will be defined as `with sharing` and will extend our familiar `Util_Query`

utility class, thereby allowing us to use the methods contained within the `Util_Query` class:

```
public with sharing class AssetSelector extends Util_Query { ... }
```

2. Once we have our class definition, we will add a constant, denoted by a designation of `public static final String`, for a `assetsByAccount` variable. We will be grabbing some pertinent info about the asset records that are associated with a given account record:

```
public static final String assetsByAccount = 'SELECT Id, Name,
Department__c, Description, Is_Public_Domain__c, Object_Id__c, Asset_URL__c,
Primary_Image_Small__c FROM Asset WHERE AccountId = :accountId LIMIT :lim
OFFSET :offset';
```

3. Notice that there are three **bind variables**, which allow us to use defined local variables in our query: `accountId`, `lim`, and `offset`. These variables represent the ID of the account we are pulling asset records for, the **limit** we are imposing on how many asset records to pull at a given time, and the number of asset records to **offset** our query results by.

> **Note**
>
> Within Apex, `limit` is defined as a reserved word, meaning we cannot name a variable for it. As a result, we utilize a shortened version of the word to be clear in our meaning.

4. Now that we have our query string of `assetsByAccount` defined, let's use it in a method. Create a `public` method, `retrieveAssetsByAccount`, that returns a list of asset records. This method will accept three parameters, an `Id` called `accountId`, an `Integer` called `lim`, and an `Integer` called `offset`:

```
public List<Asset> retrieveAssetsByAccount(Id accountId, Integer lim,
Integer offset) { ... }
```

5. Having our `retrieveAssetsByAccount` method defined, we can define our **bind variables**. Recall that `Util_Query`, implemented in *Chapter 3, Working with a Selector Class*, has a method, `queryWithBinds`, that allows us to specify bind variables in a

dynamic SOQL query utilizing a `Map<String, Object>` parameter called `bindMap`. The bind variables that we want to include are `accountId`, `lim` for limit, and `offset`:

```
Map<String, Object> bindMap = new Map<String, Object>{
   'accountId' => accountId,
   'lim' => lim,
   'offset' => offset
};
```

6. Once we have our `bindMap` variable defined, we can return a list of `Asset` sObject records with our `queryWithBinds` method, which we access via the extended `Util_Query` class:

```
return (List<Asset>) queryWithBinds(assetsByAccount, bindMap,
AccessLevel.SYSTEM_MODE);
```

7. Additionally, within our `AssetSelector` class, we are going to want to include a method that utilizes an **aggregate SOQL query** to count the total number of asset records. We will use this when determining how many records to load. This will look like the following:

```
public Integer countAssets(Id accountId) {
   return [SELECT COUNT() FROM Asset WHERE AccountId = :accountId];
}
```

8. This concludes our `AssetSelector` class. Next, we will be writing our **service class**, titled `DisplayAssetsService`.
9. Create a new Apex class called `DisplayAssetsService`. This class will be `public with sharing`, contain a `@TestVisible private` class variable of type `AssetSelector` called `selector`, which will be defined as a `new AssetSelector()` instance, and contain two methods. The first method, `getAssetsByAccount`, will return a list of asset records and accept our familiar three parameters: `accountId`, `lim` for limit, and `offset`:

```
public List<Asset> getAssetsByAccount(Id accountId, Integer lim, Integer
offset){
   return selector.retrieveAssetsByAccount(accountId, lim, offset);
}
```

10. Within this method, we are calling the `retrieveAssetsByAccount` instance method of the `AssetSelector` class. We do this by using dot notation with the instance of the **selector class**, `selector`.
11. Our second method will be constructed similarly, and will return the `Integer` results of the `countAssets` instance method:

```
public Integer getAssetCount(Id accountId) {
    return selector.countAssets(accountId);
}
```

12. To round out our Apex classes for this chapter, we will lastly build the `DisplayAssetsController` class to interface with our LWC. Start by defining a `public with sharing class` called `DisplayAssetsController`.
13. At the top of your class definition, add a `@TestVisible private static` instance of the `DisplayAssetsService` class called `service`:

```
@TestVisible private static DisplayAssetsService service = new
DisplayAssetsService();
```

14. This will allow us to call the **non-static methods** of our `DisplayAssetsService` class in a **static context**, which we will explore in the next steps.
15. Next, we are going to add two `public static` methods, the first returning a list of asset records, and the second returning an integer. Recall that, because we are exposing these methods to our LWC and caching their results on the frontend, we must mark them as `@AuraEnabled(cacheable=true)`.
16. Let's look at the `returnAssetsByAccount` method first. This method will accept three parameters: `String accountIdString`, `Integer lim` for limit, and `Integer offset`. Within a **try-catch block**, we will first cast `accountIdString` as an `Id` to ensure that our frontend is indeed passing in an appropriate `Id` value, and then we will return the results of the `getAssetsByAccount` method of the `DisplayAssetsService` class:

```
@AuraEnabled(cacheable=true)
public static List<Asset> returnAssetsByAccount(String accountIdString,
Integer lim, Integer offset){
    try {
        Id accountId = Id.valueOf(accountIdString);
        return service.getAssetsByAccount(accountId, lim, offset);
```

```
    } catch (Exception e) {
        throw new AuraHandledException(e.getMessage());
    }
}
```

17. Note that we use the static instance of the `DisplayAssetsService` class, `service`, to call the non-static, or instance, method `getAssetsByAccount`.
18. Wrapping up the controller class, we will write a similar method, `returnAssetCount`, that receives a `String` parameter, `accountIdString`, and returns the result of the `getAssetCount` method of the `DisplayAssetsService` class:

```
@AuraEnabled(cacheable=true)
public static Integer returnAssetCount(String accountIdString) {
    try {
        Id accountId = Id.valueOf(accountIdString);
        return service.getAssetCount(accountId);
    } catch (Exception e) {
        throw new AuraHandledException(e.getMessage());
    }
}
```

19. Again, we use the static instance of the `DisplayAssetsService` class, `service`, to call the non-static, or instance, method `getAssetCount`.

> **Note**
>
> For conciseness and to give you practice in making changes to existing files, I have combined the methods of *Chapters 8*, *9*, and *10* into the sample Apex files for *Chapter 8*. If you are planning on deploying the Apex classes in the `force-app/chapter08/default/classes` directory, you will need to comment out the methods for *Chapter 9, Creating Custom Lightning Web Components*, and *Chapter 10, Designing Polymorphic Lightning Web Components*, which are notated in the sample files.

See also

- The sample files for the Apex classes contained in this chapter are located at `https://github.com/PacktPublishing/Salesforce-Lightning-Web-Component-Cookbook/tree/main/force-app/chapter08/default/classes`
- The Salesforce Developer Docs article on static and instance methods, variables, and initialization code can be found at `https://developer.salesforce.com/docs/atlas.en-us.apexcode.meta/apexcode/apex_classes_static.htm`
- The Salesforce Developer Docs article on how to dynamically pass bind variables to a SOQL query can be found at `https://help.salesforce.com/s/articleView?id=release-notes.rn_apex_bind_var_soql.htm&release=242&type=5`
- The GitHub directory for the Apex classes for this chapter is located at `https://github.com/PacktPublishing/Salesforce-Lightning-Web-Component-Cookbook/tree/main/force-app/chapter08/default/classes`

Configuring LWCs for different form factors

Having written the Apex for our component, we are ready to begin the frontend work. Recall that we are building a Salesforce org for a fictional art broker, where an account record represents a museum, and an asset record represents a work of art. It has been requested that there be a visual representation of assets associated with a given account on its record page – our end users want to be able to describe a requested work of art to a potential procurer without having to leave the **Account** page. This can be achieved using a `lightning-datatable` that shows our available asset records, as well as a `lightning-carousel-image` that will display the asset that our end users have selected. Additionally, when the end user clicks on the image, they should be taken to the information page for the asset on **The Metropolitan Museum of Art**'s website. It has been requested that there be a slightly different view for the broker's mobile and desktop client where the mobile client shows a smaller, less detailed table than the desktop client. This is achievable through configuration on a single component using **form factor** designations. To begin to understand developing for different form factors, let's dive in!

How to do it...

1. Start by creating a new LWC called `displayAssetsOnAccount`. Similar to previous chapters, we will be looking at the `.js-meta.xml` file first.
2. Once you have opened your `displayAssetsOnAccount.js-meta.xml` file, edit the file to expose the LWC to a `lightning__RecordPage` by adding the following targets under the `apiVersion` tag:

```
<?xml version="1.0" encoding="UTF-8"?>
<LightningComponentBundle xmlns="http://soap.sforce.com/2006/04/metadata">
    <apiVersion>65.0</apiVersion>
    <isExposed>true</isExposed>
    <targets>
        <target>lightning__RecordPage</target>
    </targets>
</LightningComponentBundle>
```

3. Next, we will add `targetConfigs` tags. Like previous chapters, we want to expose this LWC only on the **Lightning record page** for a specific sObject – in this case, `Account` – which we specify here along with **supported form factors**:

```
<LightningComponentBundle xmlns="http://soap.sforce.com/2006/04/metadata">
    <apiVersion>65.0</apiVersion>
    <isExposed>true</isExposed>
    <targets>
        <target>lightning__RecordPage</target>
    </targets>
    <targetConfigs>
        <targetConfig targets="lightning__RecordPage">
            <objects>
                <object>Account</object>
            </objects>
            <supportedFormFactors>
                <supportedFormFactor type="Large" />
                <supportedFormFactor type="Small" />
```

```
            </supportedFormFactors>
        </targetConfig>
    </targetConfigs>
</LightningComponentBundle>
```

4. Note that we have added two `supportedFormFactor` tags, `Large` and `Small`, which allow us to specify on which devices our component will appear. Because we are building our component to be flexible across devices, we specify both `Large` (desktop) and `Small` (mobile) form factors, although some of our other components, such as the **Top Accounts** page from *Chapter 3, Working with a Selector Class*, may look best on desktop! Next, open your `displayAssetsOnAccount.js` file. We know that we need to display different information based on what form factor we are viewing an account record on, but how does the LWC know what device we are on? This is easily handled in `import` statements with the `@salesforce/client/formFactor` scoped module. While we are looking at our import statements, let's also import the Apex methods that we wrote in the previous recipe, as well as our decorators and the `c/notifUtils` notifications utility from *Chapter 4, Synchronous and Asynchronous Processing in Components*. The top of our JavaScript class will look like the following:

```
import { LightningElement, api, wire } from 'lwc';
import returnAssetsByAccount from '@salesforce/apex/
DisplayAssetsController.returnAssetsByAccount';
import returnAssetCount from '@salesforce/apex/
DisplayAssetsController.returnAssetCount';
import FORM_FACTOR from '@salesforce/client/formFactor';
import Utilities from 'c/notifUtils';
let utility;
```

5. We will add a couple more imports to our LWC toolkit later in the recipe, but for now, this will suffice.
6. Next, navigate to your displayAssetsOnAccount.html file. Like many of our components, this LWC will be housed in a **lightning-card** element that is displayed when our data is loaded. Start by adding your lightning-card component tags within an lwc:if directive that checks if an assetsForDatatable variable is truthy:

```
<template lwc:if={assetsForDatatable}>
    <lightning-card class="displayAssetComp" icon-name="utility:brush"
variant="base">
        <div slot="title">
```

```
            Assets
        </div>
        <div class="slds-p-bottom_medium">
            <!-- Card Body -->
        </div>
    </lightning-card>
</template>
<template lwc:else>
    <lightning-spinner
        alternative-text="Loading"
        size="xx-small"
        variant="base"
    ></lightning-spinner>
</template>
```

7. Remember, it is common practice to display a **lightning-spinner** element while our data is loading.
8. To display images of the artworks that our end users select, we will be using a **lightning-carousel-image** element. While we could display the image using img tags, the lightning-carousel-image component is usable on its own and has many desirable features for our use case, such as a caption, alt text, and other accessibility features, as well as the ability to click into a given link. Rather than reinventing the wheel, which we will be doing in *Chapter 9, Creating Custom Lightning Web Components*, for now, we will use a new-to-us component that checks the necessary boxes. First, add an outer div tag with a class of carousel between the card body div tags in the lightning-card element, and then populate it with a lightning-carousel-image tag:

```
<div class="carousel">
<lightning-carousel-image
class="carouselImage"
src={selectedAsset.Primary_Image_Small__c}
header={selectedAsset.Name}
description={selectedAsset.Description}
alternative-text={selectedAsset.Name}
href={selectedAsset.Asset_URL_c}
onclick={handleOpenAssetPage}
aria-disabled="true"
></lightning-carousel-image>
</div>
```

9. Notice that we have a JavaScript object, selectedAsset, with a variety of properties being accessed using dot notation. This structuring allows us to use one variable for multiple attribute values. Additionally, note that we have two accessibility features: alternative-text and aria-disabled. While we will be going into accessibility features in depth in *Chapter 11, Writing Accessible Lightning Web Components*, for now, all we need to know is that alternative-text (alt-text) is text that describes an image to a user who is using a screen-reader, and aria-disabled lets the screen-reader know that the element should be perceivable, but not editable.
10. Next, within the card body div tags in the lightning-card element, add a set of div tags with a class of datatable, and add the following **lightning-datatable** element:

```
<div class="datatable">
    <lightning-datatable
        class="slds-p-horizontal_medium"
        key-field="Id"
        data={assetsForDatatable}
        columns={assetColumns}
        selected-rows={selectedRows}
        max-row-selection="1"
        onrowselection={updateCarousel}
        enable-infinite-loading
        onloadmore={loadMoreAssets}
    ></lightning-datatable>
</div>
```

11. Notice that we have set the `max-row-selection` attribute to `1`, meaning our `lightning-datatable` will have radio buttons. We have also added two new-to-us attributes, `enable-infinite-loading` and `onloadmore`, which we will need to prepare for the *Enabling lazy loading via infinite scroll* recipe later in the chapter.
12. Now that we have the base HTML and JavaScript files built out for the `displayAssetsOnAccount` LWC, let's add one more file to differentiate between what our component should look like on a desktop form factor versus a mobile form factor. Create a new JavaScript file within the `displayAssetsOnAccount` LWC folder by right-clicking on the folder name and selecting **New File...**. Name this file `assetColumns.js`, including the `.js` suffix so that VSCode recognizes that this is a JavaScript file.
13. Within the `assetColumns.js` file, we are going to have two constants available for export, `WIDE_COLUMNS_DEFINITION` and `NARROW_COLUMNS_DEFINITION`. These definitions

will look like column definitions for the `lightning-datatable` elements we used in *Chapter 2, Writing Apex for Lightning Web Components*, and *Chapter 6, Composing Lightning Web Components*, but we will be using an importable JavaScript file to store them, which will keep our LWC files tidy. This will be imported in the way we have been importing the `c/notifsUtil` component we wrote in *Chapter 4, Synchronous and Asynchronous Processing in Components*. Within your `assetColumns.js` file, start with the following definition:

```
export const WIDE_COLUMNS_DEFINITION = [
  {
    type: 'text',
    fieldName: 'Name',
    label: 'Name'
  },
  {
    type: 'text',
    fieldName: 'Department__c',
    label: 'Department'
  },
  {
    type: 'text',
    fieldName: 'Object_ID__c',
    label: 'Asset Id'
  },
  {
    type: 'text',
    fieldName: 'Is_Public_Domain__c',
    label: 'Public Domain?'
  }
];
```

14. Next, copy your `WIDE_COLUMNS_DEFINITION` variable declaration and paste it at the bottom of your assetsColumns file, changing the pasted constant's name to `NARROW_COLUMNS_DEFINITION` and removing the objects representing the **Department** and **Asset Id** columns. To sum up what we have done, we created two separate sets of column values: one that will be used with a `Large` form factor, and one that will be used with a `Small` form factor.

15. Return to your `displayAssetsOnAccount.js` file and import the new column definitions:

```
import { WIDE_COLUMNS_DEFINITION, NARROW_COLUMNS_DEFINITION } from './
assetsColumns';
```

16. In the `import` statement, we have imported the two constants from the `assetsColumns` file.
17. Next, add the following variables to the start of your `displayAssetsOnAccount.js` class:

```
@api recordId
scrollingAssets = [];
assetsForDatatable = [];
selectedAsset;
selectedRows = [];
offset = 0;
limit = 5;
componentWidth;
componentWidthPixels;
error;
get assetColumns() {
    if(FORM_FACTOR == 'Large') {
        return WIDE_COLUMNS_DEFINITION;
    } else {
        return NARROW_COLUMNS_DEFINITION;
    }
}
```

18. The **JavaScript getter** for `assetColumns` will dynamically choose which column definition to use based on the form factor provided by our imports. Voila!
19. You should now be able to deploy and load an empty component without error, although at this point, we haven't defined `assetsForDatatable` beyond an empty array, so you will see the `lightning-spinner`. To test, drop your component on the Lightning page for the `Account` sObject, and log in to your device on a desktop and a phone using the Salesforce mobile app.

Figure 8.1: The unpopulated lightning-datatable element as seen on desktop under lightning-spinner

20. This will be similarly displayed on a mobile device, but with two fewer columns:

Figure 8.2: The unpopulated lightning-datatable element as seen on mobile under lightning-spinner

> **Note**
>
> If you are unable to see these column differences upon deployment, make sure that the `assetColumns.js` file is within your `displayAssetsOnAccount` LWC folder, or edit your import to match the relative path of this file's location.

21. The last thing we will do in this recipe is set our own styling for our component using **Cascading Style Sheets** (**CSS**). You'll notice that in the `displayAssetsOnAccount.html` file, within the `lightning-card` tag, the `div` tags, and the `lightning-carousel-image` tag, we have included custom classes. These will make it easy to apply styling.
22. Create a new CSS file within the `displayAssetsOnAccount` LWC folder by right-clicking on the folder name and selecting **New File...**. Name this file `displayAssetsOnAccount.css`, including the `.css` suffix, so that VSCode recognizes that this is a CSS file. Unlike the `assetColumns.js` file, we will not need to import this file, as it is a CSS file with the same name as the LWC, which will be applied automatically.
23. To start the file, let's review the CSS selectors, documentation for which is included in the *See also* section of this recipe. To select a class, we preface it with a period character

(`.`), such that a `myCoolClass` class will be selected by using `.myCoolClass`. Let's start with the `carousel` class:

```
.carousel
{
    width: 40%;
    margin-inline: auto;
}
```

24. This CSS snippet will set the width of the `carousel` classed `div` to 40% of its container and center it horizontally.
25. Next, let's define the CSS class for `carouselImage`:

```
.carouselImage
{
    margin-top: auto;
    margin-bottom: auto;
}
```

26. Now we have set the relative position of the `lightning-carousel-image`, classed by `carouselImage`, centering it vertically and horizontally within its container.
27. Finally, we will set the styles for `lightning-datatable`, classed by `datatable`:

```
.datatable
{
    height: 10rem;
    margin-inline: auto;
}
```

28. We have set the height of `lightning-datatable` to 10 **rem units**, meaning that it is 10 times the height of the font size of the root element. This means that if the font size changes due to style updates from Salesforce, our component will scale with it. Neat!

There's more

With the annual release cycles for Salesforce, there is always a possibility that the styles within **Salesforce Lightning Design System** (**SLDS**) will change. In fact, **SLDS 2** was moved into beta halfway through the writing of this book! This is why it is beneficial to use relative units, such as `em` and `rem`, in custom CSS classes. If Salesforce updates their styling, our component will update as well. Although we can override SLDS classes in custom CSS files, we shouldn't. If we override an SLDS class and it changes, or worse, goes away completely, we may break our components and have a hard time tracking down how to fix them! Further reading on this topic is in the *See also* section for this recipe.

See also

- The GitHub directory containing the `displayAssetsOnAccount` files is located at `https://github.com/PacktPublishing/Salesforce-Lightning-Web-Component-Cookbook/tree/main/force-app/chapter08/default/lwc/displayAssetsOnAccount`
- The Salesforce Developer Docs article titled *Configure Your Component for Different Form Factors* is located at `https://developer.salesforce.com/docs/platform/lwc/guide/use-config-form-factors.html`
- The Salesforce Developer Docs article titled *Access Client Form Factor* is located at `https://developer.salesforce.com/docs/platform/lwc/guide/create-client-form-factor.html`
- The Salesforce Developer Docs page on the `lightning-carousel-image` component is located at `https://developer.salesforce.com/docs/component-library/bundle/lightning-carousel-image/example`
- The Mozilla MDN Web Docs article on `aria-disabled` is available at `https://developer.mozilla.org/en-US/docs/Web/Accessibility/ARIA/Reference/Attributes/aria-disabled`
- There is a Trailhead module for Salesforce mobile app customization located at `https://trailhead.salesforce.com/content/learn/modules/salesforce1_mobile_app`
- The Salesforce Developer Docs page on component CSS files is located at `https://developer.salesforce.com/docs/platform/lwc/guide/create-components-css-file.html`
- The Mozilla MDN Docs page on CSS selectors is available at `https://developer.mozilla.org/en-US/docs/Web/CSS/CSS_selectors`
- The Salesforce Developer Docs article on styling components with Lightning Design System is located at `https://developer.salesforce.com/docs/platform/lwc/guide/create-components-css-slds.html`
- The website for SLDS 1 is located at `https://v1.lightningdesignsystem.com`

- The website for SLDS 2, in beta as of the writing of this chapter, is located at `https://lightningdesignsystem.com/`
- The Salesforce Developer Docs article on anti-patterns for styling components can be found at `https://developer.salesforce.com/docs/platform/lwc/guide/create-components-css-antipatterns.html`

Enabling lazy loading via infinite scroll

Now that we have built out the shell of our LWC, it's time to add the functionality. Because we can have many assets associated with an account, we might not want to load each asset when the page loads. Enter **lazy loading**. Lazy loading allows us to render parts of a page's content as they are needed by the end user. This can help to decrease page load times and save system resources. To start, let's finish our JavaScript file.

Getting started

Before we can start, we need to think through how we are going to accomplish the task at hand by looking at the variables we added earlier in the chapter. We know we are going to pass a `recordId`, representing the `recordId` of the Account record page that the LWC resides on, into two exposed Apex methods, but how do we go about this best? We know that we only need to get our count of asset records once on page load, so we can wire the `returnAssetCount` method, but how will we load more records with the `returnAssetsByAccount` method? To **lazy load** the records from the start of our sorted query results, we need to start with an offset of 0 records and a limit of 5 records, and as we scroll through the `lightning-datatable`, we will increase the offset by 5 to grab the next five records until we reach the end of our list. We can achieve this through **imperative Apex**. Let's go!

How to do it...

1. Return to the `displayAssetsOnAccount.js` file. Start by writing your wire function for `returnAssetCount`:

```
@wire(returnAssetCount, { accountIdString : '$recordId'})
totalAssets;
```

2. Next, add an **asynchronous function**, `getAssets`, that will contain our **imperative Apex** call. We are placing this call in its own function so that we can use it as needed.

```
async getAssets() {
    return await returnAssetsByAccount({ accountIdString : this.recordId,
```

```
  lim : this.limit, offset : this.offset });
}
```

3. After writing the `getAssets` function, we can utilize it in a `connectedCallback` function that loads our first five (or fewer) asset records on page load. We will also use the `connectedCallback` function to initialize the `notifUtils` component that we imported earlier in the chapter. This will look like the following:

```
async connectedCallback() {
   utility = new Utilities(this);
   try {
       this.returnedAssets = await this.getAssets();
       this.selectedAsset = this.returnedAssets[0];
       this.selectedRows = [this.selectedAsset.Id]
       this.error = undefined;
   } catch (error) {
       this.error = error;
       utility.showNotif('There has been an error loading assets!',
this.error.message, 'error');
   }
}
```

4. Notice that in the highlighted line of code, we are using **array syntax** to place `this.selectedAsset.Id` as a singular object in a JavaScript array.
5. We will make some further modifications to this function in due time, but for now, we should see the first chunk of asset records being displayed.
6. Depending on the assets you have associated with your account, you might see the following error:

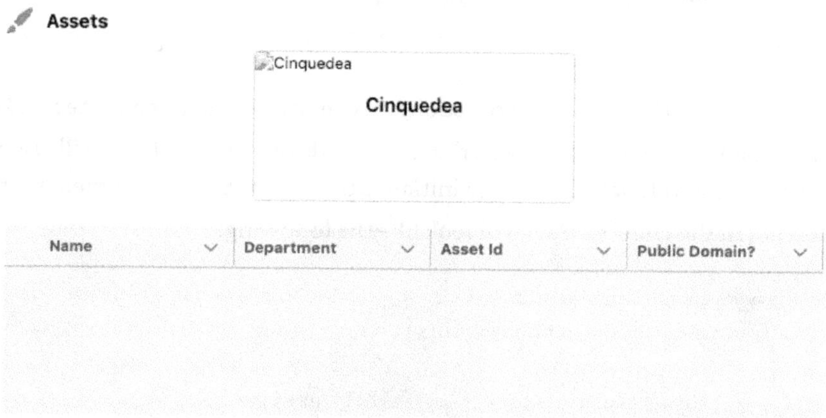

Figure 8.3: Something's not quite right! We have a broken image and can't see the lightning-datatable values

7. Let's add a `console.log` statement to the code to see what `selectedAsset` looks like. We get something like the following:

```
{
"Id": "02iaj000000Dl fRAAS",
"Name": "Cinquedea",
"Department__c": "Arms and Armor",
"Is_Public_Domain__c": false,
"Object_ID__c": "33531",
"Asset_URL__c": "https://www.metmuseum.org/art/collection/search/33531"
}
```

8. If we look at the HTML file, we notice that we are missing a `Primary_Image_Small__c` property in the JavaScript object we have viewed. This is because this artwork is not in the **public domain** and therefore cannot be displayed! So, what can we do? We queried for this field in Apex, but if the value is `null`, it doesn't appear in our JavaScript. Let's make an asset formatter function to ensure we always have a value for this property, and let's import an image as a **static resource** so that we don't break the `lightning-carousel-image` component.
9. Start by uploading a picture of your choice to Salesforce as a static resource. If you'd rather, there is a lovely picture of my cat, Gizmo, included in the GitHub repository under the `force-app/chapter00/default/staticresources` directory. You can deploy

this folder to your Salesforce Developer org or name your preferred image `NoImageFound.png` and upload it.

10. Once you have created a static resource called `NoImageFound`, we can add the following to the list of imports in the `displayAssetsOnAccount.js` file:

```
import NO_IMAGE_FOUND from '@salesforce/resourceUrl/NoImageFound';
```

11. We can then utilize this static resource in our code:

```
formatAssets(tempAssets) {
    tempAssets.forEach(asset => {
        if( !asset.hasOwnProperty('Primary_Image_Small__c')) {
            asset['Primary_Image_Small__c'] = NO_IMAGE_FOUND;
            if(!asset.Is_Public_Domain__c) {
                asset['Description'] = 'This image is not in the public domain, 
so it cannot be displayed here.';
            }
        }
    });
    return tempAssets;
}
```

12. Line by line, we are iterating over a list of asset records, checking if they have the `Primary_Image_Small__c` property and adding the static resource image if not, and adding a description that says if an item is not in the public domain.
13. Now, we must add our new function to `connectedCallback`. Edit the contents of the `try` block in the `connectedCallback` function to the following:

```
const returnedAssets = await this.getAssets();
let tempAssets = JSON.parse(JSON.stringify(returnedAssets));
this.assetsForDatatable = this.formatAssets(tempAssets);
this.selectedAsset = this.assetsForDatatable[0];
this.selectedRows = [this.selectedAsset.Id]
this.error = undefined;
```

14. Notice that we cannot pass in `returnedAssets` to the `formatAssets` function directly; we must first clone it utilizing `JSON.parse(JSON.stringify(returnedAssets))`, which is a simple, albeit goofy-looking, way to clone complex lists of JavaScript objects within LWCs. If we don't complete this step, we will receive an error similar to **Uncaught**

TypeError: 'set' on proxy: trap returned falsish for property 'Primary_Image_Small__c'. The reason for this error is that we cannot manipulate the results of an Apex call directly. We designate this variable as a `const` so we don't forget!

15. Now, we can deploy without fear:

Figure 8.4: A populated lightning-carousel-image and lightning-datatable

16. Ah! Much better. And doesn't Gizmo look lovely!
17. Now that we have a fallback for if an asset doesn't have a value for the `Primary_Image_Small__c` property, we can populate the rest of our values via lazy loading. In a `lightning-datatable`, more records load when infinite-scroll is enabled and the end user scrolls to the bottom of the component. Recall that we have already defined this behavior in the HTML file; all we need to do is define the `loadMoreAssets` function:

```
async loadMoreAssets() {
    if(this.offset < this.totalAssets.data) {
        try {
            this.offset += this.limit;
            const returnedAssets = await this.getAssets();
            let tempAssets = JSON.parse(JSON.stringify(returnedAssets));
            this.assetsForDatatable =
[...this.assetsForDatatable, ...this.formatAssets(tempAssets)];
            this.error = undefined;
        } catch (error) {
```

```
            this.error = error;
            utility.showNotif('There has been an error loading more assets!',
    this.error.message, 'error');
        }
      }
    }
```

18. Line by line, we first check to see if we have reached the end of the queried asset records, represented by the `Integer` value returned by our wired variable, `this.totalAssets.data`. In the next line, we increase the number of records we are offsetting by 5, or the `limit` variable we are returning. Finally, we retrieve and format our next chunk of asset *records* for assignment. If there's an error that is caught, we use the `notifUtils` component to display a toast message. Remember, as we learned in *Chapter 4, Synchronous and Asynchronous Processing in Components*, we can use the **spread operator (...)** to combine two arrays into one.
19. Now, all we have left to do is update the image that is displayed in the `lightning-carousel-image` based on what asset record is selected. As we look back at the `displayAssetsOnAccount.html` file, we see that we call a function called `updateCarousel` when a new row is selected in the `lightning-datatable`. This function will look like the following:

```
    updateCarousel(event) {
       let selectedAssetRows = event.detail.selectedRows;
       this.selectedAsset = selectedAssetRows[0];
       this.selectedRows = [this.selectedAsset.Id];
    }
```

20. We now have a fully functional component that displays four columns on desktop:

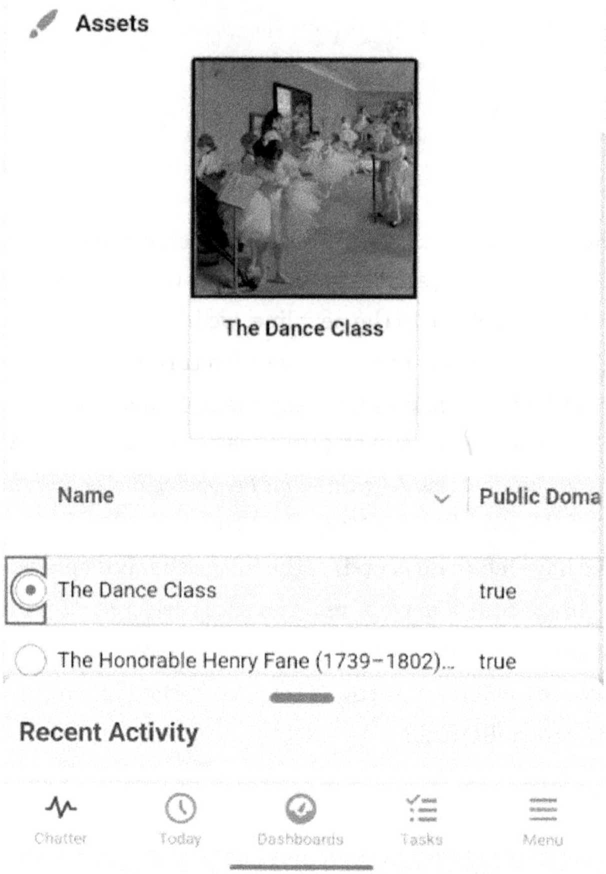

Figure 8.5: A screenshot of our component on a desktop form factor displaying The Dance Class, a public domain painting by Edgar Degas (1874)

21. It displays two columns on mobile via the Salesforce app:

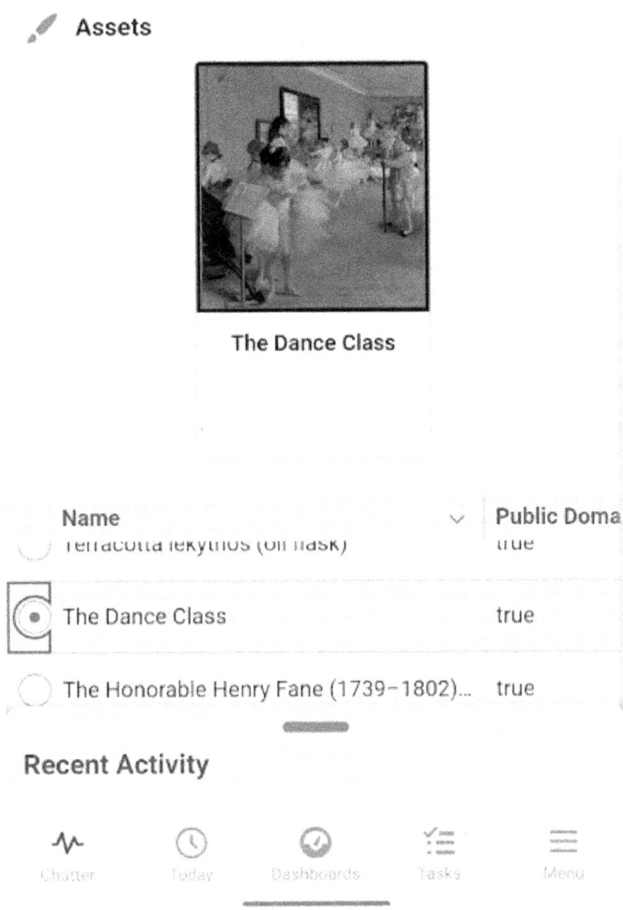

Figure 8.6: A screenshot of our component on a desktop form factor displaying The Dance Class, a public domain painting by Edgar Degas (1874)

There's more

Now that we have this component under our belts, there's one function we missed from the HTML file! If you look at the `lightning-carousel-image` tag, there's an `onclick` attribute that calls a `handleOpenAssetPage` function. We are going to use this function to open the information page from **The Metropolitan Museum of Art** for the selected artwork in a new tab. If you remember, we're already querying for the `Asset_URL__c` value in the Apex selector, which is already stored under the `href={selectedAsset.Asset_URL__c}` attribute in the HTML tag. So, how do we go about opening this URL in a new tab?

1. Return to the `displayAssetsOnAccount.js` file and add a new `handleOpenAssetPage` function:

```
handleOpenAssetPage() {
    window.open(this.selectedAsset.Asset_URL__c, '_blank').focus();
}
```

2. In this line of code, `window` is an **interface** representing the window that contains the **DOM document**. We utilize the open function of this interface to open a specified URL parameter, while the `'_blank'` target parameter indicates that we would like to open this URL in a new tab.
3. Note that this action may be prevented by **Lightning Locker**, which we learned about in *Chapter 7, Building Secure Components with Lightning Locker and Lightning Web Security*. In the event that this code doesn't work, we can use the **NavigationMixin** module to facilitate this navigation.
4. Rather than navigating to **The Metropolitan Museum of Art's** information page for the given asset, we will navigate to the Asset record page directly. The reason for this slight change is that we will not have the necessary permissions to display `www.metmuseum.org` in an **i-frame**!
5. To use `NavigationMixin`, start by importing it and extending your `DisplayAssetsOnAccount` class with it:

```
import { NavigationMixin } from 'lightning/navigation';
export default class DisplayAssetsOnAccount extends
NavigationMixin(LightningElement) { ... }
```

6. Next, edit your `handleOpenAssetPage` function to the following:

```
handleOpenAssetPage() {
    this[NavigationMixin.Navigate]({
        type: 'standard__recordPage',
        attributes: {
            recordId: this.selectedAsset.Id ,
            actionName: 'view'
        },
```

```
    });
}
```

7. Now we can easily navigate from the account record page to a selected asset record page from the component!

See also

- The Salesforce Developer Docs article on the `lightning-datatable` component is located at `https://developer.salesforce.com/docs/component-library/bundle/lightning-datatable/example`
- The Mozilla MDN Docs page on lazy loading is located at `https://developer.mozilla.org/en-US/docs/Web/Performance/Guides/Lazy_loading`
- The Mozilla MDN Docs page on the `window.open()` function is located at `https://developer.mozilla.org/en-US/docs/Web/API/Window/open`
- The Salesforce Developer Docs page for examples using `NavigationMixin` is located at `https://developer.salesforce.com/docs/platform/lwc/guide/use-navigate-page-types.html`

Building a DOM reactive LWC

Now that we have learned how to build components for multiple form factors, there are some situations in which you may want to display the same component in different ways depending on where it is placed on a page or even adjust how the component is displayed as the page is resized. So, how can we do this?

How to do it...

1. We will return once again to our `displayAssetsOnAccount.js` file. At the bottom of the file, add a `resizeFunction` function defined as an **arrow function**:

```
resizeFunction = () => {
    //...new code goes here!
}
```

2. Recall that within the `displayAssetsOnAccount.html` file, we added a class, `displayAssetsComp`, to the `lightning-card` tag. This will allow us to use a **querySelector** to access and manipulate this DOM element, like so:

```
let component = this.template.querySelector('.displayAssetComp');
```

3. Next, up at the very top of the JavaScript file, we defined two variables called `componentWidthPixels` and `componentWidth`. Now is their time to shine! We are going to define these variables as follows:

```
this.componentWidthPixels = component.getBoundingClientRect().width;
if(this.componentWidthPixels < 600) {
    this.componentWidth = 'Narrow';
} else {
    this.componentWidth = 'Wide';
}
```

4. We will be accessing the `width` property of the value returned by the `.getBoundingClientRect()` function to get the width of the `lightning-card` in pixels. So, what does the function name mean? Well, this function returns a rectangle that is the smallest rectangle that can contain the entire element, including its borders and any applied padding. This is known as a **bounding rectangle**, which can be visualized as follows:

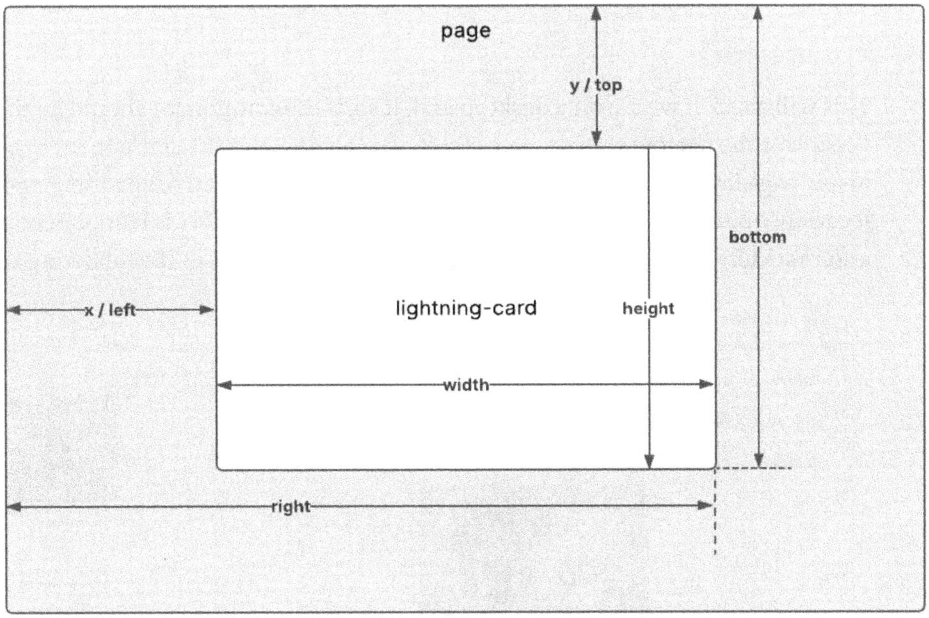

Figure 8.7: A diagram representing the bounding rectangle that encapsulates our lightning-card element

5. We access the `width` property to determine how wide our component is. If the width is above 600 pixels, we deem it `Large`; otherwise, it is `Small`.
6. Now that we know how to get the width of our component, we need to update the `connectedCallback` function to add an **eventListener** to the component. Whereas in Chapter 6, Composing Lightning Web Components, we learned about declarative eventing, this is an example of **programmatic eventing**. Add the following line before the `try-catch` block in the `connectedCallback` function:

```
window.addEventListener('resize', this.resizeFunction);
```

7. This line of code will run the arrow function as the window determines it is being resized, providing an updated `componentWidth` for us.
8. Finally, update the getter for `assetColumns` to the following:

```
get assetColumns() {
   if(FORM_FACTOR == 'Large' && this.componentWidth == 'Wide') {
      return WIDE_COLUMNS_DEFINITION;
   } else {
      return NARROW_COLUMNS_DEFINITION;
```

```
    }
}
```

9. This will check if we are on a desktop and, if so, if the component should be the wide version or the narrow version. As a result, we can now put the component in a main area in our page layout or in a sidebar, and it will display differently depending on its location. Additionally, if we minimize the screen width, the wide component will automatically switch to the narrow version. We can see this in the following screenshot:

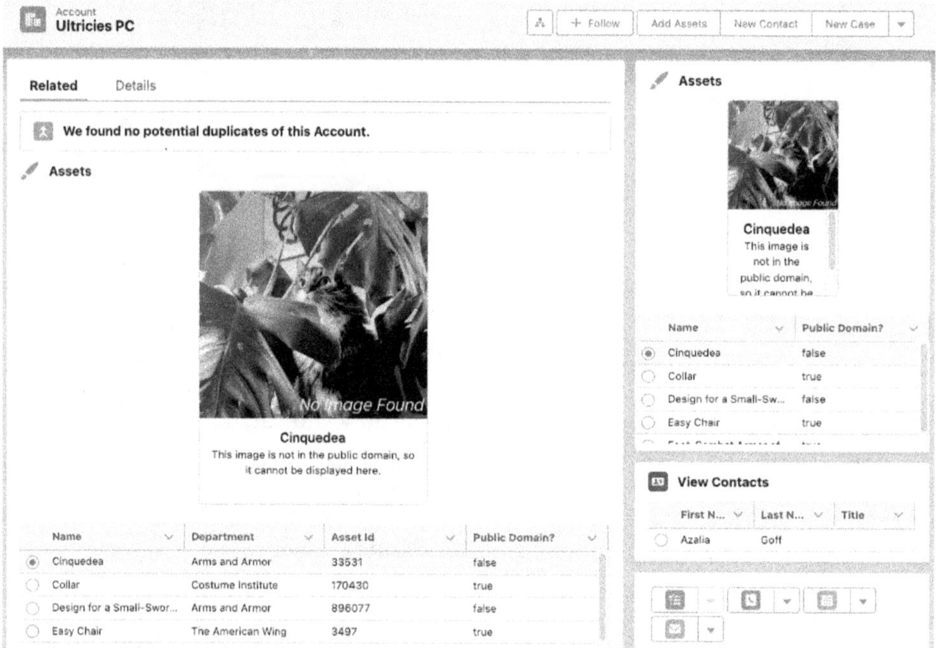

Figure 8.8: A screenshot of the same displayAssetsOnAccount component in the main slot of the Account page layout and the sidebar slot

See also

- The Salesforce Developers Docs article on accessing elements the component owns is located at `https://developer.salesforce.com/docs/platform/lwc/guide/create-components-dom-work.html`
- The Mozilla MDN Docs page on the .getBoundingClientRect() function is available at `https://developer.mozilla.org/en-US/docs/Web/API/Element/getBoundingClientRect`
- The Salesforce Developers Docs guide to event handling is located at `https://developer.salesforce.com/docs/platform/lwc/guide/events-handling.html`

Working with media queries

Our last recipe of the chapter has to do with conditionally applying styling based on form factor using **CSS media queries**. We are going to be working with our in-browser developer tools to make this work, which will be a good warm-up for *Chapter 15, Debugging Lightning Web Components*.

How it works...

1. Return to the `displayAssetsOnAccount.css` file that we created in the *Configuring LWCs for different form factors* recipe. Add the following CSS classes to the bottom of your file:

```
@media screen and (orientation: portrait) { ... }
@media screen and (orientation: landscape) { ... }
```

2. Add a `--slds-c-card-color-background` style to each of these classes, and pick a different color for each. Here's an example:

```
@media screen and (max-width: 30em) and (orientation: portrait) {
    :host {
        --slds-c-card-color-background: rebeccapurple;
    }
}
@media screen and (max-width: 60em) and (orientation: landscape) {
    :host {
        --slds-c-card-color-background: lightblue;
    }
}
```

3. Remember, we wouldn't usually want to override SLDS attributes, but we'll make an exception in this case for a quick demo.
4. Open your browser's developer tools feature and set the form factor to mobile. In Google Chrome, this is achievable by pressing *Ctrl* + *Shift* + *C* on Windows or *Cmd* + *Shift* + *C* on Mac, and selecting the **Form Factor** icon:

Figure 8.9: The Form Factor icon in Google Chrome developer tools

5. Optionally, you can complete this step in the **Salesforce One** app as well.
6. Once the updated CSS file has been deployed, you can see the difference, with portrait mode showing a dark purple background:

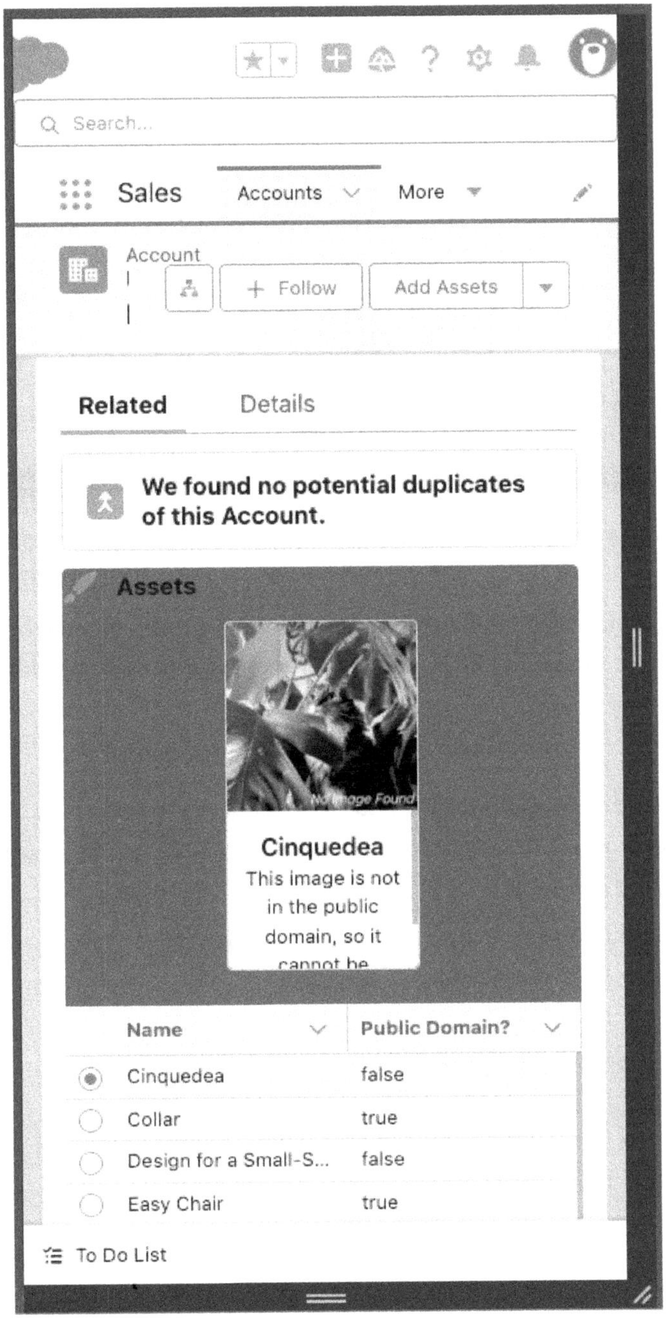

Figure 8.10: A screenshot showing a dark background, seen as purple in the org, for the lightning-card component as it is displayed in portrait mode

7. Here it is with a light blue background being displayed in landscape mode:

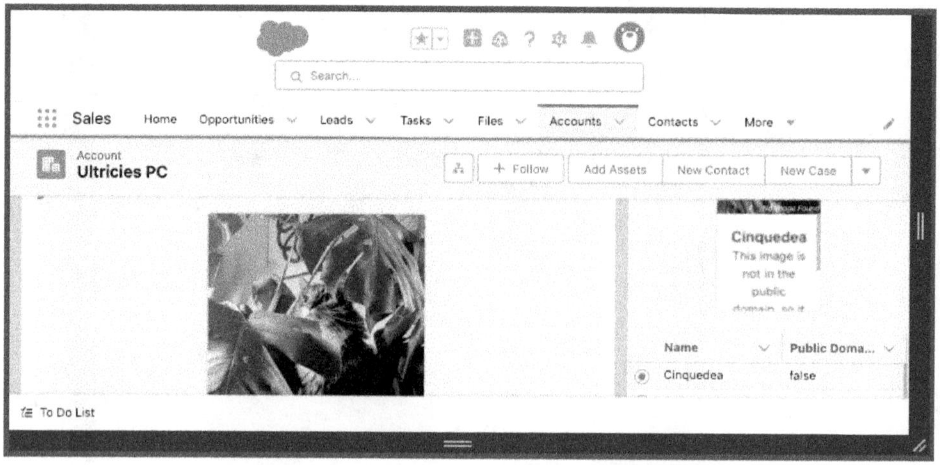

Figure 8.11: A screenshot showing a light background, seen as light blue in the org, for the lightning-card component as it is displayed in landscape mode

8. There you have it, a brief introduction to media queries! While these have mostly fallen out of favor for use in LWCs with the addition of form factor modules, you may still run into them.

See also

- The Mozilla MDN Docs page on CSS media queries is available at `https://developer.mozilla.org/en-US/docs/Web/CSS/CSS_media_queries/Using_media_queries`
- The story behind `rebeccapurple` can be read at `https://meyerweb.com/eric/thoughts/2014/06/19/rebeccapurple/`

Get this book's PDF version and more

Scan the QR code (or go to `packtpub.com/unlock`). Search for this book by name, confirm the edition, and then follow the steps on the page.

UNLOCK NOW

Note: Keep your invoice handy. Purchases made directly from Packt don't require an invoice.

9

Creating Custom Lightning Web Components

In the course of **Lightning Web Component** (**LWC**) development, there may be times when the base components do not meet the requirements laid out by the powers that be. As developers, we want to execute the vision properly, so how can we go about building components that don't yet exist? And, more importantly, how can we make them reusable?

Over the next two chapters, we will build two custom components that will increase our familiarity with the **Salesforce Lightning Design System** (**SLDS**) and send our confidence in building components soaring. In this chapter, we will be extending the `LightningDatatable` class in JavaScript to build a custom `lightning-datatable` component that allows for picklist selection within a column, while in *Chapter 10, Constructing Polymorphic Lightning Web Components*, we will be building a new search component that provides an ID for a found **Contact** or **Customer** record. These components will be built on the `displayAssetsOnAccount` component from *Chapter 8, Implementing Reactivity in Lightning Web Components*, which will give us a good idea of how we can build components for reuse across our org.

We are going to be covering the following main recipes:

- Extending base components for added functionality
- Modifying existing components in place
- Editing and saving the datatable row values

Technical requirements

The recipes for this book can be found at `https://github.com/PacktPublishing/Salesforce-Lightning-Web-Component-Cookbook`, where each chapter has its own folder under the `force-`

app folder. This GitHub repository is structured in the form of a **Salesforce DX project**, which will allow you to easily fork the repository for deployment in a free **Salesforce Developer Edition** org. The code for this chapter is located at `https://github.com/PacktPublishing/Salesforce-Lightning-Web-Component-Cookbook/tree/main/force-app/chapter09`.

The components in this book require the use of an **integrated development environment** (**IDE**), such as **Visual Studio Code** (**VSCode**) or **Salesforce Code Builder**. Detailed instructions for setting up an IDE are located in *Chapter 1, Getting Ready for Lightning Web Component,* in the *Setting up your IDE* section.

If you are building the projects in this cookbook as written, you will need to seed your Salesforce Developer Edition org with test data. Detailed instructions for seeding your org are located in *Chapter 1, Getting Ready for Lightning Web Component,* in the *Setting up the Salesforce Lightning Web Components Cookbook org* section.

Lastly, the edition of Salesforce required to implement the recipes in this book must be **Developer**, **Performance**, **Unlimited**, **Enterprise**, or **Database.com**. You can sign up for a free Salesforce Developer Edition org at `https://developer.salesforce.com/signup`.

Extending base components for added functionality

Sometimes, we may come across a use case where the functionality we are seeking to implement doesn't exist. In order to build custom components, we can take one of two approaches: we can extend the functionality of an existing component, or we can build a new component. We will be focusing on the latter in the next chapter when we examine how to build components that house multiple types of **sObjects**. For now, we will be extending the functionality of one of our favorite components, `lightning-datatable`. In our use case, we want our end users to be able to view some common fields on a given **Asset** record from its parent **Account** page. We started building this functionality in *Chapter 8, Implementing Reactivity in Lightning Web Components,* allowing representatives of our organization to easily see information about **Asset** records that are assigned to a given **Account**. What if we want to edit the fields that are viewable in our `lightning-datatable` component? This is achievable with some fiddling, but what if one of those fields needing an update is a picklist? This is not possible with the base component! We will need to add a custom column type. Let's get started by creating our column type first.

How to do it...

1. Create a new LWC called `picklistDatatable`, and open the `picklistDatatable.js` file. This JavaScript file is going to start a little bit differently than what we're used to from

earlier chapters in this cookbook. Rather than importing the `LightningElement` class at the top of our file, we are going to import `LightningDatatable` like so:

```
import LightningDatatable from 'lightning/datatable';
```

2. Further, instead of extending our default class, `PicklistDatatable`, by `LightningElement`, we are going to extend it by `LightningDatatable`:

```
export default class PicklistDatatable extends LightningDatatable { ... }
```

This slight change will allow us to extend the functionality of the `LightningDatatable` class and create a new column type.

3. After we have defined our JavaScript class, we are going to define two more imports: two HTML files called `picklistPlaceholder` and `picklistSelector`. We will create and define these files momentarily. To import these HTML files, we would use the following:

```
import picklistPlaceholder from './picklistPlaceholder.html';
import picklistSelector from './picklistSelector.html';
```

4. To round out our JavaScript file, within our class definition, we are going to instantiate and define a static variable, `customTypes`, that will define our picklist column's internal attributes:

```
static customTypes = {
   picklistColumn : {
      template : picklistPlaceholder,
      editTemplate: picklistSelector,
      standardCellLayout: true,
      typeAttributes: ['label', 'placeholder', 'options', 'value']
   }
};
```

What we are doing here is defining the HTML template that our column will use when at rest, using the HTML contained in our `picklistPlaceholder` file, and the HTML template that our column will use when editing, `picklistSelector`. We are also defining the attributes that our column will have, such as the `label` drop-down column, its placeholder, options for our dropdown, and the selected value.

5. Having completed our `picklistDatatable.js` file, let's create our `picklistPlaceholder.html` and `picklistSelector.html` files. We are going to start with `picklistPlaceholder`. Right-click on your `picklistDatatable` folder within your file structure in VSCode, and select **New File...**. Name the file `picklistPlaceholder.html`, being sure to include the `.html` suffix so that VSCode understands what kind of file we are creating.
6. Within your `picklistPlaceholder.html` file, add the following tags:

```
<template>
    <span class="slds-truncate" title={typeAttributes.label}
>{typeAttributes.label}</span>
</template>
```

   This is the first time we have encountered the `span` tag within our cookbook adventures. This tag represents a container that we can utilize to style an **inline element**. The definition for our `span` tag includes the `class` attribute, which contains an **SLDS style class** that truncates our text if it passes the width of its containing element, and the `title` attribute, which produces a tooltip that displays title text when an end user hovers their mouse over the contained text. This line of markup, nested between our `template` root tags, will style the label of our selected picklist value when our drop-down column is at rest.

7. Following a similar process, we are going to create our `picklistSelector.html` file in the same folder. Right-click on your `picklistDatatable` folder within your file structure in VSCode, and select **New File...**. Name the file `picklistSelector.html`, being sure to include the `.html` suffix.
8. Enter the following markup, which will display a drop-down `lightning-combobox` component when we are editing our picklist value for a given row:

```
<template>
    <lightning-combobox name="picklist"
        data-inputable="true"
        label={typeAttributes.label}
        placeholder={typeAttributes.placeholder}
        options={typeAttributes.options}
        variant="label-hidden">
    </lightning-combobox>
</template>
```

Note that, again, we have placed our `lightning-combobox` tag between root `template` tags. These `template` tags tell Salesforce that we are rendering an LWC in the **shadow DOM**. Recall from *Chapter 6, Composing Lightning Web Components*, that the shadow **DOM** (short for **document object model**) is what Salesforce uses to encapsulate the internal workings of an LWC, which helps to prevent it from being manipulated by malicious code.

The attributes that we have defined in our `lightning-combobox` tag include `data-inputable`, which allows us to edit the value in each row of the `lightning-datatable` component that houses our picklist column, as well as a `name` attribute for our element, a `placeholder` attribute that displays when we click on the dropdown, and our drop-down options. Our last attribute, `variant`, is set to `"label-hidden"` so that a label doesn't appear for our `lightning-combobox` element, which would affect the styling of our column.

9. Check your `picklistDatatable.html` file and verify that it has just two `template` tags. We don't need to make any changes here, as our `picklistPlaceholder.html` and `picklistSelector.html` files will be doing the heavy lifting for our column. We can optionally delete this file.

See also

- The Salesforce documentation on extending the `LightningDatatable` class is available at `https://developer.salesforce.com/docs/platform/lwc/guide/data-table-custom-types.html`
- The Salesforce documentation on making custom editable types for the `LightningDatatable` class is located at `https://developer.salesforce.com/docs/platform/lwc/guide/data-table-custom-types-editable.html`

Modifying existing components in place

For most of this cookbook, we have been writing code from scratch. So, what happens when you're on an assignment, and you must modify legacy code? Being able to sight-read code and know when and where to make changes is something that takes practice, so we are going to simulate a requirements change to get comfortable with the process. We are going to practice by adding our `picklist-datatable` component to the existing `displayAssetsOnAccount` component. We will do this by swapping out the existing `lightning-datatable` component for our `picklist-datatable` component.

How to do it...

1. To complete our project, we are going to continue by opening the `displayAssetsOnAccount` component that we built in *Chapter 8, Implementing Reactivity in Lightning Web Components*. We can either copy this LWC into a new folder or modify the existing component, whichever is preferred. I have opted to copy the LWC and its contents into a new folder and renamed it `displayAssetsOnAccountEditable` to differentiate between what we wrote in the previous chapter and what we will write in this chapter. You may choose to keep your recipes organized by chapter. In the context of client or customer work, I would modify the existing file while using a source tracking solution such as **Git**.
2. We are going to be enhancing the functionality of our existing component to add our `lightning-combobox` drop-down column to our `lightning-datatable` component. This will allow us to edit a picklist field on the **Asset** object directly from the **Account** record page.

   > **Note**
   >
   > This chapter builds on the code from previous chapters, including *Chapter 4, Synchronous and Asynchronous Processing in Components, Chapter 5, Accessing External Data Sources via Lightning Web Component*, and *Chapter 8, Implementing Reactivity in Lightning Web Components*. If you are looking to build the whole project for this chapter, you will need to complete the setup steps outlined in *Chapter 1, Getting Ready for Lightning Web Component Development*, to seed your org with appropriate data, as well as deploying the directories at `force-app/chapter04`, `force-app/chapter05`, and `force-app/chapter08` in the GitHub repository to your Developer Edition org.

3. Once you have either opened or copied and renamed your LWC, enter the `displayAssetsOnAccount.html` file (`displayAssetsOnAccountEditable.html` if you copied and renamed). Replace the `lightning-datatable` tag with the following:

```
<c-picklist-datatable
   class="slds-p-horizontal_medium"
   id="editable-datatable"
   key-field="Id"
   data={assetsForDatatable}
   columns={assetColumns}
```

```
    oncellchange={handleInlineEdit}
    onsave={handleInlineEditSave}
    oncancel={handleInlineEditCancel}
    draft-values={draftValues}
    selected-rows={selectedRows}
    max-row-selection="1"
    onrowselection={updateCarousel}
    enable-infinite-loading
    onloadmore={loadMoreAssets}
></c-picklist-datatable>
```

You'll notice that this tag, `c-picklist-datatable`, has similar attributes to the original `lightning-datatable` tag, with the additions of `oncellchange`, `onsave`, `oncancel`, and `draft-values`. These attributes go hand in hand with making a column editable, which we will take care of in the next step.

4. Navigate to the `assetsColumns.js` file. Replace the **Public Domain** column within the `WIDE_COLUMNS_DEFINITION` array with the following, which will add a column where each row contains a `lightning-combobox` component, provided by our new `picklistDatatable` LWC:

```
{
    type: 'picklistColumn',
    fieldName: 'DisplayStatus',
    label: 'Display Status',
    editable: true,
    typeAttributes : {
        label: {fieldName: 'statusLabel'},
        value: {fieldName: 'statusValue'},
        placeholder: {fieldName: 'statusPlaceholder'},
        options: {fieldName: 'statusOptions'}
    }
}
```

Notice that we have familiar properties for our column: `type`, `fieldName`, and `label`, with the addition of the `editable` property. Notice that we also have an additional property of `typeAttributes`, which is a JavaScript object containing the properties we defined in the `typeAttributes` array for our `picklistColumn` definition in the `picklistDatatable.js` file. We will have to define some properties for each row in our `lightning-datatable` component, including `statusLabel`, `statusValue`, `statusPlaceholder`, and `statusOptions`, so you won't see much of a change yet! Let's start configuring our new column so that we can tell what we're looking at.

5. Right under the class signature contained in your `displayAssetsOnAccount.js` file (`displayAssetsOnAccountEditable.js` if you copied the file), add two more variable declarations:

```
statusPickvals = [];
draftValues = [];
```

These two variables will hold the list of picklist values contained in the **Status** field on our **Asset** sObject, and the edited values that we will be saving, respectively. We are setting them to empty arrays so that we can easily add values in the form of JavaScript objects to them.

6. Next, we are going to add a few more imports to the top of our file:

```
import { getPicklistValues } from 'lightning/uiObjectInfoApi';
import { notifyRecordUpdateAvailable } from 'lightning/uiRecordApi';
import STATUS_FIELD from "@salesforce/schema/Asset.Status";
```

The first two imports, `getPicklistValues` and `notifyRecordUpdateAvailable`, are functions that are provided by the `lightning/uiRecordApi` wire adapters. These wire adapters are provided by Salesforce and allow us to easily grab and parse org data and metadata. The third import, under the `@salesforce` module, is an example of how we obtain references to an sObject field, in this case, `Asset.Status`.

7. Now that we have our `STATUS_FIELD` field reference and the `getPicklistValues` wire adapter, we can wire a function, `pickvals`. Place the following under your `connectedCallback` function:

```
@wire(getPicklistValues, { recordTypeId: '012000000000000AAA', fieldApiName:
STATUS_FIELD })
pickvals(result) {
   if(result.data) {
      let tempPickvals = result.data.values;
      tempPickvals.forEach(val => this.statusPickvals.push({label:
val.label, value: val.value}));
   } else if (result.error) {
```

```
            this.error = result.error;
            utility.showNotif('There has been an error loading pickvals!',
    this.error.message, 'error');
        }
    }
```

8. Let's take a look at the previous code snippet and break it down line by line. We are doing the following:
    - Setting the `recordTypeId` and `fieldApiName` parameters for our wire adapter
    - Wiring a `pickvals` function that receives a stream of data, `results`, from our `getPicklistValues` wire service
    - Declaring a block-scoped variable, `tempPickvals`, which is defined as the `values` property of the stream of data received by our wired function, `pickvals`
    - Iterating over our `tempPickvals` array and pushing a new JavaScript object, formed by taking the `label` and `value` attributes from each item in the collection, into the `statusPickvals` array
    - Handling any errors that pop up by displaying a toast message with our `c/notifUtils` component from *Chapter 4, Synchronous and Asynchronous Processing in Components*

> **Note**
>
> You may have noticed that we hardcoded a `recordTypeId` value of `012000000000000AAA` into our wire adapter. While it is usually best practice not to hardcode values, this use case is correct as of the time of writing of this book. The ID of `012000000000000AAA` represents a **master record type**, which is used when there is no **default record type** defined. Because we have no defined record types on the **Asset** sObject, we use the ID of the master record type. This is called out in the documentation for the `getPicklistValues` wire adapter, which is linked in the *See also* section of this recipe.

9. If you deploy now, you'll notice that clicking on the **Display Status** column will pull up an empty combobox. This is because we need to define `statusLabel`, `statusValue`, `statusPlaceholder`, and `statusOptions` for each row, as called out in the `typeAttributes` property of our `picklistColumn` definition in the `assetsColumns.js` file. Navigate to the `formatAssets` function in the `displayAssetsOnAccountEditable.js` file, and add the following property definitions to the end of the `tempAssets.forEach( ... )` iterator:

```
asset.statusLabel = asset.Status;
asset.statusValue = asset.Status;
asset.statusPlaceholder = asset.Status;
asset.statusOptions = this.statusPickvals;
```

10. Deploy one more time, and you'll now see an appropriate dropdown with the **On Display**, **Off Display**, and **On Loan** options, which correspond to the available picklist values for the `Asset.Status` field.

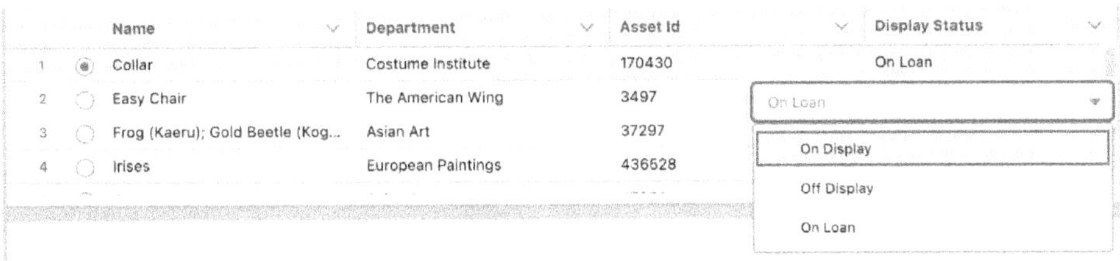

Figure 9.1: The updated c-picklist-datatable component, showing a combobox dropdown that displays appropriate picklist values

11. You may notice that our placeholder, **On Loan**, also appears in the dropdown. Ideally, this would not be the case, as we don't want to assign the same value that is already assigned, as this would cause an unnecessary update to our record. We can account for this by using the JavaScript `filter()` function, like so:

```
asset.statusOptions = this.statusPickvals.filter(val => val.value !=
asset.statusValue);
```

This will remove the current assigned value from our `statusOptions` array, thus preventing unnecessary updates through the UI.

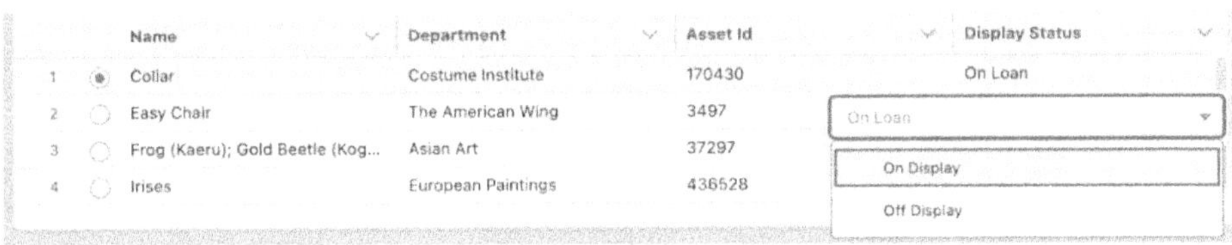

Figure 9.2: The updated c-picklist-datatable component, showing a combobox dropdown that displays only picklist values that can be newly assigned

Now that we have our drop-down functionality working, we must handle our edits appropriately, which we will be doing in the next recipe.

See also

- The Salesforce documentation on the UI API is located at `https://developer.salesforce.com/docs/platform/lwc/guide/reference-ui-api.html`

- The Salesforce documentation for the `@salesforce` module is available at `https://developer.salesforce.com/docs/platform/lwc/guide/reference-salesforce-modules.html`
- The Salesforce documentation on the provided wire adapters is available at `https://developer.salesforce.com/docs/platform/lwc/guide/reference-wire-adapters-picklist-values.html`

Editing and saving the datatable row values

So far in this chapter, we have created a new column type and designated it as *editable* in our `picklist-datatable` component. We know what this looks like in theory, but what does it look like in practice? We know that we want to edit a column, but how do we make it editable on the backend? We will have to track the new values that we want to save, and we will have to store the previous values in case we change our minds and hit the **Cancel** button. Once we hit the **Save** button, we will need to update our records via imperative Apex and refresh the values in our `picklist-datatable` component so that they contain the most up-to-date information.

How to do it...

We are going to continue building out the functionality in our `displayAssetsOnAccountEditable.js` file so that we can easily build our Apex to match. Let's begin:

1. Return to your `displayAssetsOnAccountEditable.html` file, and inspect the attributes within the `c-picklist-datatable` tag. Note the following attributes:

    - `oncellchange={handleInlineEdit}`
    - `onsave={handleInlineEditSave}`
    - `oncancel={handleInlineEditCancel}`
    - `draft-values={draftValues}`

    The first three **event attributes**, denoted by the prefix of on followed by the event name, such as `onevent`, define the functions to be called when an event is fired, and the fourth attribute holds the draft values that we are planning on saving. We are first going to define the `handleInlineEdit` function, which will allow us to define our `draftValues` variable. From there, we will be able to define what happens when we press the **Cancel** or **Save** buttons that are provided by making our `picklist-datatable` component editable.

2. At the top of your `displayAssetsOnAccountEditable.js` file, add the `draftValues` variable as a class variable:

```
draftValues = [];
```

We are defining this as an empty array so that we can easily push new draft values into it.

3. Next, add a function definition for `handleInlineEdit`. This function will take a parameter of `event`, which will be passed in when one of the cell values of our `picklist-datatable` component changes:

```
HandleInlineEdit(event) { ... }
```

4. In the first line of our function definition, let's grab the `draftValues` property from our event. The `draftValues` property is a built-in property that allows us to see which cell was just changed. We are going to grab the zeroth index of this property, which is in the format of an array, because we can only edit one cell at a time:

```
let draftValue = event.detail.draftValues[0];
```

Note that we are able to use the `draftValues` property because we have indicated that this column contains a custom component.

5. After we have grabbed our `draftValues` property, we need to pull the full record so that we can gain additional context to make sure we are displaying the right selection. This context is stored in our `assetsForDatatable` class variable, and we can use the `findIndex()` function in JavaScript to select the index of our edited record:

```
let draftValueIndex = this.assetsForDatatable.findIndex(draft => draft.Id
=== draftValue.Id);
let tempAsset = this.assetsForDatatable[draftValueIndex];
```

6. Recall that we want to track the old picklist value for our record in case we hit the **Cancel** button, so that we can restore the `picklist-datatable` component to its original state. We can do this by adding a new set of properties to the JavaScript object,

`tempAsset`, that represents our edited record. We want to do this before we assign new values so that we don't overwrite the old values:

```
tempAsset.oldLabel = tempAsset.statusLabel;
tempAsset.oldValue = tempAsset.statusValue;
tempAsset.oldPlaceholder = tempAsset.statusPlaceholder;
tempAsset.oldOptions = tempAsset.statusOptions;
```

7. Now that we have our old values locked in, we can overwrite the existing properties:

```
tempAsset.statusLabel = draftValue.Status;
tempAsset.statusValue = draftValue.Status;
tempAsset.statusPlaceholder = draftValue.Status;
tempAsset.statusOptions = this.statusPickvals.filter(val => val.value !==
tempAsset.statusValue);
```

8. Having prepared our `tempAsset` object to match the edited values, as well as store the previous values, we can overwrite the object in `draftValueIndex` with our `tempAsset` object:

```
this.assetsForDatatable[draftValueIndex] = tempAsset;
```

9. To round out this function, we also need to add our `draftValue` property to our `draftValues` array. To do this, we need to make sure that the ID for `draftValue` does not already exist in the array. If it does, we need to replace the existing value. We do this so that if we edit the value twice, we only track the most recent edits:

```
let draftIndex = this.draftValues.findIndex(draft => draft.Id ===
draftValue.Id);
if(draftIndex < 0) {
   this.draftValues.push(draftValue);
} else {
   this.draftValues[draftIndex] = draftValue;
}
```

10. Now, what happens if we hit the **Cancel** button? We need to return any changed rows in `assetsForDatatable` to their original state and clear our `draftValues` array. We can do

this using the `forEach()` function in JavaScript. Create a new function, `handleInlineEditCancel`, in your `displayAssetsOnAccountEditable.js` file:

```
handleInlineEditCancel() {
    this.draftValues.forEach(draft => {
        let draftValueIndex = this.assetsForDatatable.findIndex(draftValue =>
draft.Id === draftValue.Id);
        let tempAsset = this.assetsForDatatable[draftValueIndex];
        tempAsset.statusLabel = tempAsset.oldLabel;
        tempAsset.statusValue = tempAsset.oldValue;
        tempAsset.statusPlaceholder = tempAsset.oldPlaceholder;
        tempAsset.statusOptions = tempAsset.oldOptions;
        this.assetsForDatatable[draftValueIndex] = tempAsset;
    });
    this.draftValues = [];
}
```

11. Finally, we can save our values. We will take a momentary departure from our LWC files to ensure that our Apex is ready to accept the new values. Go to the `DisplayAssetsController` and `DisplayAssetsService` classes from *Chapter 8, Implementing Reactivity in Lightning Web Components*. If your journey with this book is starting in the current chapter, these files can be found in the `force-app/chapter08/classes` directory in your forked repository. We are going to jump around between these two files for a moment, starting with the `DisplayAssetsService` class.
12. At the bottom of your `DisplayAssetsService` class, add a **wrapper class** called `DisplayAssetWrapper`. Recall that we discussed wrapper classes in depth in *Chapter 2, Writing Apex for Lightning Web Components*, and *Chapter 3, Working with a Selector Class*. This wrapper class will have two members – `String Id` and `String Status`:

```
public class DisplayAssetWrapper {
    String Id;
    String Status;
}
```

We will use this wrapper class to hold the data passed in from our JavaScript file, `displayAssetsOnAccountEditable.js`.

13. Next, we must build a method to accept wrappers from our `displayAssetsOnAccountEditable.js` file in our `DisplayAssetsController` class. This will be similar to other **controller class** methods that we have written:

```
@AuraEnabled
public static void updateAssetWrappers(String jsonToParse) {
    try {
        List<DisplayAssetsService.DisplayAssetWrapper> assetWrappers =
(List<DisplayAssetsService.DisplayAssetWrapper>)
JSON.deserialize(jsonToParse,
List<DisplayAssetsService.DisplayAssetWrapper>.Class)
        service.saveAssetWrappers(assetWrappers);
    } catch (Exception e) {
        throw new AuraHandledException(e.getMessage());
    }
}
```

In this method, we accept a JSON string that we parse into our `DisplayAssetWrapper` wrapper class. Remember: we don't want this method to be `@AuraEnabled(cacheable=true)` because we cannot complete DML with a `cacheable` method, but because we are exposing this method to our JavaScript, we need the `@AuraEnabled` decorator.

14. Let's return to our **service class**, `DisplayAssetsService`. Once we have parsed our JSON string into a list of wrappers, we need to iterate over and transform those wrappers into updatable **Asset** records:

```
public void saveAssetWrappers(List<DisplayAssetWrapper> wrapperList) {
    List<Asset> assetsToUpdate = new List<Asset>();
    for(DisplayAssetWrapper wrapper : wrapperList) {
        Asset assetToUpdate = new Asset(Id = wrapper.Id, Status =
wrapper.Status);
        assetsToUpdate.add(assetToUpdate);
    }
    //update assets here
}
```

15. If you recall, we built a **persistence layer class** called `Assets` in *Chapter 5, Accessing External Data Sources via Lightning Web Component*. If you are joining us in the current chapter, this file is available in the `force-app/chapter05/classes` directory. We can

add a method to this class to update the **Asset** records in our `assetsToUpdate` list so that all our database interactions for the **Asset** object happen in the same class. The reasoning behind having a specific persistence layer class for each sObject is that it promotes code reuse, which reduces the amount of code that needs to change if we make an update to how we handle our DML for the sObject. Add the following method to the bottom of your `Assets` class:

```
public void updateAssets(List<Asset> assetsToUpdate) {
   try{
      updateRecords(assetsToUpdate);
   } catch (Exception e) {
      //error processing
   }
}
```

16. Return to your `DisplayAssetsService` class for a final time. At the top of your class, add a private, non-static instance of the `Assets` class as a class variable:

```
@TestVisible private Assets assets = new Assets();
```

17. Replace the `//update assets here` comment line in the `saveAssetWrappers` method we wrote in *step 14* with the following:

```
this.assets.updateAssets(assetsToUpdate);
```

This will call our persistence layer method and update our **Asset** records.

18. Now that we have modified our Apex classes to allow us to update an **Asset** record from our `displayAssetsOnAccountEditable` component, we can call this method imperatively in our JavaScript. Return once more to your `displayAssetsOnAccountEditable.js` file, and import our newly created controller method:

```
import updateAssetWrappers from '@salesforce/apex/
DisplayAssetsController.updateAssetWrappers';
```

19. Next, create a new asynchronous function, `handleInlineEditSave`, where we will stringify our `draftValues` array and imperatively call our `updateAssetWrappers` method:

```
async handleInlineEditSave() {
    let jsonToParse = JSON.stringify(this.draftValues);
    try {
        await updateAssetWrappers({ jsonToParse : jsonToParse});
        this.refreshAssets();
    } catch(error) {
        this.error = error;
        utility.showNotif('There has been an error saving assets!',
this.error.message, 'error');
    }
}
```

20. You'll notice that we have a yet-to-be-defined function, `refreshAssets`, that is called after we update our **Asset** records. Let's take a moment to think through what needs to happen here. We need to update the cache for the **Asset** records that we updated, and we need to clear our `draftValues` array. We can do this with the built-in `notifyRecordUpdateAvailable` function, which takes an array of ID strings as a parameter. Start by importing this function from the `lightning/uiRecordApi` module at the top of your file:

```
import { notifyRecordUpdateAvailable } from 'lightning/uiRecordApi';
```

21. Now that we have imported our function, we can use it in our `refreshAssets` function, along with the `forEach()` function in JavaScript, which will allow us to pull all of the IDs for records that have changed:

```
async refreshAssets() {
    let idsToUpdate = [];
    this.draftValues.forEach(draft => idsToUpdate.push({recordId :
draft.Id}));
    await notifyRecordUpdateAvailable(idsToUpdate);
```

```
    this.draftValues = [];
}
```

22. Wonderful! Now, we can deploy our code and see our updates to the functionality, which is illustrated in the following screenshot:

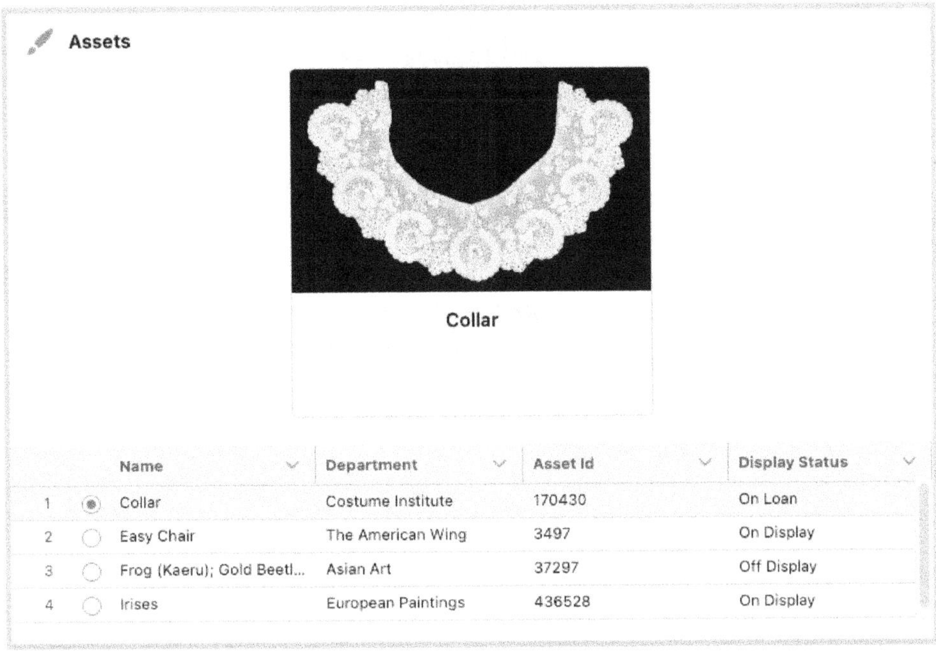

Figure 9.3: The updated c-picklist-datatable component, showing that several records have had their display status edited

See also

- The Salesforce documentation on inline editing within a lightning-datatable component is located at `https://developer.salesforce.com/docs/platform/lwc/guide/data-table-inline-edit.html`
- The Salesforce documentation on the lightning/uiRecordApi module is located at `https://developer.salesforce.com/docs/platform/lwc/guide/reference-lightning-ui-api-record.html`
- The documentation for the notifyRecordUpdateAvailable function can be found at `https://developer.salesforce.com/docs/platform/lwc/guide/reference-notify-record-update.html`

Get this book's PDF version and more

Scan the QR code (or go to `packtpub.com/unlock`). Search for this book by name, confirm the edition, and then follow the steps on the page.

UNLOCK NOW

Note: Keep your invoice handy. Purchases made directly from Packt don't require an invoice.

10

Designing Polymorphic Lightning Web Components

So far in this cookbook, we have learned a few different ways to use **wrapper classes**. We have seen how to represent various data structures, including representations of singular sObject types and lists of similar sObjects, as well as the representations of relationships between data structures through nested wrappers. So, what happens if we want to represent multiple sObjects with the same wrapper? Because we represent the properties of our wrapper class with primitive values, such as strings, integers, and Booleans, we can easily substitute values from different sObject types.

Over the course of this chapter, we are going to explore the concept of **polymorphism** in Salesforce, which can be loosely defined as performing the same action on different sObjects. We will use the concept of **polymorphic serialization** to display multiple sObject types in the same manner on the frontend, at which point we will utilize abstract Apex classes to determine what the type of an sObject is at runtime and, therefore, what actions to take on save. This will allow us to manipulate different sObjects in similar ways, allowing us to insert junction object relationships between multiple sObjects within a single LWC. We will do this all while becoming familiar with editing existing code, adding modifications to components from *Chapter 8, Implementing Reactivity in Lightning Web Components*, as well as the components from *Chapter 9, Creating Custom Lightning Web Components*.

We are going to be covering the following main recipes:

- Expressing complex object models using wrappers
- Polymorphism in Apex
- Arranging SLDS elements
- Reusing custom components

- Inserting a custom component into a datatable column
- Utilizing polymorphic Apex classes

Technical requirements

The recipes for this book can be found at `https://github.com/PacktPublishing/Salesforce-Lightning-Web-Component-Cookbook`, where each chapter has its own folder under the `force-app` folder. This GitHub repository is structured in the form of a Salesforce DX project, which will allow you to easily fork the repository for deployment in a free Salesforce Developer Edition org. The code for *Chapter 10, Designing Polymorphic Lightning Web Components*, is located at `https://github.com/PacktPublishing/Salesforce-Lightning-Web-Component-Cookbook/tree/main/force-app/chapter10`.

The components in this book require the use of an **integrated development environment** (**IDE**), such as **Visual Studio Code** (**VS Code**) or **Salesforce Code Builder**. Detailed instructions for setting up an IDE are located in *Chapter 1, Getting Ready for Lightning Web Component*, in the *Setting up your IDE* section.

If you are building the projects in this cookbook as written, you will need to seed your Salesforce Developer Edition org with test data. Detailed instructions for seeding your org are located in *Chapter 1, Getting Ready for Lightning Web Component*, in the *Setting up the Salesforce Lightning Web Components Cookbook org* section.

Lastly, the edition of Salesforce required to implement the recipes in this book must be Developer, Performance, Unlimited, Enterprise, or Database.com. You can sign up for a free Salesforce Developer Edition org at `https://developer.salesforce.com/signup`.

Expressing complex object models using wrappers

Recall in *Chapter 9, Creating Custom Lightning Web Components*, we added simple custom functionality to the `lightning-datatable` component that we built in *Chapter 8, Implementing Reactivity in Lightning Web Components*. In this chapter, we will be building a more complex extension for this component that we will also be able to use in custom components across our org.

Imagine in our fictional use case, where we are developers at an art broker that sends artworks to different museums and collectors, that we need to track the most recent consumer inquiries for each artwork. We want to extend the component we have built over the last two chapters, `displayAssetsOnAccount`, to allow our end users to do this easily: they should be able to view an artwork and some information about it, edit its display status, and update each artwork with the most recent consumer inquiry (`Consumer_Inquiry__c`), all from the **account** record page. We want our end users to be able to search for a consumer, either a contact or a customer, right from the `account` object, and create a relationship between the asset and the consumer on a `Consumer Inquiry` custom sObject. This sObject will be related to either a contact or a customer sObject record, depending on which is selected. This will allow our users to easily find and disseminate information about an asset that is attached to a given account to a consumer whose interest is tracked. We can see this functionality implemented in *Figure 10.1* within the `Most Recent Consumer Inquiry` column:

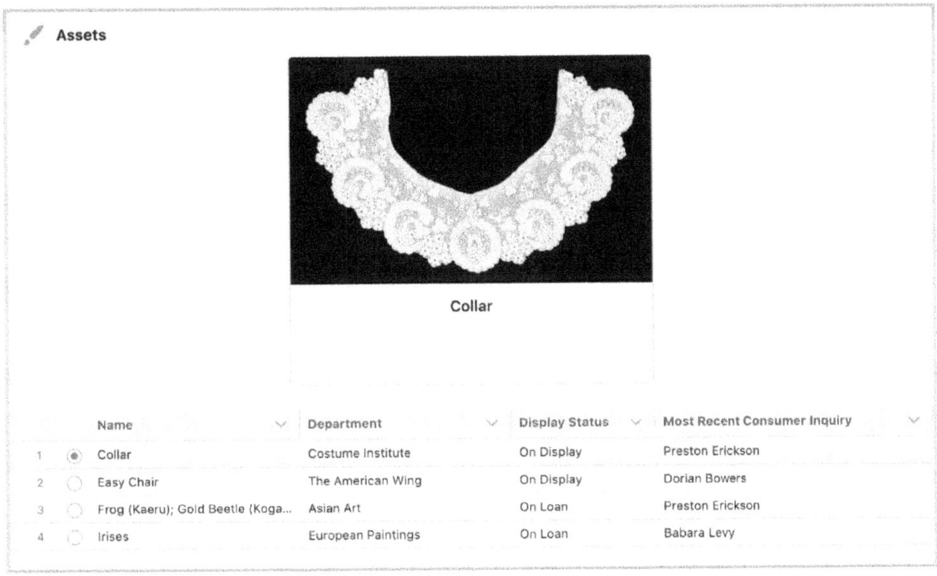

Figure 10.1: A screenshot of a new rendition of the displayAssetsOnAccount component, including the Most Recent consumer inquiry (Consumer_Inquiry__c) column

To refresh, we are utilizing the standard account sObject to track our museums, the standard asset sObject to track our artworks, and the standard contact sObject to track the relationships we have with our museums. For our most recent requirement, it was determined that we want to track private collectors as well, so we will be introducing the use of the standard customer sObject in this chapter. We want to view contact and customer records in the same component, but how can we accomplish this?

Getting started

At the start of this chapter, we briefly introduced the concept of polymorphism, defined in this chapter as performing the same actions on sObjects of different types. **Polymorphic serialization**, a concept that serializes distinct subclasses with a common superclass into JSON while preserving subclass specific attributes, can be applied in Apex with creative use of wrapper classes.

If you haven't done so already, take a moment to set up your org using the instructions in *Chapter 1, Getting Ready for Lightning Web Component*, in the *Setting up the Salesforce Lightning Web Components Cookbook org* recipe. This will populate your org with a set of test accounts, assets, contacts, and customers for use in the following recipes.

The recipes in this chapter build on the code for *Chapter 6, Composing Lightning Web Components*, *Chapter 8, Implementing Reactivity in Lightning Web Components*, and *Chapter 9, Creating Custom Lightning Web Components*. If you are joining us in this chapter, take a moment to deploy the `force-app/chapter06_setup` directory, the `force-app/chapter08` directory, and the `force-app/chapter09` directory to your Developer Edition Org.

How to do it...

Let's begin by writing our **selector classes**. We will need to build a selector class for each of the objects we are searching for in our custom component. We are going to start by adding a method to the class we built in *Chapter 6, Composing Lightning Web Components*, `contactSelector`:

1. Open your `contactSelector` class. If you are joining us in the current chapter, you can access this class by deploying the directory at `force-app/chapter06_setup` into your Salesforce Developer Edition org.
2. Below the existing method, add a non-static method, `searchContacts`, that returns a `list` of `Contact` records. This method will accept a `String` type called `searchTerm` as a parameter:

```
public List<Contact> searchContacts(String searchTerm) { ... }
```

3. Within this method, we are going to build a `String` query, `contactSearchString`, for use as a parameter in the `query` method of our extended `Util_Query` class. To do this, first, we must prepare our `searchTerm` by adding wildcards before and after. It is important to note that we must enclose our `searchTerm` and its corresponding wildcards with single quotation marks for the structure of our query, and we must escape our single quotes with forward slashes:

```
String userInput = '\'%' + String.escapeSingleQuotes(searchTerm) + '%\'';
String contactSearchString = 'SELECT Name, Title, Account.Name FROM Contact
WHERE Name LIKE ' + userInput + ' ORDER BY Name ASC';
List<Contact> queryResult = (List<Contact>) query(contactSearchString,
```

```
AccessLevel.SYSTEM_MODE);
return queryResult;
```

> Note
>
> It is important to remember that running this query in `SYSTEM_MODE` could expose contact data to users who shouldn't see it. To enforce **field-level security** (**FLS**), it is possible to query in `USER_MODE` instead. We are using `SYSTEM_MODE` here because we want end users to be able to access minimal information about all `Contact` records in the org, but in a real-world scenario, we would likely use `USER_MODE`.

4. We are grabbing the `Name`, `Title`, and `Account Name` fields from `Contact` records where our `Name` value matches our user `searchTerm`.

> Note
>
> The reason that we are utilizing the `query` method of the `Util_Query` class rather than the `queryWithBinds` method or `search` method is so we can add wildcards and single quotations to our input. We are not able to easily do this with a **bind variable**. We can also write this method in a simpler way without extending the `Util_Query` class, but we will see how easily this pattern lends itself to writing unit tests in *Chapter 13, Testing Apex with Mocking and Stubbing.*

5. Next, we will be creating a new Apex class, `CustomerSelector`. Like `ContactSelector`, we will be extending the `Util_Query` class so that we can easily stub the results of our query in our test classes:

```
public with sharing class CustomerSelector extends Util_Query { ... }
```

6. Add a `searchCustomers` method. This will mimic our `searchContacts` method, but will return a list of `Customer` records, and will retrieve the `Name` and `TotalLifetimeValue` fields from the `Customer` sObject:

```
public List<Customer> searchCustomers(String searchTerm) {
   String userInput = '\'%' + String.escapeSingleQuotes(searchTerm) + '%\'';
   String customerSearchString = 'SELECT Id, Name, TotalLifeTimeValue FROM
Customer WHERE Name LIKE '+ userInput + ' ORDER BY Name ASC';
```

```
    List<Customer> queryResult = (List<Customer>) query(customerSearchString,
AccessLevel.SYSTEM_MODE);
    return queryResult;
}
```

7. We need to use the `escapeSingleQuotes` method of the default `String` class to escape our input to ensure that there will be no **SOQL injection**, where an end user enters malicious SOQL into our LWC in an attempt to manipulate our database.
8. Now that we have our selector classes written, we are going to write a singular **service class**, `RecentConsumerService`. This service class will call each of our selector classes and prepare the results for ingestion by our LWC by **serializing** them into a wrapper class:

```
public with sharing class RecentConsumerService { ... }
```

9. Initialize an instance of each of our selector classes as a `@TestVisible private` class variable:

```
@TestVisible private ContactSelector conSelect = new ContactSelector();
@TestVisible private CustomerSelector cusSelect = new CustomerSelector();
```

10. At the bottom of your class file, add a subclass: a **wrapper class** called `ConsumerWrapper`. We will be adding four class variables to start, all `@AuraEnabled public String` variables, called `label`, `value`, `type`, and `fact`:

```
@AuraEnabled public String label;
@AuraEnabled public String value;
@AuraEnabled public String type;
@AuraEnabled public String fact;
```

11. Next, we are going to build a **constructor** for our wrapper class. Recall that a constructor allows us to define the values that will make up the instances of our wrapper class:

```
public ConsumerWrapper(sObject sObj) {
    this.label = (String) sObj.get('Name');
    this.value = sObj.Id;
    this.type = String.valueOf(sObj.getSObjectType());
    this.fact = this.type == 'Contact' ? new ContactConsumer(this.assetId,
sObj).getFact() : new CustomerConsumer(this.assetId, sObj).getFact();
```

```
}
```

Line by line, we are defining our constructor and its parameter, defining our `label` attribute as the `Name` field on our given sObject, setting the `value` attribute to the `ID` of our sObject, setting the `type` attribute to the `sObjectType` of our sObject, and, finally, setting the `fact` attribute to a field that carries a fact about our consumer. Depending on whether our consumer is a contact or a customer, we will return a different value, which we will be building infrastructure for in the next recipe. For now, know that we will be using the `getFact` method of an **abstract class**, `Consumer`, which is extended by either the `ContactConsumer` or `CustomerConsumer` **concrete class** to illustrate the concept of polymorphism in Apex.

12. Next, let's write our service method. Within this method, we will call each of our two selector class methods, `ContactSelector.searchContacts` and `CustomerSelector.searchCustomers`. We will then take the results of these two method calls and wrap them:

```
public List<ConsumerWrapper> wrapSearchedConsumers(String searchTerm) {
   List<ConsumerWrapper> consumerWrappers = new List<ConsumerWrapper>();
   List<sObject> sObjectsToWrap = new List<sObject>();
   List<sObject> contactsToWrap = (List<sObject>)
conSelect.searchContacts(searchTerm);
   List<sObject> customersToWrap = (List<sObject>)
cusSelect.searchCustomers(searchTerm);
   sObjectsToWrap.addAll(contactsToWrap);
   sObjectsToWrap.addAll(customersToWrap);
   for(sObject sObj : sObjectsToWrap) {
      consumerWrappers.add(new ConsumerWrapper(sObj));
   }
   return consumerWrappers;
}
```

13. Finally, let's build our controller class. Create a new Apex class called `RecentConsumerController`:

```
public with sharing class RecentConsumerController { ... }
```

14. This controller will have a class variable of a `@TestVisible private static` instance of the `RecentConsumerService` class called `service`:

```
@TestVisible private static RecentConsumerService service = new
RecentConsumerService();
```

15. The singular method in this class will be called `returnSearchedConsumerWrappers`:

```
@AuraEnabled(cacheable=true)
public static List<RecentConsumerService.ConsumerWrapper>
returnSearchedConsumerWrappers(String searchTerm){
    try {
        return service.wrapSearchedConsumers(
searchTerm);
    } catch (Exception e) {
        throw new AuraHandledException(e.getMessage());
    }
}
```

Now that we have our main classes written, let's learn a little bit more about polymorphism in Apex before we dive into polymorphic serialization.

See also

- The classes for this chapter are available at `https://github.com/PacktPublishing/Salesforce-Lightning-Web-Component-Cookbook/tree/main/force-app/chapter10/default/classes`
- The Salesforce Developers documentation on comparison operators in SOQL is located at `https://developer.salesforce.com/docs/atlas.en-us.soql_sosl.meta/soql_sosl/sforce_api_calls_soql_select_comparisonoperators.htm`
- The Salesforce Developers documentation on SOQL injection is located at `https://developer.salesforce.com/docs/atlas.en-us.apexcode.meta/apexcode/pages_security_tips_soql_injection.htm`

Polymorphism in Apex

In our previous recipe, we left some unexplained code in our service class, `DisplayAssetsService`. We will be clarifying this as we create an abstract `Consumer` class that will allow us to generate a `Consumer Inquiry` sObject record for insertion, relating either a

`Contact` or a `Customer` sObject record to our asset. What does *abstract* mean in this context? How does this relate to the broader chapter theme of polymorphism? Let's find out.

How to do it...

Recall that we said that we will be using the `getFact` method of an **abstract class**, `Consumer`, which is extended by either the `ContactConsumer` or `CustomerConsumer` class. This occurs in the following line in the inner class, `ConsumerWrapper`, of the `DisplayAssetsService` class:

```
this.fact = this.type == 'Contact' ? new ContactConsumer(this.assetId,
sObj).getFact() : new CustomerConsumer(this.assetId, sObj).getFact();
```

We will be starting by building the abstract `Consumer` class:

1. Start by creating a new Apex class called `Consumer`. We will be defining `Consumer` as an **abstract class**:

   ```
   public abstract class Consumer { ... }
   ```

   The `abstract` keyword means that we will not be able to create instances of this superclass directly but must instead use concrete subclasses, which we will define momentarily, to extend this class. In this way, we can use our abstract class as a template for behavior among its related subclasses. We will see an example of this later in this recipe.

2. Define two abstract methods, `getFact`, which returns a `String` object, and `getConsumerInquiry`, which will return a `Consumer_Inquiry__c` record:

   ```
   public abstract String getFact();
   public abstract Consumer_Inquiry__c getConsumerInquiry();
   ```

   Notice that these **abstract methods** cannot have a method body. We must override these methods in our concrete subclasses, allowing us to implement a modest example of polymorphism in Apex. This means we can use the same methods for different sObjects. All abstract methods must be overridden in their respective subclasses.

   We can also have **concrete methods**, which have defined bodies and lack the `abstract` keyword in their signature. These methods can be used by subclasses, and do not need overriding, although their signatures can be changed through **method overloading**.

> **Note**
>
> There are a few key differences between **method overloading** and **method overriding**.
>
> Method overloading occurs in a single class, where methods with the same name are defined with different parameters. When we extend an abstract superclass that contains a concrete method, the concrete method is accessible by the subclass and can therefore be overloaded.
>
> Method overriding is when a subclass extends an abstract superclass and redefines its abstract methods with new signatures.
>
> To rephrase, method overloading, or compile-time polymorphism, extends the functionality of existing methods, while method overriding, or runtime polymorphism, changes the behavior of the methods depending on the subclass that is extending the abstract superclass.

3. Next, we will define our first **concrete subclass**. A concrete subclass is a non-abstract class that, in this case, extends an abstract superclass. It can also be a class that implements a virtual interface. These classes can be instantiated, and they allow the methods of the **abstract superclass** to be used.
4. Create a new `public with sharing` Apex class called `ContactConsumer`. This class will extend the abstract `Consumer` class:

```
public with sharing class ContactConsumer extends Consumer { ... }
```

5. Next, we will declare our class variables:

```
public Id assetId;
public Id consumerId;
public Contact consumer;
```

6. We will be defining these variables in our constructor that accepts an `Id` record called `assetId` and an `SObject` record, `consumer`:

```
public ContactConsumer(Id assetId, SObject consumer) {
    this.assetId = assetId;
    this.consumerId = consumerId;
```

```
    this.consumer = (Contact) consumer;
}
```

Notice that we are casting our sObject as a `Contact` before assigning it to our class variable, `consumer`. We do this so that we can easily access the fields of the `Contact` sObject without having to use computationally expensive methods of the `System` and `Object` classes provided by Salesforce, such as **getDescribe**.

7. Next, we override the `getFact` method of the `Consumer` class:

```
public override String getFact() {
   return this.consumer.Account.Name;
}
```

We want to ensure that when we search for a consumer and find a `Contact` record, we have the name of the `Account` record that our contact is associated with as our "fact" about them.

8. After overriding the `getFact` method, we must override the `getConsumerInquiry` method:

```
public override Consumer_Inquiry__c getConsumerInquiry() {
   return new Consumer_Inquiry__c(Asset__c = this.assetId, Contact__c =
this.consumerId);
}
```

This method ensures that we populate the appropriate lookup relationship field, `Contact__c`, on our new `Consumer_Inquiry__c` record.

9. Now that we have defined our **overridden methods**, we can do the same for our `CustomerConsumer` class. Create a new `public with sharing` Apex class, `CustomerConsumer`, which will also extend the `Consumer` class:

```
public with sharing class CustomerConsumer extends Consumer { ... }
```

10. Similar to the `ContactConsumer` class, we will have three class variables:

```
public Id assetId;
public Id consumerId;
public Customer consumer;
```

11. We will also have a constructor:

```
public CustomerConsumer(Id assetId, SObject consumer) {
    this.assetId = assetId;
    this.consumerId = consumerId;
    this.consumer = (Customer) consumer;
}
```

Notice that we cast our `consumer` parameter as a `Customer`, again, to avoid using expensive calls such as `getDescribe`.

12. Next, we override our `getFact` method, which will give us the customer's `TotalLifetimeValue`, representing their lifetime spend, as their fact:

```
public override String getFact() {
    return String.valueOf(this.consumer.TotalLifeTimeValue);
}
```

Note that we must use the `String.valueOf()` method rather than casting directly as a `String` object. This is because an `Integer` object cannot be cast as a `String` object.

13. Finally, we override our `getConsumerInquiry` method:

```
public override Consumer_Inquiry__c getConsumerInquiry() {
    return new Consumer_Inquiry__c(Asset__c = this.assetId, Customer__c =
this.consumerId);
}
```

This method ensures that we populate the appropriate lookup relationship field, `Customer__c`, on our new `Consumer_Inquiry__c` record.

We will be coming back to these classes later in the chapter.

See also

- The Salesforce Developer documentation on Apex classes is available at `https://developer.salesforce.com/docs/atlas.en-us.apexcode.meta/apexcode/apex_classes_understanding.htm`

- The Salesforce Developer documentation on extending Apex classes is available at `https://developer.salesforce.com/docs/atlas.en-us.apexcode.meta/apexcode/apex_classes_extending.htm`
- An example of extending classes can be found at `https://developer.salesforce.com/docs/atlas.en-us.apexcode.meta/apexcode/apex_classes_example.htm`

Arranging SLDS elements

Now that we have the base for our component, let's start building our LWC. We want to be able to display a drop-down menu that displays both contact and customer records, each with its own fact and icon for context. This functionality, pictured in *Figure 10.2*, doesn't exist in Salesforce's base components, so we will need to build it from scratch.

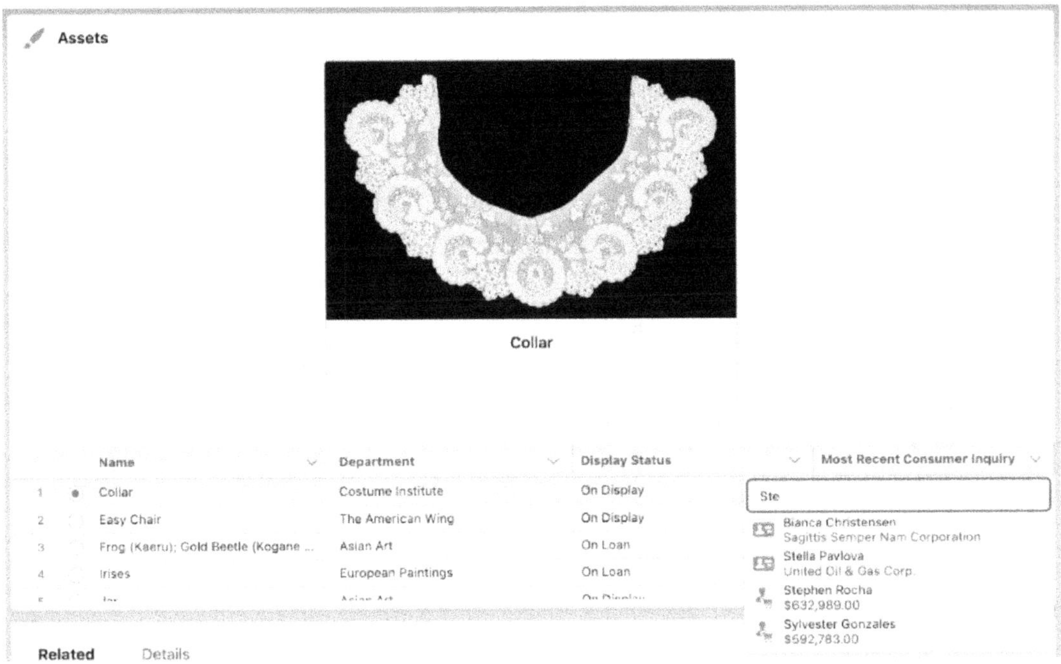

Figure 10.2: A screenshot of a new rendition of the displayAssetsOnAccount component, including the Most Recent Consumer Inquiry column showing the drop-down functionality that we will be building

When functionality doesn't exist, how do we build it? We can take individual component building blocks from the **SLDS library** and use them to build out what we need.

How to do it...

Start by opening the SLDS library, linked within the *See also* section. We will be using this documentation throughout this exercise:

1. Create a new LWC called `polymorphicDropdown`. This will be the component we will build for reuse across the rest of the recipes in this chapter, and will serve as the vehicle for our example of **polymorphic serialization**. Let's begin by importing and adding an `@api` decorated variable to our `polymorphicDropdown` JavaScript file, `dropdownOptions`:

   ```
   import { LightningElement, api } from 'lwc';
   export default class SearchableDropdown extends LightningElement {
       @api dropdownOptions;
   }
   ```

   This variable will allow us to reuse this element easily by allowing us to pass specified drop-down options in from a parent component.

2. We will come back to our JavaScript file in a moment, but for now, let's take a look at the `polymorphicDropdown.html` file, which we will use to build out our drop-down options. Because we are going to be passing in our options, we will worry about the search functionality in a little bit.
3. Open up the SLDS library and find the **Combobox** documentation. Navigate to the **Storybook** for the Combobox component, which, as of the writing of this chapter, is linked at the bottom of the example on the **Usage** tab in the **SLDS2** documentation, and familiarize yourself with the layout of the documentation. If you are using **SLDS1**, look over the examples under **Component Blueprints** for the **Combobox** component. Additionally, let's look one more time at the requirements. We will be building the drop-down portion of this component:

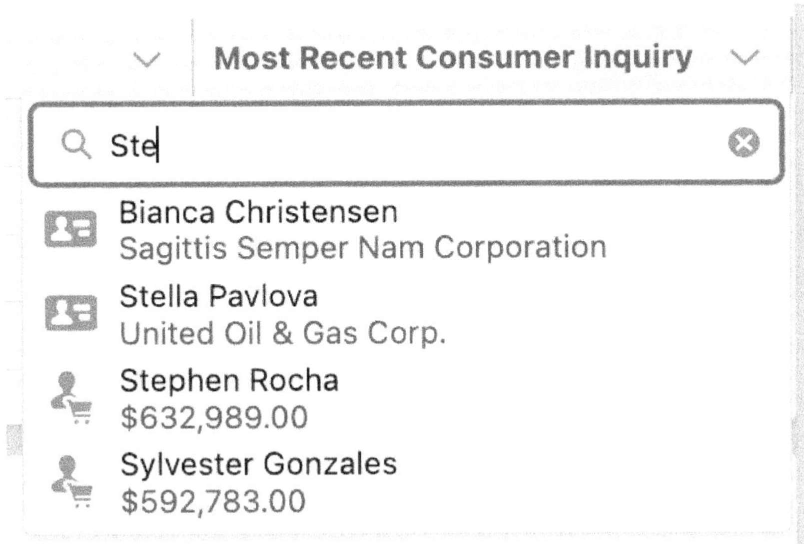

Figure 10.3: A screenshot of the functionality we will be building, showing a search input and a drop-down box showing two Contact records and two Customer records, each with a corresponding icon and either the account name for a Contact record or the total lifetime value for a Customer record

4. We are going to display our contacts with the standard `utility:contact` icon, and our customers with the standard `utility:customer` icon. The `Contact` fact will be the name of the account that is associated with the contact, and the `Customer` fact will be their lifetime total spend. We know what we need to build, but how do we do it?
5. We know that we need to have a repeating element, so let's add a template `for:each` directive that iterates over our `dropdownOptions` variable between our document `template` tags:

```
<template>
  <template for:each={dropdownOptions} for:item="option">
  </template>
</template>
```

6. Next, we are going to take what we have gleaned from the SLDS documentation and implement it. We know that we need a `div` to represent each drop-down item, so let's start there. Place the following within your template `for:each` directive tags:

```
<div
  data-id={option.value}
```

```
    key={option.value}
    class="slds-media slds-listbox__option"
    role="option"
    onclick={selectOption}
>
</div>
```

7. Line by line, we are do the following:
   - Setting **data-id** for our `div` tag, which will be accessible via the `event.currentTarget.dataset.Id` variable in our JavaScript file
   - Setting the `key` field for our iteration, which must be a unique value
   - Defining the styling for our `div`, which includes the `slds-media` and `slds-listbox__option` classes that tell our HTML file that our `div` is a `listbox` item with an icon
   - Setting the role of our `div` to `"option"`, which sets us up to use our `div` as an option in a listbox
   - Defining an `onclick` event handler that will call a function, `selectOption`
8. Next, we need to define the individual elements of our `listbox` option. These pieces include our icon, our title, and our meta, with our `title` element being the name of our consumer, and the `meta` element being the fact about our consumer. We will start with our `icon` element:

```
<div class="slds-media__figure slds-listbox__option-icon slds-p-
horizontal_medium slds-align_absolute-center">
    <span class="slds-icon_container">
        <lightning-icon
            icon-name={option.icon}
            alternative-text={option.altText}
            size="small"
        ></lightning-icon>
    </span>
</div>
```

Notice that we use the `slds-media__figure` and `slds-listbox__option-icon` classes to tell our icon where to sit within our dropdown. We also add horizontal padding to our icon and center it. We are using the `span` tags to enclose a piece of text or an element of a document, in this case, our **lightning-icon** tag. We are going to determine the icon and its alt text at runtime using the `icon` and `altText` attributes of the iterator variable option, which we will define in our JavaScript.

9. Next, we must add our text. Below our `icon div` tag, but within our `option div` tag, add the following:

```
<div class="slds-media__body">
  <span title={option.label}>{option.label}</span>
  <span class="slds-listbox__option-meta">{option.fact}</span>
</div>
```

10. The `slds-media__body` class within our encasing `div` will place our text in the right spot within our `options div`, while our `span` tags will format the text appropriately. The `title` attribute of the first span adds a **tooltip**, which will display our label when we hover over the span with our mouse, while `slds-listbox__option-meta` adds our fact as a **meta text** below the label:

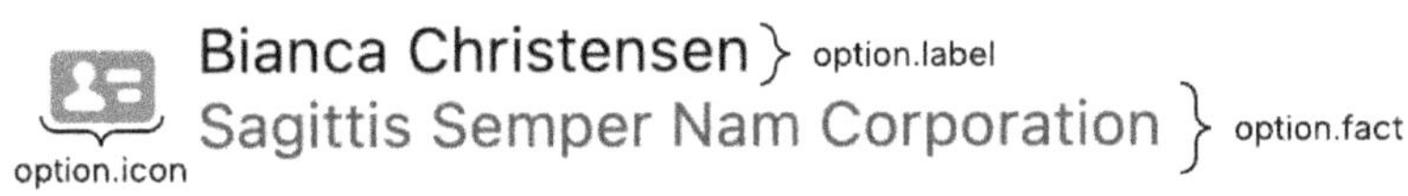

Figure 10.4: A screenshot showing where the text contained in each span lives within our option div

11. Now that we have our frontend built out, let's connect it to our database with the necessary JavaScript. Open your `polymorphicDropdown.js` file one more time. Under our earlier declaration of the `dropdownOptions` variable, we will add a function, `selectOption`, that takes a parameter of an event:

```
selectOption(event) {
  let selectedOption = event.currentTarget.dataset.id;
  let tempOptions = this.dropdownOptions;
  let selectedElement = tempOptions.find(option => option.value ===
selectedOption);
  const setSelectionEvent = new CustomEvent('setselection', {
    bubbles : false,
    composed : false,
    detail: {
      selectedElement : selectedElement
    }
  });
```

```
        this.dispatchEvent(setSelectionEvent);
    }
```

12. Since the `option` `div` tag in our utilizes the `data-id` attribute, we can use `event.currentTarget.dataset.id` to get the `option.value` of our selected option. We then want to filter our options for the selected value using the `find` method in JavaScript, at which point, we pass the whole `option` object back up in an event, `setSelectionEvent`.

> **Note**
>
> Recall that we learned in *Chapter 6, Composing Lightning Web Components,* that `bubbles : false` and `composed : false` are the default state for event configuration in LWCs, and therefore, this configuration does not need to be written out. We are doing so here for clarity.

See also

- The code for the `polymorphicDropdown` component is located at `https://github.com/PacktPublishing/Salesforce-Lightning-Web-Component-Cookbook/tree/main/force-app/chapter10/default/lwc/polymorphicDropdown`
- The SLDS1 documentation is located at `https://v1.lightningdesignsystem.com`
- The SLDS2 documentation is located at `https://lightningdesignsystem.com`
- The Mozilla MDN documentation on data attributes is located at `https://developer.mozilla.org/en-US/docs/Web/HTML/How_to/Use_data_attributes`
- The Mozilla MDN documentation on span elements is available at `https://developer.mozilla.org/en-US/docs/Web/HTML/Reference/Elements/span`
- A Salesforce Developer's video about utilizing data attributes within LWCs can be found at `https://youtube.com/watch?v=EgvMGcq0Xu8`

Reusing custom components

Now that we have our custom drop-down component, let's use it! We are going to pair our custom drop-down functionality with an input that will provide search functionality for both the `Contact` and `Customer` sObjects using polymorphic serialization. Let's get started.

How to do it...

Like other components, we can insert an instance of our `polymorphicDropdown` component within the **DOM** in our HTML and consume the events that are fired from it in a parent component. We will also need to pass in our `@api` decorated `dropdownOptions` variable into the `polymorphicDropdown` component:

1. Create a new LWC called `consumerSearchWithDropdown`, and open the resulting HTML file.

2. Add the following within your `document` template tags:

```
<div class="slds-form-element">
    <div class="slds-form-element__control">
        <lightning-input
            data-inputable="true"
            onchange={sendSearch}
            value={displayedOption}
            type="search"
            variant="label-hidden"
        ></lightning-input>
        <template lwc:if={searchResults}>
            <c-polymorphic-dropdown
                dropdown-options={searchResults}
                onsetselection={handleSelection}
            ></c-polymorphic-dropdown>
        </template>
    </div>
</div>
```

3. We are creating a `form` element with controls that contains a **lightning-input** tag for which we will be writing a search function, `sendSearch`, and if that search function returns values, we will display our `polymorphicDropdown` component with the results of that search. Notice that we are utilizing a **kebab case** variant, `c-polymorphic-dropdown`, to place our `polymorphicDropdown` component within the DOM.

4. Next, open your `consumerSearchWithDropdown.js` file. Import the `api` decorator, as well as the `returnSearchedConsumerWrappers` method of the `RecentConsumerController` class, and our `c/notifUtils` component from *Chapter 4, Synchronous and Asynchronous Processing in Components*. Additionally, add the `connectedCallback` that initializes a `utility` variable with our imported `notifUtils`:

```
import { LightningElement, api } from 'lwc';
import returnSearchedConsumerWrappers from '@salesforce/apex/
RecentConsumerController.returnSearchedConsumerWrappers';
import Utilities from 'c/notifUtils';
let utility;
export default class ConsumerSearchWithDropdown extends LightningElement {
    connectedCallback() {
        utility = new Utilities(this);
```

```
    }
}
```

5. Above our `connectedCallback` function, but within our class definition, we will add a private variable, `_value`, as well as an `api` decorated **getter and setter** for a corresponding public variable, `value`:

```
_value;
@api
get value() {
   return this._value;
} set value(val) {
   this._value = val;
}
```

6. We will use this chunk of code to set and return a selected value from our options so that we can pass in the value that is selected in our `polymorphicDropdown` component. We will see this in our next component.
7. Next, let's add some class variables. I have added mine below the getter for our `value` variable:

```
searchResults;
debounceTimeout;
selectedOption;
displayedOption;
```

Three of these variables are self-explanatory, but what about the `debounceTimeout` variable? **Debouncing** is a technique that allows us to add a delay in our search so that we don't overwhelm the server with how fast we are typing. This will add a slight delay to our search function so that we don't send a query with every letter that we type.

8. Speaking of our search functionality, let's add a function, `sendSearch`, which will accept a parameter of an event. To start, let's add a `try/catch` block within our function:

```
sendSearch(event) {
   try {
      // code will go here…
   } catch(error) {
      utility.showNotif('There has been an error searching!', error.message,
'error');
```

```
    }
}
```

9. Within the `try` block, we are first going to define a variable, `searchTerm`, which will hold the `detail.value` property of the event:

```
let searchTerm = event.detail.value;
```

10. Next, we want to only send our search if there are three or more characters, so that we can effectively use the `WHERE` clause of our SOQL query. Let's add an `if/else` block that determines whether we will run our search:

```
if(searchTerm.length > 2) {
    // more code will go here...
} else {
    this.searchResults = undefined;
}
```

11. If the `searchTerm` is three characters or longer, we will populate our `searchResults` array; otherwise, our `searchResults` will remain `undefined`.
12. Finally, within the `if` block, let's add our search and debounce functionality:

```
if(this.debounceTimeout) {
    clearTimeout(this.debounceTimeout);
}
// eslint-disable-next-line @lwc/lwc/no-async-operation
this.debounceTimeout = setTimeout(() => {
    try {
        this.search(searchTerm);
    } catch(error) {
        utility.showNotif('There has been an error returning consumers!',
error, 'error');
    }
}, 300);
```

13. If `debounceTimeout` exists, we are going to clear it using the built-in JavaScript function, `clearTimeout`. Once our `debounceTimeout` variable is clear, we will utilize the `setTimeout` function to set a delay of 300 milliseconds to allow our server to catch up

with our typing. We will try to search with a function we will write in a moment, and if that function fails, we will display a toast message via our `notifUtils` component.

> **Note**
>
> You'll notice that we have a line that is commented out and highlighted in the preceding code sample, `// eslint-disable-next-line @lwc/lwc/no-async-operation`. This comment tells our local linter to ignore the next line, specifically, the `@lwc/lwc/no-async-operation` rule. If we remove this line of code and run **ESLint**, we will get the following error message: `error Restricted async operation "setTimeout" @lwc/lwc/no-async-operation`. This rule restricts certain asynchronous operations, such as `setTimeout`, because similar actions can be taken with the use of a **callback hook**, such as `renderedCallback` or `connectedCallback`. However, because we are debouncing our search as we type, we will utilize the `eslint-disable-next-line` functionality. More information about this rule can be found at `https://github.com/salesforce/eslint-plugin-lwc/blob/master/docs/rules/no-async-operation.md`.

14. Now that we have a debounce on our search functionality, let's write the asynchronous function that will perform our search. As we saw in our `sendSearch` function, we will be accepting `searchTerm` as a parameter. Once again, we will start this function off with a `try/catch` block:

```
async search(searchTerm) {
    try{
        // code will go here...
    } catch(error) {
        utility.showNotif('There has been an error loading consumers!', error,
'error');
    }
}
```

15. Within our `try` block, we are going to call our Apex method and then process the results for display in our LWC. Remember, we are passing the results down into our `polymorphicDropdown` component, and we need the `label`, `value`, `icon`, `altText`, and

`fact` properties to do so. The `label`, `value`, and `fact` property values are baked in with our wrapper class, so we need to add our `icon` and `altText` properties:

```
const searchedConsumers = await returnSearchedConsumerWrappers({searchTerm :
searchTerm});
let tempConsumers = JSON.parse(JSON.stringify(searchedConsumers));
let results = [];
tempConsumers.forEach(consumer => {
    if(consumer.type === 'Contact') {
        consumer.icon = 'utility:contact';
        consumer.altText = 'Contact';
    } else if (consumer.type === 'Customer') {
        consumer.icon = 'utility:customer';
        consumer.altText = 'Customer';
        consumer.fact = new Intl.NumberFormat("en-US", {style: "currency",
currency: 'USD'}).format(consumer.fact);
    }
    results.push(consumer);
})
if(results.length > 0) {
    this.searchResults = results.sort((a, b) => {
        return (a.label > b.label) ? 1 : -1;
    });
}
```

16. Notice that we determine whether the consumer is a contact or a customer and assign an `icon` and an `altText` value appropriately, utilizing a modest example of polymorphic serialization, which must be completed manually in JavaScript. Additionally, if the consumer is a customer, we want to format their `TotalLifetimeValue` number value appropriately, which is highlighted in the preceding code block. Once we have assigned these values, we sort our results and assign them to the `searchResults` class variable so they can be displayed on our frontend.

> **Note**
>
> The highlighted line of code in the preceding snippet allows us to define how our number will be displayed, and it can be changed based on the locale. Currently, the line of code sets our number formatting to `en-US` styled currency in USD.
>
> The documentation for the `Intl.NumberFormat` object in JavaScript is located at `https://developer.mozilla.org/en-US/docs/Web/JavaScript/Reference/Global_Objects/Intl/NumberFormat`.

17. Once we have `searchResults` populated, we need to specify what happens when one of those results is selected. Create a function, `handleSelection`, that accepts a parameter of an event. This function will set our `selectedOption` and our `displayedOption` values, clear `searchResults`, and dispatch an event to the parent component:

```
handleSelection(event) {
    this.selectedOption = event.detail.selectedElement[0];
    this.displayedOption = this.selectedOption.label;
    this.searchResults = undefined;
    const setSearchSelectionEvent = new CustomEvent('setsearchvalue', {
        bubbles : true,
        composed : true,
        detail: {
            selectedElement : this.selectedOption
        }
    });
    this.dispatchEvent(setSearchSelectionEvent);
}
```

18. Let's deploy what we have so far. You can add this standalone functionality to the **Account** record page to test it for now. We will be adding it to a custom `lightning-datatable` in the next recipe.

See also

- The GitHub repository for the Salesforce ESLint project is located at `https://github.com/salesforce/eslint-plugin-lwc/tree/master`

- There is an example of using within a Salesforce LWC in the Salesforce documentation at `https://developer.salesforce.com/docs/platform/lwc/guide/apex-wire-method.html`
- A brief description of polymorphism in Salesforce can be found within the Developer docs at `https://developer.salesforce.com/docs/atlas.en-us.soql_sosl.meta/soql_sosl/sforce_api_calls_soql_relationships_and_polymorph_keys.htm`

Inserting a custom component into a datatable column

Now that we have our base functionality of a search dropdown for multiple sObject types, let's put it inside the **lightning-datatable** that we have been working on for the last two chapters. We started with our `displayAssetsOnAccount` component in *Chapter 8, Implementing Reactivity in Lightning Web Components,* and we made it editable with a custom picklist datatable in `displayAssetsOnAccountEditable` in *Chapter 9, Creating Custom Lightning Web Components.*

How to do it...

In this recipe, we will be adding one more editable column to the functionality we built in *Chapter 9, Creating Custom Lightning Web Components,* to expand on our repertoire of custom components:

1. Start by opening the `picklistDatatable` custom component that we created in *Chapter 9, Creating Custom Lightning Web Components.* If you are joining us in this chapter, this component is in the `force-app/chapter09/default/lwc/picklistDatatable` directory of the GitHub repository. We are going to begin by creating two new HTML template files within this LWC folder, `consumerEdit` and `consumerInquiry`. Let's start with `consumerInquiry.html`:

```
<template>
    <span class="slds-truncate" title={typeAttributes.label}>
        {typeAttributes.label}
    </span>
</template>
```

2. Within this file, we are going to add opening and closing `template` tags as well as a span that displays the `label` property of **typeAttributes**. Similar to our `picklistPlaceholder.html` file in the same folder, this is going to be our placeholder

template, which will display our most recent consumer inquiry (`Consumer_Inquiry__c`) info when we are not editing the value.

3. Next, let's create our `consumerEdit.html` file:

```
<template>
   <c-consumer-search-with-dropdown value={typeAttributes.value} data-
inputable="true"></c-consumer-search-with-dropdown>
</template>
```

4. Once again, we add `template` tags so that our browser recognizes our LWC, and within those tags, we add our `c-consumer-search-with-dropdown` component. We set the `value` attribute to the `value` property of `typeAttributes`, and we set the **data-inputable** attribute to `"true"`, which will allow us to edit and set our `value`.
5. Next, enter the `picklistDatatable.js` file. Under the imports of our `picklistPlaceholder` and `picklistSelector` HTML files, but before the definition of our class, import our `consumerInquiry` and `consumerEdit` HTML files:

```
import consumerInquiry from './consumerInquiry.html';
import consumerEdit from './consumerEdit.html';
```

6. Remember, the `consumerInquiry` and `consumerEdit` HTML files must be in the `picklistDatatable` folder for this import to work.
7. Within the definition for our `static customTypes` object, add the following, making sure to place a comma after the curly brackets surrounding the definition for our `picklistColumn`:

```
searchColumn : {
   template : consumerInquiry,
   editTemplate: consumerEdit,
   standardCellLayout: true,
   typeAttributes: ['label', 'placeholder', 'value']
}
```

8. This will set our default template to our `consumerInquiry` file, and our edit template to the `consumerEdit` file, while defining our `typeAttributes`.
9. Now that we have added our editable consumerInquiry column definition to our picklistDatatable, let's implement it. We can either modify the file that we wrote in

Chapter 9, Creating Custom Lightning Web Components, or copy it into a new folder and file structure, such as `displayAssetsOnAccountWithConsumer`, as I have opted to do to clearly differentiate the code from each chapter. If you are copying your existing code into a new folder, be sure to update the name of each of your files to match your LWC, as well as to update the name of the class in your JavaScript file.

10. First, let's add our new editable column to our `assetsColumns.js` file. In the `WIDE_COLUMNS_DEFINITION` constant, remove the **Asset Id** column, and tack on our `searchColumn` behind our `picklistColumn`. We are also going to make a slight modification to the `picklistColumn` definition, highlighted below, to make it so that only one row is editable at a time:

```
{
    type: 'picklistColumn',
    fieldName: 'DisplayStatus',
    label: 'Display Status',
    editable: {fieldName : 'statusEditable'},
    typeAttributes : {
        label: {fieldName: 'statusLabel'},
        value: {fieldName: 'statusValue'},
        placeholder: {fieldName: 'statusPlaceholder'},
        options: {fieldName: 'statusOptions'}
    }
},
{
    type: 'searchColumn',
    fieldName: 'Consumer',
    label: 'Most Recent Consumer Inquiry',
    editable: {fieldName : 'consumerEditable'},
    typeAttributes : {
        label: {fieldName: 'consumerLabel'},
        value: {fieldName: 'consumerValue'}
    }
}
```

11. This will add our custom `searchColumn` into our custom datatable, and set both the `picklistColumn` and `searchColumns` to be editable when specified.

12. Continue by opening your `displayAssetsOnAccountWithConsumer` HTML file, and add the following attributes to your `c-picklist-datatable` tag:

```
hide-checkbox-column={checkboxColumnHidden}
onsetsearchvalue={handleSearchSelection}
```

13. These two attributes allow us to optionally display the checkbox column in our **lightning-datatable**, as well as to define what happens when our `setsearchvalue` event in our `consumerSearchWithDropdown` component from earlier in this chapter is captured.

14. Next, open your `displayAssetsOnAccountWithConsumer.js` file, and add the following class variables before your getter for the `assetColumns` variable:

```
searchedLabel;
searchedValue;
checkboxColumnHidden = false;
```

15. Within our `connectedCallback` function, we are going to make some slight modifications. Recall that we are setting our first row in the datatable to be selected via radio button upon load. We only want the row that is selected by **radio button** to be editable so that we don't have competing changes, so when a row is selected, we are going to set the `consumerEditable` and `statusEditable` properties of the row to `true`. Add the following highlighted lines, shown here in context:

```
if(this.assetsForDatatable.length > 0) {
   this.selectedAsset = this.assetsForDatatable[0];
   this.selectedRows = [this.selectedAsset?.Id];
   this.assetsForDatatable[0].consumerEditable = true;
   this.assetsForDatatable[0].statusEditable = true;
}
```

16. This snippet checks to make sure we have **Assets** in our datatable, and, if so, selects the zeroth index of the `assetsForDatatable` array and sets its properties as specified.

17. Next, we need to modify our `formatAssets` function. Add the following at the end of your `forEach` method, within its defining brackets:

```
asset.statusEditable = false;
asset.consumerEditable = false;
```

```
if(Object.hasOwn(asset, 'Consumer_Inquiries__r') === false) {
    asset.consumerLabel = undefined;
    asset.consumerValue = asset.Id;
    return;
}
```

18. This snippet will ensure that only our selected row is editable by setting our `statusEditable` and `consumerEditable` attributes to `false` by default. Additionally, we will set `consumerLabel` as `undefined` if there are no related `Consumer_Inquiry__c` objects for our selected asset, and we will set `consumerValue` as the `Id` value of our asset. We set this `Id` value here to ensure that each row has a defined `consumerValue`, so we don't experience errors. If there are no `Consumer_Inquiry__c` objects, we finally use `return` to move to the next value in our `forEach` loop.
19. In the event that there are `Consumer_Inquiry__c` objects associated with the asset, we need to do a little more processing. Below the `if` block, still within our `forEach` method definition, add the following:

```
asset.mostRecentInquiry = asset.Consumer_Inquiries__r[0];
if(Object.hasOwn(asset.mostRecentInquiry, 'Contact__c')) {
    asset.consumerLabel = asset.mostRecentInquiry.Contact__r.Name;
    asset.consumerValue = asset.mostRecentInquiry.Contact__c;
}
if(Object.hasOwn(asset.mostRecentInquiry, 'Customer__c')) {
    asset.consumerLabel = asset.mostRecentInquiry.Customer__r.Name;
    asset.consumerValue = asset.mostRecentInquiry.Customer__c;
}
```

20. We want to get the most recent inquiry, which will be the zeroth index of our `Consumer_Inquiries__r` array, as defined by the sort preferences in our Apex selector class. Based on whether the `mostRecentInquiry` object has a `Contact__c` property or a `Customer__c` property, we will assign our `consumerLabel` and `consumerValue` properties accordingly.
21. Next, we must modify our `updateCarousel` function, used to determine which photograph to display in our `lightning-carousel` element based on which row is

selected, to additionally only allow edits on the selected row. Add the following highlighted lines, shown here in context:

```
updateCarousel(event) {
   let selectedAssetRows = event.detail.selectedRows;
   this.selectedAsset = selectedAssetRows[0];
   this.assetsForDatatable.forEach(asset => {
      if(asset.Id === this.selectedAsset.Id) {
         asset.consumerEditable = true;
         asset.statusEditable = true;
      } else {
         asset.consumerEditable = false;
         asset.statusEditable = false;
      }
   });
   this.assetsForDatatable = [...this.assetsForDatatable];
   this.selectedRows = [this.selectedAsset.Id];
}
```

This snippet sets the selected row to editable, while setting all other rows to uneditable.

22. Now that we have decided which rows are editable, let's ensure that we can use our search functionality to edit. Add a new function, `handleSearchSelection`. Recall that we have already placed this in our HTML file, and will need to define it for our search functionality to work:

```
handleSearchSelection(event) {
   let searchSelection = event.detail.selectedElement;
   this.searchedLabel = searchSelection.label;
   this.searchedValue = searchSelection.value;
}
```

Here, we are accessing the properties that we defined in our `setsearchvalue` event earlier in the chapter.

23. Once we have set our selected row to editable and enabled edit functionality, we need to update our `handleInlineEdit` function. The first thing that we will do is add this line to the top of our function:

```
this.checkboxColumnHidden = true;
```

This will ensure that if we have edited a column in our row, we will not be able to select and edit additional rows. Blocking this functionality through the user interface makes our work easier.

24. Recall that our `handleInlineEdit` function grabs a singular `draftValue`, based on the row that is edited, and assigns properties to a temporary `Asset` object, `tempAsset`, for storage:

```
handleInlineEdit(event) {
    this.checkboxColumnHidden = true;
    let draftValue = event.detail.draftValues[0];
    let draftValueIndex = this.assetsForDatatable.findIndex(draft => draft.Id
=== draftValue.Id);
    let tempAsset = this.assetsForDatatable[draftValueIndex];
    tempAsset.oldLabel = tempAsset.statusLabel;
    tempAsset.oldValue = tempAsset.statusValue;
    tempAsset.oldPlaceholder = tempAsset.statusPlaceholder;
    tempAsset.oldOptions = tempAsset.statusOptions;
    tempAsset.statusLabel = draftValue.DisplayStatus;
    tempAsset.statusValue = draftValue.DisplayStatus;
    tempAsset.statusPlaceholder = draftValue.DisplayStatus;
    tempAsset.statusOptions = this.statusPickvals.filter(val
=> val.value !== tempAsset.statusValue);
    this.assetsForDatatable[draftValueIndex] = tempAsset;
    let draftIndex = this.draftValues.findIndex(draft => draft.Id ===
draftValue.Id);
    if(draftIndex < 0) {
      this.draftValues.push(tempAsset);
    } else {
      this.draftValues[draftIndex] = tempAsset;
    }
}
```

25. We are going to take the highlighted portion of the existing code snippet and put it inside an `if/else if` block, where we complete a different operation based on whether `draftValue` is an edit to our `Consumer` column or our `DisplayStatus` column:

```
if(Object.hasOwn(draftValue, 'Consumer')) {
    tempAsset.oldConsumerValue = tempAsset.consumerValue;
    tempAsset.oldConsumerLabel = tempAsset.consumerLabel;
```

```
        tempAsset.consumerLabel = this.searchedLabel;
        tempAsset.consumerValue = this.searchedValue;
    } else if (Object.hasOwn(draftValue, 'DisplayStatus')) {
        tempAsset.oldStatusLabel = tempAsset.statusLabel;
        tempAsset.oldStatusValue = tempAsset.statusValue;
        tempAsset.oldStatusPlaceholder = tempAsset.statusPlaceholder;
        tempAsset.oldStatusOptions = tempAsset.statusOptions;
        tempAsset.statusLabel = draftValue.DisplayStatus;
        tempAsset.statusValue = draftValue.DisplayStatus;
        tempAsset.statusPlaceholder = draftValue.DisplayStatus;
        tempAsset.statusOptions = this.statusPickvals.filter(val
    => val.value !== tempAsset.statusValue);
    } else {
        return;
    }
```

26. Finally, we can deploy our changes to test. We will need to make a few more modifications to get our LWC working and saving properly, but for now, you should be able to search for a contact or a customer within your datatable.

See also

- The GitHub repository for the `displayAssetsOnAccountWithConsumer` LWC is located at `https://github.com/PacktPublishing/Salesforce-Lightning-Web-Component-Cookbook/tree/main/force-app/chapter10/default/lwc/displayAssetsOnAccountWithConsumer`
- The GitHub repository for *Chapter 9, Creating Custom Lightning Web Components* LWC, `displayAssetsOnAccountEditable`, is available at `https://github.com/PacktPublishing/Salesforce-Lightning-Web-Component-Cookbook/tree/main/force-app/chapter09/default/lwc/displayAssetsOnAccountEditable`
- The GitHub repository for the *Chapter 8, Implementing Reactivity in Lightning Web Components* component, `displayAssetsOnAccount`, is available at `https://github.com/PacktPublishing/Salesforce-Lightning-Web-Component-Cookbook/tree/main/force-app/chapter08/default/lwc/displayAssetsOnAccount`

- The Salesforce Developers documentation on the `lightning-datatable` element is available at `https://developer.salesforce.com/docs/component-library/bundle/lightning-datatable/documentation`
- The Mozilla MDN documentation for the `Object.hasOwn()` method is available at `https://developer.mozilla.org/en-US/docs/Web/JavaScript/Reference/Global_Objects/Object/hasOwn`

Utilizing polymorphic Apex classes

Now that we have our LWC built, we need to make some final tweaks to our service class, `DisplayAssetsService`, as well as create the `ConsumerInquiries` class that will allow us to insert a `Consumer_Inquiry__c` sObject, relating either a `Contact` or a `Customer` sObject record to our asset. So, how can we accomplish this?

How to do it...

1. Start by creating a new Apex class, `ConsumerInquiries`. This class will serve as our **persistence layer class**, allowing us to make changes to the database. This class will extend our `Util_DML` class from *Chapter 5, Accessing External Data Sources via Lightning Web Component*:

```
public with sharing class ConsumerInquiries extends Util_DML {
   public void insertInquiries(List<Consumer_Inquiry__c> inquiriesToInsert)
{
      try{
         insertRecords(inquiriesToInsert);
      } catch (Exception e) {
         //error processing
      }
   }
}
```

2. Notice that we call the `insertRecords` method of the extended `Util_DML` class.
3. Next, return to your `DisplayAssetsService` class from *Chapter 8, Implementing Reactivity in Lightning Web Components*. At the top of your class, add one more class variable, `inquiries`:

```
@TestVisible private ConsumerInquiries inquiries = new ConsumerInquiries();
```

4. Recall that we created the `saveAssetWrappers` method in *Chapter 9, Creating Custom Lightning Web Components*. This is the method we will be modifying. Within the `for` loop, add the highlighted lines of code:

```
for(DisplayAssetWrapper wrapper : wrapperList) {
   if(wrapper.statusValue != null && wrapper.statusValue != '') {
       Asset assetToUpdate = new Asset(Id = wrapper.Id, Status =
wrapper.statusValue);
       assetsToUpdate.add(assetToUpdate);
   }
   if(wrapper.consumerValue != null && wrapper.consumerValue != '') {
       Id consumerId = Id.valueOf(wrapper.consumerValue);
       Consumer_Inquiry__c newInquiry;
       Consumer newConsumer;
       switch on
consumerId.getSObjectType().getDescribe().getName().toLowerCase() {
           when 'contact' {
               newConsumer = new ContactConsumer(wrapper.Id, new Contact(Id =
consumerId));
               newInquiry = newConsumer.getConsumerInquiry();
           }
           when 'customer' {
               newConsumer = new CustomerConsumer(wrapper.Id, new Customer(Id
= consumerId));
               newInquiry = newConsumer.getConsumerInquiry();
           }
           when else {
               continue;
           }
       }
       inquiriesToInsert.add(newInquiry);
   }
}
```

5. Within these highlighted lines of code, we use the internal `getSObjectType`, **getDescribe**, and `getName` methods to determine which type of sObject we are updating. We use a `switch` statement on the result of these method calls to determine which subclass of the abstract `Consumer` superclass we are instantiating, and thus which field

we are assigning our `consumerId` to on the `newInquiry` record of the `Consumer_Inquiry__c` type.

6. Deploy your changes to your Salesforce Developer Edition org and verify the functionality.

See also

- The GitHub repository for the `ConsumerInquiries` class is located at `https://github.com/PacktPublishing/Salesforce-Lightning-Web-Component-Cookbook/blob/main/force-app/chapter10/default/classes/ConsumerInquiries.cls`
- The GitHub repository for the `DisplayAssetsService` class is available at `https://github.com/PacktPublishing/Salesforce-Lightning-Web-Component-Cookbook/blob/main/force-app/chapter08/default/classes/DisplayAssetsService.cls`

11

Writing Accessible Lightning Web Components

On their **Product Accessibility Status** page, Salesforce states that approximately 15% of the world's population is living with some form of disability. I am one of them. You might be, too, either now or in the future. The beautiful thing about life is that we do not have the ability to predict every aspect of our futures, and that includes aspects of our health, wellness, and ability. Disabilities can be visible or invisible, and they can be temporary or permanent. As we age, the likelihood of the occurrence of some form of disability rises, whether due to the blessing of growing old or due to an injury or illness of some kind.

Thankfully, we live in an age where assistive technologies and accommodations exist that allow folks with disabilities to participate in society in ways that we wouldn't have been able to in previous generations. This chapter is nominally about building applications compatible with these technologies, but I hope that you will take away that accessible systems behoove us all. They allow us to interact with the world and each other in a way that grants everyone dignity.

We are going to cover the following main recipes in this chapter:

- Testing behavior across operating systems and browsers
- Applying accessibility principles to custom LWCs
- Writing it right: avoiding common pitfalls

Technical requirements

The recipes for this book can be found at `https://github.com/PacktPublishing/Salesforce-Lightning-Web-Component-Cookbook`, where each chapter has its own folder under the `force-app` folder. This GitHub repository is structured in the form of a Salesforce DX project, which will allow you to easily fork the repository for deployment in a free Salesforce Developer Edition org. The code for *Chapter 11, Writing Accessible Lightning Web Components*, is located at `https://github.com/PacktPublishing/Salesforce-Lightning-Web-Component-Cookbook/tree/main/force-app/chapter11` and `https://github.com/PacktPublishing/Salesforce-Lightning-Web-Component-Cookbook/tree/main/force-app/chapter11_setup`.

The components in this book require the use of an **integrated development environment** (**IDE**), such as **Visual Studio Code** (**VS Code**) or **Salesforce Code Builder**. Detailed instructions for setting up an IDE are located in *Chapter 1, Getting Ready for Lightning Web Component*, in the *Setting up your IDE* section.

If you are building the projects in this cookbook as written, you will need to seed your Salesforce Developer Edition org with test data. Detailed instructions for seeding your org are located in *Chapter 1, Getting Ready for Lightning Web Component*, in the *Setting up the Salesforce Lightning Web Components Cookbook org* section.

Lastly, the edition of Salesforce required to implement the recipes in this book must be Developer, Performance, Unlimited, Enterprise, or Database.com. You can sign up for a free Salesforce Developer Edition org at `https://developer.salesforce.com/signup`.

Why should we care about making our applications accessible?

Well, not only is it an international best practice development standard, but in the USA, it's the law. In the USA, the **Americans with Disabilities Act** (**ADA**) requires that public places, including the web, be accessible.

According to the *2025 Mid-Year ADA Website Lawsuit Report* published by EcomBack, an organization that audits and provides fixes for accessibility issues on websites, there were 94 accessibility lawsuits brought against organizations that used Salesforce Commerce Cloud to build out their websites from just January to June in 2025.

In addition to being a jurisdictional legal requirement, it's simply the right thing to do. Accessibility features benefit not only persons with disabilities, but the general populace as well. Have you ever watched a movie with subtitles? This is an accessibility feature! Have you used hotkeys to navigate between tabs or applications on your computer? Another accessibility feature. These accessibility features range from handy to crucial in allowing all users to interact with various forms of media.

To help developers make sites accessible, the **World Wide Web Consortium** (**W3C**) leads the **Web Accessibility Initiative** (**WAI**), which offers accessibility resources. Salesforce follows W3C's **Web Content Accessibility Guidelines 2.2** (**WCAG 2.2**) recommendations, which can be seen implemented throughout the SLDS library, and in the company's Product Accessibility Conformance Reports. To learn more about ADA, go to `https://www.ada.gov/`.

Information about the W3C WAI is available at `https://www.w3.org/WAI/`.

The standards adhered to by Salesforce can be found at `https://www.w3.org/TR/WCAG22/`.

Salesforce's **Product Accessibility Status** page can be found at `https://www.salesforce.com/company/legal/508_accessibility/`.

To learn about how other companies are handling issues of accessibility, you can visit Apple's Accessibility Framework documentation, located at `https://developer.apple.com/documentation/accessibility`.

To read the EcomBack *2025 Mid-Year ADA Website Lawsuit Report*, you can visit `https://www.ecomback.com/ada-website-lawsuits-recap-report/2025-mid-year-ada-website-lawsuit-report`.

Testing behavior across operating systems and browsers

Now that we know a little bit about why we should be applying accessibility principles in developing our LWCs, let's learn how to test our components to check whether they are accessible. One of the greatest skills you can have as a Salesforce developer is empathy for your end users. The easiest way to develop this muscle is to shadow your end users to understand their pain points. If the ability to shadow your end users or peek in on user acceptance testing is beyond your reach, you can and should be testing your components as you build them and before you ship them. We are going to test two components today for accessibility to learn how to go about doing so, and to ensure that we are not only compliant but also compassionate in our development practices.

Getting started

To save us some time, I have built two Lightning Web Components and a **Lightning app** that we can use to test them. To show an example of how we can reuse the queries of a **selector class**, I have reused the methods of the `AccountSelector` that we built in *Chapter 3, Working with a Selector Class.*

If you are joining us in this chapter, you will need to deploy the files in the `force-app/chapter03` directory to deploy this app, as well as complete the setup required for test data, outlined in the *Setting up the Salesforce Lightning Web Components Cookbook org* recipe contained within *Chapter 1, Getting Ready for Lightning Web Component Development.* These steps will ensure that you have the necessary data to complete this exercise.

If you have been building along with me, verify that you have the `AccountSelector` and `Util_Query` Apex classes in your org before continuing, as the metadata we will be deploying in the `force-app/chapter11_setup` directory is dependent on these.

Once you have verified that these classes exist in your Developer Edition org, either through deployment from your forked repository or having been built by you, deploy the `force-app/chapter11_setup` directory into your Developer Edition org.

Finally, once the *Chapter 11, Writing Accessible Lightning Web Components,* setup files have been deployed, you will notice that we have deployed a **permission set**, `View Accessibility Test App`. Assign this permission set to your user to ensure that you will have access to the Lightning app called `Accessible vs. Inaccessible Test`. Verify that you have the ability to view the `Accessible vs. Inaccessible Test` app, accessed via the Salesforce **App Launcher**, and you're ready to test!

How to do it...

Once again, verify that you have access to the `Accessible vs. Inaccessible Test` app. You should see the following remarkably similar tables:

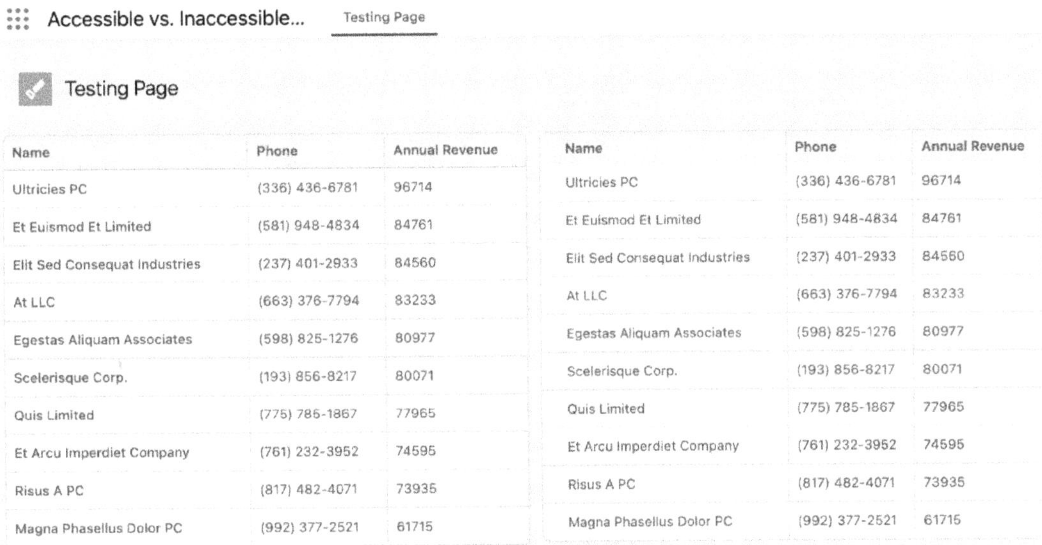

Name	Phone	Annual Revenue
Ultricies PC	(336) 436-6781	96714
Et Euismod Et Limited	(581) 948-4834	84761
Elit Sed Consequat Industries	(237) 401-2933	84560
At LLC	(663) 376-7794	83233
Egestas Aliquam Associates	(598) 825-1276	80977
Scelerisque Corp.	(193) 856-8217	80071
Quis Limited	(775) 785-1867	77965
Et Arcu Imperdiet Company	(761) 232-3952	74595
Risus A PC	(817) 482-4071	73935
Magna Phasellus Dolor PC	(992) 377-2521	61715

Name	Phone	Annual Revenue
Ultricies PC	(336) 436-6781	96714
Et Euismod Et Limited	(581) 948-4834	84761
Elit Sed Consequat Industries	(237) 401-2933	84560
At LLC	(663) 376-7794	83233
Egestas Aliquam Associates	(598) 825-1276	80977
Scelerisque Corp.	(193) 856-8217	80071
Quis Limited	(775) 785-1867	77965
Et Arcu Imperdiet Company	(761) 232-3952	74595
Risus A PC	(817) 482-4071	73935
Magna Phasellus Dolor PC	(992) 377-2521	61715

Figure 11.1: The Accessible vs. Inaccessible Test app showing the top 10 accounts by annual revenue in descending order in two tables

Aside from some minor formatting differences, these tables contain the same data. The main difference is that the one on the left is created with a `lightning-datatable` component, and the other is created using the `<table>` tag in HTML. This will become important as we experiment!

Let's get started:

1. Navigate to the `Accessible vs. Inaccessible Test` app in your browser and open your operating system's VoiceOver functionality. For Windows computers, this is achieved by pressing *Win* + *Ctrl* + *Enter* to open **Narrator**, while for Macintosh devices, you can press *Cmd* + *F5* to open **VoiceOver**. We will be utilizing these tools to read our screen back to us. In a professional environment, or as an end user, we may utilize a screen-reading tool such as **Job Access With Speech** (**JAWS**) or **NonVisual Desktop Access** (**NVDA**) to complete similar testing. You may be prompted to enter a tutorial or to set up the software. If this is the case, feel free to skip or complete the tutorial and select the defaults for the program setup.
2. On Windows, you will see the following window, letting you know that you have turned on Narrator, as well as giving you options to customize it:

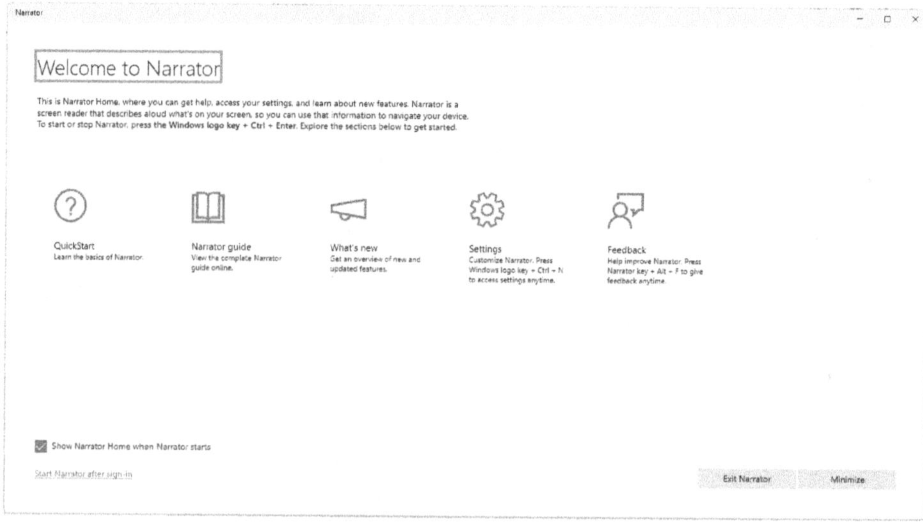

Figure 11.2: The Welcome to Narrator screen

3. Narrator will automatically start, and you can exit by pressing the **Exit Narrator** button in the bottom-right corner of this window.
4. Note that you will need to turn **Scan Mode** off in order to complete this tutorial. This can be achieved by pressing *Caps Lock* + *Spacebar*.
5. On a Mac, you will see the following popup:

Figure 11.3: The Welcome to VoiceOver popup

6. Select the **Use VoiceOver** button, or press the *V* key to continue.
7. Tab into the left-hand table utilizing the *Tab* key. This should work on either Windows or macOS. You should hear vocalizations for each item your screen reader focuses on.

When you enter the table, you should see something like the following if you are utilizing a Mac:

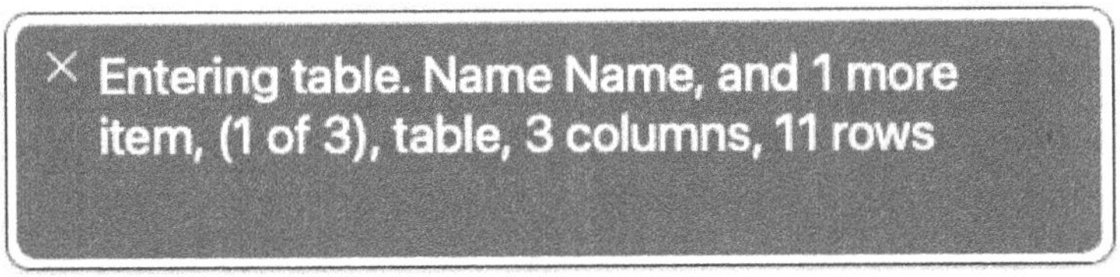

Figure 11.4: A VoiceOver modal that states that we have entered the table

> **Note**
>
> If you are utilizing Google Chrome to complete this exercise, you may notice that the table header is announced multiple times when the focus is set. This is a known issue in Chromium that is, as of the writing of this chapter, untriaged (`https://issues.chromium.org/issues/341800520`).

8. Notice that once you have focused on the left-hand table, you can navigate within the table on Windows using the *Caps Lock* + *Arrow* keys if you have turned off **Scan Mode**, or on macOS using *Ctrl* + *Option* + *Arrow*. As you navigate the table, you will see that when you enter a new row, the `Name` value in the first column is read, as well as the value in the current focus cell. When you enter a new column, the column name is read, as well as the value in the current focus cell.

> **Note**
>
> Depending on your particular combination of operating system and browser, you may see slightly different behavior than described when completing this exercise. This is to be expected. There can be slight differences in how screen-reading tools process the information presented by the browser, which is why it's important to test apps across multiple combinations. **Accessibility Developer Guide** has information on the most common operating system and browser combinations, located at `https://www.accessibility-developer-guide.com/knowledge/screen-readers/relevant-combinations/`.

9. Try tabbing into the table on the right-hand side. Depending on your browser, you might not be able to! In testing for this chapter, I was not able to navigate into the second table in Google Chrome on macOS or Windows, and I was only intermittently

able to navigate into the second table in Mozilla Firefox. This is because this table uses the `<table>`, `<th>`, `<tr>`, and `<td>` tags in HTML without assigning the necessary attributes to each tag. We will be fixing this in the next recipe.

10. Try to navigate to other apps and pages within your Salesforce org and test them for accessibility. To follow a link on Windows, you can press *Caps Lock* + *Enter*, while on macOS, you can press *Ctrl* + *Option* + *Spacebar*.
11. Because all our components up until this point have been built with **Lightning base components**, you'll find that they are mostly navigable with screen reader technologies. This is because, in addition to providing base styling, Lightning base components handle the HTML and CSS required to make our applications accessible.

> Note
>
> You may notice that the `lightning-tree-grid` containing the `assetsByTag` component, which we built in *Chapter 4, Synchronous and Asynchronous Processing in Components*, has some trouble rendering with a screen reader. This is a known gap in Salesforce's accessibility offerings.

12. When you are ready, exit your accessibility narration tool using the same keys you used to open it; for Windows, press *Win* + *Ctrl* + *Enter*, and press *Cmd* + *F5* for macOS.

See also

- The code required from *Chapter 3, Working With a Selector Class*, is located at `https://github.com/PacktPublishing/Salesforce-Lightning-Web-Component-Cookbook/tree/main/force-app/chapter03`
- The setup code for *Chapter 11, Writing Accessible Lightning Web Components*, is located at `https://github.com/PacktPublishing/Salesforce-Lightning-Web-Component-Cookbook/tree/main/force-app/chapter11_setup`
- To access the Microsoft Complete Guide to Narrator, you can visit `https://support.microsoft.com/en-us/windows/complete-guide-to-narrator-e4397a0d-ef4f-b386-d8ae-c172f109bdb1`
- To access the Apple guide to VoiceOver, you can visit `https://support.apple.com/guide/voiceover/welcome/mac`
- More information about JAWS is available at `https://vispero.com/jaws-screen-reader-software/`

- More information about NVDA is available at `https://www.nvaccess.org/download/`
- To read about the benefits of developing with Lightning base components, visit `https://developer.salesforce.com/docs/atlas.en-us.lightning.meta/lightning/lightning_overview.htm`
- Known issues in Salesforce's accessibility offerings are listed at `https://help.salesforce.com/s/articleView?id=xcloud.accessibility_lex_known_issues.htm&type=5`

Applying accessibility principles to custom LWCs

Now that we understand not only the legal issues that come with shipping an inaccessible app, but also how important readability by a screen reader is to usability for some end users, we know that we need to fix our inaccessible component. We have determined that most Lightning base components have accessibility elements built in, but how can we add these elements to any vanilla HTML within our custom LWCs? Let's take a look.

How to do it...

We are going to be expanding on the `inaccessibleTable` component that we deployed to our Developer Edition org at the start of the chapter:

1. Open your forked repository in VS Code to the `inaccessibleTable` file, which is located in the `force-app/chapter11_setup/default/lwc/inaccessibleTable` directory.
2. Examine the sample `inaccessibleTable` file and its structure. Notice that we utilize the `<table>`, `<th>`, `<tr>`, and `<td>` tags to structure the table we see in the `Accessible vs. Inaccessible Test` app. Notice that we utilize SLDS classes in our opening `<table>` tag to style our HTML table to match our `lightning-datatable`.
3. Compare this file to the sample `accessibleDatatable` file, which uses a `lightning-datatable` component to structure our data. Remember, a Lightning base component, such as `lightning-datatable`, is rendered as HTML in our browser, with Salesforce doing the translation for us. As a result, our `inaccessibleTable` file is roughly what our browser renders, minus the key accessibility features. Neat!
4. Copy the files in the `force-app/chapter11_setup/default/lwc/inaccessibleTable` directory into a new LWC file and rename the copied files to match an LWC named **accessibleTable**. We are going to be editing this file so we can easily compare it to our `inaccessibleTable` component when we are finished. Once we are done, it should look

like the `accessibleTable` sample component in the `force-app/chapter11/default/lwc/accessibleTable` directory.

5. Edit the Lightning page for our `Testing` page within the `Accessible vs. Inaccessible` app. This can be achieved by hitting **Edit Page** after exposing the **Setup** drop-down menu by clicking the gear in the top-right corner while within the app on your browser. Edit the page to include the `accessibleTable` component, placing it above the `inaccessibleTable` component. This will allow us to see our changes as we deploy them and easily compare them. Be sure to save your Lightning page before returning to our app.

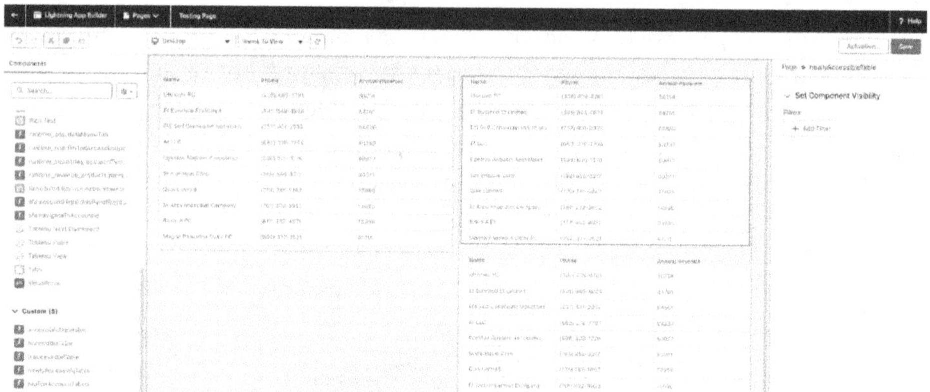

Figure 11.5: An overview of a screenshot of the Lightning App Builder showing that we have placed the accessibleTable component above our inaccessibleTable component

6. Now, our `Accessible vs. Inaccessible Test` app should look like the following:

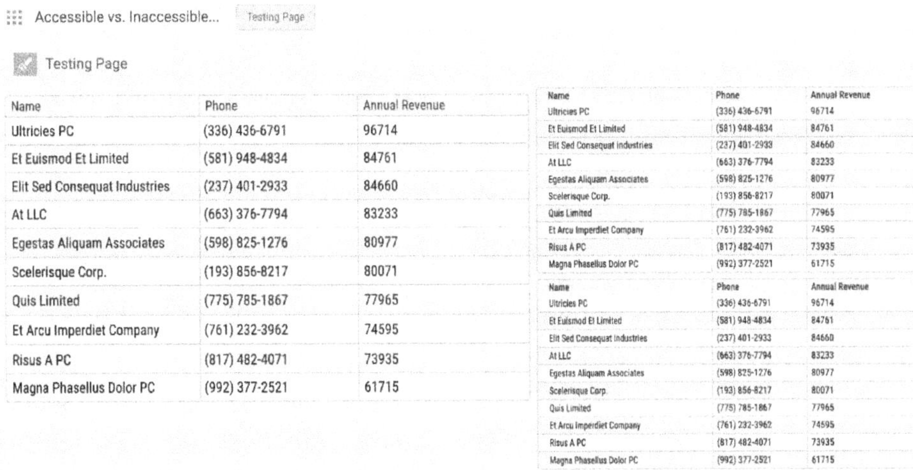

Accessible vs. Inaccessible... Testing Page

Testing Page

Name	Phone	Annual Revenue
Ultricies PC	(336) 436-6791	96714
Et Euismod Et Limited	(581) 948-4834	84761
Elit Sed Consequat Industries	(237) 401-2933	84660
At LLC	(663) 376-7794	83233
Egestas Aliquam Associates	(598) 825-1276	80977
Scelerisque Corp.	(193) 856-8217	80071
Quis Limited	(775) 785-1867	77965
Et Arcu Imperdiet Company	(761) 232-3962	74595
Risus A PC	(817) 482-4071	73935
Magna Phasellus Dolor PC	(992) 377-2521	61715

Name	Phone	Annual Revenue
Ultricies PC	(336) 436-6791	96714
Et Euismod Et Limited	(581) 948-4834	84761
Elit Sed Consequat Industries	(237) 401-2933	84660
At LLC	(663) 376-7794	83233
Egestas Aliquam Associates	(598) 825-1276	80977
Scelerisque Corp.	(193) 856-8217	80071
Quis Limited	(775) 785-1867	77965
Et Arcu Imperdiet Company	(761) 232-3962	74595
Risus A PC	(817) 482-4071	73935
Magna Phasellus Dolor PC	(992) 377-2521	61715

Name	Phone	Annual Revenue
Ultricies PC	(336) 436-6791	96714
Et Euismod Et Limited	(581) 948-4834	84761
Elit Sed Consequat Industries	(237) 401-2933	84660
At LLC	(663) 376-7794	83233
Egestas Aliquam Associates	(598) 825-1276	80977
Scelerisque Corp.	(193) 856-8217	80071
Quis Limited	(775) 785-1867	77965
Et Arcu Imperdiet Company	(761) 232-3962	74595
Risus A PC	(817) 482-4071	73935
Magna Phasellus Dolor PC	(992) 377-2521	61715

Figure 11.6: The modified Accessible vs. Inaccessible Test app

7. Navigate to the Mozilla MDN Developer documents page for the `<th>` tag. This is linked in the *See also* section of this recipe, but I encourage you to get familiar with your preferred web search tool!
8. Notice that we need to add a `scope="col"` attribute to each of our `<th>` tags to associate the header with each cell contained within the column. Add this attribute to each of the `<th>` tags in your `accessibleTable.html` file:

```
<th scope="col">
    <!--additional header code here-->
</th>
```

9. Deploy your changes, and return to your `Accessible vs. Inaccessible Test` app.
10. Turn on the accessibility voiceover for your operating system. Again, this is achieved on Windows by pressing *Win* + *Ctrl* + *Enter* to open Narrator, and *Cmd* + *F5* to open VoiceOver for Macintosh devices.
11. Attempt to tab into the upper-right table. Likely, you will have no luck, but we've made a bit of progress.
12. Tab back into our accessible table on the left-hand side of the `Accessible vs. Inaccessible Test` app, represented by the `accessibleDatatable` LWC. Notice that we enter the table on the `Ultricies PC` cell, which is in the top-left corner of our table. We

want to mimic this behavior on our right-hand `accessibleTable` table. In order to do so, we must appropriately set the `tabindex` attribute for our table.

13. Turn off your voiceover and return to VS Code. Enter the `accessibleTable.html` file, where we will be adding a `tabindex="0"` attribute to our opening `<table>` tag:

```
<table class="slds-table slds-table_cell-buffer slds-table_bordered slds-
table_col-bordered slds-table_fixed-layout" tabindex="0">
```

14. Deploy your changes and refresh your `Accessible vs. Inaccessible Test` app upon the deployment's success.
15. Turn on voiceover and attempt to tab into the `accessibleTable` table. You'll see that it highlights the whole table!

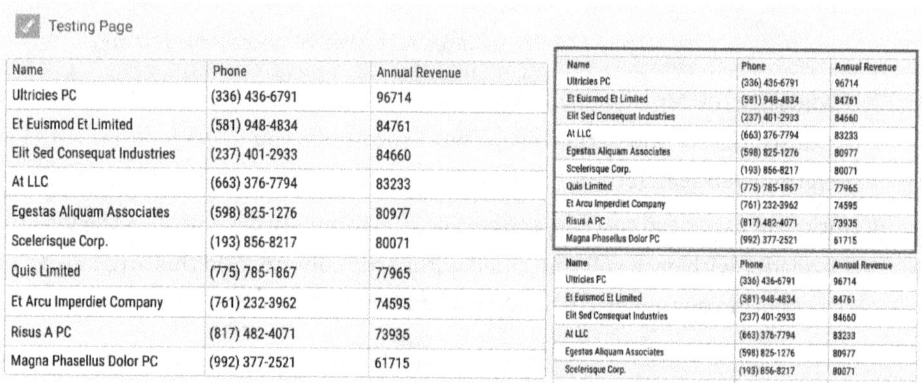

Name	Phone	Annual Revenue
Ultricies PC	(336) 436-6791	96714
Et Euismod Et Limited	(581) 948-4834	84761
Elit Sed Consequat Industries	(237) 401-2933	84660
At LLC	(663) 376-7794	83233
Egestas Aliquam Associates	(598) 825-1276	80977
Scelerisque Corp.	(193) 856-8217	80071
Quis Limited	(775) 785-1867	77965
Et Arcu Imperdiet Company	(761) 232-3962	74595
Risus A PC	(817) 482-4071	73935
Magna Phasellus Dolor PC	(992) 377-2521	61715

Figure 11.7: A screenshot of the entire accessibleTable table highlighted via focus

16. What we have done is set `tabindex`, which tells our browser that our table should be sequentially focusable. When we want an element on our page to be able to be tabbed to, we set `tabindex="0"`. When we don't want it to be tabbed to, we set `tabindex="-1"`.
17. Turn off voiceover and return to VS Code. Change your `tabindex` attribute in the `<table>` tag to `tabindex="-1"` and add a `tabindex="0"` attribute to the `<td>` tag that encloses our account name, represented by `{it.value.Name}`:

```
<td class="slds-truncate" tabindex="0">
   {it.value.Name}
</td>
```

18. Deploy your changes, return to your browser, and let's try again. Open your narration tool and tab into the right-hand `accessibleTable`. Hit the *Tab* key a few more times, and you'll notice that our browser's focus lands on every account name in order! This isn't quite right. Close the narration tool one more time, and let's think about what needs to happen.
19. Return to your `accessibleTable.html` file and look at the markup between our `<tbody>` tags. Recall that in *Chapter 3, Working with a Selector Class,* we briefly discussed the **iterator directive** in LWCs. This is similar to the `for:each` directive in that it allows us to create repetitive markup, with a few added features. One of these features is that we can use an `lwc:if` directive to determine whether we are currently rendering the first or last object in the list we are iterating over. We know we only want to focus on the first row in the first column when we tab into `accessibleTable`, so let's rewrite our iterator to include an `lwc:if` directive.
20. Within the `<tr>` tag, add an `lwc:if` directive that checks whether we are looking at the first element of the list:

```
<tr lwc:if={it.first} class="slds-hint-parent" key={it.value.Id}>
    <td class="slds-truncate" tabindex="0">
        {it.value.Name}
    </td>
    <td class="slds-truncate">
        {it.value.Phone}
    </td>
    <td class="slds-truncate">
        {it.value.AnnualRevenue}
    </td>
</tr>
```

21. Copy your entire `<tr>` tag and its contained `<td>` tags, and paste it immediately below your existing `<tr>` tag. You should have two sets of opening and closing `<tr>` tags now.
22. In the second `<tr>` tag, change your `lwc:if` directive to an `lwc:else` directive, and remove the `tabindex="0"` attribute from your first `<td>` tag:

```
<tr lwc:else class="slds-hint-parent" key={it.value.Id}>
    <td class="slds-truncate">
        {it.value.Name}
    </td>
    <td class="slds-truncate">
```

```
            {it.value.Phone}
        </td>
        <td class="slds-truncate">
            {it.value.AnnualRevenue}
        </td>
    </tr>
```

23. This will help us ensure that we focus on the first table cell within the right-hand `accessibleTable` when we tab into it.
24. Deploy your changes and return to your browser. Turn on your narration tool one more time, and tab in. Note that once we tab into `accessibleTable`, we can navigate within the table on Windows using the *Caps Lock* + *Arrow* keys, or on macOS, using *Ctrl* + *Option* + *Arrow*.

See also

- The code for the `inaccessibleTable` component is located at `https://github.com/PacktPublishing/Salesforce-Lightning-Web-Component-Cookbook/tree/main/force-app/chapter11_setup/default/lwc/inaccessibleTable`
- The code for the `accessibleDatatable` component is located at `https://github.com/PacktPublishing/Salesforce-Lightning-Web-Component-Cookbook/tree/main/force-app/chapter11_setup/default/lwc/accessibleDatatable`
- The sample code for the modified `accessibleTable` component is located at `https://github.com/PacktPublishing/Salesforce-Lightning-Web-Component-Cookbook/tree/main/force-app/chapter11/default/lwc/accessibleTable`
- The Mozilla MDN Developer documents page for the `<th>` tag is located at `https://developer.mozilla.org/en-US/docs/Web/HTML/Reference/Elements/th`
- The Mozilla MDN Developer documents page for the `tabindex` attribute is located at `https://developer.mozilla.org/en-US/docs/Web/HTML/Reference/Global_attributes/tabindex`
- The Salesforce documentation on the iterator directive is available at `https://developer.salesforce.com/docs/platform/lwc/guide/create-lists.html#iterator`
- The SLDS 1 documentation that breaks down the HTML required to create a `lightning-datatable` element is located at `https://v1.lightningdesignsystem.com/components/data-tables/`

- The Mozilla MDN Developer Docs reference for ARIA states and properties (attributes) can be found at `https://developer.mozilla.org/en-US/docs/Web/Accessibility/ARIA/Reference/Attributes`
- The WAI tutorials on building accessible tables are located at `https://www.w3.org/WAI/tutorials/tables/`

Writing it right: avoiding common pitfalls

What we have accomplished here is a modest example of how to make an element of a custom application more accessible. While Salesforce does most of the work for us, there are times when we need to do the heavy lifting ourselves, usually when building out custom elements from default HTML tags using SLDS styling.

One thing that I must mention: we did so without the use of **Accessible Rich Internet Applications** (**ARIA**) attributes. When most people hear the words "accessibility on the web," their minds jump to ARIA. While ARIA is an important tool to keep in our back pocket, it is not the be-all and end-all accessibility solution. In fact, implementing ARIA improperly can make applications less accessible!

In order to illustrate this, let's return to our `accessibleTable.html` file.

How to do it...

Now that we are educated on the value of accessibility, both from a business perspective and a human perspective, we are excited to implement all the measures! We once heard that ARIA is the way to do this, so we are going to try our hand at implementing some `aria-label` properties:

1. Open your `accessibleTable.html` file one last time.
2. In each of your `<th>` tags, add an `aria-label="header"` attribute:

```
<th scope="col" aria-label="header">
    <!--column name-->
</th>
```

3. Additionally, in each of your `<td>` tags, add an `aria-label="cell"` attribute.
4. Deploy your changes, and refresh your `Accessible vs. Inaccessible Test` app.
5. Turn on your voiceover tool one last time and tab through `accessibleTable`.
6. You'll notice that every time you navigate within the table on Windows using the *Caps Lock* + *Arrow* keys, or on macOS using *Ctrl* + *Option* + *Arrow*, you are now being told **header**, **cell**, or sometimes both! This is a confusing user experience. An `aria-label` can

be used to name an element, but this is not a good application. We have already designated our headers and cells using the HTML tags of <th> and <td>, which means we are including redundant information that isn't relevant to the user experience.

7. In the event that we misuse an `aria-label` attribute on something such as an input or a link, we can make our forms impossible to navigate with a screen reader. Not only that, but some screen readers will read the `aria-label` value over the inner content of the tags! This means that instead of getting the phone number for `Ultricies PC`, our screen reader-using colleague may just be told **cell** over and over again. I experienced this behavior while testing the code for this chapter on a Windows PC in both Google Chrome and Mozilla Firefox, for example. While we have built a relatively low-stakes table for demonstrative purposes, this impact could be devastating on something such as a government or medical form.
8. An appropriate use of `aria-label` would be something like this:

```
<button aria-label="Search">🔍</button>
```

9. In this case, our *Search* button is an emoji of a magnifying glass, which would not be easy to discern with or without a screen reader. Your end user may not be able to tell that it's a button, but the `aria-label` is there to give guidance.
10. To bring us full circle, this is where I must issue a reminder that, in the case of building a Salesforce Lightning Web Component with a **Search** button, it would be beneficial for us to instead use the following:

```
<lightning-button-icon icon-name="utility:search" alternative-text="Search"
title="Search"></lightning-button-icon>
```

11. This snippet, using a Lightning base component, will have the necessary accessibility features included.

See also

- The Mozilla MDN Developer documentation on the `aria-label` attribute is available at `https://developer.mozilla.org/en-US/docs/Web/Accessibility/ARIA/Reference/Attributes/aria-label`
- To read a piece on common accessibility mistakes put out by Vispero, the maker of JAWS, visit `https://vispero.com/resources/ten-common-web-accessibility-issues/`

- To learn more about ARIA bad practices, the Accessibility Developer Guide has the following blog: `https://www.accessibility-developer-guide.com/knowledge/aria/bad-practices/`
- The *5 Common Misconceptions about WAI-ARIA and Accessibility* blog post by the Bureau of Internet Accessibility is available at `https://www.boia.org/blog/5-common-misconceptions-about-wai-aria-and-accessibility`
- To read the guidance *No ARIA is better than Bad ARIA*, visit `https://www.w3.org/WAI/ARIA/apg/practices/read-me-first/#no_aria_better_bad_aria`

Get this book's PDF version and more

Scan the QR code (or go to `packtpub.com/unlock`). Search for this book by name, confirm the edition, and then follow the steps on the page.

UNLOCK NOW

Note: Keep your invoice handy. Purchases made directly from Packt don't require an invoice.

Part 4

Preparing Lightning Web Components for Production

Having gained familiarity with a variety of topics in Lightning Web Component development, we need to ensure that our components are ready for prime time. Salesforce mandates a minimum 75% code coverage in every org to deploy Apex to a production environment, with many organizations mandating coverage in the 90-95% range. You will learn how to unit test your code with mocking and stubbing, both by implementing the stub provider and utilizing the open source apex-mockery, allowing for quick and thorough testing of your Apex. You will also learn the basics of testing your LWCs with the Jest testing framework. Finally, you will become familiar with the most common types of errors in Apex and LWC development, so that you can spot them in your own code when they inevitably arise.

This part has the following chapters:

- *Chapter 12, Migrating Aura to Lightning Web Components*
- *Chapter 13, Testing Apex with Mocking and Stubbing*
- *Chapter 14, Testing Lightning Web Components with Jest*
- *Chapter 15, Debugging Lightning Web Components*

12

Migrating Aura to Lightning Web Components

Over the lifetime of the Salesforce product, there have been three major frontend frameworks: Visualforce, **Aura components** (**Lightning components**), and **Lightning Web Components** (**LWCs**). Each framework utilizes modified HTML to build a user interface, with the possibility of adding additional functionality with JavaScript. While the preferred and modern method of frontend development is LWCs, you will absolutely run into the older frameworks in modern Salesforce orgs. This is because there are some pieces of functionality, such as PDF generation and certain **iframe** content, that must be written in either Visualforce or Aura. As a result, we will be spending this chapter learning how to translate from one of these frameworks, Aura components, into LWCs.

We are going to be covering the following main recipes:

- Deciding when to migrate and with what tools
- Translating Lightning components into LWCs
- Rewriting JavaScript for Lightning

Technical requirements

The recipes for this book can be found at `https://github.com/PacktPublishing/Salesforce-Lightning-Web-Component-Cookbook`, where each chapter has its own folder under the `force-app` folder. This GitHub repository is structured in the form of a Salesforce DX project, which will allow you to easily fork the repository for deployment in a free Salesforce Developer Edition org. The code for this chapter is located at `https://github.com/PacktPublishing/Salesforce-Lightning-Web-Component-Cookbook/tree/main/force-app/chapter12`.

The components in this book require the use of an **Integrated Development Environment (IDE)**, such as **Visual Studio Code (VSCode)** or **Salesforce Code Builder**. Detailed instructions for setting up an IDE are located in *Chapter 1, Getting Ready for Lightning Web Components*, in the *Setting up your IDE* section.

If you are building the projects in this cookbook as written, you will need to seed your Salesforce Developer Edition org with test data. Detailed instructions for seeding your org are located in *Chapter 1, Getting Ready for Lightning Web Components*, in the *Setting up the Salesforce Lightning Web Components Cookbook org* section.

Lastly, the edition of Salesforce required to implement the recipes in this book must be Developer, Performance, Unlimited, Enterprise, or Database.com. You can sign up for a free Salesforce Developer Edition org at `https://developer.salesforce.com/signup`.

Deciding when to migrate and with what tools

As of the writing of this chapter, there is no plan in place to sunset Aura components, but it should be noted that LWCs are the modern and thus preferred solution. What makes this the case? LWCs inherit the global attributes and events from HTML, making them more accessible and more functional than their corresponding Aura components. In addition to these benefits, LWCs are easier to write, as they utilize vanilla JavaScript and HTML.

Getting started

There are several factors that contribute to whether an Aura component should be migrated to an LWC, including, but not limited to, the speed of the component, its maintainability, and existing dependencies. When tracing these dependencies, it is important to bear in mind that you can nest an LWC within an Aura component, but not the other way around. In effect, LWCs are backward-compatible. This means that when you are evaluating the order in which to refactor components, you should start with the innermost child components when possible. Another easy place to start is by migrating Aura components that only render a given user interface.

On the other hand, components that should not be migrated include those that do not yet have full support in LWC. As of the writing of this chapter, there are thankfully few of these! One example is that LWC quick actions are currently only supported from record pages, so quick actions from list views must be completed with an Aura component.

> Note
>
> A question I receive frequently from those studying for the **Salesforce Certified Platform Developer** exam, formerly known as **Platform Developer I**, or **PD1**, is whether knowledge of **Visualforce** is still a valuable skill. While Visualforce predates Aura components, it is still the easiest way to consistently generate a PDF from scratch in

> Salesforce! For this reason, you are likely to continue to run into Visualforce until PDF generation functionality is brought forward into LWCs.

Now that we know a little bit about when to migrate, we need to know what tools are available for migration.

How to do it...

In the Spring '26 release, the Salesforce Developer Experience Model Context Protocol Tools for LWC (DX MCP Tools for LWC) set will be in beta, meaning that it is not yet generally available, but we can play around with it in a Developer Edition org. Use of the DX MCP Tools for LWC in its beta form is at the sole discretion of a Salesforce customer, who must agree to Salesforce's Beta Services Terms. This is a fancy way of saying: don't try this on your work computer just yet!

1. To use the DX MCP server, Salesforce recommends utilizing the **Agentforce Vibes extension** and passing in the `aura-experts` and `lwc-experts` toolsets utilizing the `--toolsets` flag. Once this is set up, you can ask questions such as *"What Aura components are user interface only?"* or *"What Aura component should I migrate to LWC?"* to get yourself started.
2. Because this feature is currently in beta, assuming you have purchased this cookbook in early 2026, it is safe to say that you want to be able to learn how to complete this migration on your own as well. In the next recipe, we will be going through how to complete this migration.

See also

- To determine whether a new component should be written as an LWC or an Aura component, review `https://developer.salesforce.com/docs/platform/lwc/guide/get-started-lwc-or-aura.html`
- The Mozilla MDN Developer Docs on global attributes in HTML tags are available at `https://developer.mozilla.org/en-US/docs/Web/HTML/Reference/Global_attributes`
- The Mozilla MDN Developer Docs on events in HTML tags are available at `https://developer.mozilla.org/en-US/docs/Web/API/Document_Object_Model/Events`
- To determine your migration strategy, you can visit `https://developer.salesforce.com/docs/platform/lwc/guide/migrate-strategy.html`
- The docs for the DX MCP Tools for LWC are located at `https://developer.salesforce.com/docs/platform/lwc/guide/mcp-aura.html`

Translating Lightning components into LWCs

While generative AI tools can be helpful for development, the most effective developers I have met, whether they use generative AI or not, have a solid understanding of the foundations. For that reason, we are once again going to translate a component from one framework to another so that we can understand its innermost workings.

Imagine once again that you are a developer at an art broker that utilizes Salesforce to keep track of its artworks and their current locations. You partner with museums and collectors to send your collection for viewing all over the world, and you would like to make it a little easier for your representatives to grab the location of a museum, represented by the account sObject.

Figure 12.1: The Capture Geolocation quick action on the Account Record page

In order to do this, your end users had previously requested a quick action on the account **Record** page that allows them to capture the geolocation of their internet-connected device when they arrive at a given museum. This component was originally written as an Aura component, but, since picking up this cookbook and learning the benefits of LWCs, you know that it should be refactored into an LWC.

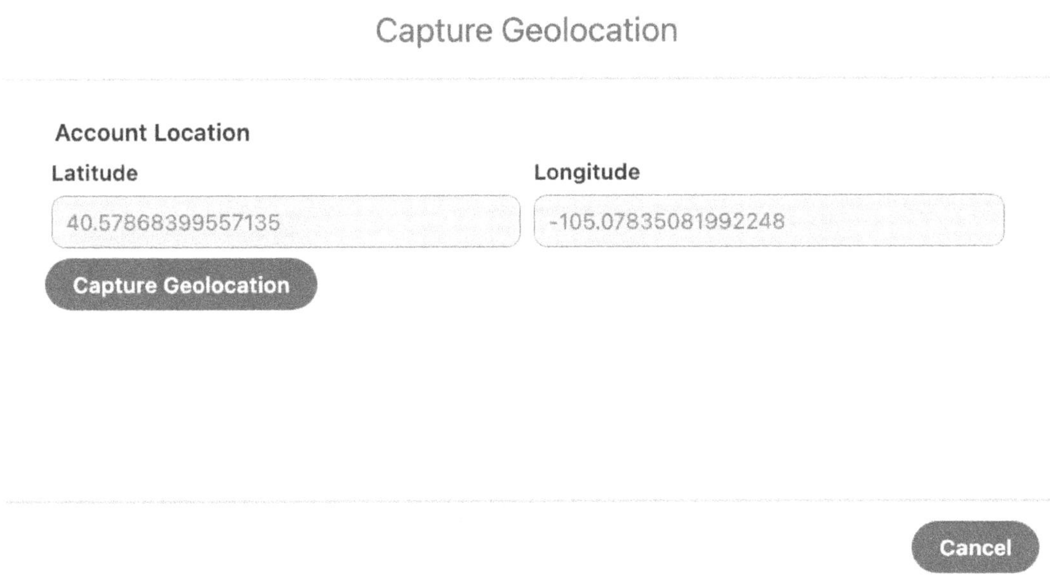

Figure 12.2: The modal displayed by the Capture Geolocation quick action on the Account Record page, which brings up the geolocation of the coffee shop where the bulk of this cookbook was written!

This Aura component is already built for you, and we will be deploying it in the next steps.

Getting started

To deploy the starting Aura component to your Salesforce Developer Edition org, fork the repository if you haven't already. Instructions on doing so are located in Chapter 1, *Getting Ready for Lightning Web Components*, in the *Setting up your IDE* section.

Once you have completed these steps, deploy the `force-app/chapter12_setup` directory into your Salesforce Developer Edition org. This will deploy the necessary Aura component, as well as its **controller class** and **service class**, the necessary **quick action**, and the page layout needed to complete this exercise.

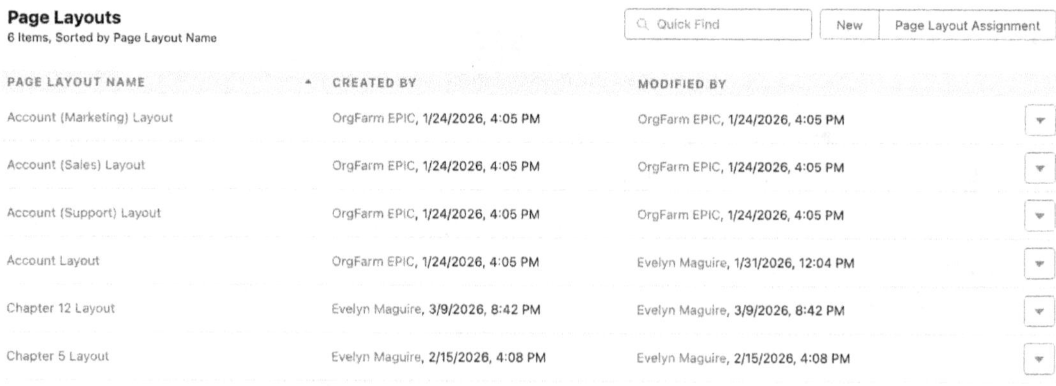

Figure 12.3: A screenshot of the account page layouts with the recently deployed Chapter 12 Layout at the bottom

Don't forget to assign **Chapter 12 Layout** as your default account layout or add the **Capture Geolocation** quick action to your preferred account layout so you can see the button.

Now that we have deployed the Aura component that we are going to be translating, let's examine the CaptureAccountGeolocation.cmp file first. We notice that there are several features being implemented in our Aura component, such as the ability to use our component in a Lightning quick action and the ability to pull in our `recordId`. Also, we are utilizing the `CaptureAccountGeolocationController` Apex class as our Aura controller:

```
<aura:component implements='force:lightningQuickAction,force:hasRecordId'
controller='CaptureAccountGeolocationController' >
   <!--rest of code here-->
</aura:component>
```

The Aura controller acts much in the same way as an LWC controller class does. In fact, we will be using the same Apex class as the controller class for our LWC!

Going down line by line, we notice that we define our attributes:

```
<aura:attribute name='latitude' type='Decimal' />
<aura:attribute name='longitude' type='Decimal' />
<aura:attribute name='recordId' type='String' />
```

In our LWC translation, these will be defined as class variables in our JavaScript file.

These attributes are followed by calling our `doInit` function, which we will focus on in the next recipe:

```
<aura:handler name='init' value='{!this}' action='{!c.doInit}' />
```

Finally, before our closing tag, we have our Lightning tags that represent an `inputLocation` and a **lightning-button**:

```
<lightning:inputLocation label='Account Location' latitude='{!v.latitude}'
longitude='{!v.longitude}' disabled='true'/>
<lightning:button variant='brand' label='Capture Geolocation' onclick='{!
c.captureGeolocation}' />
```

Notice also that the corresponding .cmp-meta.xml file merely contains an API version and a description.

We will spend this recipe focusing on translating this .cmp file into a .html file, while migrating the start of the JavaScript functionality. The bulk of the JavaScript will be handled in the next recipe.

How to do it...

Now that we are familiar with the general structure of the Aura .cmp file, let's get started!

1. To start, let's create two new LWCs, `captureAccountGeolocationLauncher` and `captureAccountGeolocationModal`. We know from *Chapter 7, Building Secure Components with Lightning Locker and Lightning Web Security*, that we will need to have a launcher component to pair with our Lightning quick action that houses a modal component, with our launcher passing key information into our modal.
2. Our `captureAccountGeolocationLauncher.html` file will remain empty except for the default template tags:

    ```
    <template>
    </template>
    ```

3. Open the `captureAccountGeolocationLauncher.js` file. First, we need to handle our imports and class definition:

    ```
    import { LightningElement, api } from 'lwc';
    import captureAccountGeolocationModal from 'c/
    captureAccountGeolocationModal';
    ```

```
import { NavigationMixin } from 'lightning/navigation';
export default class CaptureAccountGeolocationLauncher extends
NavigationMixin(LightningElement) { ... }
```

Notice that we are importing the `api` decorator, our `captureAccountGeolocationModal` component, and the `NavigationMixin` module, which we also extend in our class definition.

4. Within our class, we know that we need to grab the `recordId` of the record page we are currently on, which we know is provided by Salesforce using the following:

```
@api recordId;
```

5. Also, as we did in *Chapter 7, Building Secure Components with Lightning Locker and Lightning Web Security*, we must implement the `@api`-decorated `invoke` function to launch our modal:

```
@api invoke() {
    captureAccountGeolocationModal.open({
        size: 'large',
        description: 'A modal to grab the current device\'s geolocation for
the specified Account.',
        content: {recordId : this.recordId},
        onsavesuccess: (event) => {
            event.stopPropagation();
            this.handleSaveSuccess(this.recordId);
        }
    })
}
```

6. Notice that the `content` object that we are passing in defines a `recordId: this.recordId` property, thus passing the `recordId` from our record page to our launcher component and finally to our modal component for processing.
7. Finally, we must write our `handleSaveSuccess` function, which we call in our `invoke` function. We will be using the **NavigationMixin** module, which we explored in *Chapter 6, Composing Lightning Web Components*. This function will return us to the account

record page of the record that we are currently looking at, which results in a refresh of key values:

```
handleSaveSuccess(id) {
   this[NavigationMixin.Navigate]({
      type: 'standard__recordPage',
      attributes: {
         recordId: id,
         objectApiName: 'Account',
         actionName: 'view'
      }
   });
}
```

8. Next, let's modify our `captureAccountGeolocationLauncher.js-meta.xml` file, which will allow us to place our modal launcher as a quick action on the account page:

```
<?xml version="1.0" encoding="UTF-8"?>
<LightningComponentBundle xmlns="http://soap.sforce.com/2006/04/metadata">
   <apiVersion>65.0</apiVersion>
   <isExposed>true</isExposed>
   <targets>
      <target>lightning__RecordAction</target>
   </targets>
   <targetConfigs>
      <targetConfig targets="lightning__RecordAction">
         <actionType>Action</actionType>
         <objects>
            <object>Account</object>
         </objects>
      </targetConfig>
   </targetConfigs>
</LightningComponentBundle>
```

9. Deploy your changes and add your LWC as a quick action on the account sObject called **Capture Geolocation LWC** to differentiate it from our Aura component. This can be accomplished by going to **Setup > Object Manager > Account > Buttons Links, and Actions > New Actions**.

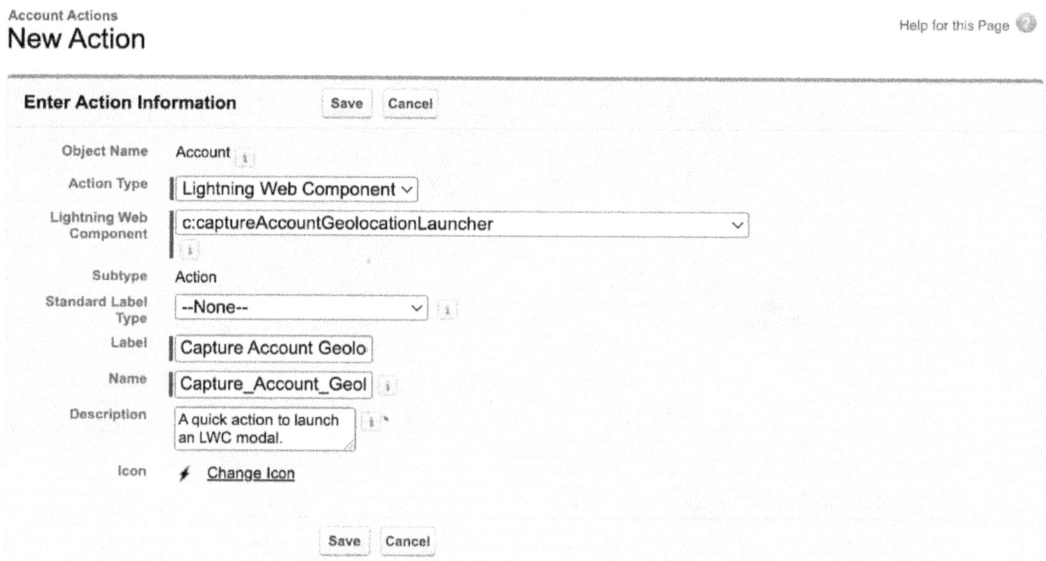

Figure 12.4: The New Action form on the account

Note that your modal won't do anything just yet, but we will be able to test as we go.

1. Now, open the `captureAccountGeolocationModal.html` file, while keeping the `CaptureAccountGeolocation.cmp` file open. We will be referring to this Aura Component throughout this exercise.
2. We know that we need a modal header that matches the name of our component to match the format of our Aura component, so let's start by adding a `lightning-modal-header` tag between our open and close template tags:

```
<lightning-modal-header label='Capture Geolocation LWC'></lightning-modal-
header>
```

3. Next, we will add our `lightning-modal-body` tags:

```
<lightning-modal-body>
    <!--modal body here-->
</lightning-modal-body>
```

4. We see that in our Aura component, we use the `lightning:inputLocation` and `lightning:button` elements to define the inside of our modal body. Salesforce provides

a handy map of Aura-to-LWC tags, linked in the *See also* portion of this recipe. As a result, we need to add a **lightning-input-location** tag. We have the following:

CaptureAccountGeolocation.cmp

```
<lightning:inputLocation label='Account Location' latitude='{!v.latitude}'
longitude='{!v.longitude}' disabled='true'/>
```

5. This translates to the following:

   CaptureAccountGeolocationModal.html

```
<lightning-input-location label='Account Location' latitude={latitude}
longitude={longitude} disabled ></lightning-input-location>
```

6. We also need to add a `lightning-button` tag. We have the following:

   CaptureAccountGeolocation.cmp

```
<lightning:button variant='brand' label='Capture Geolocation' onclick='{!
c.captureGeolocation}' />
```

7. Which translates to the following:

   CaptureAccountGeolocationModal.html

```
<lightning-button variant='brand' label='Capture Geolocation' title='Capture
Geolocation' onclick={captureGeolocation} class='slds-m-left_x-small'></
lightning-button>
```

8. Notice that there are some key, highlighted differences between the structuring of the attribute values within the Aura component tags and the LWC tags, which we will be discussing in the next section. Deploy your changes so far, and be sure to take a breather!

How it works...

Aura components use what are called **value providers** to encapsulate related values. The two types of value providers for an Aura component are **v** (**view**) and **c** (**controller**). The v value provider relates to the values that are defined in our component's markup as attributes, which in our case are the `v.latitude` and `v.longitude` expressions, whereas the c value provider allows us to wire up events and their handlers for our component, such as the `c.captureGeolocation` expression. We use expression syntax, `{!expression}`, to access the results of these expressions dynamically. We will dive deeper into what this looks like in practice in the *Rewriting JavaScript for Lightning* recipe.

See also

- For the Salesforce map for migrating Aura components to LWCs, see `https://developer.salesforce.com/docs/platform/lwc/guide/migrate-map-aura-lwc-components.html`
- The Salesforce developer documentation for `force:lightningQuickAction` is available at `https://developer.salesforce.com/docs/component-library/bundle/force:lightningQuickAction/documentation`
- The Salesforce developer documentation for `force:hasRecordId` is available at `https://developer.salesforce.com/docs/component-library/bundle/force:hasRecordId/documentation`
- The Salesforce developer documentation on value providers is available at `https://developer.salesforce.com/docs/atlas.en-us.lightning.meta/lightning/expr_source.htm`

Rewriting JavaScript for Lightning

Now that we have our markup sorted, we need to add our functionality. Recall our attributes and our handler from the CaptureAccountGeolocation.cmp file:

```
<!--define attributes-->
<aura:attribute name='latitude' type='Decimal' />
<aura:attribute name='longitude' type='Decimal' />
<aura:attribute name='recordId' type='String' />
<!--call doInit-->
<aura:handler name='init' value='{!this}' action='{!c.doInit}' />
```

These elements will lay the foundation of our `captureAccountGeolocationModal.js` file.

How to do it...

We began to migrate our JavaScript in the last recipe, so let's go ahead and finish what we started! We will be working in the `captureAccountGeolocationModal.js` file:

1. First, let's handle our imports. We are inheriting the `content` object from our nested `captureAccountGeolocationLauncher` component, so first, we must import our `api` decorator:

```
import { api } from 'lwc';
```

2. We also need to import the `updateGeolocation` method from the existing Apex controller, `CaptureAccountGeolocationController`:

```
import updateGeolocation from '@salesforce/apex/
CaptureAccountGeolocationController.updateGeolocation';
```

3. Let's also import the `Utilities` component from our *Chapter 4, Synchronous and Asynchronous Processing in Components,* toast notification utility, and define a variable for it:

```
import Utilities from 'c/notifUtils';
let utility;
```

> **Note**
>
> If you are just joining us in this chapter, this toast notification utility can easily be deployed by deploying the files from the forked repository at the `force-app/chapter04/default/lwc/notifUtils` and `force-app/chapter04/default/staticresources` directories. These files will help you in debugging by showing you the error message in a human-readable format if something goes wrong.

4. Finally, if you recall from *Chapter 7, Building Secure Components with Lightning Locker and Lightning Web Security,* we will be extending the `LightningModal` component from the `'lightning/modal'` module rather than the `LightningElement` component in our class definition:

```
import LightningModal from 'lightning/modal';
export default class CaptureAccountGeolocationLWC extends LightningModal
{ ... }
```

5. In all, the top of our `captureAccountGeolocationModal.js` file will look as follows:

```
import { api } from 'lwc';
import LightningModal from 'lightning/modal';
import updateGeolocation from '@salesforce/apex/
CaptureAccountGeolocationController.updateGeolocation';
import Utilities from 'c/notifUtils';
let utility;
```

```
export default class CaptureAccountGeolocationLWC extends LightningModal
{ ... }
```

6. To accommodate our toast notification utility, let's recall that we need a `connectedCallback` function, where we will set `mainObject` in our utilities class as the global `this`:

```
connectedCallback() {
    utility = new Utilities(this);
    //...further code here...
}
```

7. We also know that we are accepting `recordId` as part of the `content` object that is passed in from our parental `captureAccountGeolocationLauncher` component, so we need to have a public variable, an `@api`-decorated `content`, as a class variable above our `connectedCallback` function:

```
@api content;
```

8. Now that we have a rough class outline, let's go back to the attributes listed in our Aura .cmp file:

CaptureAccountGeolocation.cmp

```
<aura:attribute name='latitude' type='Decimal' />
<aura:attribute name='longitude' type='Decimal' />
<aura:attribute name='recordId' type='String' />
```

9. We know that we need to define each of these attributes as a class variable, for starters. Return to your `captureAccountGeolocationModal.js` file and add these below your `@api content` definition, before your `connectedCallback` function:

```
recordId;
latitude;
longitude;
```

10. We also know that our `recordId` should be equal to the `recordId` property of the `content` object. We want to put this assignation inside of our `connectedCallback` so

that we have a `recordId` once our `captureAccountGeolocationModal` component is inserted into the **DOM**, but not before:

```
this.recordId = this.content.recordId;
```

From here, it gets a little bit tricky. There are two JavaScript files for our given Aura component, and if you're working with a homegrown component, there may be more. How do the functionalities of these files map to one another?

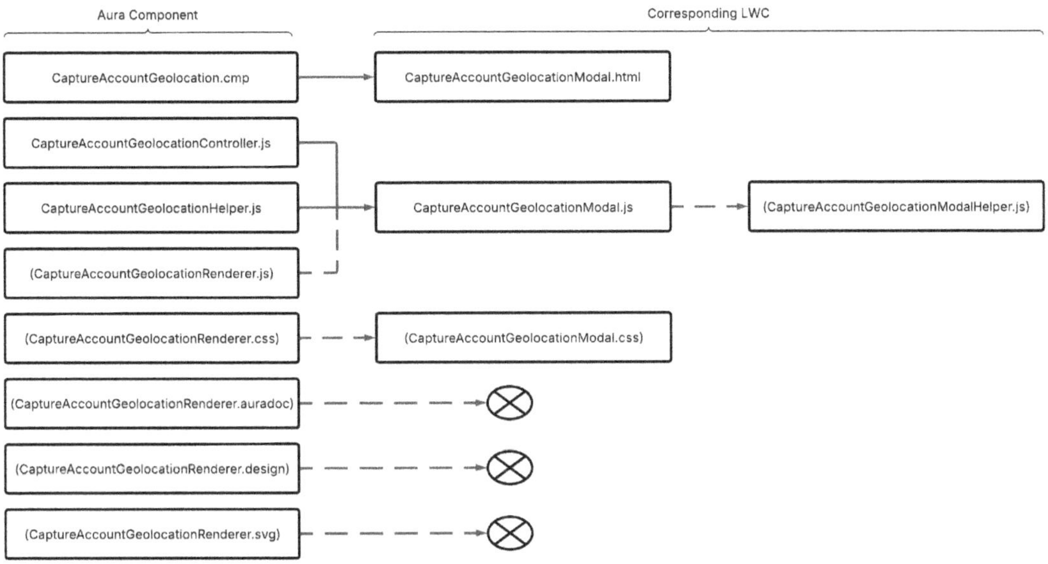

Figure 12.5: A diagram showing how the various files of an Aura component would map to an analogous LWC

Simply, the `.cmp` file maps to the `.html` file, the JavaScript files map to one or more JavaScript files, and, if we had one, the CSS file would map to a CSS file. Any files for documentation (`.auradoc`), design (`.design`), or iconography (`.svg`) do not have direct mappings at this time.

So, how do we map our Aura JavaScript files into one or more LWC files?

1. First, let's look at our `CaptureAccountGeolocationController.js` file. Notice that there are two functions, `doInit` and `captureGeolocation`. We will be coming back to the latter in a second, but for now, recall that `c.doInit` is called by `aura:handler` in our `CaptureAccountGeolocation.cmp` file:

   CaptureAccountGeolocation.cmp

   ```
   <aura:handler name='init' value='{!this}' action='{!c.doInit}' />
   ```

2. Essentially, what this line of markup means is that we are running the controller's `doInit` function on the `init` event, which occurs when the component is constructed, but before rendering. As a result, we are going to be putting the contents of the `doInit` function of our Aura component within our `connectedCallback` in our LWC, as they are roughly equivalent. Let's trace the path that our `init` event handler takes. We see in our controller file that the `doInit` function calls a **helper function**, `findGeolocation`:
   CaptureAccountGeolocationController.js

```
doInit : function(component, event, helper) {
    helper.findGeolocation(component, event, helper);
    console.log('doInit called');
}
```

We see this function in our helper file, which has been shortened here for clarity:

CaptureAccountGeolocationHelper.js

```
findGeolocation : function(component, event) {
    //finds the geolocation of the user's device
    //prompts user to allow location access if not already allowed
    if (navigator.geolocation) {
        navigator.geolocation.getCurrentPosition(
            (position) => {
                component.set('v.latitude', position.coords.latitude);
                component.set('v.longitude', position.coords.longitude);
            },
            (error) => {
                //toast notification and dismissal code here...
            }
        );
    } else {
        //toast notification and dismissal code here...
    }
},
```

We see that we are using the JavaScript **navigator interface** to grab the geolocation of the end user's device. First, we check to see whether the end user has granted `navigator.geolocation` access so that we can avoid a **null pointer exception** when retrieving the latitude and longitude of the device. We then use the view value provider, `v`, to set the values of our `latitude` and `longitude` attributes.

Now that we have a baseline understanding of what's going on, we are going to be translating this into vanilla JavaScript and using our homegrown toast notification utility:

> **Note**
>
> You may notice that, although there is quick action dismissal baked into the Aura component, there is a **known issue** where `$A.get('e.force:closeQuickAction').fire()` no longer works in console apps. This is expected behavior, which can be reported at the following known issue: `https://help.salesforce.com/s/issue?id=a028c00000gAyIEAA0&title=after-winter-20-release-forceclosequickaction-event-has-stopped-working-in-lightning-console-apps`. The workaround is simply to close the modal if it does not close on its own, and to use a validation rule to prevent the saving of a blank geolocation if necessary.

3. Open your `CaptureAccountGeolocationModal.js` file. We know that we need to add a `findGeolocation` function, so let's do that below our `connectedCallback`:

```
findGeolocation() {
   if (navigator.geolocation) {
      navigator.geolocation.getCurrentPosition(
         (position) => {
            this.latitude = parseFloat(
               position.coords.latitude
            );
            this.longitude = parseFloat(
               position.coords.longitude
            );
         },
         (error) => {
            utility.showNotif(
               'There has been an error capturing geolocation!',
               error.message,
               'error'
            );
            this.close();
         }
```

```
        );
    }
    else {
        utility.showNotif(
            'There has been an error loading geolocation!',
            'Ensure that you have enabled location.',
            'error');
        this.close();
    }
}
```

Notice the slight differences, called out in the highlighted chunks. We use our homegrown toast utility, `utility.showNotif(...)`, and rather than using `$A.get('e.force:closeQuickAction')`, we use `this.close()`, which is a built-in function of the `Modal` component provided by Salesforce.

4. In order to call this function when our component is inserted into the DOM, we must add a reference to it to our `connectedCallback` function:

```
connectedCallback() {
    utility = new Utilities(this);
    this.recordId = this.content.recordId;
    this.findGeolocation();
}
```

5. Now that we have our `doInit` function translated, let's go back to our `CaptureAccountGeolocation.cmp` file and take a closer look at our `lightning:button` tag:

```
<lightning:button variant='brand' label='Capture Geolocation' onclick='{!
c.captureGeolocation}' />
```

We see that we are using the controller value provider, `c`, to call a function, `captureGeolocation`. Let's take a look:

CaptureAccountGeolocationController.js

```
captureGeolocation : function(component, event, helper) {
    helper.captureHelper(component, event);
}
```

This calls a helper function, `captureHelper`, which is where things get a little tricky again.

6. Open the `CaptureAccountGeolocationHelper.js` file. We will be translating this line by line to gain an understanding.
7. Alongside the `CaptureAccountGeolocationHelper.js` file, open the `captureAccountGeolocationModal.js` file. Create an asynchronous function, `captureGeolocation`, that accepts a parameter of an `event`:

   captureAccountGeolocationModal.js

   ```
   async captureGeolocation(event) { ... }
   ```

8. Return to the `CaptureAccountGeolocationHelper.js` file and look at the first few lines of the `try catch` block:

   CaptureAccountGeolocationHelper.js

   ```
   var action = component.get('c.updateGeolocation');
   ```

   This line of JavaScript creates a reference, `action`, to the `CaptureAccountGeolocationController.updateGeolocation` Apex method. We know this because of the controller value provider, `c`, in the `'c.updateGeolocation'` expression.

9. We then use the JavaScript `setParams` method to set our Apex parameters:

   ```
   action.setParams({
      'accountId' : component.get('v.recordId'),
      'lat' : component.get('v.latitude'),
      'lng' : component.get('v.longitude')
   });
   ```

10. Then, we set our **callback method** using the JavaScript method, `setCallback`:

    ```
    action.setCallback(this, function(response) {
       var state = response.getState();
       if (state === 'SUCCESS') {
          alert('Geolocation Saved!');
       }
       else {
          throw new Error('There has been an error capturing geolocation!');
    ```

```
    }
});
```

This callback method determines what action is taken when the Apex action is complete. In our case, we want to either send a positive alert or throw an error to be caught by our `try catch` block.

11. Finally, we enqueue our action:

```
$A.enqueueAction(action);
```

12. Navigate to the record page we are currently on, thereby refreshing our data:

```
var navigationEvent = $A.get('e.force:navigateToSObject');
navigationEvent.setParams({
    'recordId': component.get('v.recordId'),
    'slideDevName': 'detail'
});
navigationEvent.fire();
```

13. Lastly, we close our quick action modal:

```
$A.get('e.force:closeQuickAction').fire();
```

14. If we catch the error in our `try` block, we fire an error toast event.
15. Now that we know what's going on, let's translate it. Luckily, the JavaScript for the LWC is much simpler in comparison:

captureAccountGeolocationModal.js

```
try{
    await updateGeolocation({accountId: this.recordId, lat: this.lat, lng:
this.lng});
    utility.showNotif('Geolocation has been saved!', 'Success!', 'success');
    const successEvent = new CustomEvent(
        'savesuccess', {
            bubbles: false,
            composed: false,
            detail: event.detail.id
        });
    this.dispatchEvent(successEvent);
    this.close();
```

```
} catch(error) {
   utility.showNotif('There has been an error capturing geolocation!',
error.message, 'error');
}
```

Rather than using the controller value provider as we did in our Aura component, we can utilize imperative Apex to call our Apex method, and our toast utility to show a toast success notification.

Recall that our navigation happens in our `captureAccountGeolocationLauncher` component, so we must send an event to our parental component, and rather than firing a `force:closeQuickAction` event, we can use `this.close()`.

16. Deploy your changes, and test your **Capture Geolocation LWC** quick action:

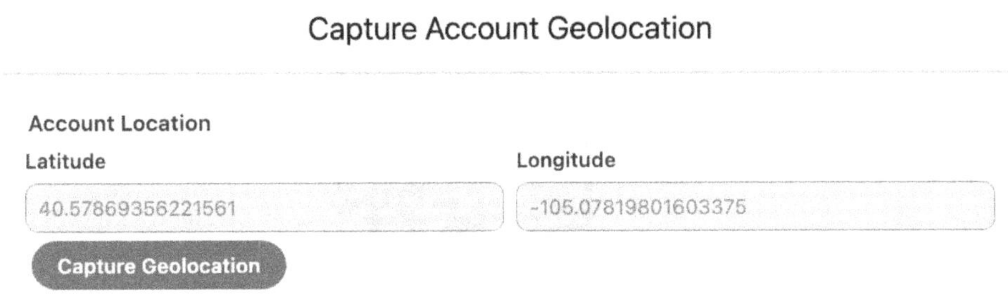

Figure 12.6: The completed Capture Account Geolocation LWC modal component

See also

- The Salesforce developer documentation on the `init` handler is located at `https://developer.salesforce.com/docs/atlas.en-us.lightning.meta/lightning/js_cb_init_handler.htm`
- A Salesforce Developer blog post about expressions in Aura components is available at `https://developer.salesforce.com/blogs/2019/01/explaining-expressions-in-the-aura-framework-part-1`
- The Mozilla MDN Developer Docs documentation for the Navigator interface is available at `https://developer.mozilla.org/en-US/docs/Web/API/Navigator`
- The Salesforce documentation on the `setCallback` method can be found here: `https://developer.salesforce.com/docs/atlas.en-us.lightning.meta/lightning/ref_jsapi_action_setCallback.htm`

- Documentation on throwing an error in an Aura component is available at `https://developer.salesforce.com/docs/atlas.en-us.lightning.meta/lightning/js_throw_error.htm`
- Finally, the `force:closeQuickAction` documentation can be found at `https://developer.salesforce.com/docs/component-library/bundle/force:closeQuickAction`

Get this book's PDF version and more

Scan the QR code (or go to `packtpub.com/unlock`). Search for this book by name, confirm the edition, and then follow the steps on the page.

UNLOCK NOW

Note: Keep your invoice handy. Purchases made directly from Packt don't require an invoice.

13

Testing Apex with Mocking and Stubbing

Now that we have our LWCs and corresponding Apex written, it's time to write test classes. "What! I thought this cookbook was about Lightning Web Components!" is what I am sure you are thinking to yourself right now. In order to deploy the Apex that accompanies our LWCs, we must have a minimum of 75% test class coverage, so Apex tests are fair game! We're going to begin to learn an advanced Apex testing technique called **mocking** and **stubbing**, which plays nicely with the **selector pattern** that we have been using in this cookbook, introduced in *Chapter 3, Working with a Selector Class*. Neat!

The purpose of using mocking and stubbing is to allow us to unit test our code. **Unit testing** allows us to test each chunk of code as an individual unit so we can verify that our methods are working as expected. By using mocking and stubbing, we ensure that only the code we need to hit the database executes a true DML statement, which has the added benefit of making our test suite execution really, really fast. There are some limits on what types of methods can be unit tested, which we will uncover in this chapter, but largely, we have written our queries to be mockable.

We are going to be covering the following main recipes:

- Mocking query results
- Implementing the stub provider
- Unit testing with the stub provider
- Utilizing `apex-mockery` for unit testing

Technical requirements

The recipes for this book can be found at `https://github.com/PacktPublishing/Salesforce-Lightning-Web-Component-Cookbook`, where each chapter has its own folder under the `force-app` folder. This GitHub repository is structured in the form of a Salesforce DX project, which will allow you to easily fork the repository for deployment in a free Salesforce Developer Edition org. The code for *Chapter 13, Testing Apex with Mocking and Stubbing*, is located at `https://github.com/PacktPublishing/Salesforce-Lightning-Web-Component-Cookbook/tree/main/force-app/chapter13`.

The components in this book require the use of an **integrated development environment** (**IDE**), such as **Visual Studio Code** (**VS Code**) or **Salesforce Code Builder**. Detailed instructions for setting up an IDE are located in *Chapter 1, Getting Ready for Lightning Web Component*, in the *Setting up your IDE* section.

If you are building the projects in this cookbook as written, you will need to seed your Salesforce Developer Edition org with test data. Detailed instructions for seeding your org are located in *Chapter 1, Getting Ready for Lightning Web Component*, in the *Setting up the Salesforce Lightning Web Components Cookbook org* section.

Lastly, the edition of Salesforce required to implement the recipes in this book must be Developer, Performance, Unlimited, Enterprise, or Database.com. You can sign up for a free Salesforce Developer Edition org at `https://developer.salesforce.com/signup`.

Mocking query results

Let's start with a standard definition of mocks and stubs, as there is much heated debate about the definition of each term in the software industry.

We are going to use the definition provided by Salesforce in the *Advanced Apex Testing* module in Trailhead, linked in the *See also* section of this recipe. In short, a **mock** is a fake object that we use to isolate the code that we are testing in a test class, while a **stub** replaces an individual method by creating an anonymous subclass of the Apex class that we are testing at runtime. To phrase this differently, a stub gives hardcoded, specific data so we can run a test, while a mock makes sure a method was called in the way that it was expected to be called.

A common example of a stub in Salesforce is `HttpCalloutMock`, which, when implemented in our Apex test class, allows us to **inject** a fake HTTP `Response` value into our test method.

How to do it...

To create a fake sObject for use in our test methods, first, we need to create a unique 18-character Salesforce ID:

1. Start by creating a new Apex class, `Util_FakeIdGenerator`. This class will have one `private static` class variable, `Integer idsGenerated = 0`, and two `static` methods, each returning an `Id` object, each with different parameters, and each with the method name of `getFakeId`. This is a technique known as **method overloading**, where methods with the same name can perform distinct functions based on the parameters that they receive.
2. We'll start with our second `getFakeId` method, because we will be calling it in our first. Start by adding a parameter of an `SObjectType` object called `sObjType` to your method definition. So far, it should look like this:

```
public static Id getFakeId(SObjectType sObjType) {
}
```

3. On the first line of the body of your method, increment the `static` class variable of `idsGenerated` by one using the ++ operator. Because this is a `static` variable, the `idsGenerated` variable will remain the same across all instances of the `Util_FakeIdGenerator` class for the duration of the transaction. In a practical sense, what this means is that if we run all our test classes at once, each mocked sObject that appears in our tests will have a unique ID based on the sequence in which it was generated. Our first line of the method will look like this:

```
idsGenerated++;
```

4. On the second line of our method body, grab the `String keyPrefix` of the `sObjType` value that we passed in as a parameter. We can do this using a built-in non-static method of the `sObjectType` class, `getDescribe`, followed by the non-static `getKeyPrefix` method of the `DescribeSObjectResult` class. We can do this in one line, as follows:

```
String keyPrefix = sObjType.getDescribe().getKeyPrefix();
```

5. Next, we are going to grab the `String` value of our class variable, `idsGenerated`, so that we can manipulate it as text. We can do this using the static `valueOf` method of the `String` class:

```
String idsGenStr = String.valueOf(idsGenerated);
```

6. Lastly, we are going to use these two values to generate our mocked ID. There are several ways to do this, but my favorite involves the non-static `leftPad` method of the `String` class. The `leftPad` method adds a specified character (or a `String` value) to the left of our rightmost character until our string reaches a certain character length. We can verify this with the following anonymous Apex snippet:

```
String myCoolString = '123';
String myPaddedString = myCoolString.leftPad(10, '0');
System.debug(10 == myPaddedString.length()); //true
System.debug('0000000123' == myPaddedString); //true
```

So, if we want to get a 15-character ID, how can we generate this? Let's do some thinking.

The `keyPrefix` value in Salesforce is equal to 3 characters, so we have 12 characters left to populate with zeros in order to generate an ID. If we have an integer of `1` for our first ID generated, we know we need 12 more characters to get to 15 after we subtract our single character. Thus, our `return` statement will look like the following:

```
return Id.valueOf(keyPrefix + idsGenStr.leftPad(13-idsGenStr.length(),
'0'));
```

We can test this with the following anonymous Apex snippet:

```
Account acct = new Account();
SObjectType acctType = acct.getSObjectType();
System.debug(Util_FakeIdGenerator.getFakeId(acctType));
```

When we check our logs, we get something similar to the following as a debug statement:

```
00:00:00:000 USER_DEBUG [4]|DEBUG|001000000000001AAA
```

As we see, casting the `String` value as an ID using the static `valueOf` method of the `Id` class adds our 3-character suffix, yielding our classic 18-character Salesforce ID.

7. Now, what if we want to handle grabbing our `sObjectType` within our `Util_FakeIdGenerator` class, so we don't have to handle it before calling our `getFakeId` method? This is where the concept of **method overloading** comes in.
8. Above your `getFakeId` method, create another `getFakeId` method, but this time, with a parameter of an sObject called `sObj`. For our `return` statement, call the other `getFakeId` method on your `sObj` sObject after calling the `getSObjectType` method on it, as we did in the second line in the preceding anonymous Apex snippet. This will look like the following:

```
public static Id getFakeId(SObject sObj) {
    return getFakeId(sObj.getSObjectType());
}
```

Now, we have two `getFakeId` methods, one that operates on an sObject record, such as an **Account** or **Asset** record, and one that operates on an `sObjectType` record, optionally pulled directly from our sObject record. The resulting mocked sObject IDs can be passed into our stubbed methods.

See also

- The sample file for the `Util_FakeIdGenerator` class is located under the `force-app/chapter00/default/classes/Util_FakeIdGenerator.cls` directory in your forked repository for comparison. This file is located at `https://github.com/PacktPublishing/Salesforce-Lightning-Web-Component-Cookbook/blob/main/force-app/chapter00/default/classes/Util_FakeIdGenerator.cls`.
- The *Advanced Apex Testing* module on Trailhead is located at `https://trailhead.salesforce.com/content/learn/modules/unit-testing-on-the-lightning-platform`.
- The documentation for the `SObjectType` class is located at `https://developer.salesforce.com/docs/atlas.en-us.apexref.meta/apexref/apex_class_Schema_SObjectType.htm`.
- The documentation for the `DescribeSObjectResult` class is located at `https://developer.salesforce.com/docs/atlas.en-us.apexref.meta/apexref/apex_methods_system_sobject_describe.htm`.

- The documentation for the `String` class is located at `https://developer.salesforce.com/docs/atlas.en-us.apexref.meta/apexref/apex_methods_system_string.htm`.
- For further reading on the difference between mocks and stubs, see Martin Fowler's seminal essay, *Mocks Aren't Stubs*, at `https://martinfowler.com/articles/mocksArentStubs.html`.

Implementing the stub provider

Now that we have a way of mocking our sObjects with a fake ID that Salesforce will recognize, we can use Salesforce's **stub API**. As stated earlier in the chapter, there are several mocking and stubbing frameworks that can be used for unit testing, one of which we will cover in the next recipe, but this example serves to demonstrate a use case for the stub API in a small-to-mid-sized org. We will get into enterprise use cases later in this chapter.

How to do it...

Salesforce's stub API is provided so that a mocking framework can be implemented, so that classes can be tested in isolation. In an enterprise org, we would use a **factory pattern** to achieve this, but for now, we will start by implementing the stub provider to gain an understanding of this advanced Apex functionality. We will be writing a test class for the `AccountService` class that we wrote in *Chapter 3, Working with a Selector Class*. If you are joining us in this chapter, you can deploy the `force-app/chapter03` directory to your Salesforce Developer Edition org for this purpose:

1. To get started, we must implement the `System.StubProvider` **interface class** in an Apex test class, which we will call `AccountServiceMockProvider`. We can do this in our class definition using the `implements` keyword, like so:

```
@isTest
public class AccountServiceMockProvider implements System.StubProvider {
}
```

2. Next, we need to implement the `handleMethodCall` method of the `StubProvider` interface. This must be done in every mock provider class, as the `handleMethodCall` method defines the behavior of a stubbed method, while the `StubProvider` interface

defines the behavior of the class. In every implementation, the `handleMethodCall` method will have the following signature:

```
public Object handleMethodCall(Object stubbedObject, String
stubbedMethodName, Type returnType, List<Type> listOfParamTypes,
List<String> listOfParamNames, List<Object> listOfArgs) {
}
```

3. The parameters represent the following:
   - `Object stubbedObject` represents the stubbed class
   - `String stubbedMethodName` represents the name of the stubbed method that was called
   - `System.Type returnType` represents the return type of the stubbed method that was called
   - `List<SystemType> listOfParamTypes` represents a list of the parameter types of the stubbed method that was called
   - `List<String> listOfParamNames` represents a list of the parameter names of the stubbed method that was called
   - `List<Object> listOfArgs` represents the actual argument values that were passed into the called stubbed method at runtime

   These parameters can be used to determine which method was invoked on the stubbed object.

4. Because we are testing our `AccountService` class, which has one distinct method, we will utilize the `stubbedMethodName` parameter to determine which method was called. If we were to test our `Util_FakeIdGenerator` class, which has two methods with the same name, we would also need to check which parameters were passed in using the `listOfParamTypes`, `listOfParamNames`, or `listOfArgs` variables. Because we are only testing the one method (for now!), we will use an Apex `switch` statement on the `stubbedMethodName` variable, like so:

```
switch on stubbedMethodName {
   when 'getTopAccountWrappers' {
   } when else {
      return null;
```

```
    }
}
```

As we build out our `AccountService` class, we can easily add more values here by adding more `when` blocks to our `switch` statement. We can also do an `if-else` block here, but a `switch` statement offers modest performance gains.

5. Inside our `when 'getTopAccountWrappers'` block, we need to return a mocked `AccountWrapper`. How do we go about doing that? Let's take a look at the documentation for the `Test.createStubQueryRows` method, linked in the *See also* section for this recipe. This method will allow us to create an instance of a stubbed `sObjectType` that we can use to provide testing results, and it accepts two parameters: an `SObjectType` record, `targetType`, and a `List<Map<String, Object>>` collection, `fieldMapWithRelationshipKeysForMultipleRows`.
6. Let's start by building out our `List<Map<String, Object>>` collection, which will contain a list of mocked `Account` records with field values designated by `Map<String, Object>`, where `String` represents the field name, and `Object` represents a primitive type for the field value. We will accomplish this with a classic `for` loop:

```
List<Map<String, Object>> accountMaps = new List<Map<String, Object>>();
for(Integer ii = 9; ii > -1; ii--) {
    Account acct = new Account(Name = 'Account ' + ii);
    Id mockedId = Util_FakeIdGenerator.getFakeId(acct);
    Decimal annualRev = ii * 100000;
    Map<String, Object> accountMap = new Map<String, Object> {
        'Id' => mockedId,
        'Name' => acct.Name,
        'AnnualRevenue' => annualRev,
        'Phone' => '555-555-5555',
        'BillingCity' => 'Denver',
        'BillingState' => 'Colorado',
        'BillingCountry' => 'USA',
        'Museum_Office__latitude__s' => 37.790197,
        'Museum_Office__longitude__s' => -122.396879
    };
    accountMaps.add(accountMap);
}
```

Writing a backward `for` loop, where we start at `9` and decrease to `0`, will ensure that our mocked accounts appear in order of descending annual revenue, where our `AnnualRevenue` variable is equal to `index ii` multiplied by 100,000. Like many pieces of code, there are several other ways we could write this, such as the following:

```
for(Integer ii = 0; ii < 10; ii++) {
   Account acct = new Account(Name = 'Account ' + ii);
   Id mockedId = Util_FakeIdGenerator.getFakeId(acct);
   Decimal annualRev = (10-ii) * 100000;
   ...
}
```

This depends on personal preference and how you like to visualize your data in your mind.

7. Once we have `List<Map<String, Object>> accountMaps` populated with our top 10 `Account` records in descending order, we are going to use the `Test.createStubQueryRows` method, which returns a `List<sObject>`, to transform them into `List<Account>` objects with casting:

```
List<Account> acctsToWrap = (List<Account>)
Test.createStubQueryRows(Account.getSObjectType(), accountMaps);
```

8. Finally, we iterate over our `acctsToWrap` list and wrap them using the following:

```
List<AccountService.AccountWrapper> wrappedAccounts = new
List<AccountService.AccountWrapper>();
for (Account acct : acctsToWrap) {
   wrappedAccounts.add(new AccountService.AccountWrapper(acct));
}
return wrappedAccounts;
```

This allows us to pass our mocked account wrappers into our stubbed method.

See also

- The sample file for the `AccountServiceMockProvider` class is located under the `force-app/chapter13/default/classes/AccountSelectorMockProvider .cls` directory in your forked repository for comparison. This file is located at `https://github.com/PacktPublishing/Salesforce-Lightning-Web-Component-Cookbook/blob/main/force-app/chapter13/default/classes/AccountServiceMockProvider.cls`.
- The sample file for the `AccountService` class is located under the `force-app/chapter03/default/classes/AccountService.cls` directory in your forked repository for comparison. This file is located at `https://github.com/PacktPublishing/Salesforce-Lightning-Web-Component-Cookbook/blob/main/force-app/chapter03/default/classes/AccountService.cls`.
- The *Build a Mocking Framework with the Stub API* documentation in the Salesforce Developer Docs is located at `https://developer.salesforce.com/docs/atlas.en-us.apexcode.meta/apexcode/apex_testing_stub_api.htm`.
- The documentation for the `StubProvider` interface class is located at `https://developer.salesforce.com/docs/atlas.en-us.apexref.meta/apexref/apex_interface_System_StubProvider.htm`.
- The documentation for the `Test` class, specifically the `Test.createStubQueryRow` method, is available at `https://developer.salesforce.com/docs/atlas.en-us.apexref.meta/apexref/apex_methods_system_test.htm#apex_System_Test_createStubQueryRow`.

Unit testing with the stub provider

Now that we have a list of mocked account wrappers to test with, let's build a `Util_Mocker` class that returns a stubbed class so we can test them.

Getting started

1. Create a new Apex class, `Util_Mocker`, with one public static method that returns an object and accepts a `Type` parameter, called `typetoMock`, and call this method `createMock`.

> **Note**
>
> This sample class is included in the `force-app/chapter00/default/classes` directory, with the pieces we are about to write commented out. If you are deploying the whole repository and running all tests, you will encounter a **null pointer exception** error until these lines are included.

2. Inside this method, place another `switch` statement with a switch on the value of `String.valueOf(typeToMock)`. When the `switch` value is equal to `AccountService`, return the result of the `Test.createStub` method, and pass in the parameters of `typeToMock` and a newly instantiated `AccountServiceMockProvider` class, like so:

```
public with sharing class Util_Mocker {
    public static Object createMock(Type typeToMock) {
        switch on String.valueOf(typeToMock) {
            when 'AccountService' {
                return Test.createStub(typeToMock, new
AccountServiceMockProvider());
            }
            when else {
                return null;
            }
        }
    }
}
```

As we grow our org, we can add additional mock provider classes to our `switch` statement. Again, if we were working in an enterprise org, we would want to do this with a factory pattern or an existing library, such as `fflib` or `apex-mockery`, which we will be exploring in the next recipe.

How to do it...

Now that we have our Util_Mocker class, we can write our test methods. For the sake of brevity, we will not be writing the whole test class, but let's verify that our modest mocking and stubbing implementation works:

1. Start by creating a new Apex class, a test class called AccountTest, and define a test method called testMockedSelectorTopTenAccounts:

```
@IsTest
public with sharing class AccountTest {
    @IsTest
    static void testMockedSelectortopTenAccounts() {
    }
}
```

2. On the first line of the body of your test method, instantiate an AccountService object called mockService:

```
AccountService mockService =
(AccountService)Util_Mocker.createMock(AccountService.class);
```

   From left to right, we are declaring an AccountService object called mockService and setting it equal to an AccountService casting of the result of the Util_Mocker.createMock method performed on the AccountService.class object. Now, we have our stubbed Apex class.

3. Because we have already defined the result for our stubbed getTopAccountWrappers method in our AccountServiceMockProvider class, all we must do is call the method on our mocked class, mockService. We do this with the instance of our class, as our getTopAccountWrappers method is non-static. This is important to note, as only non-static methods can be stubbed. It's all coming together now!

```
Test.startTest();
    List<AccountService.AccountWrapper> resultWrappers =
```

```
mockService.getTopAccountWrappers();
Test.stopTest();
```

4. Lastly, we write our **assert statements**, which we can do in a `for` loop to ensure that our mocked account wrappers are in the order in which we specified them:

```
for(Integer jj = 0; jj < 10; jj++) {
   Assert.isTrue(resultWrappers[jj].Name == 'Account ' + (9 - jj), 'Verify
that the resultString contains each of the inserted accounts, and that they
are sorted in the correct order. Account ' + jj);
}
```

Doing our asserts in this format allows us to check every mocked `Account` record and ensure that they are in the correct order.

See also

- The sample file for the `AccountTest` class, which I have named `Chapter3Tests_StubProvider` for clarity, is located under `force-app/chapter13/default/classes/Chapter3Tests_StubProvider.cls` in your forked repository for comparison. This file is located at `https://github.com/PacktPublishing/Salesforce-Lightning-Web-Component-Cookbook/blob/main/force-app/chapter13/default/classes/Chapter3Tests_StubProvider.cls`.
- The documentation for the Salesforce provided `Test` class is available at `https://developer.salesforce.com/docs/atlas.en-us.apexref.meta/apexref/apex_methods_system_test.htm`.

Utilizing apex-mockery for unit testing

Now that we have a basic understanding of implementing the stub provider provided by Salesforce, we can expand our knowledge by utilizing a common mocking and stubbing library, the open source `apex-mockery` library. `apex-mockery` has the benefit of being lightweight compared to a predecessor, `fflib`, which is a common Apex enterprise pattern.

apex-mockery licensed under a BSD 3-Clause, available here:

Copyright (c) 2022, Salesforce.com, Inc. All rights reserved.

Getting started

We've already introduced the concepts of stubs and mocks, but to round out our understanding of the workings of `apex-mockery`, we need to add one more concept: spies. A **spy** effectively enables us to take a peek at what's happening with a given method, which allows us to dictate what should be happening. For example, if we spy on a **selector class** method, we can dictate that this method return a certain set of values. We will look at an example of this shortly.

To get started, we need to deploy the `apex-mockery` library to our Salesforce Developer Edition org. This can easily be done by following the **README Installation** link, `https://github.com/salesforce/apex-mockery/tree/main?tab=readme-ov-file#installation`, and selecting the **Deploy to Salesforce** button. This should not be deployed to a production org without buy-in, thorough testing, and a plan for migration, so ensure you are logged in to your Developer Edition org!

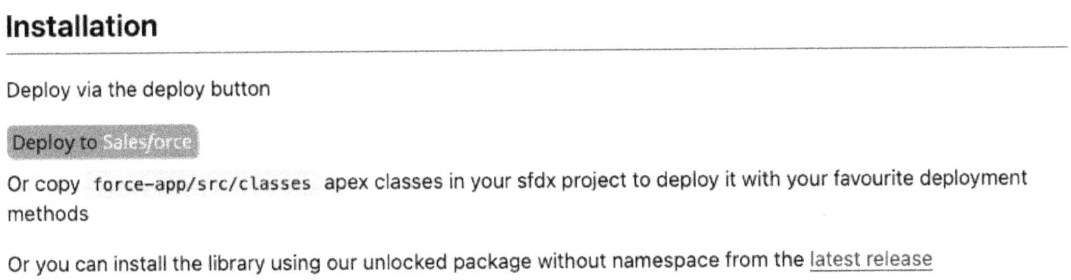

Figure 13.1: A screenshot of the Installation header under the README for apex-mockery

Once you have selected this button, you will be prompted to log in to your Developer Edition org, at which point you will be able to deploy by pressing the **Deploy** button in the top-right corner of your screen:

Figure 13.2: A screenshot of the GitHub Salesforce Deploy Tool deploying apex-mockery to the cookbook org

Now, we are ready to write our unit tests with `apex-mockery`.

> **Note**
>
> If you attempted to deploy the entire cookbook `force-app` directory before this point, you would have gotten an error such as **Invalid type: Mock** or **Invalid type: MethodSpy**. This is because the cookbook repository does not include the necessary files for `apex-mockery`. The solution is to deploy `apex-mockery` or to deploy individual chapter directories as needed.

How to do it...

We are going to be writing three methods to accompany our *Chapter 3, Working with a Selector Class*, code. While I have written example test classes for most of the rest of the cookbook for your viewing pleasure, we will be focusing on writing unit tests for the `TopAccountsController`, `AccountService`, and `AccountSelector` classes. Make sure you have deployed `apex-mockery` to your Salesforce Developer Edition org, and let's get started:

1. Start by creating a new Apex class. I have called mine `Chapter3Tests_Mockery` for clarity, but you will likely want to go with something more specific, such as `TopAccountsControllerTest`, and annotate it with the `@IsTest` declaration:

```
@IsTest
public without sharing class TopAccountsControllerTest { ... }
```

2. We are going to start by writing a test for our `AccountSelector.topTenAccountsByRevenue` method. Create an `@IsTest` annotated `static void` method called `selector_it_should_return_accounts`:

```
@IsTest
static void selector_it_should_return_accounts() { ... }
```

3. Next, we are going to create a list of mocked account records. We will be using this snippet in the other two methods in the test class as well:

```
List<Account> accountsToReturn = new List<Account>();
for(Integer ii = 0; ii < 10; ii++) {
    Account acct = new Account(Name = 'Account ' + ii);
    acct.Id = Util_FakeIdGenerator.getFakeId(new Account());
    acct.AnnualRevenue = ii * 100000;
    acct.Museum_Office__Latitude__s = 37.790197;
    acct.Museum_Office__Longitude__s = -122.396879;
    accountsToReturn.add(acct);
}
```

4. In a production org, we would likely have an sObject utility that would allow us to generate a type of mocked sObject with a method call. This would help to reduce code repetition and promote reuse. For now, as this is beyond the scope of this cookbook, we will come back to this snippet. We will call this our **preparation** before we dive into the

Arrange, Act, Assert pattern, where we arrange our data, act on it, and then assert the results.

5. Now that we have our data prepared, we must arrange it. If we had an sObject utility, we would be able to do these two steps at the same time, but for clarity and the sake of time, we are keeping them separate.
6. First, we create a `utilQueryMock` using the `Mock` class, provided by `apex-mockery`:

```
Mock utilQueryMock = Mock.forType(Util_Query.class);
```

7. Next, we create our `MethodSpy`, `querySpy`. This is going to allow us to peek in on what's happening when we call the `query` method of the `Util_Query` class that we wrote in *Chapter 3, Working with a Selector Class*:

```
MethodSpy querySpy = utilQueryMock.spyOn('query');
```

8. Following the pattern laid out in the `apex-mockery` docs, linked in the *See also* section of this recipe, we then create an instance of our `AccountSelector` class:

```
AccountSelector myAccountSelector = new AccountSelector();
```

9. Lastly, for our arrangement, we utilize the instance method of the `MethodSpy` class, `returnsOnce`, which is provided by the `apex-mockery` library:

```
querySpy.returnsOnce(accountsToReturn);
```

10. In doing so, we specify that when we peek in on our `query` method call, we want it to return the `accountsToReturn` that we prepared at the top of our method.
11. After arranging our data, we want to act on it. Here is where we call the method we are testing, the `topTenAccountsByRevenue` instance method of the `AccountSelector` class:

```
List<Account> myAccounts = myAccountSelector.topTenAccountsByRevenue();
```

12. Notice that we use the `myAccountSelector` instance that we created a few lines prior, as the `topTenAccountsByRevenue` method is non-static. Remember, we can't stub static methods!

13. Finally, we can assert and check that our accounts were returned:

```
for(Integer jj; jj < 10; jj++) {
   Integer accountNumber = 9 - jj;
   Account currentAccount = myAccounts[jj];
   Assert.isTrue(
      currentAccount.Name.contains(
         String.valueOf(accountNumber)
      ),
      'Accounts should be in order.'
   );
   Assert.isTrue(
      currentAccount.AnnualRevenue == accountNumber * 100000,
      'Accounts should have appropriate annual revenue.'
   );
}
```

14. Deploy your test class and run it, and you should see that we have 100% test coverage for our `AccountSelector` class:

```
=== Apex Code Coverage for Test Run 707g5000005H8xD
TEST NAME                                              CLASS BEING TESTED      OUTCOME  PERCENT  MESSAGE  RUNTIME (MS)
─────────────────────────────────────────────────────  ──────────────────────  ───────  ───────  ───────  ────────────
Chapter3Tests_Mockery.selector_it_should_return_accounts  Util_Query           Pass     33%               98
Chapter3Tests_Mockery.selector_it_should_return_accounts  Util_MockIDGenerator Pass     100%              98
Chapter3Tests_Mockery.selector_it_should_return_accounts  AccountSelector      Pass     100%              98

=== Apex Code Coverage by Class
CLASSES               PERCENT  UNCOVERED LINES
────────────────────  ───────  ───────────────
AccountSelector       100%
Util_Query            33%      6,7,10,11
Util_MockIDGenerator  100%
```

Figure 13.3: A screenshot of the Apex code coverage for a given test run

15. Next, let's write a test method called `service_it_should_return_account_wrappers`:

```
@IsTest
static void service_it_should_return_account_wrappers() { ... }
```

16. We will use the same preparation we did in the previous method, but our arrangement will be a little bit different:

```
Mock accountSelectorMock = Mock.forType(AccountSelector.class);
MethodSpy topTenAccountsByRevenueSpy =
accountSelectorMock.spyOn('topTenAccountsByRevenue');
```

```
AccountService myAccountService = new AccountService();
myAccountService.accountSelect = (AccountSelector) accountSelectorMock.stub;
topTenAccountsByRevenueSpy.returnsOnce(accountsToReturn);
```

17. Line by line, we do the following:
    - Mock our `AccountSelector` class
    - Spy on our `topTenAccountsByRevenue` method of the `AccountSelector` class
    - Declare and initialize an instance of the `AccountService` class
    - Stub the `AccountSelector` class variable in our `AccountService` class
    - Specify the accounts we want to return!
18. This will allow us to manipulate multiple aspects of our code at the same time.
19. Next, we act:

```
List<AccountService.AccountWrapper> myWrappers =
myAccountService.getTopAccountWrappers();
```

20. We call the `getTopAccountWrappers` instance method from our newly created instance of the `AccountService` class, `myAccountService`.
21. Finally, we assert:

```
for(Integer jj; jj < 10; jj++) {
   Integer accountNumber = 9 - jj;
   AccountService.AccountWrapper currentWrapper = myWrappers[jj];
   Assert.isTrue(
      currentWrapper.Name.contains(
         String.valueOf(accountNumber)
      ),
      'Accounts should be in order.'
   );
   Assert.isTrue(
      currentWrapper.AnnualRevenue == accountNumber * 100000,
      'Accounts should have appropriate annual revenue.'
   );
}
```

22. Deploy your test class and run it one more time:

```
=== Apex Code Coverage for Test Run 707g5000005HIYs
TEST NAME                                                  CLASS BEING TESTED     OUTCOME  PERCENT  MESSAGE  RUNTIME (MS)
─────────────────────────────────────────────────────────  ─────────────────────  ───────  ───────  ───────  ────────────
Chapter3Tests_Mockery.service_it_should_return_account_wrappers  AccountSelector        Pass     0%                104
Chapter3Tests_Mockery.service_it_should_return_account_wrappers  Util_MockIDGenerator   Pass     100%              104
Chapter3Tests_Mockery.service_it_should_return_account_wrappers  Util_Query             Pass     0%                104
Chapter3Tests_Mockery.service_it_should_return_account_wrappers  AccountService         Pass     96%               104

=== Apex Code Coverage by Class
CLASSES               PERCENT  UNCOVERED LINES
────────────────────  ───────  ───────────────
AccountSelector       0%       4,5,7
AccountService        96%      8
Util_Query            0%       2,3,6,7,10,...
Util_MockIDGenerator  100%
```

Figure 13.4: A screenshot of Apex code coverage for a given test run, showing a passing test that has coverage on multiple classes

23. Lastly, let's create one final test method for our controller class, `TopAccountsController`. Remember, we can't stub static methods, so we have to get a little tricky! Start by writing your method definition:

```
@IsTest
static void controller_it_should_return_account_wrappers() { ... }
```

24. Input our preparation one more time by copying and pasting it from one of your other two methods, and write our arrangement:

```
Mock accountSelectorMock = Mock.forType(AccountSelector.class);
MethodSpy topTenAccountsByRevenueSpy =
accountSelectorMock.spyOn('topTenAccountsByRevenue');
AccountService myAccountService = new AccountService();
myAccountService.accountSelect = (AccountSelector) accountSelectorMock.stub;
topTenAccountsByRevenueSpy.returnsOnce(accountsToReturn);
```

25. One thing to note, our `Controller` class returns a JSON `String` value, so we must act accordingly:

```
String myWrapperJson = TopAccountsController.returnAccountWrapperList();
```

26. Now, we can assert confidently:

```
for(Integer jj; jj < 10; jj++) {
   Integer accountNumber = 9 - jj;
   Assert.isTrue(
      myWrapperJson.contains(
```

```
            String.valueOf(accountNumber)
        ),
        'Accounts should be in order.'
    );
    Assert.isTrue(
        myWrapperJson.contains(
            String.valueOf(accountNumber * 100000)
        ),
        'Accounts should have appropriate annual revenue.'
    );
}
```

27. Deploy and run all tests:

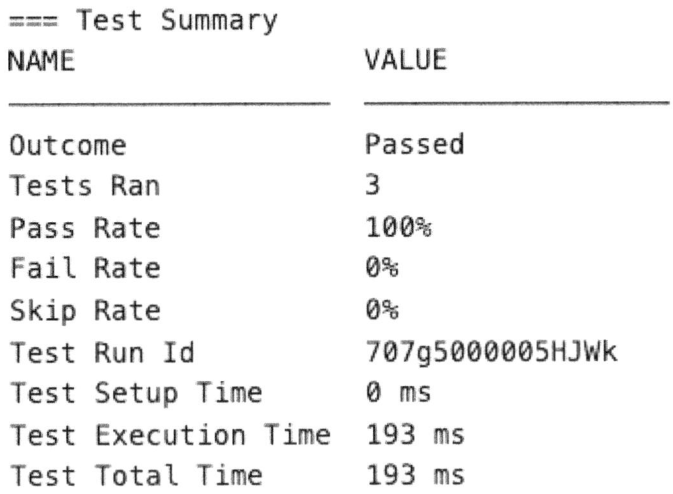

Figure 13.5: A screenshot showing three passed tests in a little under 2/10ths of a second

See also

- The sample code for this recipe is located in the repository at `force-app/chapter13/default/classes/Chapter3Tests_Mockery.cls`, or at `https://github.com/PacktPublishing/Salesforce-Lightning-Web-Component-Cookbook/blob/main/force-app/chapter13/default/classes/Chapter3Tests_Mockery.cls`
- The repository for `apex-mockery` is located at `https://github.com/salesforce/apex-mockery/tree/main`

- The Salesforce Developers blog post announcing `apex-mockery` is available at `https://developer.salesforce.com/blogs/2023/06/introducing-apex-mockery-a-unit-test-mocking-library`
- The `fflib` common library is available at `https://github.com/apex-enterprise-patterns/fflib-apex-common`
- Information about the *Arrange, Act, Assert* design pattern is available at `https://java-design-patterns.com/patterns/arrange-act-assert/`

Get this book's PDF version and more

14

Testing Lightning Web Components with Jest

Now that we have learned about several methods for testing the Apex that we pair with Lightning Web Components, it's time to test the components themselves. To do this, we will focus on some of the code that we have already written, namely the components we wrote for *Chapter 3, Working with a Selector Class*, and *Chapter 4, Synchronous and Asynchronous Processing in Components*. The tests for these two chapters will give us an idea of what needs to happen when we write our frontend tests.

We are going to be covering the following main recipes:

- Setting up for testing with Jest
- Writing tests using matchers
- Mocking controller methods
- Testing asynchronous JavaScript
- Checking element attributes

Technical requirements

The recipes for this book can be found at `https://github.com/PacktPublishing/Salesforce-Lightning-Web-Component-Cookbook`, where each chapter has its own folder under the `force-app` folder. This GitHub repository is structured in the form of a Salesforce DX project, which will allow you to easily fork the repository for deployment in a free Salesforce Developer Edition org. The code for *Chapter 14, Testing Lightning Web components*, is located within the *Chapter 4, Synchronous and Asynchronous Processing in Components*, directory at `https://github.com/`

PacktPublishing/Salesforce-Lightning-Web-Component-Cookbook/tree/main/force-app/chapter04/default/lwc/assetsByTag/__tests__.

The components in this book require the use of an **Integrated Development Environment (IDE)**, such as **Visual Studio Code (VSCode)** or **Salesforce Code Builder**. Detailed instructions for setting up an IDE are located in *Chapter 1, Getting Ready for Lightning Web Components*, in the *Setting up your IDE* section.

If you are building the projects in this cookbook as written, you will need to seed your Salesforce Developer Edition org with test data. Detailed instructions for seeding your org are located in *Chapter 1, Getting Ready for Lightning Web Component Development*, in the *Setting up the Salesforce Lightning Web Components Cookbook org* section.

Lastly, the edition of Salesforce required to implement the recipes in this book is Developer, Performance, Unlimited, Enterprise, or Database.com. You can sign up for a free Salesforce Developer Edition org at `https://developer.salesforce.com/signup`.

Setting up for testing with Jest

In order to test the frontend of our LWCs, we will be using the JavaScript testing framework, Jest. We will be building our way through five tests for a component we have built within this cookbook using Jest, ranging from testing our transformative functions to testing our Apex calls.

Getting started

To start, we will be looking at the `lightning-tree-grid` component, built in *Chapter 4, Synchronous and Asynchronous Processing in Components*.

1. Ensure that you have the code that was written for *Chapter 4, Synchronous and Asynchronous Processing in Components*, deployed. This may have been achieved either by having written the necessary components at some point on our journey together or by having deployed the sample code that was written for this cookbook. This component is highlighted in *Figure 14.1*:

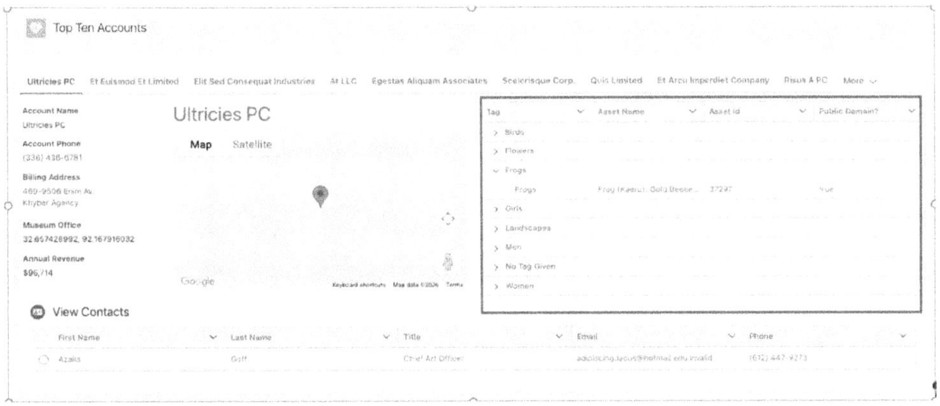

Figure 14.1: A screenshot of the Top Ten Accounts page, built in Chapters 3, 4, and 6

2. If you are joining us in this chapter, it is recommended to complete the setup in *Chapter 1, Getting Ready for Lightning Web Component Development*, in the *Setting up the Salesforce Lightning Web Components Cookbook org* recipe, to seed your org with appropriate sample data. Once these steps have been completed, deploy the `force-app/chapter03` and `force-app/chapter04` directories to your Salesforce Developer Edition org, and delete the sample directory at `force-app/chapter04/default/lwc/assetsByTag/__tests__`. The reason for this deletion is that we will be recreating the sample files in the scope of this chapter, which will give us some code to work with. The files from *Chapter 3, Working With a Selector Class*, allow us to easily display the component from *Chapter 4, Synchronous and Asynchronous Processing in Components*, on the **Top Ten Accounts** page.
3. While I do recommend exploring the content in previous chapters, we shouldn't need to do any setup beyond deployment here, as our tests will run locally, and the `force-app/chapter03` directory contains the necessary **Top Ten Accounts** page.

How to do it...

The first thing we will need to do to test with Jest is install the necessary dependencies, including **Node.js** and **npm**. If you have been following along up until this point, you will recall that we installed these tools in the *Linting for Salesforce* recipe of *Chapter 1, Getting Ready for Lightning Web Component Development*. Node.js and the related npm can be installed using the package manager at `https://nodejs.org/en/download/package-manager`. We will also need to ensure that the **Salesforce CLI** is installed, which can be accessed at `https://developer.salesforce.com/tools/salesforcecli`. Once these steps have been completed, we can get started.

1. Restart Visual Studio Code if you haven't already. This will refresh the IDE settings to ensure we are using the most recent updates.

2. Issue the following command:

```
sf force lightning lwc test setup
```

3. This will prepare the IDE for testing with Jest. If you run into upstream dependency errors, you may need to run this command instead:

```
npm install --save-dev @salesforce/sfdx-lwc-jest -force
```

4. You should see something like the following in your terminal:

```
Installing @salesforce/sfdx-lwc-jest node package...

up to date, audited 768 packages in 782ms

193 packages are looking for funding
  run `npm fund` for details

found 0 vulnerabilities
Test setup complete.
evelynmaguire@Evelyns-Laptop Salesforce-Lightning-Web-Component-Cookbook %
```

Figure 14.2: A screenshot of the installation of the @salesforce/sfdx-lwc-jest node package

5. Next, we need to create a `__tests__` folder in our desired directory. For this chapter, we will revisit the code we wrote in *Chapter 4, Synchronous and Asynchronous Processing in Components*. We are going to write a test for the `AssetsByTag` component that we wrote previously, which will show us how we can write tests for synchronous and asynchronous JavaScript, as well as imperative Apex. This can be achieved using the following command:

```
sf force lightning lwc test create -f force-app/chapter04/default/lwc/
assetsByTag/assetsByTag.js
```

6. This will create the necessary `__tests__` folder in our specified directory—in this case, `force-app/chapter04/default/lwc/assetsByTag`—and pair it with our desired LWC's JavaScript file, `assetsByTag.js`. Note that if you did not delete the `force-app/chapter04/default/lwc/assetsByTag/__tests__` directory in the *Getting started* section of this recipe, you will receive an error stating that the files already exist.
7. Once this command has been issued, you should see the template code that is provided by Salesforce:

```
import { createElement } from 'lwc';
import AssetsByTag from 'c/assetsByTag';

Run All Tests | Debug All Tests
describe('c-assets-by-tag', () => {
    afterEach(() => {
        // The jsdom instance is shared across test cases in a single file so reset the DOM
        while (document.body.firstChild) {
            document.body.removeChild(document.body.firstChild);
        }
    });

    Run Test | Debug Test
    it('TODO: test case generated by CLI command, please fill in test logic', () => {
        const element = createElement('c-assets-by-tag', {
            is: AssetsByTag
        });
        document.body.appendChild(element);
        expect(1).toBe(2);
    });
});
```

Figure 14.3: A screenshot of the template __tests__ code for the AssetsByTag.js file

8. Note that if you run the test as written, it will fail by default. This is because we assert that 1 should be equal to 2, which will never be true. This is expected behavior, as we want to replace our `TODO` annotated test with a real test.

See also

- To access the Salesforce Developer Documentation on preparing to unit test with Jest, visit `https://developer.salesforce.com/docs/platform/lwc/guide/unit-testing-using-jest-installation.html`
- The Salesforce Developer Documentation on creating unit tests with Jest is available at `https://developer.salesforce.com/docs/platform/lwc/guide/unit-testing-using-jest-create-tests.html`
- The Jest *Getting Started* documentation is located at `https://jestjs.io/docs/getting-started`
- A helpful Salesforce Developers blog on unit testing Lightning Web Components with Jest is available at `https://developer.salesforce.com/blogs/2019/03/unit-test-lightning-web-components-with-jest`

Writing tests using matchers

Similar to how we have **Assert** statements in Apex, there are **matchers** in Jest. Matchers allow us to test our code against various assumptions. If we call a function in JavaScript, we want to make sure it **matches** the expected result. To begin to understand testing in Jest, we will start by writing tests for the `tagFlattener` and `treeGridFormatter` functions. It is important to note that the returned results of the `tagFlattener` function are passed into the `treeGridFormatter` function, which is where we will begin.

Getting started

Knowing that these two functions share common data at the egress of one and the ingress of the other, we will start by creating some test data to use. Take a moment to refresh yourself on the functions of the `assetsByTag` component. Recall that we utilize the `TagSelector` Apex class to grab **Tag** records with child **Asset** records where each **Asset** is associated with a given **Account** record, as shown in the following ERD:

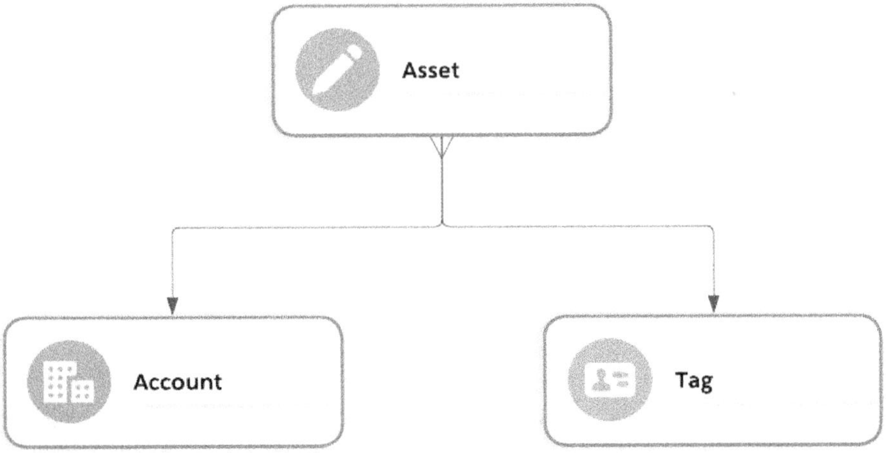

Figure 14.4: A basic entity relationship diagram showing the relationships between accounts, assets, and tags

The results of this query are transformed within the `AssetsByTagService` class and served to our LWC via the `AssetsByTagController` class using the `returnTagsWithAssetsByAccount` method. We are going to mock the data served by this Apex method so that we can test our JavaScript functions.

How to do it...

1. Within your `force-app/chapter04/default/lwc/assetsByTag/__tests__` directory, create a new folder called `data`.
2. Inside the newly created `data` folder, create a file called `returnedTagsWithAssets.json`. This file will contain sample data that we will feed into the `tagFlattener` function now, and into our mocked imperative Apex call later in this chapter.
3. Within your `returnedTagsWithAssets.json` file, enter the following:

```
[
    {
        "Id": "a03g5000001EuUnAAK",
        "Name": "Frogs",
        "Assets__r": [
            {
                "Tag__c": "a03g5000001EuUnAAK",
                "Id": "02ig50000000uwfAAA",
                "Name": "Frog (Kaeru); Gold Beetle (Kogane mushi), from the
Picture Book of Crawling Creatures (Ehon mushi erami)",
```

```
            "Department__c": "Asian Art",
            "Description": "Rogers Fund, 1918",
            "Is_Public_Domain__c": true,
            "Object_ID__c": "37297",
            "Primary_Image__c": "https://images.metmuseum.org/CRDImages/as/
original/DP135565.jpg"
          }
        ]
    }
]
```

4. This is a JSON representation of the `Frogs` tag record associated with a fictional account record, which contains a single child asset record. If you completed the org setup in *Chapter 1, Getting Ready for Lightning Web Component Development*, you should be able to see the following artwork in your Salesforce Developer Edition org.

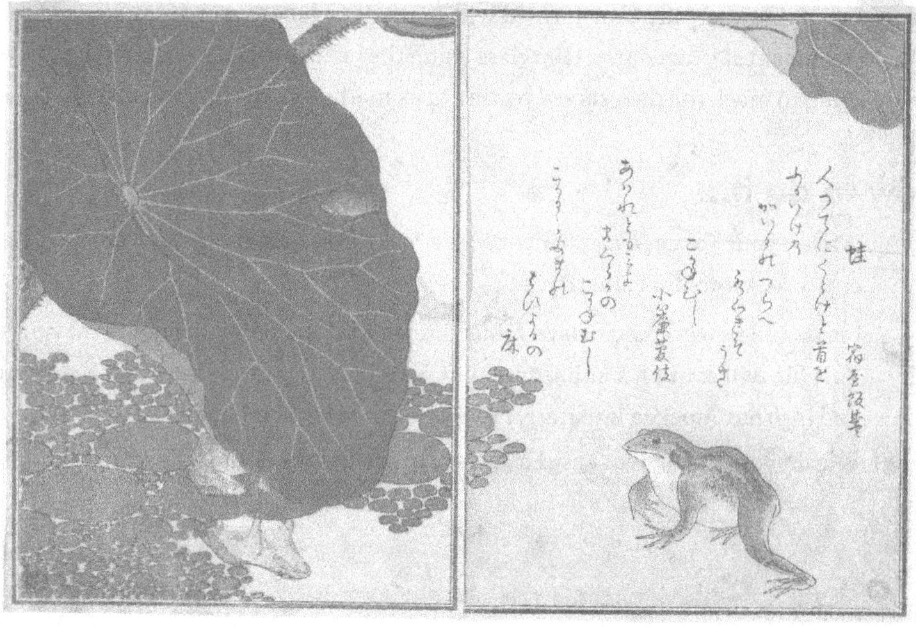

Figure 14.5: Frog (Kaeru); Gold Beetle (Kogane mushi), from the Picture Book of Crawling Creatures (Ehon mushi erami), by Kitagawa Utamaro, a public domain artwork sourced from The Metropolitan Museum of Art's Open Access collection

5. If you don't want to type this out, an easy way to grab the result of the Apex method is to add a `System.debug()` statement within your Apex controller, or a `console.log()`

statement within your LWC's JavaScript file, and copy the JSON output for the given method call. This is what I did to generate the included sample files. If, for example, we were working with an API call, we would be well served to copy a chunk of the API streaming response into our requisite JSON file. The reason for this is that building a JSON file by hand can be tricky and error-prone.

> **Note**
>
> The included sample `returnedTagsWithAssets.json` file includes data for several more tags and assets, so that we can test the sort and transform functionalities within the specified functions. We are building a pared-down version for brevity and clarity.

6. Next, create a second file within your `data` folder, this time called `flattenedAssets.json`. Populate it with the following:

```
[
    {
        "assetDepartment": "Asian Art",
        "assetId": "02ig50000000uwfAAA",
        "assetIsPublicDomain": true,
        "assetName": "Frog (Kaeru); Gold Beetle (Kogane mushi), from the
Picture Book of Crawling Creatures (Ehon mushi erami)",
        "assetObjectId": "37297",
        "assetPrimaryImage": "https://images.metmuseum.org/CRDImages/as/
original/DP135565.jpg",
        "tagId": "a03g5000001EuUnAAK",
        "tagName": "Frogs"
    }
]
```

7. This mimics the data structure that we are flattening our tags with assets into.
8. Create one last JSON file, `treeGridAssets.json`, and populate it with the following:

```
[
    {
        "tagName": "Frogs",
        "assetName" : "",
        "assetObjectId" : "Frogs",
```

```
        "assetIsPublicDomain" : "",
        "_children": [
            {
                "assetDepartment": "Asian Art",
                "assetId": "02ig50000000uwfAAA",
                "assetIsPublicDomain": true,
                "assetName": "Frog (Kaeru); Gold Beetle (Kogane mushi), from the
Picture Book of Crawling Creatures (Ehon mushi erami)",
                "assetObjectId": "37297",
                "assetPrimaryImage": "https://images.metmuseum.org/CRDImages/as/
original/DP135565.jpg",
                "tagId": "a03g5000001EuUnAAK",
                "tagName": "Frogs"
            }
        ]
    }
]
```

9. This file will represent the assets that have been formatted to fit the structure for the `lightning-tree-grid`.
10. Next, we must import our files into our test. Open the `assetsByTag.test.js` file within the `__tests__` directory. Under the `import` statements, add the following:

```
const RETURNED_TAGS_WITH_ASSETS = require('./data/
returnedTagsWithAssets.json')
const FLATTENED_ASSETS = require('./data/flattenedAssets.json');
const TREE_GRID_ASSETS = require('./data/treeGridAssets.json');
```

11. This will allow us to use our JSON files within our tests to simulate input and output data.
12. Edit the second block of code, beginning with `it('TODO:' ... )` to the following:

```
it('should flatten asset data', () => {
   const element = createElement('c-assets-by-tag',
      { is: AssetsByTag }
   );
   document.body.appendChild(element);
   const result = element.tagFlattener(RETURNED_TAGS_WITH_ASSETS);
```

```
    expect(result).toStrictEqual(FLATTENED_ASSETS);
});
```

13. Line by line, we are using `it`, an alias of the `test` function in Jest, to set a description for and define our test, defining `element` as an instance of the `assetsByTag` component, appending the component instance to the **DOM**, calling the `tagFlattener` function of the component with the `RETURNED_TAGS_WITH_ASSETS` JSON data file, and **asserting (expecting)** that the result will be equal to the data in the `FLATTENED_ASSETS` JSON file. Notice that we use the `toStrictEqual` matcher to verify the contents of the arrays defined in our JSON files, as `toStrictEqual` verifies that our values have the same object structure and type.
14. Copy this test function and paste it below. We will be writing a similar function to test the `treeGridFormatter` functionality.
15. Make the following edits to your pasted code block:

```
it('should format flattened assets for a tree grid', () => {
const element = createElement('c-assets-by-tag', { is: AssetsByTag });
document.body.appendChild(element);
const result = element.treeGridFormatter(FLATTENED_ASSETS);
expect(result).toStrictEqual(TREE_GRID_ASSETS);
});
```

16. Save your `.test.js` file and run the two tests we have written so far. This can be achieved most easily by selecting the Erlenmeyer flask icon in VSCode, which will open the **Test Explorer** menu:

Figure 14.6: The Test Explorer menu

17. These tests should pass if we formatted our JSON correctly. The tests will run locally, so there is no need to deploy. If your tests do not pass, compare the result with your expected output, and ensure that the JSON has the appropriate capitalization, as JavaScript is case sensitive.

See also

- The Jest documentation on using **matchers** can be found at `https://jestjs.io/docs/using-matchers`
- The Jest documentation on the `expect` function is available at `https://jestjs.io/docs/expect`

Mocking controller methods

Now that we know the basics of matchers, we can expand our repertoire. What happens if we need to simulate an Apex controller method call within our JavaScript? Again, similar to how we learned to test Apex, we can use a mock function. We will spend the next three recipes learning how to build our final Jest test of the chapter.

How to do it...

To start, we are going to build out a mock function to test the results of an imperative Apex call.

1. Begin by importing the `AssetsByTagController.returnTagsWithAssetsByAccount` method, as we would in a regular LWC JavaScript file:

```
import returnTagsWithAssetsByAccount from '@salesforce/apex/
AssetsByTagController.returnTagsWithAssetsByAccount';
```

2. Next, we need to mock this function. Before the `describe` function, but after the imports and constants from the previous recipe, add the following:

```
jest.mock(
    '@salesforce/apex/
AssetsByTagController.returnTagsWithAssetsByAccount',
    () => {
        return {
            default: jest.fn(),
        };
    },
    { virtual: true }
)
```

3. This will allow us to return a mocked function value, where the default return value is an empty mocked function.

4. At the bottom of your file, add one more test function:

```
it('should return, flatten, and format our returned assets by account', ()
=> { ... }
```

5. Like the previous test functions, we will begin by defining the `element` variable, an instance of the `assetsByTag` component, and appending it to the DOM:

```
const element = createElement('c-assets-by-tag', { is: AssetsByTag });
document.body.appendChild(element);
```

6. Next, we will mock the `returnTagsWithAssetsByAccount` resolved value:

```
returnTagsWithAssetsByAccount.mockResolvedValue(
   RETURNED_TAGS_WITH_ASSETS
);
```

7. After we define what our mock function will return, we can test against our expected values:

```
const result = element.getTagsWithAssets();
expect(result).toStrictEqual(TREE_GRID_ASSETS);
```

8. Save and attempt to run your test so far. It should fail. We will see why in the next recipe.

Figure 14.7: A debug output showing that our test failed, with an expected result of our JSON file not matching the received result, which is an empty JavaScript object

There's more

We now know how to mock the results of an imperative Apex call, but how would we mock a @wire service method? We will use the emit function rather than the mockResolvedValue function. Let's look, for example, at the TopAccountsController.returnAccountWrapperList Apex method from Chapter 3, Working With a Selector Class, which we have deployed in preparation for this chapter.

1. Start by deleting the existing `__tests__` folder from the `force-app/chapter03/default/lwc/topTenAccountTabset` directory so that you don't generate a duplicate file error.
2. Continue by issuing this command:

```
sf force lightning lwc test create -f force-app/chapter03/default/lwc/
topTenAccountTabset/topTenAccountTabset.js
```

3. This will create a new `__tests__` folder in the *Chapter 3, Working With a Selector Class,* directory. Add the following to your imports at the top of your `topTenAccountTabset.test.js` file to import the `returnAccountWrapperList` method:

```
import returnAccountWrapperList from '@salesforce/apex/
TopAccountsController.returnAccountWrapperList';
```

4. Below your imports, add the following constant value:

```
const ACCOUNT_WRAPPER_STRING = `[
  {
    "Id": "accountId",
    "Name": "Test Account",
    "Phone": "123-456-7890",
    "BillingCity": "Denver",
    "BillingState": "CO",
    "BillingCountry": "USA",
    "AnnualRevenue": "1000000.00"
  }
]`;
```

5. This mimics a pared-down version of the JSON structure that is returned by our wired function, `returnAccountWrapperList`. Note that we must enclose our JSON within

backtick marks (` `) to register this return value as a JSON **string**, as we are returning a string of JSON to be parsed in our JavaScript by our Apex controller method.

6. We also need to add our mock function definition below our constant:

```
jest.mock(
    '@salesforce/apex/
      TopAccountsController.returnAccountWrapperList',
    ()=>{
        const { createApexTestWireAdapter } = require("@salesforce/sfdx-lwc-
jest");
        return {
            default: createApexTestWireAdapter(jest.fn()),
        };
    },
    {virtual: true}
);
```

7. Edit the second block of text, the default `it` function with the `TODO` note, to the following:

```
it('should test wire function', () => {
    const element = createElement('c-top-ten-account-tabset', {
        is: TopTenAccountTabset
    });
    document.body.appendChild(element);
    returnAccountWrapperList.emit(
        ACCOUNT_WRAPPER_STRING
    );
    return Promise.resolve().then(() => {
        const tabs = element.shadowRoot.querySelectorAll('lightning-tab');
        expect(tabs.length).toBe(1);
        expect(tabs[0].label).toBe('Test Account');
    });
});
```

8. Once again, we are appending our component to the DOM, but this time, we emit `ACCOUNT_WRAPPER_STRING` as the result of the `@wire` function. We add a promise, which we resolve to simulate calling the resolve to simulate calling thefunction, and then we

check the `element` attributes, which we will be exploring further in the last recipe of this chapter.

See also

- The Jest documentation on manual mocking can be found at `https://jestjs.io/docs/manual-mocks`
- A Trailhead module on writing tests for Lightning Web Components is available at `https://trailhead.salesforce.com/content/learn/modules/test-lightning-web-components`
- The Salesforce Developer Docs documentation on unit testing using Jest is available at `https://developer.salesforce.com/docs/platform/lwc/guide/unit-testing-using-jest-create-tests.html`
- The Salesforce Developer Docs guide on unit testing using the wire utility can be found at `https://developer.salesforce.com/docs/platform/lwc/guide/unit-testing-using-wire-utility.html`
- The sample files for the *Chapter 3*, *Working with a Selector Class*, tests are available in the `force-app/chapter03/default/lwc/ topTenAccountTabset /__tests__` directory, or at the following GitHub link: `https://github.com/PacktPublishing/Salesforce-Lightning-Web-Component-Cookbook/tree/main/force-app/chapter03/default/lwc/topTenAccountTabset/__tests__`

Testing asynchronous JavaScript

Returning to the *Chapter 4*, *Synchronous and Asynchronous Processing in Components*, tests, the test function checking our imperative Apex is failing. As of right now, this is correct. There are a few changes that we must make to get this to return the values that we want. If we look at the assetsByTag.js file, stored within the force-app/chapter04/default/lwc/assetsByTag directory, we will see that the function we are testing has an async designation. What this means for our test, which is running synchronously, is that we need to make sure we wait for the asynchronous function to complete.

How to do it...

This is going to be a very short recipe, as the fix is quite simple.

1. Add the `async` and `await` keywords to your function, as shown in the highlighted segments:

```
it('should return, flatten, and format our returned assets by account',
async () => {
   const element = createElement('c-assets-by-tag', { is: AssetsByTag });
   document.body.appendChild(element);
   returnTagsWithAssetsByAccount.mockResolvedValue(
      RETURNED_TAGS_WITH_ASSETS
   );
   const result = await element.getTagsWithAssets();
   expect(result).toStrictEqual(TREE_GRID_ASSETS);
}
```

2. Now the test should pass.

See also

The Jest documentation for asynchronous JavaScript is available at `https://jestjs.io/docs/asynchronous`.

Checking element attributes

Now that we've tested our transformative JavaScript functions, how do we test what ends up displayed to the end user? We saw a quick example of this in the There's more section of the Mocking controller methods recipe of this chapter, but what did it mean? Let's find out.

How to do it...

We are going to add one more expect to the 'it should return, flatten, and format our returned assets by account' test function that we have been working on.

1. Add the following to your function:

```
const treeGrid = element.shadowRoot.querySelector('lightning-tree-grid');
expect(treeGrid.data).toStrictEqual(TREE_GRID_ASSETS);
```

2. What we are doing here is accessing the DOM elements via a `querySelector` that is looking for the `lightning-tree-grid`. Once we have the `treeGrid`, we access the `data` attribute and verify that its value matches the expected output.

> Note
>
> Salesforce calls out that DOM inspection tests, such as the test that we just wrote, are subject to change in their End-to-End Tests for LWC documentation (`https://developer.salesforce.com/docs/platform/lwc/guide/testing-dom-api.html`). As a result, these kinds of tests are actually not recommended, as they do not use a stable API and may break if Salesforce makes any updates to the way that LWCs are accessed via the shadow DOM. It is therefore recommended to use a tool such as **Selenium WebDriver** for end-to-end testing, which is beyond the scope of this cookbook.

See also

- The sample files for the *Chapter 4, Synchronous and Asynchronous Processing in Components*, tests are available in the `force-app/chapter04/default/lwc/assetsByTag/__tests__` directory, or at the following GitHub link: `https://github.com/PacktPublishing/Salesforce-Lightning-Web-Component-Cookbook/tree/main/force-app/chapter04/default/lwc/assetsByTag/__tests__`
- The Salesforce Developer Documentation on the **Document Object Model** (**DOM**) is available at `https://developer.salesforce.com/docs/platform/lwc/guide/create-dom-intro.html`
- The Salesforce Developer Documentation on end-to-end tests for LWCs is available at `https://developer.salesforce.com/docs/platform/lwc/guide/testing-dom-api.html`

Get this book's PDF version and more

Scan the QR code (or go to `packtpub.com/unlock`). Search for this book by name, confirm the edition, and then follow the steps on the page.

UNLOCK NOW

Note: Keep your invoice handy. Purchases made directly from Packt don't require an invoice.

Get this book's PDF version and more

[illegible] the QR code [illegible] this book [illegible] edition [illegible] the steps on the page.

15

Debugging Lightning Web Components

If you're reading this chapter, you've either made it through the cookbook (congrats!), you got stuck somewhere along the way, or you've got a tricky problem to solve. This chapter will go over some of the options for debugging your Salesforce applications, including Apex and Lightning Web Components. To prepare you to diagnose some common errors, we are going to do our best to cause them in the code that we have written in this cookbook. This will help to give us an idea of what to look for when we encounter these errors in our own projects.

We are going to be covering the following main recipes:

- Working with common debugging tools
- Knowing the limitations of debugging tools
- Preventing common errors in Apex
- Handling common errors in LWCs
- Dealing with null pointer exceptions

Technical requirements

The recipes for this book can be found at `https://github.com/PacktPublishing/Salesforce-Lightning-Web-Component-Cookbook`, where each chapter has its own folder under the `force-app` folder. This GitHub repository is structured in the form of a Salesforce DX project, which will allow you to easily fork the repository for deployment in a free Salesforce Developer Edition org. The code for *Chapter 15, Debugging Lightning Web Components*, is located within `https://github.com/PacktPublishing/Salesforce-Lightning-Web-Component-Cookbook/tree/main/force-app`.

The components in this book require the use of an **Integrated Development Environment (IDE)**, such as **Visual Studio Code (VSCode)** or **Salesforce Code Builder**. Detailed instructions for setting up an IDE are located in *Chapter 1, Getting Ready for Lightning Web Component Development*, in the *Setting up your IDE* section.

If you are building the projects in this cookbook as written, you will need to seed your Salesforce Developer Edition org with test data. Detailed instructions for seeding your org are located in *Chapter 1, Getting Ready for Lightning Web Component Development*, in the *Setting up the Salesforce Lightning Web Components Cookbook org* section.

Lastly, the edition of Salesforce required to implement the recipes in this book must be Developer, Performance, Unlimited, Enterprise, or Database.com. You can sign up for a free Salesforce Developer Edition org at `https://developer.salesforce.com/signup`.

Working with common debugging tools

When it comes to debugging Lightning Web Components, there are two main sets of tools that are used: Salesforce's provided **Debug Mode** and **Debug Logs**, and **Chrome Developer Tools (DevTools)**. While there are similar toolsets in other browsers, Chrome's DevTools are recommended for debugging LWCs, as **Google Chrome** is the preferred browser for Salesforce applications. In this recipe, we will learn how to navigate the internal and external tools recommended for LWC debugging.

How to do it...

Let's start by looking at the Salesforce native debugging tools.

1. First, let's look at Salesforce's **Debug Mode**, which is accessible via **Setup** > **Debug Mode**, and which brings up a menu that will allow us to assign **Debug Mode** to individual users:

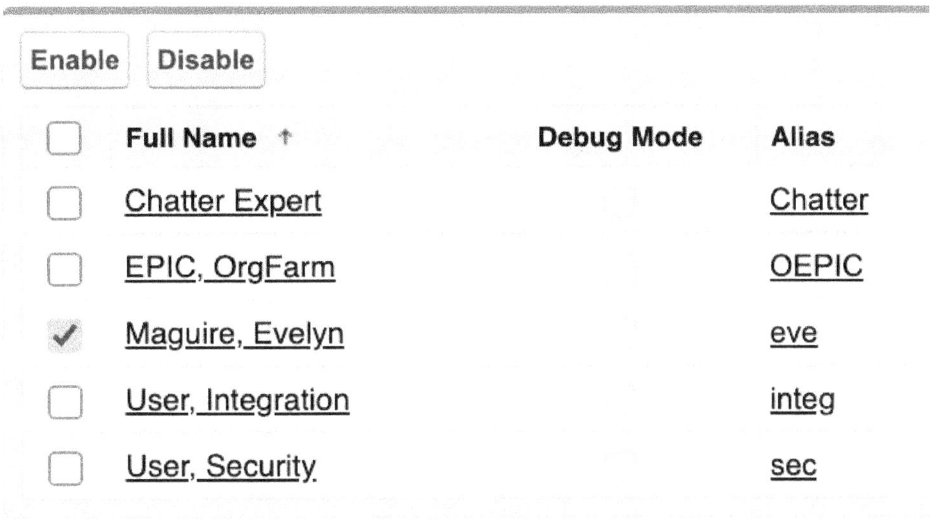

Figure 15.1: A screenshot of the Debug Mode menu, where individual users can have Debug Mode enabled or disabled

2. Once **Debug Mode** is enabled for the user, a banner will appear once weekly at the top of their Salesforce org view to notify them of the change:

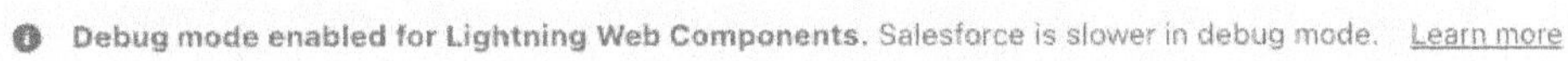

Figure 15.2: A screenshot of the Debug Mode banner that appears when Debug Mode is enabled for the running user

The benefit of using **Debug Mode** is that JavaScript output in the DevTools console isn't minified and compacted, which makes it easier to debug. Additionally, some component errors are surfaced in more detail. The disbenefit is that **Debug Mode** significantly slows down the operation of the Salesforce org for the specified user, so it is only recommended to be used while actively debugging.

3. In terms of offerings by Salesforce, there is also the option of turning on **Debug Logs** for a given user, which will log their interactions with the Salesforce org. This is where you can see messages such as **System.debug()** outputs, as well as Apex errors in jobs. To turn on **Debug Logs**, access the **Debug Logs** menu by going to **Setup** > **Debug Logs**.

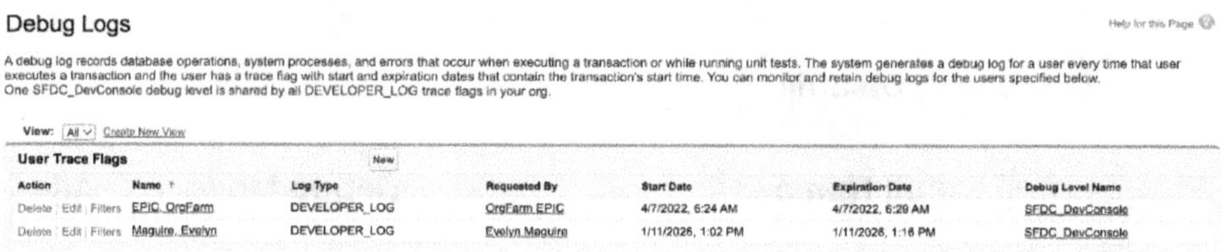

Figure 15.3: A screenshot of the Debug Logs menu, showing the debug logs that have been implemented within the Developer Edition org

4. To determine how fine the logs should be, and for what period of time they should run, we can set a **trace flag** for our desired user. The **Trace Flag** settings that follow will collect logs for our user, Evelyn, for a period of 30 minutes at the level of **SFDC_DevConsole**:

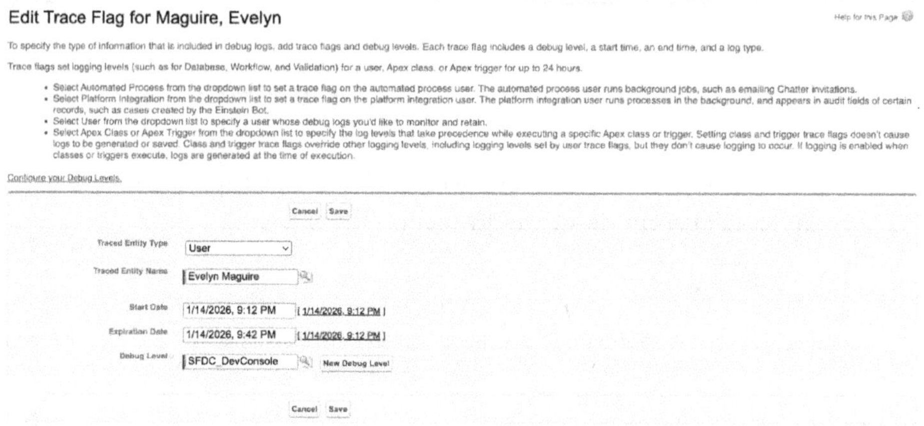

Figure 15.4: A screenshot of the Trace Flag editor for user Evelyn Maguire

These log levels can be adjusted to be as verbose as needed to debug and diagnose issues within the Salesforce org.

There's more

- Outside of Salesforce, there are browser tools that allow us to inspect our applications, such as **Chrome Developer Tools** (**DevTools**).
- To activate DevTools in Google Chrome, press *Control* + *Shift* + *I* on Windows, or *Command* + *Shift* + *I* on Mac. Alternatively, you can *right-click* on your application and select **Inspect** from the menu. This will bring up the DevTools sidebar:

Figure 15.5: A screenshot of the Top Accounts page with Debug Mode enabled and DevTools open on the right-hand side of the screen

- Once we have DevTools active, we can inspect various page elements using the **Elements** tab, read JavaScript logs in the **Console** tab, view the internal and written JavaScript in the **Sources** tab, find information about site connectivity in the **Network** tab, and more.

Figure 15.6: A screenshot of the DevTools panel under the Sources tab, with the picklistDatatable.js file selected

We will be investigating how we can effectively use these tools in subsequent recipes.

See also

- To see the Salesforce Developer Docs guide to LWC debugging, visit `https://developer.salesforce.com/docs/platform/lwc/guide/debug-intro.html`.
- To view instructions on turning on Salesforce's **Debug Mode**, see `https://developer.salesforce.com/docs/platform/lwc/guide/debug-mode-enable.html`.
- For more information on debug logs, visit `https://help.salesforce.com/s/articleView?id=platform.code_debug_log.htm&type=5`.
- To see the various debug log levels, see `https://help.salesforce.com/s/articleView?id=code_setting_debug_log_levels.htm&language=en_US&type=5`.
- The Google Chrome Developer Tools (DevTools) documentation is available at `https://developer.chrome.com/docs/devtools`.
- A Trailhead module on LWC debugging and troubleshooting is available at `https://trailhead.salesforce.com/content/learn/modules/lwc-troubleshooting`.
- A Salesforce Developers blog on how to debug Lightning Web Components is located at `https://developer.salesforce.com/blogs/2019/02/debug-your-lightning-web-components`.
- The Salesforce Developers Docs guide to debugging with DevTools is available at `https://developer.salesforce.com/docs/platform/lwc/guide/debug-dev-tools.html`.

Knowing the limitations of debugging tools

Because of the architecture of **Lightning Web Security (LWS)**, you may encounter issues while debugging. This is because **LWS** uses JavaScript proxies to enforce various security restraints on the code that runs within Salesforce, which can lead to discrepancies between a developer's code and what the browser displays. This is why the code in the **Sources** tab of **DevTools** looks different than the code in the JavaScript files for our components.

Getting started

To troubleshoot issues related to LWS, **Google Chrome** is once again the recommended browser. It is a known issue that some versions of **Mozilla Firefox** do not show breakpoints appropriately, and although Salesforce states it is working with the vendor to alleviate this, there is no estimated fix date at this time.

We will be looking at the code for *Chapter 7, Building Secure Components with Lightning Locker and Lightning Web Security*, in order to learn how to mitigate some of these issues. If you are joining us in the current chapter, you may need to deploy the forked repository code for the `force-app/chapter07` folder to your Salesforce Developer Edition org and complete the instructions for seeding your org, which are located in *Chapter 1, Getting Ready for Lightning Web Component Development*, in the *Setting up the Salesforce Lightning Web Components Cookbook org* section.

Once your *Chapter 7, Building Secure Components with Lightning Locker and Lightning Web Security*, code is deployed, assign the **Asset** sObject's **Chapter 7 Layout** to your profile so that you can see the **Change Request quick action** on the **Asset** record page:

Figure 15.7: A screenshot of the header for the Easy Chair Asset record, with the Change Request quick action highlighted

Finally, ensure that LWS is enabled in your org, and assign the deployed **permission set**, **Custom Permission: LWS Enabler**, to yourself. This will flip a **feature flag** in our quick action LWC, `changeRequestLauncher`, that forces it to display an LWS-ready component, `changeRequestModalLws`, rather than the **Lightning Locker** backwards-compatible `changeRequestModal`.

Once you have completed this setup, we are ready to explore the **distortions** enacted by LWS to enable or disable them individually for debugging. These distortions are put in place by LWS to alter the JavaScript in LWCs to prevent unsafe behavior by the end user and developer.

How to do it...

To start, navigate to an **Asset** record page and open **DevTools**.

1. Type the following command into your DevTools console. You may receive a warning not to paste code into DevTools – this is expected.

```
$LWS.namespaces.c.distortions
```

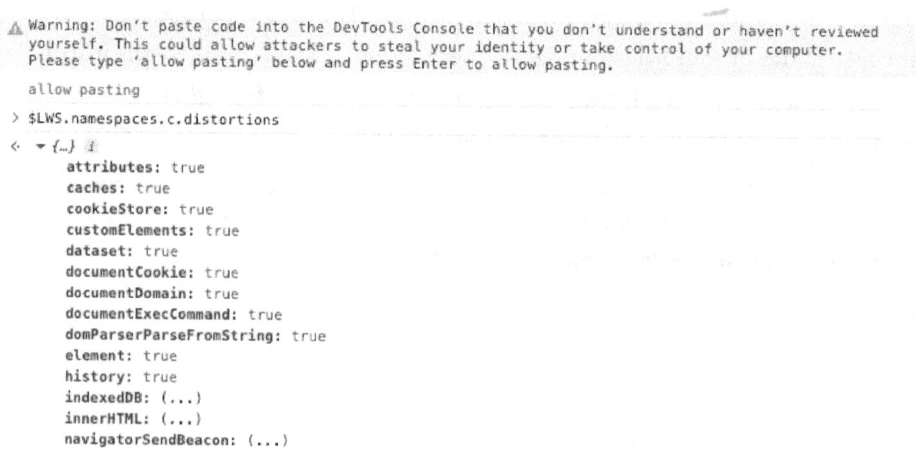

Figure 15.8: A screenshot of the DevTools console after running the command

2. You should see a list of distortions that are available. In order to disable a distortion, such as `innerHTML`, use the following command:

```
$LWS.namespaces.c.distortions.innerHTML = false
```

3. Here, `c` represents the namespace, and `innerHTML` represents the distortion. These distortions are set to `true` by default, and can be toggled off for debugging.
4. You may be wondering, how will turning off certain distortions help with debugging? Because LWS uses these distortions to isolate certain functionality from the user while namespacing certain global variables, we can tell if an individual security constraint placed by LWS is breaking our JavaScript. We can also test this using the **LWS Console**, linked in the *See also* section of this recipe:

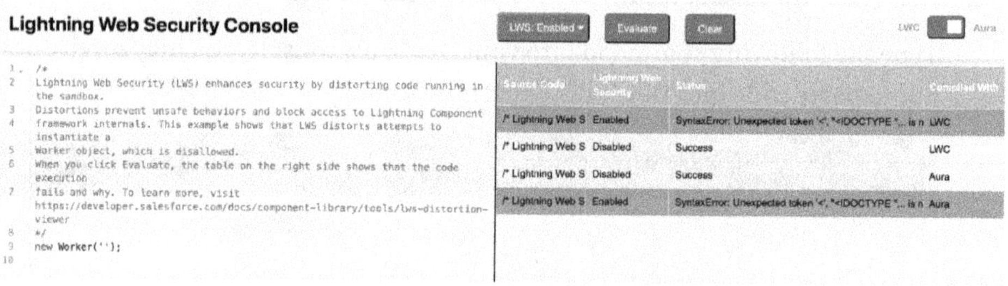

Figure 15.9: A screenshot of the Lightning Web Security Console

5. The example given in the LWS Console illustrates that instantiating `new Worker('')` will fail with LWS enabled for both Lightning Web Components and Aura components,

but will succeed when Lightning Locker is enabled. This is useful information, as a `Worker`, which will run the script contained at a specified URL, is distorted in LWS so that we are not unintentionally running malicious scripts.

See also

- The sample code for this section and *Chapter 7, Building Secure Components with Lightning Locker and Lightning Web Security*, is available at `https://github.com/PacktPublishing/Salesforce-Lightning-Web-Component-Cookbook/tree/main/force-app/chapter07`.
- For information on enabling Lightning Web Security, see `https://developer.salesforce.com/docs/platform/lightning-components-security/guide/lws-enable.html`.
- The Salesforce Developer Documents page on how LWS works can be viewed here: `https://developer.salesforce.com/docs/platform/lightning-components-security/guide/lws-architecture.html`.
- To understand the limits of debugging with LWS enabled, visit `https://developer.salesforce.com/docs/platform/lightning-components-security/guide/lws-debug-limitations.html`.
- For comprehensive guidance on troubleshooting components with LWS, see `https://developer.salesforce.com/docs/platform/lightning-components-security/guide/lws-troubleshoot.html`.
- For more information on debugging with LWS, visit `https://developer.salesforce.com/docs/platform/lwc/guide/debug-lwsec.html`.
- The Lightning Web Security Distortions guide is available at `https://developer.salesforce.com/docs/platform/lightning-components-security/guide/lws-debug-distortion-flags.html`.
- The LWS Distortions Viewer is available here: `https://developer.salesforce.com/docs/component-library/tools/lws-distortion-viewer`.
- The LWS Console is available at `https://developer.salesforce.com/tools/lws-console`

Preventing common errors in Apex

There are a number of issues that you may see in Apex, and although they will not be the bulk of the content in this chapter, we will spend this recipe learning how to mitigate them. I have baked a few not-best-practice elements into the setup code for this cookbook so we can practice refactoring.

Getting started

We will be looking at the code that is used to seed the data for a Salesforce Developer Edition org for this cookbook in order to see how some of these errors can be written, as well as how to mitigate them. If you are joining us in the current chapter, you may need to deploy the forked repository code for the `force-app/chapter00` folder to your Salesforce Developer Edition org and complete the instructions for seeding your org, which are located in *Chapter 1, Getting Ready for Lightning Web Component Development*, in the *Setting up the Salesforce Lightning Web Components Cookbook org* section.

How to do it...

The most common errors that will be faced when writing Apex for Lightning Web Components can be divided into three general categories:

- **Known knowns**, which consist of data requirements such as validation rules, and can be checked for before failure to be handled gracefully
- **Known unknowns**, which consist of operations that we know may fail, but we don't necessarily know why until runtime, such as DML or SOQL operations
- **Unknown unknowns**, which consist of bugs that we can't necessarily predict and can't catch, such as **Limit exceptions**

In the `OrgSetupClass` Apex file, located in `force-app/chapter00/default/classes/OrgSetupClass`, we have an example of a bad piece of code and an okay piece of code. Let's explore why.

1. Open the `OrgSetupClass` file, and take a moment to look over it, including the comments I have left for each method.
2. Next, open the `OrgSetupREST` Apex file, located in `force-app/chapter00/default/classes/OrgSetupREST`, to confirm that we are making an HTTP callout when we call the `getAssets` method of the `OrgSetupREST` class.

3. Return to the `OrgSetupClass` file and let's dive in. We are first going to examine the bad code, which consists of the `getPerms` method:

```
public static void getPerms() {
    Id permSetId = [SELECT Id FROM PermissionSet WHERE Name=
'Named_Credential_Access'].Id;
    Id userId = UserInfo.getUserId();
    List<PermissionSetAssignment> assignedPerms = [SELECT Id FROM
PermissionSetAssignment WHERE AssigneeId = :userId AND PermissionSet.Name =
'Named_Credential_Access'];
    if(assignedPerms.size() == 0) {
        PermissionSetAssignment psa = new PermissionSetAssignment(
            AssigneeId = userId,
            PermissionSetId = permSetId
        );
        insert psa;
    }
}
```

4. Note the first highlighted line, which assigns a value to an `Id` based on the result of a SOQL query. Although this is an efficient way to write this line of code, if the `Named_Credential_Access` permission set does not exist, this line will fail spectacularly! This falls into the **known unknowns** category. We will get a **null pointer exception** if we don't have the proper data in our org. Not only that, but because we do not have a `LIMIT` clause in our SOQL query, we might end up with too many permission set records, or not enough, ending with a **SOQL exception**. A better way to write this would be as follows:

```
List<PermissionSet> permSets = [SELECT Id FROM PermissionSet WHERE Name =
'Named_Credential_Access' LIMIT 1];
```

5. Here, we can then access the `Id` of `permSet` after checking the length of our list:

```
if(permSets.size() > 0) {
    Id permSetId = permSets[0].Id;
}
```

6. If `permSetId == null`, we can throw a custom exception, letting our end user know that they need to deploy the permission set to their org and cease operation of our Apex.

Note

Although it may seem to make sense to use a **safe navigation operator** here, such that `Id permSetId = permSets[0]?.Id`, this will not work! If we attempt to access the 0th element of a list that has no elements, we will receive a **List Index Out of Bounds** exception. Therefore, if we want to be safe, we should ensure that our list has members.

7. In the second highlighted line, we have an ever-so-slightly safer query, which assigns the results of our query to a `List<PermissionSetAssignment>`. We then check to see if our **Permission Set Assignment** record exists so that we don't attempt to assign the permission set twice. Again, this falls into the **known unknowns** category.
8. Finally, in the third highlighted line, we have an unprotected DML statement. To make this safer, we can surround it with a `try-catch` block, which will allow us to check for any **known knowns**, or validation errors.
9. Next, let's look at the `dataSetup` method of the `OrgSetupClass` class. This code is better, but still not great:

```
public static void dataSetup() {
    List<Account> setupAccounts = [SELECT Id FROM Account WHERE Name =
'Ultricies PC'];
    if(setupAccounts.size() < 1) {
        CsvReader.getAccounts();
        CsvReader.getCustomers();
    }
    try {
        Id acctId = [SELECT Id FROM Account WHERE Name = 'Ultricies PC' LIMIT
1].Id;
        if(artToImportById.size() < 100) {
            for(Integer intId : artToImportById) {
                OrgSetupREST.getAssets(intId, acctId);
            }
        }
    } catch(Exception e) {
        throw new SetupException(e.getMessage());
    }
}
```

10. In the first highlighted line, we check to see if the desired **Account** record exists and assign it to a `List<Account>` if it does. This is good! We are accounting for **known knowns** and **known unknowns** by doing this `List` assignation.
11. In the second highlighted chunk, we run a set of **DataWeave scripts** that insert the test **Account** records if our sample test account doesn't exist, thereby seeding our org with data. We check to make sure that we only insert these records once to prevent ourselves from hitting **duplicate rules**, a **known known**. We can make this code better by inserting a `try-catch` block, like so:

```
if(setupAccounts.size() < 1) {
    try{
        CsvReader.getAccounts();
        CsvReader.getCustomers();
    } catch (exception e) {
        //error handling here...
    }
}
```

12. This will help us to catch any **unknown unknown** errors, such as if the source code for the DataWeave scripts changes on us.
13. Finally, in the third highlighted chunk, note that we call an **HTTP callout** method within a `for` loop. This is admittedly not a best practice, as we will hit limits if we have more than `100` **Asset** Ids that we are attempting to query from **The Metropolitan Museum of Art's Open Access API**. The reason this is written this way is because, as of the writing of this book, the **Open Access API** only supports a single artwork being queried at a time. As a result, we add a check to ensure that `artToImportById.size() < 100`, which will ensure that we don't hit an **API limit exception**, an **unknown unknown**, which can't be caught and can only be prevented. Again, to make this safer, we could put it in a `try-catch` block to catch any **unknown unknown** errors, such as if the API goes down or changes its availability.

See also

- The sample code for this section and seeding the Salesforce Developer org with data is available at `https://github.com/PacktPublishing/Salesforce-Lightning-Web-Component-Cookbook/tree/main/force-app/chapter00`.
- The Salesforce Developer Docs guide to Apex error handling is available at `https://developer.salesforce.com/docs/platform/lwc/guide/apex-error-handling.html`.

- The Salesforce Developer Docs guide to Apex exceptions can be viewed at `https://developer.salesforce.com/docs/atlas.en-us.apexcode.meta/apexcode/apex_exception_definition.htm`.
- The Salesforce Developer Docs guide to Apex debugging is available at `https://developer.salesforce.com/docs/atlas.en-us.apexcode.meta/apexcode/apex_debugging.htm`.
- For documentation on the safe navigation operator, see `https://developer.salesforce.com/docs/atlas.en-us.apexcode.meta/apexcode/langCon_apex_SafeNavigationOperator.htm`.
- For further reading on how to debug with Apex Replay Debugger, which is beyond the scope of this cookbook, you can visit `https://trailhead.salesforce.com/content/learn/projects/find-and-fix-bugs-with-apex-replay-debugger`.

Handling common errors in LWCs

Now that we know a bit about the kinds of errors that can appear in Apex and how to prevent them, it's time to explore errors in LWCs. Like Apex, we can use `try-catch` blocks in JavaScript to prevent some errors, but what other errors should we be on the lookout for?

Getting started

We will be looking at the code for *Chapter 3, Working with a Selector Class, Chapter 4, Synchronous and Asynchronous Processing in Components*, and *Chapter 6, Composing Lightning Web Components*, in this recipe. If you are joining us in the current chapter, you may need to deploy the forked repository code for the `force-app/chapter03`, `force-app/chapter04`, and `force-app/chapter06` folders to your Salesforce Developer Edition org, and complete the instructions for seeding your org, which are located in *Chapter 1, Getting Ready for Lightning Web Component Development*, in the *Setting up the Salesforce Lightning Web Components Cookbook org* section.

Once your code is deployed, assign the **View Top Accounts App Permission Set** to yourself to gain access to the **Top Accounts custom application**.

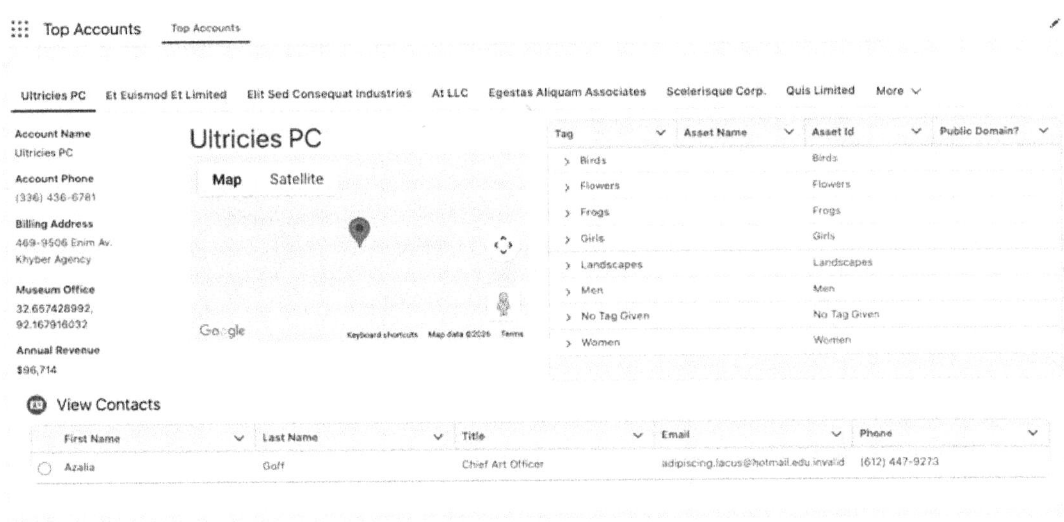

Figure 15.10: A screenshot of the Top Accounts custom application with the components from Chapter 3, Chapter 4, and Chapter 6

We will be causing errors in these components to familiarize ourselves with a few of the types of errors that are likely to be seen in LWCs, especially as you are starting out.

How to do it...

Let's start by looking at the component for *Chapter 3, Working with a Selector Class*, `topTenAccountTabset`.

1. Start by opening the `topTenAccountTabset.js` file, and refresh yourself on its content.
2. Pick a variable (any variable!) in the `@wire` decorated function, `wiredAccounts`, and remove the `this.` prefix from it. For example, I will be removing `this.` from `this._wiredAccounts` to start. Say we use this example:

```
this._wiredAccounts = result;
```

3. This becomes the following:

```
_wiredAccounts = result;
```

4. Deploy your change and refresh your **Top Accounts** application.

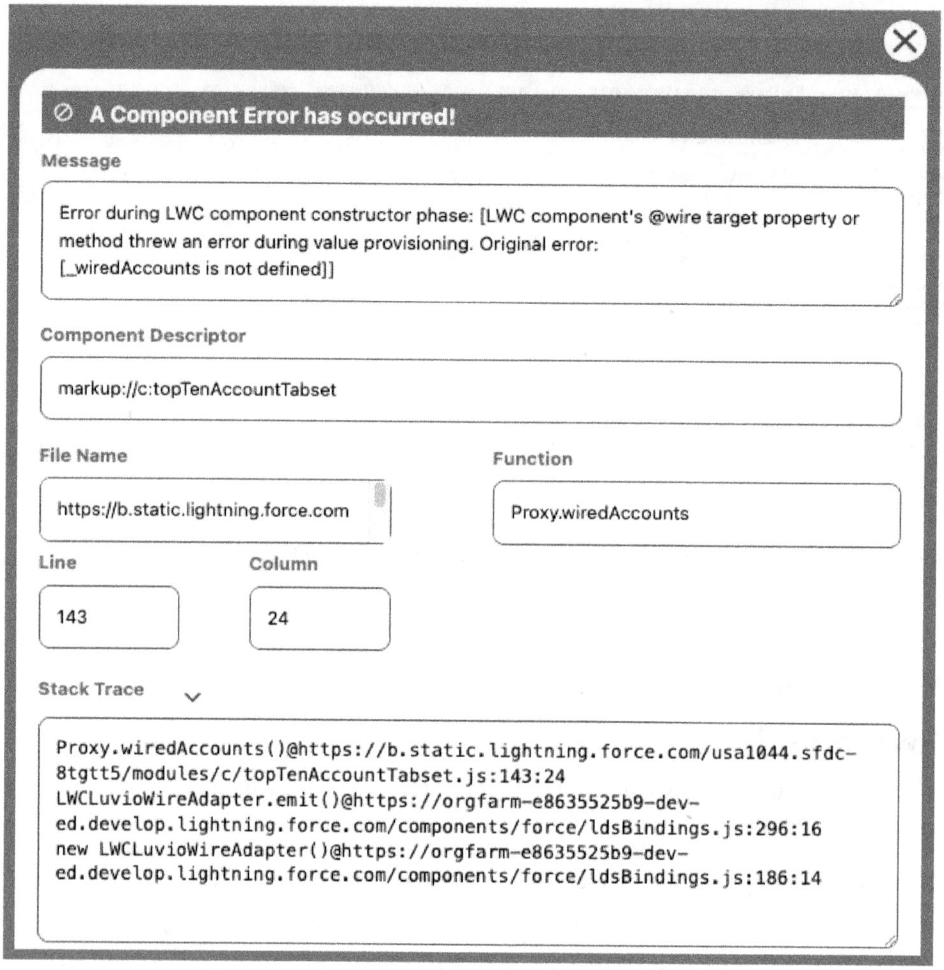

Figure 15.11: A Component Error has occurred! We receive an error popup letting us know that we have an error where _wiredAccounts is not defined

5. Looking under the **Sources** tab in DevTools, with the approximate location of `top` > `[orgname]` > `components` > `c` > `topTenAccountTabset.js`, we can see that the error occurs around line 143, which is the line directly following our change when we account for the **distortions** applied by LWS.

```
133 class TopTenAccountTabset extends lwc.LightningElement {
134   constructor(...args) {
135     super(...args);
136     this.accounts = void 0;
137     this._wiredAccounts = void 0;
138     this.error = void 0;
139   }
140   wiredAccounts(result) {
141     _wiredAccounts = result;
142     if (result.data) {
143       this.accounts = JSON.parse(result.data);
```

Figure 15.12: A screenshot of the topTenAccountTabset.js file after distortions are applied, found under the Sources tab in DevTools

6. This error occurs because of **variable scoping**. We have not defined a `_wiredAccounts` variable within the **scope** of our wired function, so we must use the `this.` prefix to access the class variable.
7. If we revert this change and remove the prefix from our accounts variable, we will receive a similar error:

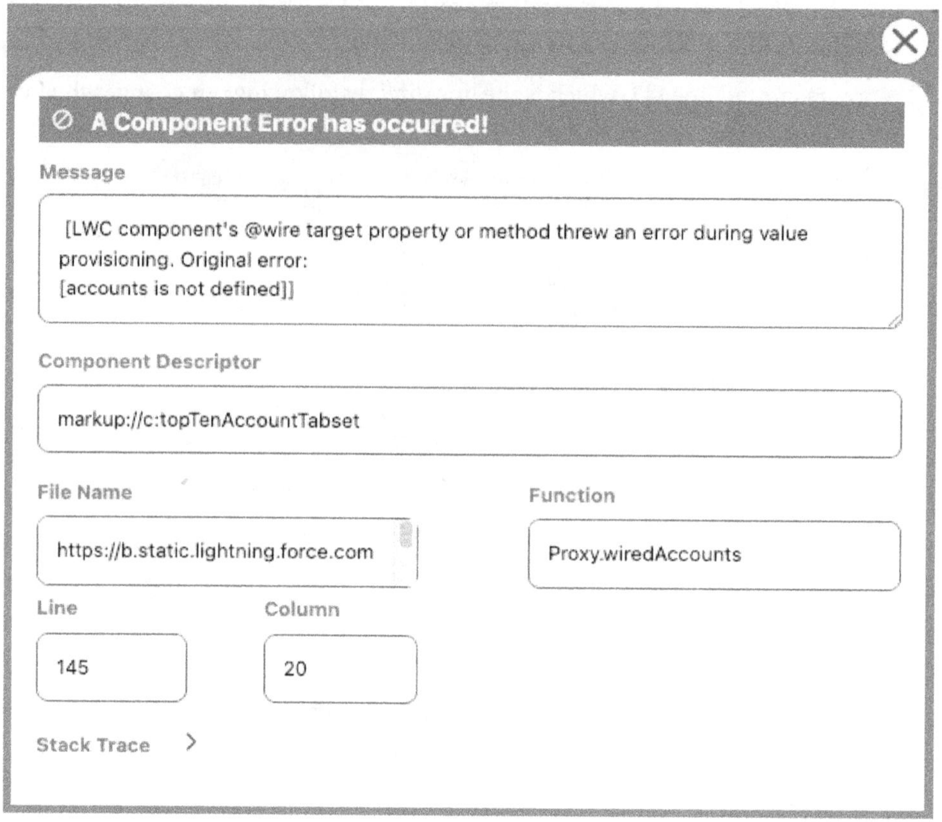

Figure 15.13: A Component Error has occurred! We receive an error popup letting us know that we have an error where accounts is not defined

8. These errors occur because JavaScript variables within a code block must be defined within the scope of that block, either with `let`, which defines a block-scoped mutable variable, `const`, which defines a block-scoped immutable variable, or the legacy `var`, which defines a global-scoped mutable variable. `var` is no longer preferred due to a phenomenon called **variable hoisting**, which means that a `var`-defined variable can be used outside of the block it is defined in. It is important to note that block-scoped variables and global-scoped variables can share names, which can be confusing, but it is allowed! It is therefore especially important to ensure that the `this` keyword is applied appropriately in our JavaScript files.

Note

It is important to note that public class fields, such as `accounts`, `_wiredAccounts`, and `error`, do not need a designation of `const`, `let`, or `var` because they are properties defined for each instance of the class. We use the `this` keyword to access the class fields within a function. More reading on this subject can be done in the MDN Developer Docs at `https://developer.mozilla.org/en-US/docs/Web/JavaScript/Reference/Classes/Public_class_fields`.

9. Revert and deploy your changes, and let's look at the files for *Chapter 4*, *Synchronous and Asynchronous Processing in Components*, namely, `assetsByTag.js`.
10. Within the `getTagsWithAssets` function, let's mimic a common typo. Say you are typing quickly, and your *Shift* key sticks. Instead of typing `tagsWithAssets`, you type `tagsWithASsets` when calling the `tagFlattener` function, like so:

```
const tagsWithAssets = await
returnTagsWithAssetsByAccount({ accountIdString : this.accountId });
this._tagsWithAssetsResult = this.tagFlattener(tagsWithASsets);
```

11. Deploy your change and refresh the **Top Accounts** application.

Figure 15.14: tagsWithASsets is not a defined error

12. Note that because we have our `notifUtils` toast notification utility, it's easy to see that we have a typo. Tools such as **code suggestions** also help with diagnosing typos like this faster than it was possible to do so previously. As IDEs add more tools, missing semicolons in Apex and case-sensitive typos in JavaScript may become a thing of the past, but they have led to enough collective frustration that they are worth calling out here.

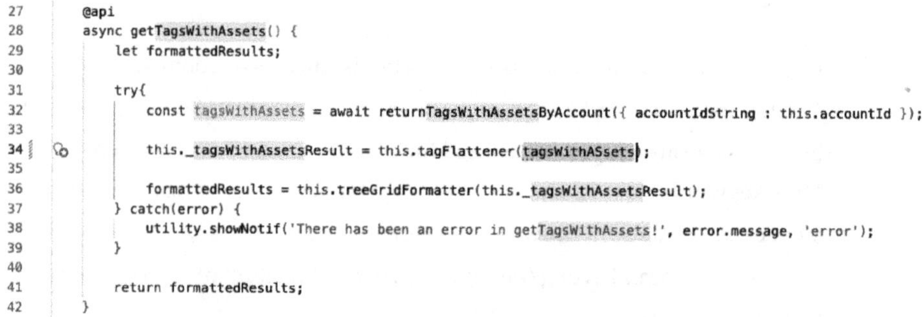

Figure 15.15: A code suggestion calls out that there is a typo in line 34 of our assetsByTag.js file

13. Revert your changes, deploy the original file, and then turn to the `tagFlattener` function in the same file.
14. In the first line of our function definition, make the following change:

```
let flattenedData = [];
```

15. This becomes the following:

```
let flattenedData;
```

16. Save and deploy your changes and refresh the **Top Accounts** application.

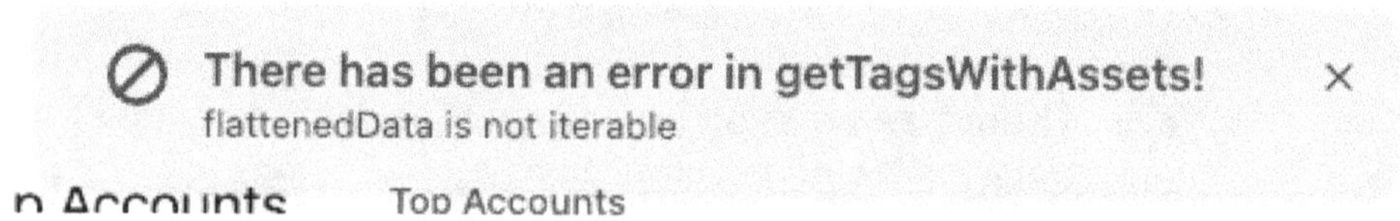

Figure 15.16: An error showing that flattenedData is not iterable

17. This error occurs because we have not defined `flattenedData` as an array before we use a **spread operator** on it in the following line of code:

```
flattenedData = [...flattenedData, ...flattenedAssets];
```

18. This is because, although we have instantiated `flattenedData`, we have not defined it on our first `for` loop pass. We can mitigate this error by defining `flattenedData` as an

array in that first line, as we did initially, or by using the **or** double pipe (||) operator to check the value in the erroring line of code:

```
flattenedData = [...(flattenedData || []), ...flattenedAssets];
```

19. This change effectively checks if `flattenedData` is **falsy** and substitutes an empty array if so.
20. Revert your changes and deploy the original file.
21. Although this is not a comprehensive list of errors, variable scoping issues and improperly defined variables are responsible for a large number of the errors we will see while writing Lightning Web Components. In the final recipe in this cookbook, we will explore how to handle the other most common type of error: the **null pointer exception**.

See also

- To see how to work with errors in JavaScript, visit `https://developer.salesforce.com/docs/platform/lwc/guide/data-error-types.html`.
- For working with errors in Lightning Data Service, visit `https://developer.salesforce.com/docs/platform/lwc/guide/data-error.html`.
- The Salesforce Developers documentation on common HTML errors is available at `https://developer.salesforce.com/docs/platform/lwc/guide/reference-template-errors.html`.
- For detailed instructions on utilizing **Debug Mode**, see `https://developer.salesforce.com/docs/platform/lwc/guide/debug-debug-mode.html`.
- A Trailhead module on LWC troubleshooting can be found here: `https://trailhead.salesforce.com/content/learn/modules/lwc-troubleshooting`.

Dealing with null pointer exceptions

If you ever get a nasty, unspecified error in Salesforce, chances are it's a **null pointer exception**. These unspecified errors can be tricky to diagnose, as the error messages can leave a lot to be desired. This is where our debugging tools come in handy.

Getting started

We will be looking at the code for *Chapter 5, Accessing External Data Sources via Lightning Web Component*, in this recipe. If you are joining us in the current chapter, you may need to deploy the forked repository code for the `force-app/chapter05` folder to your Salesforce Developer Edition org, and complete the instructions for seeding your org, which are located in *Chapter 1, Getting Ready for Lightning Web Component Development*, in the *Setting up the Salesforce Lightning Web Components Cookbook org* section.

Once your *Chapter 5, Accessing External Data Sources via Lightning Web Component*, code is deployed, assign the **Account** sObject's **Chapter 5 Layout** to your profile so that you can see the **Add Asset** quick action on the **Account** record page:

Figure 15.17: A screenshot of the header for the Ultricies PC Account record, with the Add Assets quick action highlighted

We are ready to begin.

How to do it...

We are going to start by looking at the business logic Apex class for *Chapter 5, Accessing External Data Sources via Lightning Web Component*, `AddAssetService`.

1. Refresh yourself on the contents of the file and validate that we have a `nullCheck` method towards the bottom of the file that accepts a `String` value.
2. This `nullCheck` method is used throughout the file, namely to check the values passed in for the imported asset's optional constituents (artists) and tags:

```
if(assetWrapper.constituents != null) {
    constituentToUpsert.Name = nullCheck(assetWrapper.constituents[0].name);
    constituentToUpsert.Constituent_Id__c = nullCheck(assetWrapper.constituents[0].constituentID);
    constituentToUpsert.Gender__c = nullCheck(assetWrapper.constituents[0].gender);
    constituentToUpsert.Role__c = nullCheck(assetWrapper.constituents[0].role);
    constituentToUpsert.ULAN_URL__c = nullCheck(assetWrapper.constituents[0].constituentULAN_URL);
    constituentToUpsert.Wikidata_URL__c = nullCheck(assetWrapper.constituents[0].constituentWikidata_URL);

    constituentsToUpsert.add(constituentToUpsert);
}

if(assetWrapper.tags != null) {
    tagToUpsert.Name = nullCheck(assetWrapper.tags[0].term);
    tagToUpsert.AAT__c = nullCheck(assetWrapper.tags[0].AAT_URL).removeStart(AAT_URL_STRING);
    tagToUpsert.AAT_URL__c = nullCheck(assetWrapper.tags[0].AAT_URL);
    tagToUpsert.Wikidata_URL__c = nullCheck(assetWrapper.tags[0].Wikidata_URL);

    tagsToUpsert.add(tagToUpsert);
} else {
    tagToUpsert.Name = 'No Tag Given';
    tagToUpsert.AAT__c = '99999';

    tagsToUpsert.add(tagToUpsert);
}
```

Figure 15.18: A screenshot of the AddAssetService.cls file showing the usage of the nullCheck method

3. Note that we check to make sure the `constituents` and `tags` properties of our `assetWrapper` class are not `null` and then perform a `nullCheck` on any values provided. This is because not all these values are provided by the **Open Access API**, and we don't want to encounter any unexpected errors when preparing our data for insertion.
4. Let's go ahead and remove the null checks from the `assetWrapper.constituents` block:

```
if(assetWrapper.constituents != null) {
    constituentToUpsert.Name = nullCheck(assetWrapper.constituents[0].name);
    constituentToUpsert.Constituent_Id__c =
nullCheck(assetWrapper.constituents[0].constituentID);
    constituentToUpsert.Gender__c =
nullCheck(assetWrapper.constituents[0].gender);
    constituentToUpsert.Role__c =
nullCheck(assetWrapper.constituents[0].role);
    constituentToUpsert.ULAN_URL__c =
nullCheck(assetWrapper.constituents[0].constituentULAN_URL);
    constituentToUpsert.Wikidata_URL__c =
nullCheck(assetWrapper.constituents[0].constituentWikidata_URL);
    constituentsToUpsert.add(constituentToUpsert);
}
```

5. That becomes the following:

```
    constituentToUpsert.Name = (assetWrapper.constituents[0].name);
    constituentToUpsert.Constituent_Id__c =
(assetWrapper.constituents[0].constituentID);
    constituentToUpsert.Gender__c = (assetWrapper.constituents[0].gender);
    constituentToUpsert.Role__c = (assetWrapper.constituents[0].role);
    constituentToUpsert.ULAN_URL__c =
(assetWrapper.constituents[0].constituentULAN_URL);
    constituentToUpsert.Wikidata_URL__c =
(assetWrapper.constituents[0].constituentWikidata_URL);
constituentsToUpsert.add(constituentToUpsert);
```

6. The reason we are focusing on the constituent upsertion here is that not all artists are known, and even if we have their name, we might not have their gender or other such information about them due to historical reasons. Because of this, we are more likely to encounter the error we are attempting to cause.
7. Deploy your changes and refresh the **Account** record page.

8. Just for fun, open the Developer Console in a new tab before we attempt to call the **Add Assets** flow. This will allow us to view logs locally without explicitly turning on **Debug Logs**. The Developer Console can be opened in a new tab with *Ctrl* + *Click* on Windows, *Cmd* + *Click* on Mac, or right-clicking and selecting **Open Link in New Tab**. Note that if we want to download these logs, we must turn on **Debug Logs** explicitly, but this will be fine for our purposes.

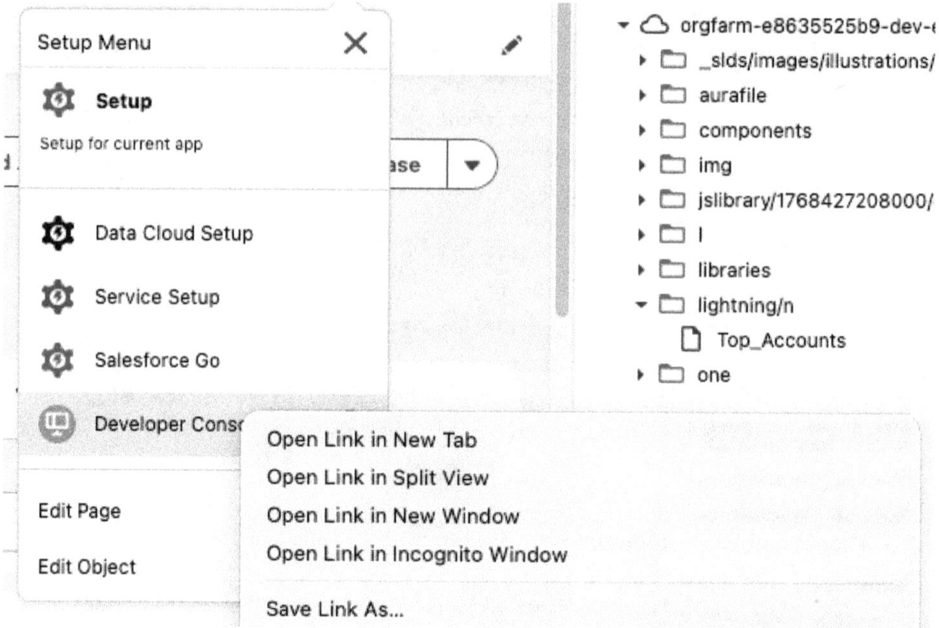

Figure 15.19: A screenshot showing that we have DevTools open, as well as the options for opening the Developer Console in a new tab

9. Enter the **Add Assets** flow and select **Medieval Art** (or your preferred department) from the drop-down menu.

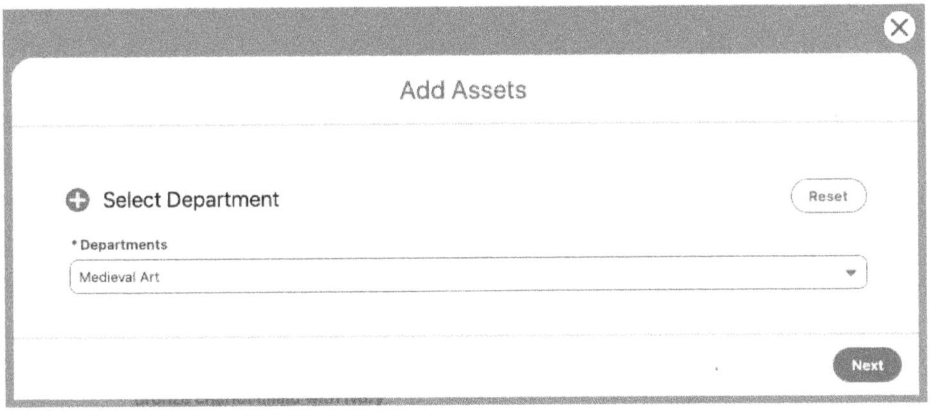

Figure 15.20: A screenshot of the Add Assets flow with the Medieval Art department selected in the addAssetDepartment component

10. Search for a relevant term. I have searched for the term "dragon" with good results. Note that the Metropolitan Museum of Art is constantly adding new works and rearranging collections, so your search results may vary. Select all artworks in the **lightning-dual-listbox**, and hit **Save**.

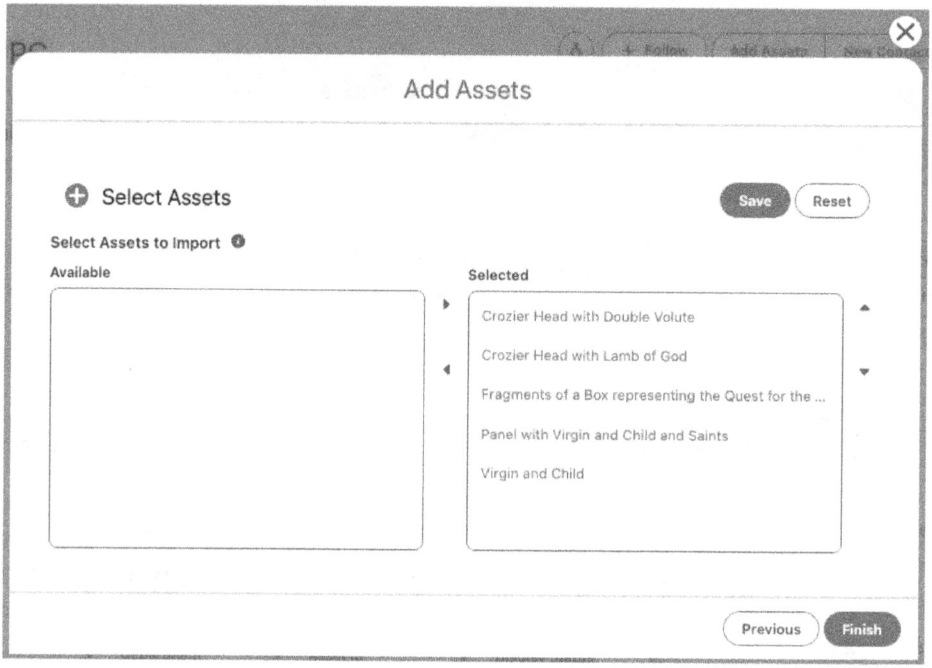

Figure 15.21: A screenshot of the Add Assets flow showing the results of the query for "dragon" under Medieval Art to be added to our Account record

11. When you hit **Save**, you should receive an error toast thanks to our `notifUtils` function:

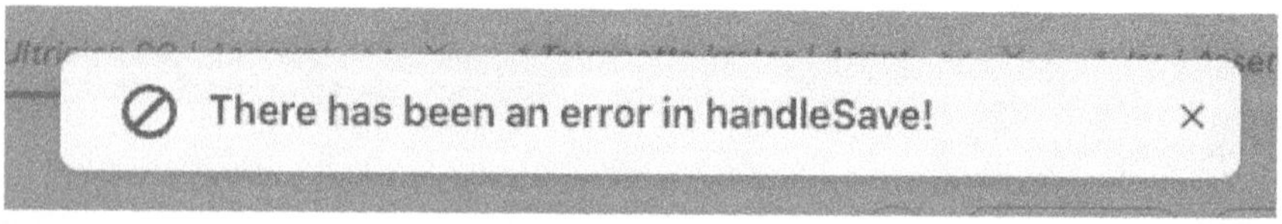

Figure 15.22: The error toast stating that there has been an error in handleSave with no given error message

12. Because we don't have an error message in our toast, let's see what this looks like in the Developer Console, where we have a **Script-thrown exception**:

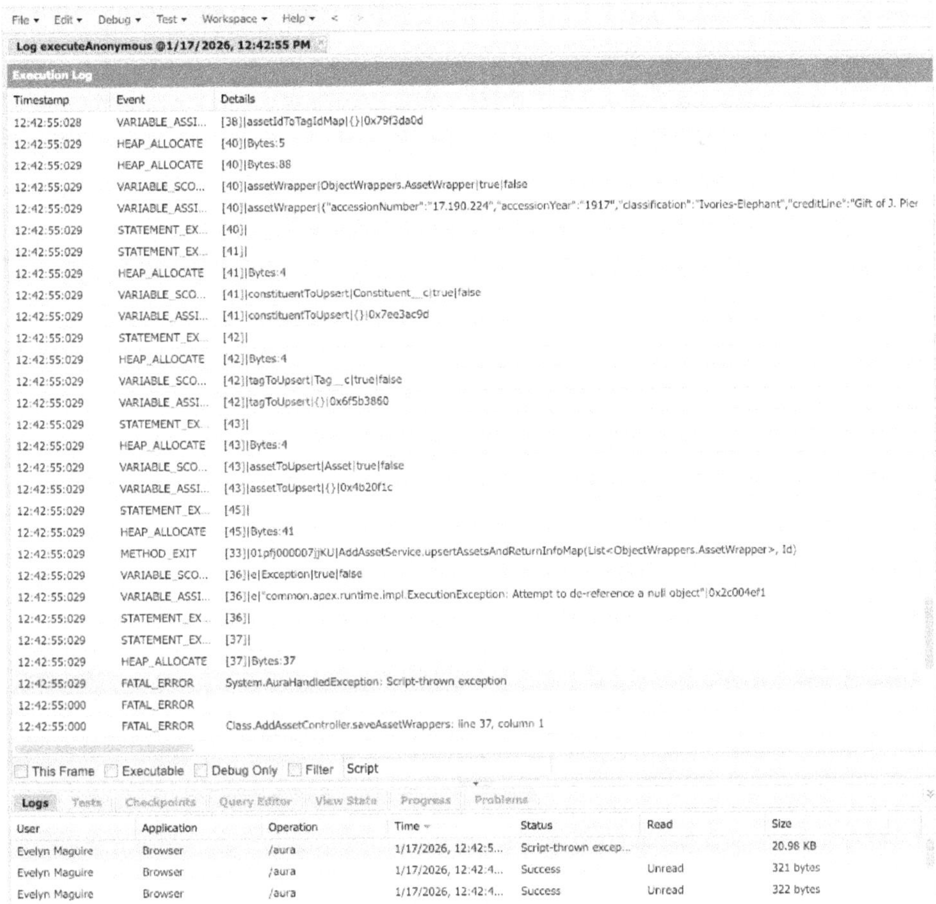

Figure 15.23: A screenshot of the Developer Console, which shows a Script-thrown exception in line 37 of AddAssetController.saveAssetWrappers

13. We notice that we have an **AuraHandledException** with a message of **Script-thrown exception**. This is because of the following lines of code in our `AddAssetController` class:

```
try{ ... } catch (Exception e) {
  throw new AuraHandledException(e.getMessage());
}
```

14. You'll notice that we catch our generic **Exception**, e, and then throw a new `AuraHandledException` with the message from our original exception. The reason for

this is so we can return our error message, **Script-thrown exception**, to our JavaScript controller so we can display it to our end user on the frontend.

15. By reading the log lines around **Script-thrown exception**, we can determine that we committed a boo-boo, resulting in an **attempt to de-reference a null object** error.
16. Let's try to break this a little more. Enter the `addAssetPicker.js` file, located at `force-app/chapter05/default/lwc/addAssetPicker/addAssetPicker.js`. We are going to remove the `try-catch` block in the `handleSave` function to try to produce a nasty error. Comment out the lines corresponding to the `try-catch` block, like so:

```
118     async handleSave() {
119         this.savePressed = true;
120         this.buttonsDisabled = true;
121 
122         let recordsToSave = this.searchResults.filter(asset => this.assetsToReturn.includes(asset.value));
123 
124         let jsonToParse = JSON.stringify(recordsToSave);
125 
126         // try {
127             const savedRecords = await saveAssetWrappers({ jsonToParse : jsonToParse, accountId : this.recordId});
128             let savedMessage = '';
129             let unsavedMessage = '';
130             let duplicateRecords = [];
131 
132             if(savedRecords == null) {
133                 duplicateRecords = recordsToSave;
134             } else {
135                 let propertyList = Object.getOwnPropertyNames(savedRecords);
136 
137                 for(let property of propertyList) {
138                     savedMessage += savedRecords[property] + ', item number ' + property + '.\n';
139                 }
140 
141                 duplicateRecords = recordsToSave.filter(record => !propertyList.includes(record.objectId));
142 
143                 utility.showNotif('You have successfully inserted the following record(s):', savedMessage, 'success');
144             }
145 
146             if(duplicateRecords.length > 0) {
147                 for(let record of duplicateRecords) {
148                     unsavedMessage += record.label + ', item number ' + record.value + '.\n';
149                 }
150 
151                 utility.showNotif('The following duplicate record(s) were not saved: ', unsavedMessage, 'info');
152             }
153         // } catch(error) {
154         //     utility.showNotif('There has been an error in handleSave!', error.message, 'error');
155         // }
156     }
```

Figure 15.24: A screenshot of the handleSave function in the addAssetPicker.js file with lines 126 and 153-155 commented out

17. Deploy these changes, refresh your **Account** record page and your **Developer Console** tab, and attempt to re-enter the **Add Assets** flow one more time using the same search criteria as before for consistency.
18. Notice that this now fails silently due to an **uncaught exception**. We can account for this by opening **DevTools**, entering the **Sources** tab, and adding a **breakpoint**: **Pause on uncaught exceptions**:

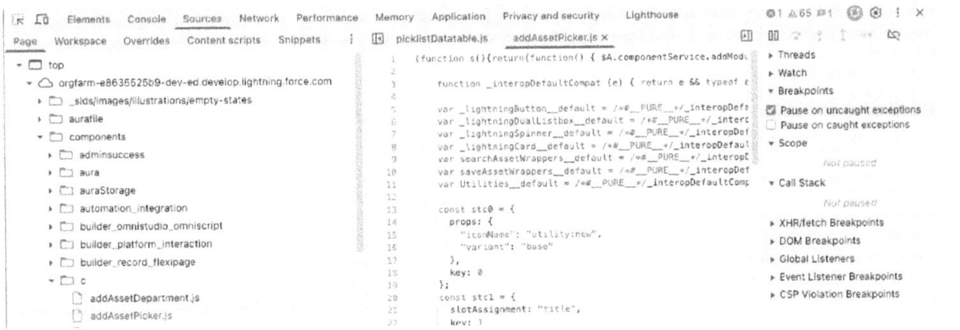

Figure 15.25: A screenshot of the DevTools Sources tab, with the option to add breakpoints highlighted

19. Refresh your **Account** record page and your **Developer Console** tab again and attempt to re-enter the **Add Assets** flow once again using the same search criteria as before for consistency. Note that we will now pause on the uncaught exception.

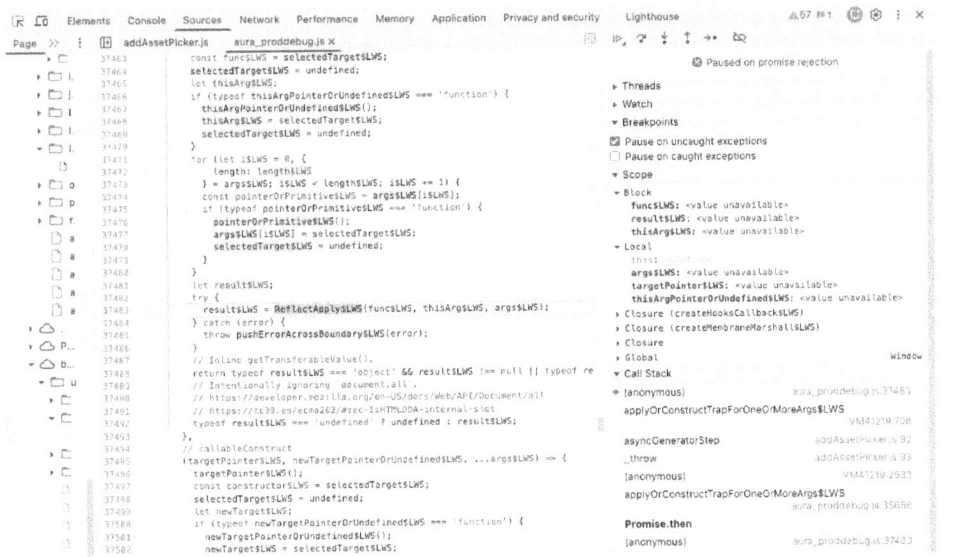

Figure 15.26: A screenshot of the DevTools Sources tab, which is paused on a promise rejection, with the options to step through the error highlighted

20. Step through the uncaught exception using the **Play/Pause** button, highlighted in the preceding screenshot, and open the **Console** tab in **DevTools**.

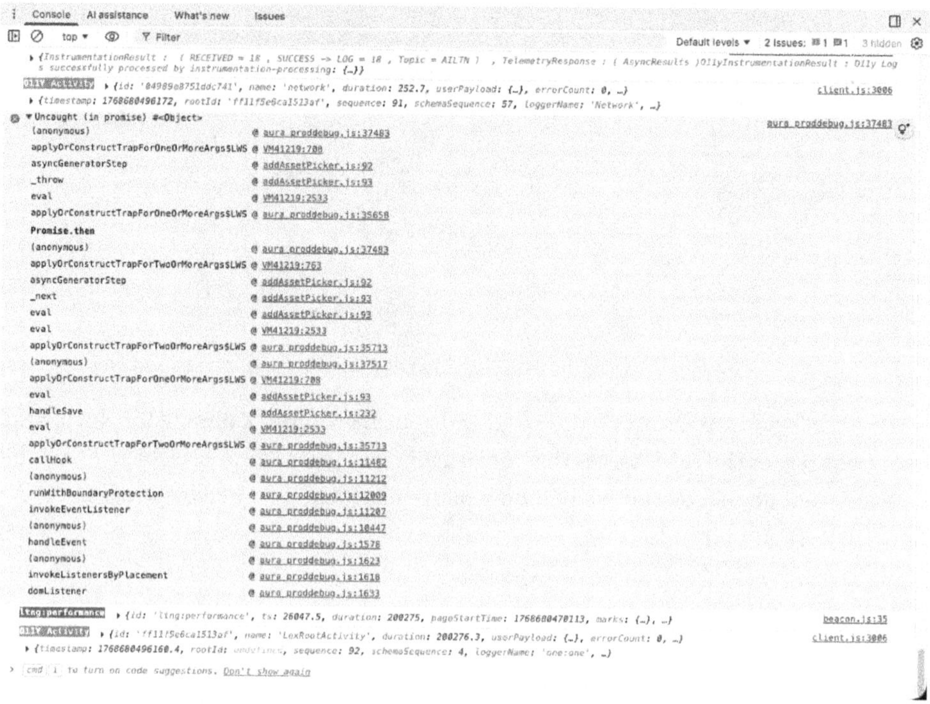

Figure 15.27: A screenshot of the DevTools Console tab, which gives us a few hints as to where our error could be, namely the distorted addAssetPicker.js lines 92, 93, and 232

21. Click on the link in the **Console** tab that states what line the error is on in `addAssetPicker.js`. Note that the line in your Console might be different than the line in mine. This will take you to the distorted `addAssetPicker.js` file in the **Sources** tab at the appropriate line. Because we have **Debug Mode** enabled, this file is formatted nicely for us, and we can begin to track down the error:

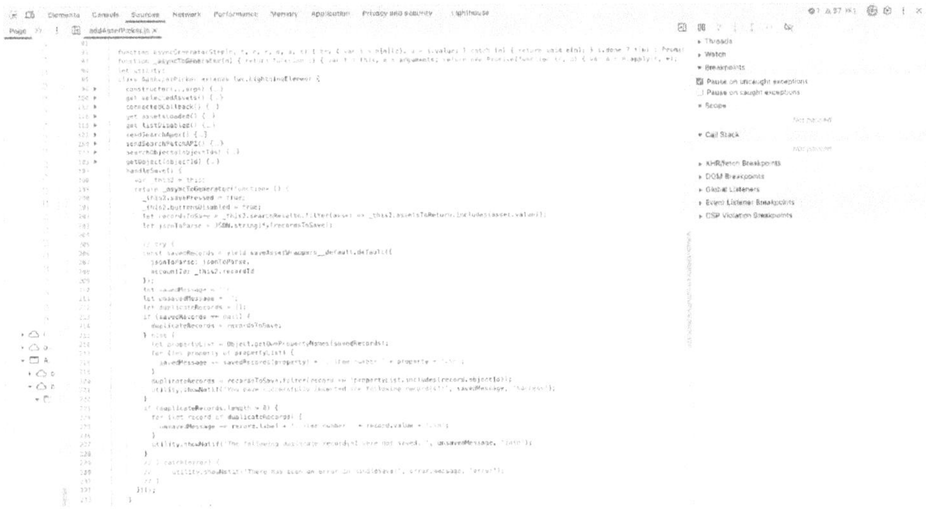

Figure 15.28: A screenshot of the DevTools Source tab, showing the beautified JavaScript file, addAssetPicker.js

22. Let's add some additional **breakpoints** to our JavaScript to try to debug this. In order to add a **manual breakpoint**, click slightly to the left of the number indicating the line of code:

Figure 15.29: A screenshot showing four manual breakpoints added to the addAssetPicker.js file

23. Refresh your **Account** record page and your **Developer Console** tab one more time and attempt to re-enter the **Add Assets** flow once again using the same search criteria as before for consistency. Note that we will now pause on the breakpoints that lead to our uncaught exception.
24. Step through the breakpoints that we have added using the **Play/Pause** button. Note that we can see the values of our variables under the **Sources** tab as they are populated:

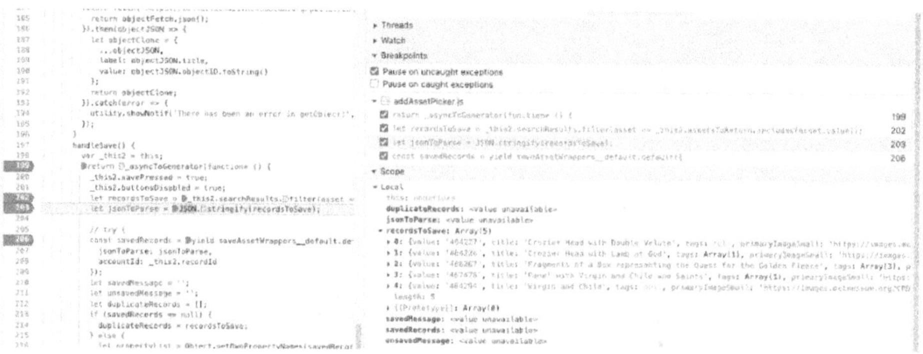

Figure 15.30: A screenshot showing the value of the recordsToSave variable at a given breakpoint

25. Using these breakpoints, we can determine that the error occurs within our imperative Apex call to `saveAssetWrappers`. Combining this knowledge with what we can see in the Developer Console and debug logs, we are able to track the source **of** the null pointer exception.
26. Revert your changes, deploy the original file, and pat yourself on the back for a job well done.

See also

For guidance on handling null pointer exceptions, see `https://help.salesforce.com/s/articleView?id=005226724&type=1`.

Get this book's PDF version and more

Scan the QR code (or go to `packtpub.com/unlock`). Search for this book by name, confirm the edition, and then follow the steps on the page.

UNLOCK NOW

Note: Keep your invoice handy. Purchases made directly from Packt don't require an invoice.

16

Unlock Your Exclusive Benefits

Your copy of this book includes the following exclusive benefits:

Follow the guide below to unlock them. The process takes only a few minutes and needs to be completed once.

Unlock this Book's Free Benefits in 3 Easy Steps

Step 1

Keep your purchase invoice ready for *Step 3*. If you have a physical copy, scan it using your phone and save it as a PDF, JPG, or PNG.

For more help on finding your invoice, visit `https://www.packtpub.com/en-us/unlock?step=1`.

> **Note**
>
> If you bought this book directly from Packt, no invoice is required. After *Step 2*, you can access your exclusive content right away.

Step 2

Scan the QR code or go to `packtpub.com/unlock`.

On the page that opens (similar to *Figure 16.1* on desktop), search for this book by name and select the correct edition.

Figure 16.1: Packt unlock landing page on desktop

Step 3

After selecting your book, sign in to your Packt account or create one for free. Then upload your invoice (PDF, PNG, or JPG, up to 10 MB). Follow the on-screen instructions to finish the process.

Need Help

If you get stuck and need help, visit `https://www.packtpub.com/unlock-benefits/help` for a detailed FAQ on how to find your invoices and more. This QR code will take you to the help page.

> **Note**
>
> If you are still facing issues, reach out to `customercare@packt.com`.

Other Books You May Enjoy

If you enjoyed this book, you may be interested in these other books by Packt:

Salesforce CRM Administration Handbook

Krzysztof Nowacki, Mateusz Twarożek

ISBN: 978-1-83508-569-1

- Discover strategies to stay up-to-date with Salesforce releases
- Integrate Salesforce products seamlessly to meet diverse business needs
- Explore Sales and Service Cloud and its transformative impact on sales and customer support operations
- Master opportunity management for successful deal closures and pipeline forecasting
- Understand Salesforce Orgs, managing users, settings, and customization
- Explore data import and export methods and data mapping
- Discover best practices, mock tests, and valuable tips and tricks to prepare for Salesforce certification

ChatGPT for Accelerating Salesforce Development

Andy Forbes, Philip Safir, Joseph Kubon, Francisco Fálder

ISBN: 978-1-83508-407-6

- Masterfully craft detailed and engaging user stories tailored for Salesforce projects
- Leverage ChatGPT to design cutting-edge features within the Salesforce ecosystem, transforming ideas into functional and intuitive solutions
- Explore the integration of ChatGPT for configuring Salesforce environments
- Write Salesforce flows with ChatGPT, enhancing workflow automation and efficiency
- Develop custom LWCs with ChatGPT's assistance
- Discover effective testing techniques using ChatGPT for optimized performance and reliability

MuleSoft for Salesforce Developers

Akshata Sawant, Arul Christhuraj Alphonse

ISBN: 978-1-83588-232-0

- Understand the fundamentals of MuleSoft APIs and integrations
- Unlock siloed data and implement the API lifecycle with MuleSoft's latest capabilities
- Get started with AnyPoint Code Builder with the capabilities of MuleSoft IDEs
- Understand DataWeave to build, secure, transform, and test MuleSoft applications
- Explore CloudHub 2.0 features along with other deployment models
- Gain expertise in MuleSoft connectors, security configuration, and integration of AI and automation
- Attain practical guidance and interview tips to achieve MCD level 1 certification

Packt is searching for authors like you

If you're interested in becoming an author for Packt, please visit `authors.packtpub.com` and apply today. We have worked with thousands of developers and tech professionals, just like you, to help them share their insight with the global tech community. You can make a general application, apply for a specific hot topic that we are recruiting an author for, or submit your own idea.

Share your thoughts

Now you've finished *Salesforce Lightning Web Component Cookbook*, we'd love to hear your thoughts! Scan the QR code below to go straight to the Amazon review page for this book and share your feedback or leave a review on the site that you purchased it from.

`https://packt.link/r/1835469868`

Your review is important to us and the tech community and will help us make sure we're delivering excellent quality content.

Index

Symbols

C

D

E

W

www.ingramcontent.com/pod-product-compliance
Lightning Source LLC
Chambersburg PA
CBHW080612090426
42761CB00011B/119